Writing the History of Nationalism

Writing History

The *Writing History* series publishes accessible overviews of particular fields in history, focusing on the practical application of theory in historical writing. Books in the series succinctly explain central concepts to demonstrate the ways in which they have informed effective historical writing. They analyse key historical texts and their producers within their institutional arrangement, and as part of a wider social discourse. The series' holistic approach means students benefit from an enhanced understanding of how to negotiate the contours of successful historical writing.

Series editors: Stefan Berger (Ruhr University Bochum, Germany), Heiko Feldner (Cardiff University, UK) and Kevin Passmore (Cardiff University, UK)

Published

Writing History (second edition), edited by Stefan Berger, Heiko Feldner & Kevin Passmore
Writing Medieval History, edited by Nancy F. Partner
Writing Early Modern History, edited by Garthine Walker
Writing Contemporary History, edited by Robert Gildea and Anne Simonin
Writing Gender History (second edition), Laura Lee Downs
Writing Postcolonial History, Rochona Majumdar
Writing the Holocaust, edited by Jean-Marc Dreyfus and Daniel Langton
Writing the History of Memory, edited by Stefan Berger and Bill Niven
Writing Material Culture History, edited by Anne Gerritsen and Giorgio Riello

Forthcoming

Writing History (third edition), edited by Stefan Berger, Heiko Feldner and Kevin Passmore
Writing Queer History, Matt Cook
Writing Transnational History, Fiona Paisley and Pamela Scully

Writing the History of Nationalism

Edited by
Stefan Berger and Eric Storm

BLOOMSBURY ACADEMIC
LONDON • NEW YORK • OXFORD • NEW DELHI • SYDNEY

BLOOMSBURY ACADEMIC
Bloomsbury Publishing Plc
50 Bedford Square, London, WC1B 3DP, UK
1385 Broadway, New York, NY 10018, USA

BLOOMSBURY, BLOOMSBURY ACADEMIC and the Diana logo are trademarks of
Bloomsbury Publishing Plc

First published in Great Britain 2019

ISBN: HB: 978-1-3500-6430-0
PB: 978-1-3500-6431-7
ePDF: 978-1-3500-6432-4
eBook: 978-1-3500-6433-1

Series: Writing History

Typeset by Newgen KnowledgeWorks Pvt. Ltd., Chennai, India

To find out more about our authors and books visit www.bloomsbury.com
and sign up for our newsletters.

CONTENTS

List of Figures vii
List of Contributors viii

1 Introduction: *Writing the History of Nationalism* – in what way, for whom and by which means? 1
Stefan Berger and Eric Storm

2 National histories and the promotion of nationalism in historiography – the pitfalls of 'methodological nationalism' 19
Stefan Berger

3 Marxism and the history of nationalism 41
Miroslav Hroch

4 Modernism and writing the history of nationalism 61
John Breuilly

5 Nations are (occasionally) forever: Alternatives to the modernist perspective 83
Aviel Roshwald

6 Cognitive and psychoanalytic approaches to nationalism 105
Steven J. Mock

7 Constructivism in the history of nationalism since 1945 131
Christian Wicke

8 Deconstructing nationalism: The cultural turn and poststructuralism 155
Gabriella Elgenius

9 Postcolonialism and the history of anti-colonial nationalism 171
Sanjay Seth

10 Gender approaches to the history of nationalism 191
Elizabeth Vlossak

11 The spatial turn and the history of nationalism: Nationalism between regionalism and transnational approaches 215
Eric Storm

12 The global turn in historical writing and the history of nationalism 239
Matthias Middell

Index 263

FIGURES

5.1 Ernst von Bandel, The *Hermannsdenkmal* (Hermann
(Arminius) Monument, 1875) in the Teutoburger Wald.
North Rhine-Westphalia, Germany 85
10.1 Guido Schmitt, *The Blacksmith of German Unity* –
Bismarck handing Germania the sword 'Unitas'.
Woodcut, *c.*1895 192

CONTRIBUTORS

Stefan Berger is Professor of Social History and Director of the Institute for Social Movements at Ruhr Universität Bochum as well as Executive Chair of the Foundation History of the Ruhr and Honorary Professor at Cardiff University. His research interests include the history of labour and social movements, of regions of heavy industry, in particular deindustrialization and industrial heritage, as well as the history of historiography and the history of nationalism and national identity. Recent publications include: *The Past as History. National Identity and Historical Consciousness in Modern Europe*, with Christoph Conrad (2015); *The History of Social Movements. A Global Perspective*, edited with Holger Nehring (2017).

John Breuilly is Emeritus Professor of Nationalism and Ethnicity at the London School of Economics. His research interests include the history of nationalism and modern Germany. Recent publications include: *The Oxford Handbook of the History of Nationalism* (2013); 'Modernisation and Nationalist Ideology', *Archiv für Sozialgeschichte 57* (2017); Modern Empires and nation-states, *Thesis Eleven* (2017). He is currently revising *19th Century Germany: Politics, Culture and Society, 1780–1918* (2001) for a second edition and writing a book on how nationalism 'travelled' the world.

Gabriella Elgenius is Associate Professor of Sociology at the University of Gothenburg and Associate Member of the Department of Sociology, University of Oxford. She is researching nationalism with reference to the radical right, diaspora and integration, and the repatriation of cultural heritage. Publications include: (with Jens Rydgren) 'Frames of Nostalgia and Belonging', *European Societies* (2018); 'Socio-Political Integration Through Diaspora Organisations and Civil Society Initiatives, in Heath (ed.), *Social Integration* (2017); 'Ethnic Bonding and Homing Desires', in Jacobsson and Korolczuk (eds), *Civil Society Revisited* (2017); (edited with Peter Aronsson), *National Museums and Nation-building in Europe 1750–2010* (2015; *Symbols of Nations and Nationalism* (2011).

Miroslav Hroch is Emeritus Professor in General History at Charles University Prague. His research during the last two decades focused on nation formation in Europe and national movements. His publications include: *European Nations. Explaining Their Formation* (2015; German orig. *Das Europa der Nationen*, 2005), *Comparative Studies in Modern European History* (2007); *Hledání souvislostí. Eseje z komparativních dějin Evropy* (2016).

Matthias Middell is Professor of Cultural History and Director of the Global and European Studies Institute at Leipzig University. He does research in the field of global and transregional history and the history of historiography. Among his most recent books are (with Steffi Marung and Katja Naumann) *In Search of Other Worlds. Towards a Cross-Regional History of Area Studies* (2018); *Handbook of Transregional Studies* (2018); (with Frank Hadler) *Handbuch einer transnationalen Geschichte Ostmitteleuropas*, Band I: *Von der Mitte des 19. Jahrhunderts bis zum Ersten Weltkrieg* (2017); (with Alan Forrest) *The Routledge Companion to the French Revolution in World History* (2015).

Steven J. Mock is Research Assistant Professor at the Balsillie School of International Affairs and Director of the Ideological Conflict Project. His research interests focus on methods for modelling the myths, symbols and rituals associated with the constructs of national and other forms of political-cultural identity, further to understanding the impact of these constructs on conflict and conflict resolution. He is the author of *Symbols of Defeat in the Construction of National Identity* (2012).

Aviel Roshwald is Professor of History at Georgetown University, Washington, DC. He is the author of the following books: *The Endurance of Nationalism: Ancient Roots and Modern Dilemmas* (2006); *Ethnic Nationalism and the Fall of Empires: Central Europe, Russia and the Middle East, 1914–1923* (2001); *Estranged Bedfellows: Britain and France in the Middle East during the Second World War* (1990). He is the co-editor, with Richard Stites, of *European Culture in the Great War: The Arts, Entertainment, and Propaganda, 1914–1918* (1999). With Matthew D'Auria and Cathie Carmichael, he is a co-editor of *The Cambridge History of Nationhood and Nationalism* (in progress). His current research focuses on comparing responses to Axis-power occupations during the Second World War across a range of European and Asian examples.

Sanjay Seth is Professor of Politics and Director of the Centre for Postcolonial Studies, Goldsmiths, University of London. He has published in the areas of modern Indian history, postcolonial theory, and social and political theory. His books include *Marxist Theory and Nationalist Politics: The Case of Colonial India* (1995), *Subject Lessons: The Western Education of Colonial India* (2007) and an edited book, *Postcolonial Theory and International Relations: A Critical Introduction* (2012). He is also a founding co-editor of the journal, *Postcolonial Studies*.

Eric Storm is Associate Professor in Modern History at Leiden University, The Netherlands. His investigations focus on Spanish cultural history and regional and national identity construction in Europe. Recent publications include *The Culture of Regionalism: Art, Architecture and International Exhibitions in France, Germany and Spain, 1890–1939* (2010) and *The Discovery of El Greco: The Nationalization of Culture versus the Rise of Modern Art* (2016). He is co-editor (with Joost Augusteijn) of *Region and State in Nineteenth-Century Europe: Nation-Building, Regional Identities and Separatism* (2012) and (with Xosé M. Núñez Seixas) of *Regionalism and Modern Europe: Identity Construction and Movements from 1890 to the Present Day* (2019).

Elizabeth Vlossak is Associate Professor in the Department of History at Brock University, Canada. Her research interests include the social and cultural history of war, gender and nationalism, and memory and the politics of commemoration. She is the author of *Marianne or Germania? Nationalizing Women in Alsace, 1870–1946* (2010), 'Traitors, heroes, martyrs, victims: Veterans of Nazi "forced conscription" in Alsace and Moselle', in *Rewriting German History: New Perspectives on Modern Germany*, ed. Nikolaus Wachsmann and Jan Rüger (2015), and 'The Civil War in France, Alsace-Lorraine, and Postwar Reconstruction in the 1870s', in *Decades of Reconstruction: Postwar Societies, State-building, and International Relations, from the Seven Years War to the Cold War*, ed. Ute Planert and James Retallack (2017). Her current work focuses on Nazi forced labour.

Christian Wicke is Assistant Professor in Political History at Utrecht University. He is interested in historical representations of nations, regions and cities. He is the author of *Helmut Kohl's Quest for Normality: His Representation of the German Nation and Himself* (2015), and recently co-edited along with Stefan Berger and Jana Golombek *Industrial Heritage and Regional Identities* (2018) as well as a special issue (also with Stefan Berger) of *The Public Historian* entitled 'Deindustrialization, Heritage and Representations of Identity' (November 2017). His current focus is on the history of urban movements in the 1970s.

1

Introduction: *Writing the History of Nationalism* – in what way, for whom and by which means?

Stefan Berger and Eric Storm

Introduction

A spectre is haunting the world (once again) – it is the spectre of nationalism. This adaptation of Karl Marx's famous quote highlights the simple fact that nationalism has been a far more powerful ideology in the modern world than Communism; so powerful that even most of the Communist regimes, for as long as they existed, developed nationalist sentiments and ideas.[1] Ever since modern nationalism and nationalist movements arose (and when they did so is a matter of some debate), it has been continuously holding the world spellbound. Hyper-nationalism led to two world wars in the first half of the twentieth century and left much of Europe in rubble. The European Union and the United Nations were attempts to overcome old nationalist enmities and develop a culture of cooperation. When the Cold War came to an end in 1989, it looked as though Eastern Europe could now join their Western European neighbours to build a peaceful and, some hoped, postnational continent, even if nationalism had been very much alive and kicking in the non-European post-Second World War world.[2]

Yet, the 1990s brought the first signs that this vision of a postnational Europe would not be easy to put into place. The Yugoslav Wars, above all, but also the more peaceful separation of ways between the Czech Republic and Slovakia as well as the rise of strong nationalist movements in post-Communist societies across Eastern Europe were signs that Eastern Europeans would not easily subscribe to the postnational vision of key

Europeanists in the West.[3] However, the latter were also challenged closer to home. On the one hand, regionalism turned to nationalism in some parts of Western Europe, notably in Scotland, Catalonia and Flanders. But nationalism also returned to mainstream politics in some of the larger West European democracies: UK Independence Party in Britain, the Front National in France, the Swedish Democrats in Sweden, the True Finns in Finland and most recently the Alternative für Deutschland in Germany are right-wing movements adapting nationalism to their cause and mobilizing in the name of the nation against an allegedly overpowering elite project of European unification.[4] As the second decade of the twentieth century draws to a close and as Europe has been commemorating the key disaster of the twentieth century, the First World War, nationalism is also back on the agenda in Europe – the one place in the world which arguably went furthest in distancing itself from 'hot' forms of nationalism after 1945. If we look at the non-European world, nationalism arguably always has been far more virulent throughout the Cold War and post-Cold War period, and with Trump in the United States, Modi in India and Abe in Japan, nationalist leaders are doing extremely well.

The field of nationalism studies and the purpose of this volume

Given the contemporary relevance of nationalism, it is little surprising that nationalism studies has been, over the last decades, a fast-growing field of studies. Much of nationalism studies has been engaging critically with the phenomenon it studies. Many scholars have a strong inner distance to nationalism. However, there have also been studies promoting nationalism, sometimes using different words for it, such as patriotism, and there is a body of literature that seeks to naturalize national sentiment and make it seem 'normal'.[5] Although the latter strategy can, of course, also build on a long and distinguished tradition, ranging all the way back to Johann Gottfried Herder and Johann Gottlieb Fichte, it seems a clear minority among scholars of nationalism today.

The renaissance of nationalism studies preceded the tearing down of the Iron Curtain by about a decade, but it was also a direct reaction to political developments. In the immediate post-Second World War world and during the heyday of the ascendancy of European integration many scholars argued that nationalism was a spent force. It could be assigned to a dead past and dead pasts are rarely the object of true fascination among historians. Yet in the 1980s nationalism returned to Europe – in a variety of different guises. The political victory of Conservative prime minister Margaret Thatcher in Britain in 1979 saw attempts to return the United Kingdom to Victorian values, although her ambitious neo-liberal programme for authors, such as Benedict Anderson, Ernest Gellner and Michael Billig,[24] are discussed in several chapters, while other fundamental contributions to the field of nationalism studies, such as Liah Greenfeld's *Five Roads to Modernity* (1992), Roger Brubaker's *Nationalism Reframed* (1996) or Timothy Edensor's *National Identity, Popular Culture and Everyday Life* (2002) are barely mentioned,[25] because they did not play a fundamental role in one specific approach. Moreover, not all approaches are in the same stage, some are already quite mature and seem to be in decline, while others are quite recent and productive. Although it cannot be excluded that older approaches provide new incentives in the future, some seem to have already borne their main fruits, such as the Marxist view (Chapter 3), the modernist interpretation (Chapter 4) and perennial understandings (Chapter 5). Constructivism (Chapter 6), postmodern (Chapter 7) and postcolonial (Chapter 8) approaches have become mainstream, but still inspire many current-day scholars. Although psychoanalytical interpretations (Chapter 9) are already quite old, there are some fresh incentives that may lead to new empirical studies related to the history of emotions. Gender approaches (Chapter 10) and the impact of the spatial (Chapter 11) and global turn (Chapter 12) on the study of nationalism are still fresh, so possibly more innovative interpretations can be expected.

We do not pretend to provide a complete overview of all possible approaches. We basically decided to start in the early 1980s with the modernist interpretation, as provided in the ground-breaking studies by Anderson, Gellner and Hobsbawm, which still form the starting point of actual debates on the origins and nature of nationalism. Since Marxist views had a very strong impact on the modernist interpretation we also included this older approach. However, the history of ideas approach with which scientific study of nationalism began is largely omitted. Pioneers, such as Carlton Hayes, Hans Kohn and Elie Kedourie, associated nationalism with the horrors of the First World War, fascism and eventually Nazi Germany. They interpreted nationalism as an ideology and as a consequence focused on the ideas of its main proponents. Thus, in his *The Historical Evolution of Modern Nationalism* (1931), Hayes described the chronological succession of various types of nationalism – humanitarian, Jacobin, traditional, liberal and integral – each of which was associated with a number of influential thinkers from a particular ideological persuasion. Thus, the 'traditional nationalism' from the Romantic era was discussed through the ideas of Burke, Bonald and Schlegel.[26] Although Kohn's *The Idea of Nationalism* (1944) focused more on the long-term political transformation that enabled the rise of nationalism, he illustrated his views largely with long digressions on the contribution of a number of famous intellectuals.[27] In *Nationalism* (1960), Kedourie presented nationalism as an ideology that was invented and disseminated by European intellectuals.[28] According to him, the nationalist doctrine came into existence by combining a few crucial ideas which had been developed by Kant, Fichte and Herder. It is obvious that this history of ideas approach was rejected by those who had less faith in the power of ideas. Marxists and modernists accordingly shifted the focus to more structural factors, such as the rise of capitalism, industrialization and modernization.

Nationalism is a broad topic and not all approaches discussed in this volume focus on the same aspects. Marxists, modernists, perennialists and constructivists primarily proposed alternative views on the origins of nationalism and the process of nation formation (the rise of a national consciousness and feelings of national solidarity). Postcolonialism, on the other hand, focuses largely on nation formation outside of Europe and North America. The most influential studies in these fields were broad overviews that presented sweeping statements on the long-term causes of nationalism. Newer approaches, for instance, constructivists interested in nationalism from below, postmodernists, psychoanalytical interpretations and many historians that study nationalism through the lens of gender or influenced by the spatial turn, on the other hand, show less interest in the rise of nationalism and instead focus on the nation-building process and on how national identities are narrated, represented and performed in everyday life. They have resulted in a large number of case studies and while they certainly have deepened our understanding in many ways, these highly nuanced, contextualized studies also tend to present a very fragmented picture.

Structure of the book

Writing the History of Nationalism is structured in a loose chronological order, while we have tried to cluster chapters that are closely related, such as those on postmodernism and postcolonialism and those on the spatial and global turn. The opening Chapter 2 by Stefan Berger sets the scene by critically analysing how nationalism has influenced history writing and how since the late eighteenth century many historians have in fact been active nation-builders. Although enlightened historians in Europe generally focused on the progress of human civilization, many of them saw their own nation as its apex or, if this was hard to sustain, deplored the lack of enlightened values to explain why their country lagged behind. During the Romantic era historians put more emphasis on differences by focusing on the specific and particular path that each nation had taken during the course of history. At about the same time, history writing was professionalized. In most parts of Europe, history chairs and departments were created; new historical institutes as well as professional journals were founded. However, in most cases this reinforced the orientation on and prioritization of national history writing. The high point of historiographical nationalism was reached in the Interwar period. This is obvious for fascist countries like Italy and Germany, but nationalism was also on the rise elsewhere. After 1945, aggressive and racial forms of nationalism largely disappeared;

nonetheless, only during the 1960s and 1970s more critical approaches to historiographical nationalism would become mainstream. Developments in North America, Australia and Japan showed many similarities with those in Europe. Western-style professional history writing was also exported to the rest of the world, although in countries like China and India it was adapted to older forms of reporting on the past. In parts of the world where oral representations of the past had been dominant, such as in large parts of Africa, Western-style history even had to create its own institutions and traditions. Nevertheless, in all these cases national history writing became and still is the dominant form of dealing with the past.

Miroslav Hroch is the author of Chapter 3 on the impact of Marxist views. He distinguishes between the interpretation of the 'national question' by those who strove towards a socialist revolution and the views of those who used the theories of Marx to study the formation of modern nations and the rise of nationalism. Marx and Engels themselves accepted the nation state as a given of the existing bourgeois order, while they considered nations without a state as relics of the past. However, they also thought that the existing nation states would be superfluous after a future socialist revolution. Lenin slightly adapted Marx's views by arguing that during the struggle against feudalism (which still existed in Russia) national movements could be useful allies of the working classes, while at a later stage – of a mature capitalist nation state – this alliance was not opportune anymore. Otto Bauer, a foremost representative of Austro-Marxism, accepted nations as 'communities of fate' and advocated their cultural autonomy within a future socialist society. Marxism also had a broad, but rather diffuse influence on many crucial contributions to the history of nationalism. One of these is to see nationalism in a negative light as an invention of the bourgeoisie and thus as a construct. The author concludes his chapter with a brief discussion of a few of the more practical contributions inspired by the Marxist worldview, such as those of Karl Deutsch, Miroslav Hroch, Tom Nairn, Michael Hechter, Benedict Anderson, Immanuel Wallerstein and Eric Hobsbawm. They all viewed nationalism as intimately connected to the rise of capitalism and thus as an inherently modern phenomenon.

In Chapter 4, John Breuilly discusses the modernist interpretation of nationalism. He first shows how after the defeat of Nazi Germany in 1945 everything that was reminiscent of exalted nationalism was condemned as archaic and reactionary, while Western national sentiment was seen as benign and nation-building in the 'Third World' was perceived as a necessity. The prevalent distinction between backward nationalism and modern nation states was challenged by the studies of Anderson, Gellner and Hobsbawm. All three basically argued that nationalism and nation states were the product of a general modernization process. Anderson focused on cultural factors, such as the role of printing and secularization, while Gellner emphasized the role of the economic transformation brought about by the rise of industrial society. Hobsbawm's and Ranger's concept of 'invention of tradition', in turn, inspired a large number of detailed historical case studies on nation-building processes throughout the globe. How these modernist theories influenced concrete historical research is illustrated with Eugen Weber's book on the nationalization of the French countryside in which he analysed how state officials and other members of the elites tried to modernize the country and thereby turned peasants into Frenchmen. Another classical study is by Miroslav Hroch, in which he distinguished three successive stages in the rise and formation of small European nations.

Chapter 5 deals with alternatives to the modernist view, that is to say, with those interpretations that emphasize that nations, national identities and nationalism have older roots and are not the product of modernization. Aviel Roshwald shows that most nationalists see nations as rooted in the mist of times, with their characters remaining largely unchanged. This position is known respectively as perennialism and essentialism. Another interpretation can be defined as primordialism, which argues that ethnicity and nationalism have always been important in human history because people have a genetic or cultural disposition to feel more akin to those people who share physical and cultural traits with them. Probably more influential among experts is the ethno-symbolist interpretation of Anthony Smith, who argues that in many cases there is a lot of continuity between modern national and earlier ethnic identities. Many historians have conducted detailed investigations, for instance, on late medieval England and France, the early modern Dutch Republic, ancient Greece and China, in order to demonstrate that national identities and even nationalism existed before the rise of modernity. Recent studies, on nation formation in Europe and Asia and on modern empires, particularly challenge the linear and secular nature of modernization as defended by scholars such as Gellner and Anderson. Modernity did not only arise in nation states and thus, according to Roshwald, the question can be raised whether nationalism necessarily needs to be modern.

Christian Wicke explores the constructivist approach to the history of nationalism in Chapter 6. Strongly influenced by Marxist, modernist and post-structural ideas, various authors began to see nations – and social reality at large – not as a given, but as constructed through discourse, myths, symbols and imaginations. Many scholars from the new multidisciplinary field of nationalism studies now examined how national elites had constructed, narrated or invented all kinds of national myths, symbols, heroes and stories. Dissatisfied with such a focus on elites, some historians have begun to study the construction of national identities from below. Although most constructivists were staunchly modernist, there were also scholars such as Anthony Smith and Victor Liebermann who applied a constructivist approach to earlier periods.

Chapter 7 by Gabriella Elgenius focuses on the impact of the cultural turn and the post-structuralist school on the history of nationalism. Inspired by post-structuralist thinkers, such as Jacques Derrida and Michel Foucault, not only did scholars see nations as constructs, but they also began to deconstruct the underlying assumptions and power relations of discourses about nations that (implicitly) distinguish insiders from outsiders. Thus, Michael Billig analyses the banal ways in which nationalism is reproduced on a daily basis, for instance, by referring to one's own nation with 'us' and 'here'. Homi Bhabha, in turn, argues that in the way in which people speak and write about the nation they often implicitly present it as a unitary phenomenon with clear boundaries that separate it from 'others'. Other scholars have examined how national commemorations, holidays and symbols were used to create unity. Craig Calhoun, another influential author, has made clear how even historians and social scientists routinely treat societies as integral wholes with distinctive identities and cultures.

In Chapter 8, Sanjay Seth discusses postcolonial interpretations of nationalism. Postcolonialism basically attacks the idea that Western knowledge since the Enlightenment was based on reason and as a consequence universally valid, whereas other cultures and knowledges were rooted in historically specific communities. Authors, such as Edward Said, argue that the knowledge and culture of the modern West, which was used to legitimize colonial domination, is also a specific product of history. From the 1980s these ideas were applied to the study of nationalism. Strongly influenced by Marxism, the subaltern studies group began to criticize the existing interpretation of Indian nationalism as primarily an elite project derived from the West, because it ignored the crucial and autonomous role of the subaltern classes. Slowly, Marxist influences on these Indian scholars were substituted by post-structural views. Partha Chatterjee, thus, argued that by adopting Western nationalism, many national liberation movements also accepted the universality of Western knowledge. In a later book, he argued that although many post-colonial states in Asia and Africa copied the material institutions of the nation state, they generally also protected the 'spiritual' domain of language, arts and family relations against Western influences, thus creating new forms of community. These postcolonial views also inspired the study of nationalism in Latin America and Africa. Finally, Seth reflects on the wider impact of postcolonial views on nationalism studies, for example, the tendency not to understand deviations of the standard modernization paradigm as anomalies.

Cognitive and psychoanalytic approaches to the history of nationalism are discussed by Steven Mock in Chapter 9. Although almost all experts agree that nationalism has to do with psychic phenomena, such as desires, sentiments, memory and imagination, few of them dare to touch upon the relationship between nationalism and the human mind, while psychologists generally disregard the nation. The overview of authors who have dealt with the relationship between the mind and the nation obviously begins with Sigmund Freud, who explained the individual's innate need to adapt to the social environment from early childhood experiences. Adorno used this view after 1945 to explain the appeal of extreme nationalism in Germany from an authoritarian upbringing. More recent theorists, such as Ernest Becker, have explained nationalism as providing sense to individual existence. It can even help overcome death anxiety by making clear that individuals, through their nation, can contribute to 'hero projects' that will live on after us. Influenced by Jacques Lacan, authors such as Slavoj Žižek and Julia Kristeva argue that the wish to protect 'our (national) way of life' is a quite natural feeling, and thus not a consequence of a kind of pathology. However, these feelings of solidarity with the nation are often combined with dislike or even hatred towards a collective enemy, which can even be converted into a scapegoat. The nation, thus, is at the same time a group of individuals linked by networks of social communication and a cognitive construct common to the minds of its members. Although many of these ideas are not unfamiliar to historians, hitherto there are only a very limited amount of historical studies that directly apply psychological concepts or theories to the study of the nationalism in the past.

The topic of Chapter 10, written by Elizabeth Vlossak, is the influence of gender studies to the history of nationalism. Influenced by Beauvoir's *Second Sex* (1949) and a new generation of feminists, women's history emerged as a new field in the 1960s. However, in the 1980s, by distinguishing between sex – which belongs to the realm of biology – and gender, which is socially and culturally constructed, the focus shifted towards the historical construction of specific 'appropriate' roles and ideals for both men and women. The lens of gender was also applied to the history of nationalism and this has resulted in a rapidly growing number of fascinating case studies. Vlossak provides an overview of recent trends by focusing on four thematic fields: citizenship, symbols, sexuality and militarism. The introduction of citizenship in the new nation states was mostly connected with conscription. Accordingly, men were supposed to play an active role in the public sphere, whereas women should protect the nation's morality at home. Nations were often depicted as a woman who generally reproduced ideas about 'typical' feminine qualities. Although the way these symbols have been defined varied greatly, they mostly were the product of male authors, politicians and artists. The perceived interests of the nation also largely determined what specific forms of sexual behaviour were stimulated, discouraged or even prohibited. Finally, nationalist warfare often had a major impact on gender roles. In the end, it becomes clear that nationalism had an enormous impact on the definition of gender roles, but that gender also influenced the way the nation was constructed, maintained and experienced.

Eric Storm examines the impact of the spatial turn on the study of nationalism in Chapter 11. Neo-liberal reforms, the end of the Cold War and the subsequent rapid process of globalization have undermined the dominant position of the nation state. The spatial turn reflects this new awareness of the arbitrariness of spatial hierarchies and existing borders. Its roots can be found in France, where in the 1970s critical thinkers began to criticize the post-structuralist emphasis on discourse – and abstract mental spaces – for ignoring how people actually dealt with ideas and concepts in their daily life. Thus, Henri Lefebvre argued that space is not static, but is used and understood differently at different times and places. Michel de Certeau focused on the agency that individuals actually have to reproduce and transform spaces in daily life. Their ideas were quickly adopted by geographers who coined the term 'spatial turn', while social scientists applied them to examine the construction and reproduction of national spaces. Historians, although largely unaware of these parallel theoretical developments, moved in the same direction by conducting empirical case studies to understand how people in the countryside actively adapted and appropriated the nation-building process to serve their own interests. Moreover, they also concluded that the nation state was not an empty space in which historical developments took place, and began to conduct studies on the interaction between local, regional and national identities. Surprisingly, the historiographical developments in the different parts of the globe developed almost separately of each other, although almost all authors make clear that the nation-building process did not weaken existing local, regional and ethnic identities, but in many cases reinforced them. Storm also pays attention to new transnational approaches to nationalism studies. Thus, historians have shown that emigrants, borders, cultural transfers and foreigners also had a strong impact on the nation-building process.

Chapter 12 is dedicated to the implications of the global turn for the history of nationalism. Matthias Middell shows how since the late eighteenth century historians have primarily concentrated on domestic instead of transnational processes in order to analyse historical change. Thus, for example, the French Revolution is related almost entirely to developments in France rather than seeing it as a result of wider Atlantic or global trends. World and global history – which have increasingly become popular since the early 1990s – aims to break with this tradition of inward looking national history writing. This global turn led to a rapidly growing interest in the trans-border movement of persons, goods, capital, ideas and epidemics. One of the implications of this new attention for transnational developments is a revision of the strict dichotomy between empires and nation states. In fact, in many European cases nation-building and imperial expansion went hand in hand. Recently, authors, such as Charles Maier, have argued that territorialization – the homogenization of space and people through state-building – is a process that is not limited to nation states and even started before the age of nationalism.[29] Moreover, national territorialization does not impede a simultaneous process of regionalization and the strengthening of transnational links. Nationalism can also be studied as a global phenomenon, for instance, by focusing on the international networks of national activists and the transnational spread of nationalist ideas. The global rise of nationalism also profoundly transformed portals of globalization, such as harbours, train stations and airports, by introducing passports, statistics and maps in order to manage the flow of people and goods. In a similar way, the rise of the welfare state, which replaced communal and private forms of charity, encouraged nation states to distinguish more sharply between citizens, foreigners and immigrants. Globalization and nationalism, as a consequence, are not opposed, but were often intertwined in very intricate ways.

Tasks for the future: The ongoing historicization of nationalism and the challenge of denationalizing history writing including the history of nationalism

In this book, the main approaches for studying the history of nationalism from the last few decades are extensively reviewed. Most influential by far was the constructivist approach. By showing that nations are constructions, they became historicized and were not taken any more as a given. By also considering gender and space as constructions, the interpretation of nationalism and its impact on society was further historicized. Overall, however, a great variety of approaches have increased our knowledge about the rise of nationalism, the formation of nations and the nation-building process in all corners of the world. Nevertheless, there are still a few topics, which are barely studied. Sometimes this is because of a dearth of primary sources, for instance, when studying nationalism from below. It has also proven difficult to establish when new trivial forms of nationalism became banalized, that is, not consciously perceived anymore. And there have been problems in developing interdisciplinary cooperation, which seems necessary for an in-depth inquiry into the role of nationalist emotions in the past. We are also still lacking more empirical studies that show how the transition from proto-nationalist feelings to modern national identities and modern nations actually occurred.[30]

A striking feature of the approaches that currently dominate the field, such as constructivism, postmodernism, postcolonialism, gender and the spatial turn, is that they all focus on differences and are based on a wide range of empirical case studies. This means that the sweeping global interpretations, written by modernist authors such as Ernest Gellner, Benedict Anderson and Eric Hobsbawm, still provide the main interpretative framework thirty-five years after they were first published. However, the overall picture has become blurred by innumerable case studies that provide revisions, nuances and additions, which in the end leads to a very fragmented field. New syntheses are badly needed and it seems that ambitious comparative studies and a global approach could at least refocus the debate.

Fortunately, there are already a few promising examples. Thus, Joep Leerssen created an open access database on Romantic nationalism in Europe, which particularly focuses on transnational contacts, networks and transfers between the various countries and national movements.[31] Erez

Manela's book on the Wilsonian moment discusses the repercussions of the Fourteen Points and the Parisian Peace Conference of 1919 in Egypt, India, China and Korea.[32] With all due modesty on behalf of one of the authors of this introduction, we should also like to mention the European Science Foundation research programme 'Representations of the Past: The Writing of National Histories in Nineteenth and Twentieth Century Europe', which ran between 2003 and 2008. It involved more than 250 scholars from twenty-nine European countries and resulted in more than a dozen publications.[33] An attempt at providing some sort of synthesis to the wealth of research results examines the main trends, similarities and differences in the writing of national history throughout the European continent.[34] The sociologist Andreas Wimmer assembled a new, global data set of all civil and interstate wars during the last two centuries in order to determine the relationship between the rise of nationalism, the formation of new nation states and military conflict. His book amounts to a highly nuanced update of the modernist interpretation.[35]

It has also become clear that the nation state is not the only possible state form in the modern world, or that a world divided into nation states means the end of history. In fact, the nation state should be seen as a quite specific product of historical developments. Moreover, it did not become dominant until the twentieth century. Before then, most states in Europe were empires or aspired to become one, whereas much of the rest of the world was colonized. This slowly began to change after the First World War – with Wilson's plea for national self-determination. It would, however, only become more effective after the collapse of the imperial dreams of Nazi-Germany and Japan in 1945.[36] Nonetheless, most colonial empires only disappeared in the 1960s, while the Soviet Empire lasted even until the early 1990s. It really was only during the second half of the twentieth century that the nation state came to dominate the globe; ironically, this is also the time when it became questionable. From the late 1980s onwards the autonomous nation state was rapidly undermined by neo-liberal policies, such as large-scale privatizations and the curtailing of the welfare state, while at the same time it was eroded from the outside by the globalization of the economy, the rapid increase of travel, tourism and migration, the growing power of transnational companies and supranational organizations such as the European Union and the rise of internet and social media.[37] However, while we may observe tendencies that have been weakening the autonomy of the nation state from the last two decades of the twentieth century onwards, we also see a remarkable resilience of the nation state and the rise of nationalism as a response to globalization.[38]

If the longevity and power of the nation state should neither be over-nor underestimated, it is also worth pointing out that most nation states hardly conform to the ideal of cultural and ethnic homogeneity. Historically, many nation states resorted to forced assimilation, oppression of minorities, population transfers and ethnic cleansing in order to create the homogeneous nation that the model seemed to require.[39] The massive trans-border flow of migrants and refugees, which has always been a quite normal phenomenon in human history, in fact contradicts the nation state model, since it both undermines the cultural unity of the nation and the sharp borders between the supposedly unique national cultures.[40] Furthermore, the opposition between nation states and empires is actually being revised. In fact, most European nation states during the nineteenth and twentieth centuries were 'nationalizing empires'.[41] Outside of Europe the boundaries between both were not that sharp either. Even in the colonies nationalizing tendencies were detectable, for instance, when mass media began to construct a collective 'national' identity for each colony, even long before the first movements of national liberation came into being.[42]

In light of the rather brief period in which the nation state model was truly hegemonic, it is surprising that nationalism had such a profound and lasting impact on the social sciences and the discipline of history. From the early nineteenth century onwards, the nation state became the dominant unit of analysis as is still very much the case. It must be admitted that recently historians and other scholars within the humanities and social sciences have become more critical about the dominant position of the nation state and have adapted their research agenda by, for instance, paying more attention to comparative history and transnational flows, or by exploring local, regional, imperial or global topics.[43] Nevertheless, most scholars continue to focus on the local, regional or imperial past of one nation state, take nation states as their basic units for comparison or study the movement of persons, ideas or goods over national borders. Berger defines this in his chapter as historiographical nationalism. However, the legacy of two centuries of national history writing from which we ought to emancipate ourselves is much more encompassing. It also entails institutional nationalism, methodological nationalism, terminological nationalism and normative nationalism.[44]

First of all, education and research is still organized along national lines. National archives collect primary sources along national lines, while national libraries do the same for secondary studies, and government agencies generate all kinds of national statistical data. Universities depend largely on their national government and national agencies for their money and research funds. Many chairs in history departments are still dedicated to national history, while many conferences, associations and journals focus on one national context. Maps and catalogues reproduce a world of bounded nation states, while history books in libraries and shops are generally ordered according to the nationality of the topic.

Historiographical and institutional nationalism mostly went hand in hand with methodological nationalism. Many studies limit the analytical focus to the boundaries of the nation state, thus largely excluding outside influences. In the social sciences, society is often equated with national society and it is used as the naturally given entity of analysis. Comparisons are generally made between nation units, thus in fact further reinforcing this methodological nationalism.[45]

A problem that affects historians probably more than other scholars is the impact of terminological nationalism. Thus, terms used to design historical epochs, such as the Victorian era, the Third Republic, the Antebellum period, the *Risorgimento*, the Tanzimat reforms and the Meiji-Restoration, are generally derived from and applicable to one national context only. Moreover, supposed turning points are different for each national case, which makes comparison even more difficult. This is even more evident by the use of concepts that allegedly only apply to one national context, such as frontier, Home Rule, *Heimat*, *laicité*, *kulak* or *swadeshi*, even if sometimes comparable political currents or movements exist, only to receive different labels in each national context. Thus, German *Sozial-Liberalismus* is known as New Liberalism in Britain, *solidarisme* in France, *regeneracionismo* in Spain, the Giolittian Era in Italy and the Progressive Movement in the United States. They are not exactly the same but they share a body of ideas and practices that make it extremely worthwhile to look in comparative and transnational ways at those phenomena.[46] But this remains a challenge, when even the various fields of our discipline are defined by nationalism. Thus the main divide in history in many countries is still between national history and international or world history, meaning everything but one's own national history including the national histories of many other parts of the world. Hence, pushing nationalism out of the way remains a major challenge for all those who aim to transcend national history writing and practice a more transnational history.

However, it is not just a question of units of analysis, infrastructure, methodology and terminology. The nation state also provides a normative framework, which is still omnipresent in the writings of historians and passes largely unacknowledged. It is understandable that as private individuals we possibly prefer to live in a (democratic) nation state. However, as professional historians we should not privilege one state form over another and instead aim to treat them on an equal basis and with a neutral tone. Nonetheless, this is generally not the case. Like Wilson, historians still routinely describe empires as 'backward', while their policies are characterized as 'foreign conquest', 'occupation', 'oppression' and 'subordination', while the creation of nation states is analysed by using much more positive terms like 'revolution', 'unification', 'war of independence', 'liberation' or 'uprising' (instead of, for instance, rebellion, secession, disruption or usurpation). Empires are described as 'multi-ethnic' or 'multi-national', thus implying that their demise was inevitable. Nation states, on the other hand, are associated with progress, equality and self-determination, and cases that do not entirely conform to the ideal type are characterized as anomalies, such as the presence of ethnic minorities or immigrants, which have to be dealt with through nation-building or assimilation policies. Even postmodern and postcolonial concepts, such as 'cross-cultural', 'othering' or 'hybrid identities', presuppose that an independent, unified and homogeneous nation state is the norm. Thus, it will not be an easy task to denationalize history writing. In order to succeed we will have to amend our way of doing research, revise our vocabulary and rewrite the story of the past in a very thorough way.

Notes

1 Roman Szporluk, *Communism and Nationalism: Karl Marx versus Friedrich List* (Oxford, 1988); Richard Pipes, *The Formation of the Soviet Union: Communism and Nationalism, 1917–1923*, rev. edn (Cambridge, MA, 1997); Walter A. Kemp, *Nationalism and Communism in Eastern Europe and the Soviet Union: A Basic Contradiction?* (Basingstoke, 1999).

2 Mike Mason, *Development and Disorder: A History of the Third World since 1945* (Hanover, 1997).

3 Sabrina P. Ramet (ed.), *The Radical Right in Central and Eastern Europe since 1989* (University Park, 1999).

4 Ruth Wodak, Majid KhosraviNik and Brigitte Mral (eds), *Right-Wing Populism in Europe: Politics and Discourse* (London, 2013).

5 Stefan Berger, *The Search for Normality. National Identity and Historical Consciousness in Germanys since 1800*, rev. edn (Oxford, 2003).

6 Raphael Samuel (ed.), *Patriotism: The Making and Unmaking of British National Identity* (London, 1989).

7 Christian Wicke, *Helmut Kohl's Quest for Normality: His Representation of the German Nation and Himself* (Oxford, 2015).

8 Silvana Patriarcha, 'Italian Neopatriotism: Debating National Identity in the 1990s', *Modern Italy* 6:1 (2001), 21–34.

9 Ernest Gellner, *Nations and Nationalism* (Ithaca, 1983); John Breuilly, 'Introduction', in Ernest Gellner, *Nations and Nationalism*, 2nd edn (Oxford, 2006), pp. XIII–LIII.

10 Benedict Anderson, *Imagined Communities: Reflections on the Origins and Spread of Nationalism* (London, 1983, rev. edn, 2006).

11 Eric Hobsbawm and Terence Ranger (eds), *The Invention of Tradition* (Cambridge, 1983).

12 John Breuilly, *Nationalism and the State*, 2nd edn (Manchester, 1993).

13 Aviel Roshwald, *The Endurance of Nationalism: Ancient Roots and Modern Dilemmas* (Cambridge, 2006).

14 Joep Leerssen, *National Thought in Europe: A Cultural History* (Amsterdam, 2006); Anne-Marie Thiesse, *La creation des identités nationales. Europe XVIIIe-XXe siècle* (Paris, 1999).

15 Eric Hobsbawm, *Nations and Nationalism since 1789: Programme, Myth, Reality* (Cambridge, 1990).

16 Oliver Zimmer, *Nationalism in Europe, 1890–1940* (Basingstoke, 2003).

17 Timothy Baycroft and Mark Hewitson (eds), *What Is a Nation? Europe 1789–1914* (Oxford, 2006).

18 John Breuilly (ed.), *The Oxford Handbook of the History of Nationalism* (Oxford, 2013).

19 Christopher Bayly, *The Birth of the Modern World, 1780–1914* (Oxford, 2004); Jürgen Osterhammel, *The Transformation of the Modern World: A Global History of the Nineteenth Century* (Princeton, 2014).

20 Anthony D. Smith, *The Nation in History: Historiographical Debates about Ethnicity and Nationalism* (Hanover, 2000).

21 Anthony D. Smith, *Nationalism: Theory, Ideology, History* (Cambridge, 2010).

22 Paul Lawrence, *Nationalism: History and Theory* (London, 2004).

23 Umut Özkirimli, *Theories of Nationalism: A Critical Introduction*, 3rd edn (Basingstoke, 2017).

24 Michael Billig, *Banal Nationalism* (London, 1995).

25 Liah Greenfeld, *Nationalism: Five Roads to Modernity* (Cambridge, MA, 1992); Roger Brubakers, *Nationalism Reframed: Nationhood and the National Question in the New Europe* (Cambridge, 1996); Tim Edensor, *National Identity, Popular Culture and Everyday Life* (London, 2002).

26 Carlton Hayes, *The Historical Evolution of Modern Nationalism* (New York, rev. edn, 1961 [originally published in 1931]).

27 Hans Kohn, *The Idea of Nationalism: A Study in Its Origin and Background* (London, 1944).

28 Elie Kedourie, *Nationalism* (London, 1960).

29 Charles S. Maier, 'Consigning the Twentieth Century to History: Alternative Narratives for the Modern Era', *American Historical Review* 105 (2000), 807–31.

30 See David A. Bell, *The Cult of the Nation in France: Inventing Nationalism, 1680–1800* (Cambridge, 2001); Charles S. Maier, *Once within Border: Territories of Power, Wealth and Belonging since 1500* (Cambridge, 2016).

31 Joep Leerssen (ed.), *Encyclopedia of Romantic Nationalism* (Amsterdam, 2017); the online database can be accessed here: https://ernie.uva.nl/viewer.p/21 and here: http://romanticnationalism.net.

32 Erez Manela, *The Wilsonian Moment: Self-Determination and the International Origins of Anticolonial Nationalism* (Oxford, 2007).

33 See the nine-volume book series *Writing the Nation*, with Stefan Berger, Christoph Conrad and Guy Marchal as general editors, published between 2008 and 2015, and Stefan Berger, Linas Eriksonas and Andrew Mycock (eds), *Narrating the Nation: Representations in History, Media and the Arts* (Oxford, 2008); Stefan Berger, Chris Lorenz and Billie Melman, *Popularising National Pasts, 1800 to the Present* (London, 2012), Stefan Berger and Andrew Mycock (ed.), Europe and Its National Histories, special issue of *Storia della Storiografia* 50 (2007).

34 Stefan Berger with Christoph Conrad, *The Past as History: National Identity and Historical Consciousness in Modern Europe* (Basingstoke, 2015).

35 Andreas Wimmer, *Waves of War: Nationalism, State Formation and Ethnic Exclusion in the Modern World* (Cambridge, 2013); Andreas Wimmer, *Nation-Building: Why Some Countries Come Together While Others Fall Apart* (Princeton, 2018).

36 Ian Buruma, *Wages of Guilt: Memories of War in Germany and Japan* (London, 1994); Patrick Finney (ed.), *Remembering the Second World War* (London, 2017).

37 Philipp Ther, *Europe since 1989: A History* (Princeton, 2016).
38 Liah Greenfeld (ed.), *Globalisation of Nationalism: The Motive-Force Behind 21st Century Politics* (London, 2016); Samuel Skipper, *Assessing the Role of Globalisation in the Rise of New Right Attitudes in Germany and Italy* (Hamburg, 2016).
39 Hans-Rudolf Wicker, *Rethinking Nationalism and Ethnicity: The Struggle for Meaning and Order in Europe* (London, 1997).
40 Alperhan Babacan and Supriya Singh (eds), *Migration, Belonging and the Nation State* (Cambridge 2010); Christian Joppke, *Immigration and the Nation State: The United States, Germany and Britain* (Oxford, 1999).
41 Stefan Berger and Alexei Miller (eds), *Nationalizing Empires* (Budapest, 2015); Siniša Malešević, 'Empires and Nation-States: Beyond the Dichotomy', *Thesis Eleven* (April 2017), 3–10.
42 Donald Malcolm Reid, *Whose Pharaohs? Archaeology, Museums and Egyptian National Identity from Napoleon to World War I* (Berkeley, 2003); Abigail McGowan, *Crafting the Nation in Colonial India* (Basingstoke, 2009).
43 Pierre-Yves Saunier, *Transnational History* (Basingstoke, 2013).
44 Some of the following paragraphs are partially based on: Eric Storm, 'A New Dawn in Nationalism Studies? Some Fresh Incentives to Overcome Methodological Nationalism', *European History Quarterly* 48:1 (2018), 113–29.
45 Daniel Chernillo, 'The Critique of Methodological Nationalism: Theory and History', *Thesis Eleven* 106:1 (2011), 98–117; Anna Amelina, Devimsal D. Nurgiz, Thomas Faist and Nina Glick-Schiller (eds), *Beyond Methodological Nationalism: Research Methodologies for Cross-Border Studies* (London, 2012).
46 Margrit Pernau and Dominic Sachsenmaier (eds), *Global Conceptual History: A Reader* (London, 2016); Willibald Steinmetz, Michael Freeden and Javier Férnandez-Sebástian (eds), *Conceptual History in the European Space* (Oxford, 2017); Reinhart Koselleck, *The Practice of Conceptual History: Timing History, Spacing Concepts* (Stanford, 2002).

2

National histories and the promotion of nationalism in historiography – the pitfalls of 'methodological nationalism'

Stefan Berger

The promotion of nationalism and the writing of history have been closely aligned ever since the emergence of modern nationalism in the late eighteenth century.[1] For nationalism and its promoters the past was a crucial terrain in which to anchor the national imagination and history was the foundational slab on which to build the national 'home'. This chapter seeks to analyse this symbiotic relationship between history writing and nationalism from the eighteenth century to the present day, starting off with Enlightenment historiography, moving to Romantic history writing and further to a fully professionalized and, by and large, 'historist' form of national history writing in the second half of the long nineteenth century. The first half of the twentieth century, with the two world wars, represents the high point of historiographical nationalism – with historians in the vanguard of those justifying and legitimating war, ethnic cleansing and genocide. It contributed to a situation that left Europe and large parts of the world in smouldering ruins in 1945. Yet there was no immediate break with historiographical nationalism after 1945. In the West, as we shall see, we can at best talk about a delayed break – with a more critical historiography wary of historiographical nationalism gaining ground in the 1960s and 1970s. The momentous processes of decolonization after the Second World War saw the rise of nationalism in the postcolonial worlds of Africa and Asia with its accompanying examples of historiographical nationalism, derivative of, but not identical to Western historiographical nationalisms. And in the West, the process of de-nationalizing historiography developed from the 1980s alongside a variety of efforts to renationalize historical writing – indicating that historiographical nationalism was far from being a spent force in the heartlands of modern nationalism. The chapter concludes by asking what future national historiographies will have in the twenty-first century.

Enlightenment national historiographies

Of course, there were forms of history writing that are older than the period of the Enlightenment. They can be traced back to ancient times and many of the tropes, metaphors and ideas about 'national character' go back at least to the writings about nation during the Middle Ages.[2] However, two developments that came together during the second half of the eighteenth century gave historiographical nationalism a new significance.[3] First, the meaning of nation changed in that it now became more common to refer to nation as a fixed territorial unit in which all the people living there, regardless of social status, were seen as equal members of the nation.[4] Second, history as a university discipline freed itself from the shackles of theology and began, from its early centres, such as the University of Göttingen, to develop a self-understanding as a professional 'science'. Its representatives increasingly claimed that they, because of their professional training, were the only ones who could speak authoritatively about the past.[5] Both developments together mark a qualitative shift from pre-modern to modern forms of historiographical nationalism.

The majority of Enlightenment histories were outwardly not interested in national history in itself. Rather, they focussed on tracing the path of progress and civilization through world history. The philosophical mode of history writing championed by Enlightenment historians did not look for national peculiarities, but for the manifestations of the universal spirit of progress.[6] The latter, however, they often found in particular nations and their histories. If we take the example of Voltaire, his attempt to write universal history, the *Essai sur les moeurs et l'esprit des nations* (Essay on the Manners and the Spirit of Nations, written in the 1740s and 1750s but published only in 1756 and 1769), was informed by a desire to identify in world history a succession of peoples and nations that had fostered progress in history. Voltaire extended his gaze well beyond Europe to include countries such as Persia, China, India and the Arab world. While Voltaire was capable of evaluating non-Europeans positively, his universal history was still Western-centric in that it left the reader in no doubt where human reason had settled to build its progressive home – in Europe and especially in France. Voltaire's history of France under Louis XIV portrayed his own country as a shining example of Enlightenment values and a new zenith in the universal history of civilization. Comparing it to the Athens of Pericles, the Rome of Augustus and the Florence of the Medicis, his comparative and universal framework of history writing served a nationalist purpose – to emphasize the moral and civilizational superiority of his native France over all other nations of the world.[7]

And indeed, despite the penchant of Enlightenment historians to look for universalisms and employ comparative and transnational methods, they did practice a lot of national history writing that was often underpinned by nationalist motives. In Scotland, one of the foremost representatives of the Scottish Enlightenment, William Robertson published his *History of Scotland* (1759) in which his native country ascends from a brutal dark age through a range of unhappy religious and political cleavages during the sixteenth and seventeenth centuries to arrive at economic prosperity and political peace that it had found in its union with England. Like Voltaire's contemporary France, Robertson's contemporary Scotland (and Britain) rode at the helm of progress in world history and were therefore blessed before all other nations.[8] And both authors could 'prove' this through a thorough examination of history. In other countries of Europe that could not so easily claim superiority and national excellence, Enlightenment historians used a similar approach to history writing to underline the need to transform their nations in line with Enlightenment principles and pave the way for future national greatness. Thus, eighteenth-century Spanish historians were obsessed with notions of Spanish 'backwardness' and the negative influence of the Catholic Church on national development. The Inquisition and imperial overstretch summed up where Spanish national history had gone wrong.[9] The nationalist agenda of those historians was to transform Spain in a way that would make it a fit home for progressive ideas and practices that would ennoble Spain before all other nations like it was ennobling France and Britain in the eyes of Voltaire and Robertson, respectively.

Romantic nationalism and its impact on history writing

There was no radical break between Enlightenment and Romantic history writing. The towering figure of Johann Gottfried Herder demonstrates how closely aligned the worlds of the Enlightenment and Romanticism were. A dedicated pupil of Immanuel Kant, Herder was steeped in Enlightenment thought, yet he also became one of its sharpest critics. In particular he argued that its universalism could easily turn into an oppressive cage, in which all the nations of the world would find themselves measured by the same standards and supposed to follow the same benchmarks. This, in the eyes of Herder, was not in line with the wonderful diversity of nations and national characters that made God's creation so colourful, exciting and beautiful.

In strongly organicist language, often comparing the world to a tree and its branches to the different nations, Herder outlined a different purpose for national history writing – one that the legions of Romantic national historians were set to explore during the nineteenth century. That purpose was to find and describe what made nations particular, specific and peculiar, what could explain, in other words, their unique national character that made them different from others.[10] It is ironic that this search for particularity was often the basis of historiographical nationalism in the nineteenth century. Once historians had located particularity, it was not difficult to link such particularity to sentiments of superiority, often making their own nations better than others. In Herder's thoughts, such historiographical nationalism did, at times, find some reflection, but on the whole he tended to be adamant that each nation had its own specific value that was not morally or civilizationally better or worse than that of other nations. It was just different and such difference, according to Herder, was part of God's plan for the world. His deeply theological and religious sentiments were to inform historism[11] to a significant extent and were mirrored in the writings of Leopold von Ranke, often perceived across Europe as the father-figure of modern historical writing.[12]

The search for particularity in historical writing was an important defence against the expansionist universalism of the French Revolution and Napoleon Bonaparte. National history was mobilized across Europe to defend the European nations against Napoleon's imperial designs.[13] Johann Gottlieb Fichte, for example, explicitly demanded a German national history that could counter the aggression of Napoleon's armies: 'Amongst the means to strengthen the German spirit it would be a powerful one to have an enthusiastic history of the Germans, which would be a national as well as a people's book just like the Bible or the Song Book.'[14] Such defensive mechanisms against expansionist universalism would, in the eyes of Romantic national historians, first of all have to seek to define the territory of the nation, something that, in large parts of Europe and the Americas, was by no means a clear-cut case in the nineteenth century. Where borderlands were contested, historiographical nationalism provided historically founded claims on those borderlands. History wars over territories often preceded and accompanied 'real' wars fought over territory.[15]

Regions and their histories often became building blocks of nations and regional histories were brought into line with national histories. Continuing the organicist language of Herder, Romantic national historians could portray nations as the branches of a tree and regions as the twigs and leaves hanging off the branches. The national imagination found expression in the description of and meaning given to landscapes.[16] Territories were invariably connected to states and to state power, and national historians of powerful nation states could hang their national histories on continuous state histories and those representing those states, in particular monarchies and parliaments as well as constitutions.[17]

There were, however, an awful lot of nations where independent statehood was either interrupted or where it had never existed. Their historians had to look for alternatives on which to construct national histories, and they often found such an alternative in the people of an imagined national territory. These people, often peasants, artisans or burghers, formed the backbone of constructions of national character that had remained different from those who had ruled over them and had prevented them from forming their own nation state. In fact, the declared or undeclared aim of much national history writing in the nineteenth century became the formation of an independent nation state and the promotion of nationalism that would work towards the formation of such a nation state. Constructions of notions of 'centuries of darkness' that a people had endured under foreign rule served the purpose of rallying these people, whose national character had allegedly survived during those centuries of oppression, to the cause of nation state formation. Such 'people's histories' were often oppositional histories in that they were opposed to a given territorial and political order, whereas statist histories that could rely on existing states often legitimated existing territorial and political orders. But there were also statist histories that were oppositional in that they affirmed the territorial but contested the political order. And the diverse people's histories were often deeply contested between rival historiographical traditions that had different ideas about national character, national territory and political order.[18]

Romantic national histories also established a 'rise and decline' pattern of national histories that sought to push the origins of the nation as far back into the dim and distant past as possible and then narrated it as a history of rise and decline and (prospective) rise again to national greatness. The longue durée was important for historiographical nationalism as it allowed national historians to posit a long pedigree of nations that served to distinguish them from other nations. Medievalism was one of the most enduring characteristics of Romantic national history writing, especially in those cases where 'big' middle ages allowed national historians to claim superiority over other national histories.[19] Canons of national heroes and enemies were constructed that could build on earlier pre-modern attempts to define those groups.[20]

In forms of liberal national history writing across Europe, historians traced the progressive extension of the idea of liberty throughout the ages.[21] Early socialist history writing, both deeply national and Romantic in its form and sentiment, sought to relate social class to the nation, often incorporating the working classes into the nation. Religion had already become an important part of national history writing during the Reformation and the subsequent wars of religion. In Romantic national history writing, the relationship between religion and nation was often described as a symbiotic one – with religion being nationalized and the nation sacralized. The gendering of national histories became all-pervasive with the misfortunes of nations often explained with reference to the bourgeois gender order being threatened. Thus, for example, the Polish national historian Joachim Lelewel explained all the misfortunes of the Polish nation, ultimately leading even to the disappearance of Poland from the map of Europe, with reference to the foreign-born wives of the Polish kings who meddled into the affairs of the state – instead of looking after their husbands, children and homes.[22]

The patterning of national histories everywhere was deeply influenced by the generations of Romantic national historians of the nineteenth century. Latin American national historians, for example, also busied themselves with constructing national histories that underpinned nationalist ambitions. In Brazil Francisco Adolfo de Varnhagen, the Viscount of Porto Seguro, published a multi-volume *Historia Geral do Brasil* between 1854 and 1857 that aimed to legitimate the independent state and its ruling royal family. Celebrating the country's Portuguese heritage, he emphasized Brazil's territorial integrity and its greatness that was built not only on conquest but also on Catholicism and the construction of the peculiar Brazilian character on three races that had played a role in the formation of the Brazilian people. Notions of racial or social equality were, however, not included in this vision. Rather to the contrary, Varnhagen provided an outspoken justification for what was still, at the time, a slave-owning society. Varnhagen provided a historical national master narrative for Brazil that was nationalist in its ambition but proudly professional in that he stressed that his history was based on years of archival research.[23]

The professionalization of historical writing and historiographical nationalism

Romantic national historians laid the groundwork on which professional historians could construct their own national histories, for the symbiotic relationship between nationalism and history writing increased with professionalization. True, professional university-based historians accused their Romantic predecessors of peddling in national myths and not respecting the professional standards of source criticism and archival work. But, on balance, their national narratives were as nationalist, or even more so than the ones produced by their Romantic predecessors. In an age of increasing mass nationalism, historians often saw themselves as prophets of the nation who served, through their professionalism, their nation. Of course, historiographical nationalism was also a very effective means of generating funding. Those in power and in control of the purse-strings could be motivated to fund generously historical research if they thought that the unique authority of the historical sciences would further their own national ambitions.

The building of institutions was a crucial precondition for the strength and durability of historiographical nationalism.[24] University seminars and history departments as well as historical institutes in the academies became the most important institutions for national history writing. Antiquarian societies, amateur circles and historical societies professionalized themselves in the course of the nineteenth century. Civil society organizations stood next to state-sponsored ones, and many promoted a strong sense of nation-ness and historiographical nationalism, even if they were not located in nation states but in larger empires. Historical archives became important backbones of national historical master narratives. The collection and publication of national historical sources became a prominent feature of historical activities across Europe. The *Monumenta Germaniae Historica* was launched in 1819, and its seal immediately indicated its nationalist intentions: an oak wreath included the words 'Sanctus amor patriae dat animum' (The sacred love of the fatherland inspires). Historical journals were established as outlets of professional historians' work that was often national(ist) in orientation. National libraries and national museums also engaged with national historical master narratives and national themes were among the most popular in nineteenth-century history competitions. National dictionaries sought to organize knowledge around the principle of the nation.[25]

The strong drive towards professionalization in the second half of the long nineteenth century meant that the borderlines towards so-called amateurs, that is, literary writers or anyone not having had a sound training as a professional historian and working in a professional capacity as a historian, were pushed out of the discourse of a national historical master narrative. This did not necessarily mean that these were less influential, as the huge impact of historical novels, theatre, opera, history painting and other genres and also academic disciplines, such as literary history, theology or sociology demonstrates, but the professional historians increasingly claimed that it was only them who could speak authoritatively about the past and therefore their exclusionary practice grew stronger. In their endeavour to set themselves up as the only ones who could speak authoritatively about the past, they were partially successful, as other genres and other disciplines now turned to history and historians for legitimation, authenticity and authority. In France, the most important history textbook for use in secondary schools in the nineteenth century was penned by one of the best-known university historians, Ernest Lavisse, who has been described as 'instituteur national'.[26]

The strong emphasis on national history in an increasingly professionalized history writing meant that the Enlightenment interest in universal, comparative and transnational history became much weaker and in particular the latter's concern with non-European histories became almost extinct. In the German lands, August Ludwig von Heeren has been described as the last proponent of world history. His voice had largely been silenced after the 1830s.[27] However, national history was never the only show in town, as both regional and transnational history, including imperial, universal and global history,[28] remained minority traditions in historiographies whose mainstream was deeply committed to national history writing.

If the nineteenth-century profession was deeply committed to the promotion of nationalism, there were also burgeoning transnational practices. Before 1914, aspiring historians from many parts of the world went to study in what were regarded as the centres for historical studies, that is, universities in Germany and in France, notably Berlin, Munich, Leipzig and Paris. The Belgian historian Paul Fredericq travelled through England and Scotland to take note of the diverse ways in which historical studies and research were organized.[29] World historical congresses were organized regularly after 1898 in which the historical profession presented itself as a self-consciously transnational community even if that transnationalism made the congresses often into platforms for historiographical nationalism.[30] As the example of the Romanian historian Nicolae Iorga demonstrates, historiographical transnationalism and nationalism could go together very well: Iorga occupied a chair for world history at the University of Bucharest from 1892 until 1940, yet he wrote panegyrics about the alleged organic peasant community of Romania forming the backbone of the Romanian nation. He not only promoted the comparative history of South-Eastern Europe but also insisted that national history was the highest form of history writing as it stilled the social need for providing the nation with historical consciousness.[31]

In multi-national empires and multi-national states alike, historiographies began to nationalize themselves, threatening existing territorial orders and state structures. The diverse national historiographies in the Austro-Hungarian Empire or the different national historiographies in Spain after 1898 are good examples for this explosive potential of national historiographies. Thus, for example, the narratives that Germans and Czechs in Bohemia constructed were mutually exclusive and built around the alleged antagonism between the Slav and the German element in Bohemia. Palacký's history of the Czech nation constructed an age-old national antagonism between Czechs and Germans in Bohemia and Moravia.[32] However, there are also nationalizing tendencies in historical writing that could strengthen imperial designs and ambitions, as was the case in Britain, France, Russia and Germany where nineteenth-century empires used imperial and national history to devise national cores and peripheries in the pursuit of both national and imperial glory.[33]

By the end of the long nineteenth century, professional historians had a strong feeling of their own importance in society. As the Greek national historian Spyridon Lambros wrote, the pen of the historian was more important for nation formation than the guns of the military.[34] And the willingness of states to grant history a prominent and well-funded place among the sciences seemed to indicate that those in positions of power tended to agree about the usefulness of the historical sciences for the purpose of nation building. The very first issue of the *Revue Historique* that appeared in France just five years after the Franco-Prussian war also spelt out a nationalist mission: 'The study of France's past, which shall be our principal task, is today of national importance. We can give to our country the unity and moral strength it needs by revealing its historical traditions and, at the same time, the transformations that these traditions have undergone.'[35] And across the border, in Germany, Heinrich von Treitschke promoted, through his national historical writing, his publicist work and his teaching at the University of Berlin an anti-French, anti-Slav, anti-Semitic, anti-socialist, anti-Catholic, imperialist and statist self-understanding of the German nation that was deeply nationalist, aggressive and expansionist.

The culmination of historiographical nationalism in the first half of the twentieth century

Nationalist history writing was prominent in all nation states participating in the First World War. When the lights went out in Europe in the summer of 1914, the torch of historiographical nationalism provided guidance throughout four long years of war. German nationalist historians were to the fore when it came to formulating nationalist war aims.[36] In France and Britain historians indicted an alleged age-old militarist and expansionist national character that had found its true voice in historians such as Treitschke.[37] After the war Henri Pirenne, who served time as German prisoner of war, called on fellow historians to 'un-learn' their trade from the Germans and did his best to exclude German historians from international conferences, while trying to de-ethnicize his own history of Belgium that he had written under the influence of German historiography before the First World War.[38] In the interwar period a veritable history war ensued, surrounding the issue of German war guilt as specified in the Versailles Peace Treaty. The German Foreign Office created a War Guilt Department that was lavishly funded in order to counter the Allied position that Germany alone was responsible for the outbreak of the war. It hired an army of German historians and published forty volumes of documents between 1922 and 1927 to prove the point that this position was wrong. Many historians participating in this endeavour sacrificed their scholarly standards on the altar of political expediency.[39] Historians in other countries were equally willing to serve their respective national governments in the alleged national interest. But it was not only the war and its aftermath that engendered a good deal of historiographical nationalism. The emergence of a whole host of new nation states in Central, East-Central and Eastern Europe, in particular, brought with it much historiographical nationalism to stabilize and support those new nation states, such as the Baltic states, the refounded Poland, Czechoslovakia, Romania and the Irish Free state.[40]

In the interwar period historiographical nationalism was strong among fascist and right-wing authoritarian historiographies in Italy after 1923,

Portugal and Germany after 1933, and Spain after 1939. In Germany, for instance, the state-centred historiographical nationalism was augmented with a racialized people's history (Volksgeschichte) that sought to put ethnicity and race centre stage. It had risen to prominence after the First World War and flourished under the National Socialist regime.[41] In fascist Italy cooperation with the regime and support for it was also widespread among historians, although there was more opposition here than in National Socialist Germany. Benedetto Croce publishing a national history of Italy that celebrated the liberal-democratic traditions under fascism would have been unthinkable in National Socialist Germany.[42] Under the Estado Novo in Portugal, lasting from 1933 to 1974, historians celebrated the nation's glorious past during the Age of Discoveries, denounced the advances of nineteenth-century liberalism and socialism and mobilized nationalist historical consciousness in support of the regime.[43] The Franco regime in Spain purged republican historians from the universities after 1939 and installed those loyal to the Falange and to Opus Dei. History was demoted to celebrating the Spanish past and providing legitimation to the dictatorship.[44]

Historiographical nationalism also became strong again in the one country that had seen a successful socialist revolution, namely the Soviet Union. The transformation of a Tsarist Russian into Soviet historiography was achieved under the leadership of Mikhail Pokrovski. Nicknamed the 'Supreme Commander of the Army of Red Historians', he was opposed to historiographical nationalism and was a keen propagator of comparative economic history. However, under instruction from Lenin he still penned the new national master narrative for the Soviet Union, carefully avoiding excesses of historiographical nationalism and instead trying to show that the Russian national development fitted into the general development of Western nation states in world history according to the laws of history provided by Marxism–Leninism.[45] Yet under Stalin an increasingly nationalist historiography was promoted that actively sought to promote what often looked like a very traditional Russian nationalism. In 1937 Pokrovski's master narrative was replaced with the heroic *Short Course in the History of the USSR*, penned by Andrej Vasil'evic Šestakov. The book starts: 'The USSR is the land of socialism. There is only one socialist country on the globe – it is our motherland.' And it ends: 'We love our motherland and we must know her wonderful history well.'[46] In the context of the Second World War and its aftermath, Stalinist nationalism celebrated its worst excesses, putting the 'Great Patriotic War' in a long line of Russian victories against the Mongols, Teutonic Knights, Tatars, Sweden, the Ottoman Empire and Napoleon.

But historiographical nationalism in the interwar period was by no means only connected to twentieth-century totalitarianism. Liberal democracies in Europe were beleaguered between the two world wars and many succumbed to the pressures from right-wing movements, but we also find a strong liberal nationalism in countries such as Great Britain. Here historians took courage from the fact that its historical traditions were holding back the forces of illiberalism and strengthening the bulwark of liberal democracy. As George Trevelyan put it in a speech, written for George V on the occasion of the opening of parliament in 1935: 'It is to me a source of pride and thankfulness that the perfect harmony of our parliamentary system with our constitutional monarchy has survived the shocks that have in recent years destroyed other empires and other liberties.'[47] Even those who came to demolish the famous Whig history, with its central idea of the slow extension of liberty in Britain down the ages from the Magna Carta onwards, were full of admiration for British liberal institutions. Herbert Butterfield could not fully free himself from a belief in Britain's civilizational destiny,[48] and Lewis Namier remained convinced that 'Britain was the epitome of constitutional wisdom'.[49] And in Scandinavia, the beginning social democratization of the Scandinavian nation states also corresponded to the writing of national historical master narratives. Two of Norway's most famous historians, Halvdan Koht and Edvard Bull Sr, served as social-democratic ministers of Foreign Affairs, underlining the strong alliance between social democracy and history writing that dominated Scandinavian historiographies, to varying degrees, since the interwar period.[50]

The Second World War saw another high point in the history of nationalist history writing. German historians justified the expansion of the German Reich both westwards and eastwards using historical arguments, and they also endorsed National Socialist plans to ethnically cleanse East-Central Europe from Slavs and settle the area with Germans.[51] Under German occupation in the Second World War, a whole host of collaborationist historiographies sought to foster highly nationalist and right-wing historiographical agendas in a variety of established and new nation states, as well as in stateless nations, although their impact was not too strong, given the short time period they had to establish themselves. The Slovak and Croat cases are particularly interesting, as the beginnings of an independent state-promoted historiography lay in the short-lived fascist puppet states that were created by Germany in the Second World War – something that came to haunt both states after they were refounded in the 1990s.[52]

A delayed break with historiographical nationalism in the West

Amidst the ruins of the Second World War, historians across Europe were mainly concerned with rescuing elements of traditional national master narratives that, they hoped, would help to stabilize their respective nation states in a moment of crisis. In Germany, National Socialism was written out of the national tradition, which was now identified almost exclusively with the national-conservative opposition to Hitler. If many historians had critically to rethink their erstwhile support for National Socialism, they felt reassured that they had been correct in their anti-communism all along. That had been right under National Socialism and was still right in the Cold War. Anti-communism was arguably the most important bridge that allowed German historians to travel 'safely' from their commitment to National Socialism to their commitment to liberal democracy in the Federal Republic of Germany. In Italy, the resistance to Mussolini was now hailed as a 'second Risorgimento', and anti-fascism became one of the foundational myth of the Italian post-war Republic. Fascism was to a surprising extent externalized and identified with the German occupation of northern Italy that had followed the downfall of Mussolini in 1943. In France there was silence about the widespread collaboration under the Vichy regime, and instead the nation was exclusively represented by the Gaullist and Communist resistance allegedly carrying on the positive republican traditions of the country. In Communist Eastern Europe, under the influence of Stalinist historiographical nationalism, most national histories were simply painted red – with a little Marxist/Leninist gloss put over otherwise very traditionally looking national master narrative. In those countries that had been occupied during the Second World War, most historians portrayed them as victims of fascist aggression and did not ask too many questions regarding collaboration.[53]

In Western Europe it was only during the 1960s and 1970s that we see criticisms of historiographical nationalism emerging within the mainstream of historical writing. In Germany, notions of a negatively inverted German special path (Sonderweg) came to the fore that rooted National Socialism in German history and anchored the success of National Socialism firmly in German national history. In Italy, fascism was now increasingly perceived as being rooted in the nineteenth-century nationalist tradition of the Risorgimento. In France, critical questions were asked about the collaborationist Vichy regime. The turn to social history in the 1960s took place within nationalized frameworks almost everywhere, but the questions that were being asked and the topics that were being researched were no longer the traditional ones that had been prominent in the traditions of historiographical nationalism. Labour history and women's history were examples of new departures where historians either had a highly critical perspective on national history or were not interested in such a perspective.[54]

It is, however, impossible to speak about a general trend towards the denationalization of historical writing from the 1960s onwards. In fact, in many countries in Europe, we can observe a renationalization of historical writing from the 1980s onwards that happened in parallel with further critiques of methodological nationalism and a turn to more comparative, transnational and global history. In Germany, first the Historians' Controversy in the mid-1980s and then the search for national normality after reunification brought a good deal of renationalization.[55] In France, the crisis of the republican, revolutionary paradigm, so obvious in the bi-centenaire of 1989, produced an outpouring of national histories. The crisis of the Italian Republic in the midst of financial corruption and the end of Communism also rallied many historians to the national cause – among fears that Italy might simply fall apart in the early 1990s. Multi-national states such as Britain, Spain and Belgium were threatened by nationalist movements in Scotland, Catalonia and Flanders, which produced historiographical repercussions with nationalist agendas. In Eastern Europe, the end of Communism produced a revival of often very traditional nationalist history writing harking back to right-wing authoritarian historiographical traditions of the pre-Communist periods.[56]

Yet, to speak about a return of national(ist) paradigms in European historiographies from the 1980s is not to say that what is returning is the same that was there before the critical turn in historical writing in the 1960s. Self-critical and self-reflexive forms of national history writing continued almost everywhere, and among professional historians there were many who sought to challenge methodological nationalism and national(ist) forms of history writing. Histories of everyday life, historical anthropology, the new cultural history, memory history, European and global history as well as the new (critical) imperial history are just the most prominent forms of history writing that all go beyond and are critical of national paradigms in history writing and have instead promoted comparative and transnational methods of historical investigation.[57]

Decolonization and historiographical nationalism in the developing world

So far, this chapter has presented a very Eurocentric picture of historiographical nationalism. Apart from a brief mention of strong nationalist traditions in nineteenth-century Latin America, no reference was made to historiographical nationalism in other countries normally counted among the global West. However, in North America similar tendencies of historiographical nationalism can be observed both in the United States and in Canada. The European Romantic model was strong during the nineteenth century[58] – with issues of progress and geography being very much to the fore in the respective national historiographies. Like in Latin America, there was a strong 'new world' emphasis that often had a comparative European dimension and served the nationalist purpose of affirming the 'new world' vis-à-vis the old European world. The strength of transnationalism in American historiography during recent years might also have strong nationalist connotations – at least in part, for the global reach of the United States harmonizes well with a historiographical orientation that is equally global in outlook.[59]

In Australia, historiographical master narratives were, for a long time, oriented towards British history – with Australia figuring only as a small extension of Britain and its Empire. A strong national historiographical development only set in during the interwar period and it was intimately connected with the experience of the Australian and New Zealand Army Corps during the First World War. Mateship, egalitarianism and masculinity became important ingredients of a national master narrative that was strongly liberal-democratic in orientation and included, from early on, strong elements of social history. Like in Europe, the more self-critical national historiography of the 1960s and 1970s was followed by a backlash and a history war that focussed on the histories of colonization and the fate of the Australian indigenous population.[60]

Japan is the only non-Western Asian country to make it into the West and to become its own Occident complete with its own Orient. Like in many other areas, it also learnt from the West historiographically and developed a strongly nationalist professional historiography which was represented by Fukuzawa Yukichi whose *Outline of a Theory of Civilisation* (1875) was explicitly advocating nationalist history writing. Strongly attached to the Meji state, Japanese historians sought to boost national confidence in the wider population, legitimate dynastic rule and justify Japanese imperialism in East Asia. After 1945, on one level, there was a major change in that professional historiography at the universities became dominated by Marxists promoting a highly self-critical view of national history, but the new left-of-centre national master narrative in Japan could also still be strongly nationalist, in particular when it came to relations with the United States and with the attitudes towards capitalist restoration in post-war Japan.[61]

The non-European Western historiographies in different parts of the world had many overlaps and connections with European historiographical developments. The same can be said for evolving historiographies in the colonial worlds. Arguably national history writing became one of the most successful European export articles between the interwar period and the phase of massive decolonization between the end of the Second World War and the 1970s. In some parts of the world, notably China and India, Western-style professional history writing met indigenous ways of writing history and was adopted and adapted to those older forms of history writing; in other parts of the world more attuned to oral forms of representations of the past, Western-style history was also adopted but had to create its own traditions and institutions.[62]

Chinese historians even in the late nineteenth century remained, by and large, wedded to Confucian concepts of history writing, rejecting, unlike Japan, Western forms of historical knowledge production. Renewal came via Japan at the beginning of the twentieth century, when younger historians, often with training and experience in Japan, founded the *National Essence Journal* in 1905 in order to seek a cultural revival of

China through historical writing. Their nationalist ambitions called for a reconceptualization of Chinese history along Western lines. National(ist) history writing subsequently became one of the most prominent activities of Chinese historiography, with Huang Jie's Yellow History setting the tone in terms of the promotion of nationalist achievements, the longevity and superiority of the Chinese nation and a generally strongly ethnocentric view of history. In the 1930s, the historians Hu Shi and Gu Jiegang attempted to promote a National School of history writing that emphasized proud moments in Chinese history. When the Communists took over power, like in the rest of the Communist world, the national historical master narrative became underpinned with Marxist/Leninist frameworks but it remained highly nationalist.[63]

In India, the British colonial tradition ensured the setting up of Western-style universities and the training of generations of Indian historians in Western, mainly British and American, universities. Hence a strong Westernizing trend was visible in Indian colonial historiography that was, incidentally, also written to a large extent by British historians. British writing on India during the eighteenth and nineteenth centuries showed a strong fascination with the Indian subcontinent that patterned the perception of the Indian nation also for the twentieth century and laid the foundation for a strongly communalist historiography that established a Hindu and a Muslim version of Indian history. These separate national historiographies contributed to the separation between India and Pakistan in 1947. Nationalist historical writing in India was increasingly directed against British colonial rule, but it took over some of the interpretative patterns of India that had been established by British historiographical traditions. Forms of autochthonism were very prominent, arguing that ancient India already had all the elements of greatness and was even superior to European civilizations. These autochthonist arguments were very recognizable also in modern Eastern European historiographies defending themselves against the West and often self-adopted charge of 'backwardness'. It was, in other words, already a well-established trope in European historiographies before it travelled to the non-European world.[64]

From the middle of the nineteenth century, the Arab Renaissance movement took up European ideas of civilization and nationhood and sought to adapt them to an Arab context. Early nationalist writings focussed on language and culture as central ingredients of an 'Arab nation'. It was not before the 1940s and 1950s that often Western-trained historians sought to develop the concept of an Arab nation and transform it into a political reality with the help of a range of postcolonial Arab states, in particular Egypt, Syria and Iraq. Qustantine Zurayq, who was to become president of the University of Damascus, wrote Arab national history as a political mission statement for the future. Nationalist history writing in the Arab world combined with socialist ideas in Jamal Abdul Nasser's Egypt, but it struggled to find a positive rapport with rising Islamism. For Islamic movements, the concept of the nation and nationalism itself were often evil Western concepts, which were rejected and replaced with the idea of a potentially global community of Islamic believers.[65]

In sub-Saharan African history we also have many attempts to establish nationalist history writing, often by historians trained in the West. These attempts underpinned attempts by postcolonial states to legitimate their rule and territorial shape. However, almost from the beginning of Western-influenced history writing, we also see attempts to provide transnational legitimation for the struggle of independence and the creation of postcolonial nation states in Africa. The negritude movement, founded in Paris in the 1930s, is one such example and the history writing produced by supporters of the Pan-African movement is another. The constant lack of material resources in sub-Saharan Africa was one reason why historical writing and research did not flourish and why centres of historical research on sub-Saharan Africa often are located in the West rather than in Africa. Nevertheless, as the Dakar school of history writing demonstrates, there had been valiant attempts to reintroduce sub-Saharan Africa into a historiographical discourse from which colonialist ideology had often removed it.[66]

Conclusion: What paths for national history writing in the twenty-first century?

These brief comments on the development of historiographical nationalism outside of Europe just give a glimpse to what extent the promotion of nationalism through historiography was also present in other parts of the world. In the context of a volume that introduces various theories of nationalism and their impact on the writing of histories of nationalism, it seems appropriate to reflect on the fact that much historical writing in the world has been and continues to be strongly influenced by nationalist concerns. The power and longevity of the national paradigm in history writing is striking also in global comparative perspective, and it was often linked to nationalist agendas. It successfully subsumed a wide range of other forms of history writing, both spatial and non-spatial, under its remit and it was closely associated with state power and with civil society movements. Nationalist history writing was essentially contested, as different national historical master narratives often competed with each other for dominance and superiority.

Historiographical nationalism is a Janus-faced phenomenon as it could work towards emancipation and liberation from oppression, but it could also be used to justify aggression, ethnic cleansing and genocide. It is hard to neatly delineate a positive historiographical nationalism from a negative one, as both occupy a sliding scale on which they can easily move from one end to the other. The malleability and changeability, in different contexts, of historiographical nationalism makes it deeply problematical and raises the question what to do with it in the twenty-first century. A majority of academic historians in the West today reject historiographical nationalism as a means to establish the superiority of their own nation vis-à-vis others, but many still work within the confines of methodological nationalism, that is, prioritizing in their own work the nation state container. A national lens on history is still very common despite the advances of comparative, transnational and global perspectives in historical writing. And there are, of course, certain topics and themes where such a national framework of analysis might indeed be appropriate. There is no need to throw out national history altogether. However, when national history is being written with a view of promoting national identity, it would be advisable to promote a highly self-reflexive and even playful form of national history that is self-aware of its constructive potential and of alternative ways of constructing that same history. In other words, it should not posit its own construction as the only possible one and enter a field of contestation in which dialogue and debate are seen as the normal means by which to determine politically how people would like to see their national history and its relationship to identity. Changes over time are as acceptable as argumentative shifts and revisions. A move away from essentialist constructions of national history and national identity is certainly a huge advantage over past attempts authoritatively and from above to determine nationalist master narratives.

Notes

1 Andreas Wimmer and Nina Glick-Schiller, 'Methodological Nationalism and Beyond: Nation-State Building, Migration and the Social Sciences', *Global Networks* 2:4 (2002), 301–34.

2 See, e.g., Caspar Hirschi, *The Origins of Nationalism: An Alternative History from Ancient Rome to Early Modern Germany* (Cambridge, 2012); Gabrielle M. Spiegel, *The Past as Text: The Theory and Practice of Medieval Historiography* (Baltimore, 1997); Antonia Gransden, *Historical Writing in England, c. 559–1307* (Ithaca, NY, 1974); Peter Burke, *The Renaissance Sense of the Past* (New York, 1969); Daniel R. Woolf, *The Idea of History in Early Stuart England* (Toronto, 1990); Richard Helgerson, *Forms of Nationhood: The Elizabethan Writing of England* (Chicago, 1992).

3 The term 'historiographical nationalism' is used here in a broad sense and refers to methodological nationalism, that is, privileging the national container for history writing and in the sense of portraying one's own nation in history as being superior to the histories of other nations.

4 This changing perception is related to massive changes in thinking about time and history that are witnessed in the second half of the eighteenth century. See Reinhart Koselleck, 'Einleitung', in Reinhart Koselleck, Otto Brunner and Werner Conze (eds), *Geschichtliche Grundbegriffe: Historisches Lexikon zur*

politisch-sozialen Sprache, vol. 1 (Stuttgart, 1979), p. xv; François Hartog, *Régimes d'Historicité et Expériences du Temps* (Paris, 2003).

5 The emergence of the ideal of professionalism and professional historical writing is dealt with by Rolf Torstendahl, *The Rise and Propagation of Historical Professionalism* (London, 2014).

6 Hans Erich Bödecker, Georg G. Iggers, Jonathan B. Knudsen and Peter H. Reill (eds), *Aufklärung und Geschichte* (Göttingen, 1986).

7 Síofra Pierse, *Voltaire Historiographer: Narrative Paradigms* (Paris, 2008); see generally: Guido Abbatista, 'The Historical Thought of the French Philosophes', in José Rabasa, Masayuki Sato, Edoardo Tortarolo and Daniel Woolf (eds), *History of Historical Writing*, vol. 3 (Oxford, 2015), pp. 406–27.

8 Murray G. H. Pittock, 'Historiography', in Alexander Broadie (ed.), *Cambridge Companion to the Scottish Enlightenment* (Cambridge, 2003), pp. 258–79.

9 Gonzalo Pasamar, *Apologia and Criticism: Historians and the History of Spain, 1500–2000* (Bern, 2010), chapter 1.

10 H. B. Nisbet, 'Herder: the Nation in History', in Michael Branch (ed.), *National History and Identity: Approaches to the Writing of National History in the North-East Baltic Region – Nineteenth and Twentieth Centuries* (Tampere, 1999), pp. 78–96.

11 I have been using the term 'historism' rather than the more common term 'historicism' because I think it is more precise to distinguish two very different set of ideas that are associated with the term 'historicism' in the English language. On the one hand it refers to ideas set out and personified by Leopold von Ranke that circulate around the idea of the specificity of historical developments and the need to understand them in their uniqueness. On the other hand, the same term is used to describe a set of ideas associated with the philosopher Karl Popper who used it to analyse teleological historical thinking in philosophy that associated with thinkers such as Plato, Hegel and Marx. In the German language these two different set of ideas are referred to with two separate terms: 'Historismus' and Historizismus'. Hence I am taking the German term 'historism' and using it in all cases where I refer to forms of Rankean historical thinking.

12 Georg G. Iggers and James M. Powell (eds), *Leopold von Ranke and the Shaping of the Historical Discipline* (Syracuse, 1990).

13 Stanley Mellon, *The Political Uses of History: A Study of Historians in the French Revolution* (Stanford, 1958).

14 Johann Gottlieb Fichte, *Reden an die deutsche Nation* (Hamburg, 2008) [first published in 1808], p. 106.

15 Frank Hadler and Tibor Frank (eds), *Disputed Territories and Shared Pasts: Overlapping National Histories in Modern Europe* (Basingstoke, 2011).

16 François Walter, *Les Figures Paysagères de la Nation. Territoire et Paysage en Europe (16e-20e Siècle)* (Paris, 2004).

17 John Breuilly, *Myth-Making or Myth-Breaking? Nationalism and History* (Birmingham, 1997).

18 Stefan Berger with Christoph Conrad, *The Past as History: National Identity and Historical Consciousness in Modern Europe* (Basingstoke, 2015), pp. 111–13.

19 R. J. W. Evans and Guy P. Marchal (eds), *The Uses of the Middle Ages in Modern European States: History, Nationhood and the Search for Origins* (Basingstoke, 2010).

20 Linas Eriksonas, *National Heroes and National Identities. Scotland, Norway and Lithuania* (Brussels, 2004).

21 Berger with Conrad, *The Past as History*, pp. 120–3.

22 On the relationship of national historical master narratives with their class, religious and ethnic 'others' as well as on the gendering of history, compare Stefan Berger and Chris Lorenz (eds), *The Contested Nation: Ethnicity, Class, Religion and Gender in National Histories* (Basingstoke, 2008).

23 Eliana de Freitas Dutra, 'The Mirror of History and Images of the Nation: The Invention of National Identity in Brazil and Its Contrasts with Similar Enterprises in Mexico and Argentina', in Stefan Berger (ed.), *Writing the Nation: A Global Perspective* (Basingstoke, 2007), pp. 84–102. For Chile, see also Allen Woll, *A Functional Past: The Uses of History in Nineteenth-Century Chile* (Louisiana, 1982).

24 Ilaria Porciani and Lutz Raphael (eds), *Atlas of European Historiography: The Making of a Profession 1800–2005* (Basingstoke, 2010).

25 Ilaria Porciani and Jo Tollebeek (eds), *Setting the Standards: Institutions, Networks and Communities of National Historiographies* (Basingstoke, 2012).

26 Pierre Nora, 'Lavisse: instituteur national', in *Les Lieux de Mémoire*, vol. 1, ed. Pierre Nora (Paris, 1984), pp. 247–90.

27 Jürgen Osterhammel, *Geschichtswissenschaft jenseits des Nationalstaats. Studien zu Beziehungsgeschichte und Zivilisationsvergleich* (Göttingen, 2001), pp. 91–102.

28 Hervé Inglebert, *Le Monde, l'Histoire. Essai sur les Histoires Universelles* (Paris, 2014).

29 Paul Fredericq, *The Study of History in England and Scotland* (Baltimore, 1887).

30 Karl Dietrich Erdmann, *Toward a Global Community of Historians: The International Historical Congresses and the International Committee of Historical Sciences, 1898–2000* (Oxford, 2005).

31 Hans-Christian Maner, 'Die Aufhebung des Nationalen im Universalen oder die Nation als das Mass aller Dinge? Zum historiographischen Konzept Nicolae Iorgas im südost- und ostmitteleuopäischen Rahmen', in Hans-Christian Maner and Markus Krzoska (eds), *Beruf und Berufung: Geschichtswissenschaft und Nationsbildung in Ostmittel- und Südosteuropa im 19. und 20. Jahrhundert* (Berlin, 2015), pp. 239–63.

32 Milan Řepa, 'The Czechs, Germans and Sudetenland: Historiographical Dispute in the Heart of Europe', in Tibor Frank and Frank Hadler (eds), *Disputed Territories and Shared Pasts: Overlapping National Histories in Modern Europe* (Basingstoke, 2011), pp. 303–28.

33 Stefan Berger and Alexei Miller (eds), *Nationalizing Empires* (Budapest, 2015).

34 Cited in Effi Gazi, 'Theorizing and Practising "Scientific History", in Southeastern Europe (19th and 20th Centuries): Spyridon Lambros and Nicolae Iorga', in Stefan Berger and Chris Lorenz (eds), *Nationalising the Past* (Basingstoke, 2010), p. 198.

35 Gabriel Monod and Gustave Fagniez, 'Avant-propos', *Revue Historique* 1:1 (1876), 4.

36 Matthew Stibbe, 'German Historians Views of England during the First World War', in Stefan Berger, Peter Lambert and Peter Schumann (eds), *Historikerdialoge. Geschichte, Mythos und Gedächtnis im deutsch-britischen kulturellen Austausch, 1750–2000* (Göttingen, 2003), pp. 235–54.

37 Stuart Wallace, *War and the Image of Germany. British Academics, 1914–1918* (Edinburgh, 1988); Gerd Krumeich, 'Ernest Lavisse und die Kritik an der deutschen "Kultur", 1914–1918', in Wolfgang J Mommsen and Elisabeth Müller-Luckner (eds), *Kultur und Krieg: die Rolle der Intellektuellen, Künstler und Schriftsteller im Ersten Weltkrieg* (Munich, 1996), pp. 143–54.

38 Peter Schöttler, 'After the Deluge: The Impact of the Two World Wars on the Historical Work of Henri Pirenne and Marc Bloch', in Berger and Lorenz (eds), *Nationalizing the Past* (Basingstoke, 2010) pp. 404–25.

39 Holger Herwig, 'Clio Deceived: Patriotic Self-Censorship in Germany after the Great War', in Wilson (ed.), *Forging the Collective Memory* (Princeton, 1991), p. 88f.

40 Berger with Conrad, *The Past as History*, pp. 240–5.

41 Winfried Schulze and Otto-Gerhard Oexle (eds), *Deutsche Historiker im Nationalsozialismus* (Frankfurt/Main, 2000).

42 Fabio Fernandi Rizi, *Benedetto Croce and Italian Fascism* (Toronto, 2003).

43 Sérgio Campos Matos and Joana Gaspar de Freitas, 'Portugal', in Ilaria Porciani and Lutz Raphael (eds), *Atlas*, p. 124f.

44 Miquel A. Marin, *Los historiadores españoles en el franquismo 1948–1975* (Zaragoza, 2005).

45 G. M. Enteen, *The Soviet Scholar-Bureaucrat: M. N Pokrovskii and the Society of Marxist Historians* (London, 1978).

46 Cited in Anatole G. Mazour, *Modern Russian Historiography*, 2nd edn (Princeton, 1958), p. 204.

47 Cited in J. M. Hernon Jr, 'The Last Whig Historian and Consensus History: George Macaulay Trevelyan, 1876–1962', *American Historical Review* 81 (1976), 86.

48 Michael Bentley, *The Life and Thought of Herbert Butterfield* (Cambridge, 2011).

49 Thus his biographer, Linda Colley, *Lewis Namier* (London, 1989), p. 14.

50 Ragnar Björk, 'The Overlapping Histories of Sweden and Norway – the Union from 1814 to 1905', in Frank and Hadler (eds), *Disputed Territories*, pp. 17–34.

51 Karen Schönwälder, *Historiker und Politik: Geschichtswissenschaft im Nationalsozialismus* (Frankfurt/Main, 1992).

52 Adam Hudek, 'Slovakia', in Ilaria Porciani and Lutz Raphael (eds), *Atlas*, p. 152f.; Ulf Brunnbauer, 'Croatia', in Ilaria Porciani and Lutz Raphael (eds), *Atlas*, p. 102f.

53 Stefan Berger, 'A Return to the National Paradigm? National History Writing in Germany, Italy, France and Britain from 1945 to the Present', *Journal of Modern History* 77:3 (2005), 629–78; Maciej Górny, *Die Wahrheit ist auf unserer Seite'. Nation, Marxismus und Geschichte im Ostblock* (Cologne, 2011).

54 Berger, 'A Return to the National Paradigm'.

55 Stefan Berger, *The Search for Normality: National Identity and Historical Consciousness in Germany since 1800*, 2nd edn (Oxford, 2003).

56 Sorin Antohi, Balázs Trencsényi and Péter Apor (eds), *Narratives Unbound: Historical Studies in Post-Communist Eastern Europe* (Budapest, 2007).
57 Berger with Conrad, *The Past as History*, pp. 338–57.
58 Gabriele Lingelbach, *Klio macht Karriere. Die Institutionalisierung der Geschichtswissenschaft in Frankreich und den USA in der zweiten Hälfte des 19. Jahrhunderts* (Göttingen, 2003).
59 Allen Smith, 'Seven Narratives in North American History: Thinking the Nation in Canada, Quebec and the United States', in Stefan Berger (ed.), *Writing the Nation*, pp. 63–83.
60 Stuart Macintyre and Anna Clark, *The History Wars* (Melbourne, 2003).
61 Stefan Tanaka, *Japan's Orient: Rendering Pasts into History* (Berkeley, 1993).
62 Partha Chatterjee, *The Nation and Its Fragments: Colonial and Postcolonial Histories* (Princeton, NJ, 1993).
63 Q. Edward Wang, 'Between Myth and History: The Construction of a National Past in Modern Asia', in Berger (ed.), *Writing National History*, pp. 126–54; Prasenjit Duara, *Rescuing History from the Nation. Questioning Narratives of Modern China* (Chicago, 1995).
64 Radhika Seshan, 'Writing the Nation in India: Communalism and Historiography', in Stefan Berger (ed.), *Writing the Nation*, pp. 155–78; Kumkum Chatterjee, 'The King of Controversy. History and Nation-Making in Late Colonial India', *American Historical Review* 110:5 (2005), 1454–75.
65 Birgit Schaebler, 'Writing the Nation in the Arab-Speaking World, Nationally and Transnationally', in Berger (ed.), *Writing the Nation*, pp. 179–96.
66 Ibrahima Thioub, 'Writing National and Transnational History in Africa: The Example of the, "Dakar School"', in Berger (ed.), *Writing the Nation*, pp. 197–212; Paul Lovejoy, 'The Ibadan School of History and Its Critics', in Toyin Falola (ed.), *African Historiography. Essays in Honour of Jacob Ade Ajayi* (Burnt Mills, 1993); Michael Amoah, *Reconstructing the Nation in Africa: the Politics of Nationalism in Ghana* (London, 2006).

Further reading

Berger, S. (ed.), *Writing National Histories: A Global Perspective.* Basingstoke: Palgrave Macmillan, 2007.
Berger, S. and C. Lorenz (eds), *The Contested Cation: Ethnicity, Class, Religion and Gender in National Histories.* Basingstoke: Palgrave Macmillan, 2008.
Berger, S. with Christoph Conrad, *The Past as History: National Identity and Historical Consciousness in Modern Europe.* Basingstoke: Palgrave Macmillan, 2015.
Frank, T. and F. Hadler (eds), *Disputed Territories and Shared Pasts: Overlapping National Histories in Modern Europe.* Basingstoke: Palgrave Macmillan, 2011.
Iggers, G. G. and Q. E. Wang with contributions from S. Mukherjee, *A Global History of Modern Historiography.* Harlow: Pearson Longman, 2008.
Middell, M. and L. Roura i Aulinas (eds), *Transnational Challenges to National History Writing.* Basingstoke: Palgrave Macmillan, 2013.

Porciani, I. and L. Raphael (eds), *Atlas of European Historiography: The Making of a Profession, 1800–2005*. Basingstoke: Palgrave Macmillan, 2010.

Porciani, I. and J. Tollebeek (eds), *Setting the Standards: Institutions, Networks and Communities of National Historiography*. Basingstoke: Palgrave Macmillan, 2012.

Woolf, D., *A Global History of History*. Cambridge: Cambridge University Press, 2011.

3

Marxism and the history of nationalism

Miroslav Hroch[1]

Introduction

Simplification is inherent in every 'ism', especially when it is applied to both social behaviour and an interpretation of the world. There is a great risk of misunderstanding, necessitating definition in advance. This is true of both central termini of this chapter. A consensual definition of the differently misused and vague term 'nationalism' is hardly possible, which is why, in this chapter, we will follow the understanding used by orthodox Marxists themselves, albeit formulated many decades after Marx and in the context of fully formed nations. Nationalism was categorized as an ideology pretending to advocate the interests of all members of the nation, while in fact serving the egoistic interests of the ruling class of this same nation. Under certain circumstances, it has been called a smokescreen obscuring the true interests of the bourgeoisie. It is interesting to note, by the way, that the term was not in use during Karl Marx's and Friedrich Engel's lifetime in the second half of the nineteenth century. Making Marxist perceptions of this 'nationalism' the core issue of this chapter would consequently entail an unwarranted narrowing of perspective and examination. Rather than 'nationalism', it was merely the nation that was under scrutiny originally. I therefore think it legitimate to choose the term 'nation' as my point of departure and to scrutinize how 'the classic' and later Marxists understood the nation and its relevance and how they interpreted its formation in the context of European capitalist society. Originally, during all the nineteenth century and later (until the Second World War), all discussions and also research on nation and nationalism were focused on Europe, since they were regarded as genuine European phenomena. Consequently, this overview of Marxist concepts concerns above all Europe: the understanding of these terms changed distinctly during the last decades as a result of their globalization. To interpret this change is, however, not the task of this chapter.

But what do we mean by 'Marxism' in relation to the nation? There is no room here to unravel the wide spectrum of different interpretations, from orthodox Marxists, to Austro-Marxist revisionists, and today's neo-Marxists and postmodernists. Giving due consideration to the context is rather more important. The past 170 years have seen two distinct contexts, depending on historical perspective and political situation, respectively, and two corresponding 'Marxisms':

1.   The often controversial discussions and considerations regarding the nation (or the nation state respectively) as a sociopolitically given factor took place in the context of a struggle to overcome capitalism through socialism. In this climate of political conflicts, Marxists (in their capacity as socialists) judged the concept of nation by its utility for their struggle and therefore discussed the nation in relation to a socialist future. Of course, this revolutionary perspective compromised the objectivity of the analyses since social classes and their interests were foregrounded. Notably, the most intensely discussed problem was not primarily cast in terms of the 'nation', but was rather formulated as a 'national question' which needed to be resolved. It may also be possible to discern two further steps in this process: one preceding and one following the socialist revolution.

2.   Examination and discussion of nation-building and nationalism took place in sociopolitical conditions that no longer saw the 'transition to socialism' as a viable historical perspective and that no longer had the possible development and layout of the socialist nation on its agenda. Even those who adopted Marx's teachings or felt inspired by them put less and less emphasis on it as an instrument of socialist revolution.

Differentiating these contexts is useful, not least because it allows for a more nuanced look at what might otherwise generically be perceived as 'Marxism'. This differentiation sets apart Marxism as a political programme or political doctrine on the one hand and Marxism as an analytical tool or method on the other:[2]

> With the former, theoretical analysis of the 'national question' has
>   been put at the service of a political struggle for a revolutionary
>   transformation of society on its way to socialism. This struggle took
>   recourse to Marxism (and later Marxism–Leninism respectively),
>   their authors more or less identifying with these political goals. Class
>   and revolution were key concepts of these theories.

With the latter, fundamentals of Marxist theory were used as tools of academic analysis, regardless of whether an author professed socialist convictions or not. Here, Marxism presented itself as an application of research methodology and models that relate to Karl Marx's thought and use it. This application, however, is no longer used as a militant argument in the class struggle. Rather, it is used to analyse and explain historical processes – in our case the formation of modern nations and nationalism.

Theory as a means of changing the world

Although it is generally said that neither Karl Marx nor Friedrich Engels left any systematic analysis of processes of nation-building, no historical overview of the research on nationalism can do without them. They did not draft a theory, that is, they did not develop thorough definitions and did not draw systematic conclusions. Nonetheless, however, they were frequently and intensely confronted with the phenomenon of the nation, forcing them to comment on the political and social relevance of the nation, time and again. In doing so, they formulated several observations and general remarks, which in turn served as guidelines (or points of departure) to their followers on their way to formulating a theory. Central to these was the opinion that the nation (in the sense of a nation state) was an instrument of the bourgeoisie and could therefore not serve as the proletariat's object of identification ('mother country').

To be fair we should keep in mind that a theory of the nation was not on the contemporary agenda and that consequently no non-Marxist concept of the nation was formulated in the social sciences, either. The nation was generally regarded as a natural phenomenon and also as a political and social value – a possible Marxist innovation being the partial or full questioning of this naturalness.

In terminology, Marx and Engels differentiate between the 'nation' as a synonym of statehood and 'nationality' as denoting a nation living in the misery of being bereft of a state and possibly even political history. The (nation-) state was regarded as a necessary component and as the ordering principle of the capitalist society. Hand in hand, the nation state playing its temporal historical role of progress, both are walking to their doom. Marx's and Engels's attitude towards the category of the 'nation' was, therefore, ambivalent: they saw it as a historically necessary and temporarily progressive phenomenon, but did not perceive it as a norm and value in itself, as the bourgeois world did. The proletariat should be organized in 'Internationals' rather than according to nations.

The only problem that was discussed and theoretically defined even then was that of the existence (or non-existence) of nations without a state, or 'non-historical nation[s]', to put it briefly and simply. Using Hegel's dichotomy of 'barbaric' and 'civilized' nations[3] and in harmony with many German liberals of the mid-nineteenth century, Marx and Engels, besides their acknowledgement of established nations, considered nationalities without a state as 'people[s] without a history'. They were the embodiment of 'relicts of peoples' from feudal times that survived by accident and would be civilized through assimilation by big nations: the same way in which the Provençals and Bretons, the Scots or Welsh had been assimilated. These peoples do not have a bourgeoisie and therefore no hope of existing as nations. In the concrete historical situation of the revolutionary year 1848–49 this meant that the non-historical peoples of central Europe received a chance of Germanizing or Magyarizing themselves, and since they rejected that opportunity, they sided with the counter-revolution.[4] Consequently, these nations disappeared from the horizon of the 'classics', as they were not deemed sufficiently interesting to study their inclusion into a capitalist society in greater theoretical depth. The assumption that these nationalities did not have a bourgeoisie mirrored the contemporary status, but turned out to be an incorrect prognosis for the future.[5]

When speaking of the 'failure' of Marxism in examining the national issue, big nation states are not what comes to mind first and foremost. Neither Marx nor Engels questioned the national existence of the French, the Dutch or the Germans. They saw them as existing nations, headed by the bourgeoisie, and it was within their framework that the internationalist struggle of the proletarians against the bourgeoisie consequently had to take place.

Neither Marx nor his followers during the second half of the nineteenth century understood the national movements of the 'non-historical' nations (and these were the majority) as an organic part in the formation of capitalist societies. Rather, they thought of them as political complications. Focussed entirely on the political goals of the proletariat, in the sense of a peculiar idealism, they understood these national movements as some national enthusiasts' voluntarist project, which did not lend legitimacy to the Czechs', Lithuanians', Slovenians' and others' claim to national existence. They did not even pause to consider the objective social factors. In this regard, proletarian internationalists, like Marx and Engels, agreed with bourgeois liberal nationalists and the bourgeoisie of big nations.

This attitude harboured a contradiction. On the one hand, it was said that proletarians did not have a mother country (or should not have one) and that the nation was a tool of power wielded by the bourgeoisie alone. On the other hand, development towards a capitalist form was seen as a necessary consequence of progress in production/for the productive forces, which made the nation an organic, historically required component of this development. This, however, was only considered true of the 'historical' nation, that is, for those nation states and possibly for nations such as the Poles or the Magyars, which had previously owned statehood and were prepared to free themselves by revolution to pave the way to progressive capitalism.

Overcoming capitalism through socialism was likewise considered necessary, making it possible to fundamentally question the existence of the nation: the future was not one of nations.[6] These considerations, however, did not include the 'non-historical' nations, which were regarded a coincidence, an artificial product of national agitation.

This contradiction between the politically motivated rejection of national movements and the empirical fact that many of these national movements were successful remained problematic. In fact, it made the development of coherent theories of the nation or of nationalism impossible. This inner tension may not have been coincidental. It corresponded to the fundamental dualism of Karl Marx's own concept of science. On the one hand it basically was a positivistic approach, according to which science was supposed to seek and find the objective reality of society and the 'laws of its workings' ('Gesetzmässigkeiten'). On the other hand, there was the assumption that not only objective conditions but also human needs and subjective interests played a role in society.[7]

As long as the socialist movement developed under the conditions of the 'historical' nation states, which were perceived as mono-ethnic, national movements were merely a marginal phenomenon. Polemics against these 'relics of peoples' continued also at the time of the First International in the 1860s and 1870s, even though at that time, national movements grew stronger and achieved clear successes. This changed greatly towards the end of the nineteenth century, when many national movements on the territory of the multi-ethnic empires of Russia, Austria and the Ottomans proved to be successful. The small nations had become a reality. The need to accommodate this new situation through theoretical analysis rather than slogans gave rise to controversial discussions in the Second International, out of which systematic theoretical concepts have emerged.

As an orthodox Marxist, Karl Kautsky was foremost among those who analysed the question of nations at that time. He could not imagine the nation to be anything else but a national state in whose framework the national market would consolidate under the leadership of the bourgeoisie. This market needed one uniform language and therefore demanded the assimilation of all ethnic minorities that did not have a chance to build their own market under their own bourgeoisie. Therefore, as late as 1887, Kautsky still claimed that the Czech could not become a nation, since there was no Czech bourgeoisie.[8] He remained faithful to that conviction, even when, ten years later, the Czech socialist movement identified itself with their own nation.

Orthodox Marxism also determined the political practice of the Russian socialists in their relationship to national movements in Russia. The quarrel between Vladimir Lenin and Rosa Luxemburg is symptomatic in that respect. Following the failed revolution of 1905, Lenin argued in favour of cooperation between socialists and the national movements, which, in their anti-tsarist struggle, were on the side of progress. Luxemburg strongly argued against this on the grounds that the nation was merely a kind of self-organizing bourgeoisie with which the proletariat had nothing in common. In a class society, 'the nation' as a homogeneous sociopolitical entity does not exist. Neither with respect to economics, nor in the realm of morals can the bourgeoisie and the proletariat appear as a consolidated 'national' entity.[9] Therefore, Luxemburg even considered the phrase 'right to self-determination' of nationalities (of those under Russian rule) as an empty shell. These nationalities were doomed to assimilation through the logics of capitalism.[10]

Lenin argued against this orthodox position, which took recourse to Marx and Engels, arguing that social conditions had changed by the beginning of the twentieth century. The achievements of capitalism were bound to lead to the creation of the nations, whose economic foundation was control over the local market on the part of the bourgeoisie. The latter has an interest in the unity of these territories with inhabitants who speak the same language. He took recourse to Kautsky's thesis, according to which linguistically heterogeneous states tend to be backwards, while the nation state offers the best conditions for the development and well-being of capitalism. Here, Lenin named two stages of nation-building: during the first, national movements fight feudalism, thereby siding with progress and being a potential ally of the proletariat. During the second phase, the bourgeoisie is already dominant in a capitalist society and the main opposition is between itself and the proletariat. During this phase, national movements advocate the interests of the bourgeoisie and become an enemy to socialism.[11] This periodization was not only important for the practice of the Russian workers' movement, but also (freed of the political doctrine) inspiring for research on national movements in general. It should also be mentioned in this context that Lenin globalized the national question. Taking the idea of a world revolution as his starting point, he also paid attention to the suppressed peoples of Asia and of the colonized world.[12]

At the same time, but independent from this discussion, new ways for a more thorough revision of Orthodox Marxism were sought by the young social democrat Otto Bauer in his copious book *Die Nationalitätenfrage und die Sozialdemokratie* (1907; The Nationality Question and Social Democracy).[13] This was a work that for the first time attempted a Marxist, systematic interpretation of processes of nation formation. He tried to solve the political problem through scientific analysis, signalling a shift from political Marxism to Marxism as a method. One of Bauer's contemporary political goals was overcoming the divide caused by the nationality question among Austrian Social Democrats. The other was scientific testing of the already ten-year-old Austro-Marxist concept of cultural autonomy as a solution to the question of nationalities.[14] In the field of practical politics, he revised orthodox Marxism by acknowledging the right of nations to independent, 'viable' existence without a state and by counting on the nation as an independent, culturally autonomous community to take part in the shaping of a future socialist society.[15] In his eyes, the question of nationalities could not be solved without a more in-depth theoretical examination of the character and the origins of the nations.[16] This was his reaction to the debate that had continued among 'bourgeois' scientists for more than a decade. After all, the question of how a nation could be defined, that is, who could rightfully claim recognition as a full-fledged nation, was a political issue, not only for social democrats.

First and foremost, Bauer accepted the then predominant notion of a nation as a community that had been in existence for many centuries. He relativized this perennialist view by differentiating between different previous 'nations', depending on historical phase and predominant class structure: the nation of prehistoric tribes, of medieval feudalism, of early bourgeoisie, of the intellectuals – and only then did the present nation of the capitalist age follow. Consequently, this nation came into being through a long historical process in which its members experienced a shared fate and corresponding conflicts, while being in a constant exchange of information and opinions. For him, the nation was 'the community of those connected by fate into a community of character'. By the term 'community of fate', he did 'not [mean] submission to the same fate, but shared experience of the same fate' – namely 'in continued intercourse, ongoing interaction with each other'.[17] The most important medium of this interaction was and is language. This process took place under the conditions of continued class struggle, which holds a contradictory element: on the one hand, Bauer advocated the 'classic' Marxist thesis that workers of different nations had more in common with each other than with the bourgeoisie of their respective nation. On the other hand, shared experience of fate connected the workers to the other classes of their nation. This was why Bauer had certain reservations against classifying the nation as a cultural community. Culture in a (capitalist) class society would remain mainly an issue for the ruling class, but potentially workers could also participate and fully join this cultural community in the future socialist nation.[18]

The weak point in Bauer's theory is a claim made in the introduction to his book, that the question of nationalities could be interpreted by means of national character. By this, he means a 'compound of bodily and mental traits regarding which one nation is different from another'.[19] These traits are said to have developed as a result of the same historical forces and conditions exerting an influence on all members of the nation.[20] It is a justified and repeatedly raised argument that the national character can hardly be grasped empirically. It is symptomatic, by the way, that the term 'nationalism', so frequently used today (also among 'Marxists'), is not yet part of Otto Bauer's terminological toolkit.

Summing up, it can be said that Otto Bauer examined the nation regarding two aspects: On the one hand, Marxism for him was a means for solving the political problem – the question of nationalities in Austria. His solution, however, had been rendered obsolete by the disintegration of Austria-Hungary in 1918. On the other hand – regarding Marxism as a method – he attempted to elucidate a complex programmatic Marxist analysis of nation formation. It is in this theory that we find generalizations and basic tenets that later became part of the methodology of several authors who were considered Marxists. The nation is here understood as an objectively existent community (meaning the understanding is 'essentialist') that was created by a long historical development, a never-ending process of formation. Through their common history, or shared fate, its members would always be linked more closely to each other than to members of other nations, language playing an important role in the process. This community of fate was formed through its internal conflicts: the process of formation of modern nations was closely connected to the class struggle between bourgeoisie and proletariat. Since his work was only translated into English in 2000,[21] he was known to most Anglo-American authors only second hand for a long time.

Fate has a sense of irony – Otto Bauer's theory had its strongest effect (in distorted form) thanks to a Russian revolutionary whom Lenin had sent to Vienna in 1913 and charged with the task of studying Austro-Marxism. This man was the later notorious Josef Džugašvili-Stalin. He found Otto Bauer's book particularly interesting and – even though he probably did not fully understand it – wrote a critical appraisal of it: Marxism and the National Question.[22] He accepted Otto Bauer's historical dimension to the formation of nations, characterized the nation as a historically 'developed' community, but simplified Bauer's five steps of their development, reducing them down to two: the pre-capitalist one and the capitalist one. At the same time, he strictly rejected the terms 'community of character' and 'community of fate'. In tune with Bauer and in the spirit of the old Marxist tradition, he stressed that the bourgeoisie's fight for dominance of the markets was of critical importance for the generation of the nation of the present. He efficiently condensed Bauer's complicated terminological considerations into his later very famous definition: 'A nation is a historically constituted, stable community of people, formed on the basis of common language, territory, economic life and psychological make up manifested in a common culture.'[23]

Although Stalin's opinion was questioned repeatedly – for its rigourism, for its sketchy definitions of individual factors, for underestimating national consciousness – it became a scientific axiom in major parts of the world, above all in the Soviet Union and its satellites from the 1920s onwards. This forced research into adopting the only permitted concept of nation and nationalism, although this adoption was often only *pro forma*. Stalin's definition set the horizons for this research and thereby strongly limited its analytical potential insofar as it corresponded to the general decline of dogmatic Marxism as a method. Ten years after the October Revolution, Stalin's dictatorial practices of national policy that claimed to be founded in Marxism–Leninism no longer matched the theory he had formulated in pre-revolutionary times, namely that all nations have a real right to self-determination and cultural autonomy. To this was added the hypocritical distinction between 'bourgeois nationalism' and socialist 'patriotism' that survived in all states of the Soviet bloc up to the end of the twentieth century. Only from the 1960s on did a gradual revision of the Stalinist concept take place in the Soviet Union and in Eastern European countries, leading to a return to (revised) Marxism as a methodology, increasingly in harmony with Western authors who had been inspired by Marxism.

Marxism as a theory without ambitions of changing the world

After the breakdown of the Habsburg monarchy, the strength of the Austro-Marxist concept for a resolution of the nationality question could not be empirically tested. In Central and Western Europe, this effectively freed the Marxist method from the burden of responsibility of political engagement. Only in the Soviet Union (and after 1948 in East-Central Europe as well) there were political control of the orthodoxy and keepers of 'true' Marxism represented by Stalin's theses. Marxism as a political doctrine and as a theory was here declared a union and this was also true of the communist movement which was controlled by the Third International. Antonio Gramsci was among the few authors in the interwar period in the West who tried to unfurl Marxist theory further by attempting to reinterpret the proletariat as a nationally anchored people in opposition to the cosmopolitan bourgeoisie.[24]

After the Second World War, Marxism in Western Europe was a slowly dying political doctrine. With regard to the 'national question' it oscillated between the Stalinist dogmatism of the communist parties and 'neo-Marxist' revisionism. Through shifts in social structures and demographics, class differences grew more complicated. Consequently, the opposition between national 'separatism' ('bourgeois nationalism') and the unity of the working class, as well as the dichotomy of class and nation, which had been of such core importance at the beginning of the century, lost much of its relevance. The final discussions of scientists attempting to apply Marxism as a political doctrine and as a method in relation to the problems of the nationalism of their time took place in France and England in the mid-1970s, without causing much of an echo. Haupt, Löwy and Weill took a clear stance towards the constructivist perception and saw the nation as a big, social community of citizens of all classes, who longed to identify with a super-personal entity. Under the conditions of inner conflicts of interest, but also 'irrational ties' they were mobilized for the nation as a vehicle of positive values by cultural activities, such as celebrations, places of remembrance and so on. But this mobilization also contained elements of exclusion and a-social behaviour.[25]

In 1975, in the *New Left Review* Tom Nairn stated that nationalism should be understood as a 'modern Janus': as a negative, backwards-oriented, conflict-inducing force on the one hand and as a useful side effect of the national liberation movements of the nineteenth century and the anti-colonial and anti-imperial struggles of the twentieth century on the other, where it was on the side of progress. By contrast, Eric Hobsbawm emphasized the Marxist critical distance *vis-à-vis* egoistic and irrational nationalism. He warned against idealizing nationalism, even if it fights in the name of liberation. Notwithstanding the fact that the nation came into being as a result of economic processes, he cannot reconcile himself to the vision of a future socialist world as a mosaic of numerous small national states.[26] Following his study on 'invented tradition' – which primarily questions the myth of real existing traditions – his name then became unjustly associated with the claim that the nation was an invention.[27]

Independent of these politically oriented discussions, nation-building and nationalism became – even for some of the participants of these discussions – a subject of scientific enquiry. The nation and nationalism were no longer to be assessed according to abstract class criteria. Rather, their causality was to be analysed and explained in a Marxist manner. It was not always clear where the limits of this method lay or in how far authors understood the application of historical materialism as Marxist. Rather, this academic research brought together differently interpreted Marxist approaches and Marxist influences.[28] After Stalin, no sophisticated Marxist 'theory of nationalism' developed. A strong and undeniable inspiration through Marxism remained, however. The term 'inspiration' is here used to denote full or revised acceptance of some methodological approaches which are understood to be Marxist.

First of all we should consider that – apart from this inspiration in Western academic discourse – a quasi-stereotype has survived that could be called a spontaneous, unreflected heirloom of the Marxist political doctrine. I mean, above all, the survival of the former Orthodox Marxist conviction that the nation was a harmful product of historical development since, as a creation of the bourgeoisie, it inhibits the struggle of classes and harms historical progress. This opinion was cultivated intellectually: the nation was called a construct, a product of the imagination. Likewise, language and national history were instrumentalized orchestrations – not so much at the service of the bourgeoisie as serving the old-fashioned national academics, notables, members of the educated middle class.

This perception was also shared by authors who spoke up neither about socialism nor about Marxism and who had no interest in the proletariat's class struggle. This kind of anti-nationalist thinking has been termed 'Olympianism' by Kenneth Minogue, who suspects it of seeking world domination through globalization.[29] Although he understood 'nationalism' to be something positive, he still advocated the same opinion as the critics of nationalism, namely that the existence of the nation was primarily conditioned by activities and decisions of certain interest groups.

This peculiar heirloom of Marxist political doctrine had a (possibly decisive) part in helping the neologism 'nationalism' infiltrate the academic sphere from the political one. It was no deterrent that, above all, social democracy – since the turn of the century – took part in creating its originally very negative connotations. Combined with the older, almost forgotten, views expressed by Ernest Renan and German statisticians,[30] according to which the nation existed mainly by grace of its members' decision, the mainstream opinion gradually formed that the nation was created through nationalism. With a certain degree of simplification, one could therefore advocate the view that the nation was simply a product of nationalism, or even that – of the two concepts – nationalism was the one actually existent phenomenon that should therefore primarily be studied. This opinion, which was in stark contradiction to historical materialism, triggered reactions from authors who saw themselves as Marxists, as well as from those who explicitly rejected Marxism. This convergence can be illustrated by the common ground between the professed Marxist Eric Hobsbawm and the non-Marxist Ernest Gellner's idea concerning the decisive role of nationalism in nation formation.[31] The terminological mess was complete from the 1930s on, when some authors, like Carlton Hayes, started to consciously use the term 'nationalism' not as a political denunciation, but neutrally, that is, free of evaluation or judgement.[32]

Consequently, neither of the terms 'nationalism' and 'Marxism' is unambiguous. It is only in this context that Tom Nairn's oft-cited sentence should be commented upon or interpreted, according to whom 'the theory of nationalism represents Marxism's great historical failure'.[33] Insofar as we understand Marxism as a political doctrine, we can agree to that sentence: viewing the nation as an unwelcome complication on the way to socialism and as a product of bourgeois interests (later called 'nationalism') and therefore denying its right to exist was a fatal contradiction to the fundamental thesis of historical materialism, according to which the prospective social development to capitalism should be interpreted through objective conditions and material interests. If we understand Marxism as a method, however, as is mostly the case today, we should not so much speak of 'failure', as of insufficient attention to the phenomenon of the 'nation' by Marxist theory up to the beginning of the twentieth century. This, however, changed with Otto Bauer, whose concept of nation formation can neither be classified as failure nor as ignorance. To the contrary, since his time and also thanks to him, Marxism (where it has been freed from the dead weight of political doctrine) has made major contributions to the understanding of the formation of nations as large social groups. This, however, did not happen through Marxist Orthodoxy, but rather through Marxist inspiration.

So what was the nature of this Marxist inspiration for the study of nation-building and nationalism? It was in the implementation of Marxist methodological approaches, and of historical materialism respectively. It is irrelevant, in this context, whether or not authors took explicit recourse to Karl Marx or Otto Bauer. In this sense, Marxism did not inspire in the form of a compact theory, but rather in the shape of multiple patterns of interpretation, which were integrated into individual authors' analytical toolkits. If some authors are now treated here by way of example, no full development of their concepts is intended, as other chapters of this volume are reserved for this purpose. Rather, we will focus on those opinions and conclusions that were immediately derived from Marxist methodological thought.

The first theory of communication that may be counted among those inspired by Marxism is the one developed by Karl W. Deutsch, a younger compatriot of the American political scientist Hans Kohn, at the beginning of the 1950s.[34] Through quantifying research he found out that nations formed as a result of strongly intensifying, complementary communication. This communication was only possible after the rise of capitalist industrialization. Through industrialization and increased social mobility, as well as increased market relations, communication within the large group called nation, that is, between its members, gradually gained intensity and depth. The national market and the national bourgeoisie formed parallelly. After his theory had been criticized as too mechanistic, Deutsch supplemented his understanding of nation-building with the integrating effect of material and social interests.[35] In an attempt to assign abstract concepts such as opposition of interest or social communication to concrete social phenomena, Miroslav Hroch tried to determine the social structure among activists of various national movements and their territorial roots in his book *The Social Preconditions of National Revival in Europe* (1968). Thereby, he allowed for the interpretation of nation-building as a process of gradual acceptance of national identity following national agitation. Its success was first and foremost made possible by such opposing interests that lend themselves to combination with a linguistic or national difference, therefore being understood as nationally relevant. These conflicts of interest can by no means be reduced to class struggle, for instance, Estonian or Ukrainian peasants versus German or Polish landlords or Czech workers versus German industrialists, they also include the Scottish (or Catalan) periphery versus the English (or Castilian) centre.[36]

While Deutsch can be seen as the last researcher in Otto Bauer's tradition, a new wave of historical examinations of nation-building surfaced during the 1970s. They can be seen as a reaction to the decolonization process. Hobsbawm was the first to try to locate the nation as a historically conditioned phenomenon, that is, as a by-product of a general modernization process.[37] Tom Nairn was the first to render an explicit explanation for the process in his book on the looming disintegration of Great Britain. He pointed to the key role played by uneven economic development and its destabilizing role, both in multi-ethnic states and at a global level. Some regions became economically dominating, while others suffered from stagnation and started their struggle for equality, formulated as national interests. This also concerns the emancipation of the colonies.[38]

In contrast to Nairn, who stressed the unevenness of economic development and put emphasis on the political consequences of the external dependence of colonies, M. Hechter in his book on the rise of nationalism in Great Britain chose as his point of departure internal, regional dependencies that had been caused by this unevenness. His thesis that 'internal colonialism' had to be seen as the driving force behind processes of nation-building in Ireland, Scotland and Wales triggered lively discussions.[39] With this provocative neologism, he hinted that all countries had their respective economic core regions and, besides these, some 'backward' provinces, which are dependent on the core region. This dependence did not only concern the economy, but also extended to culture: the cultural dominance of the core region was also mirrored in the language-related and cultural policies of the country, which provoked the rise of so-called 'ethno-nationalism', in this case of the Celtic fringe. However, this did not exclude the decisive role played by individuals' material interests. Finding examples to counter Hechter's model was not difficult. Notably, the example of Catalonia showed that those provinces revolting against the centre were not necessarily the poorer ones, but here rather the opposite was true.[40] However, this was still a case of a nationally relevant opposition between centre and province which had been caused by uneven development. Hechter later tried to use rational choice theory as a key to understanding nationalist motivation. This motivation was not irrational but corresponded to each individual's quasi-rationally assessed interests.[41]

The fate of Benedict Anderson's theoretical approach is significant for the ambiguity of his use of Marxist concepts of nationalism.[42] The term which he coined, namely 'imagined community', sounded radically constructivist (and has, at times, been interpreted that way), although its author originally formulated it to designate the psychological fact that individuals can feel belonging to a group only if they are able to imagine other members of their group without having personal contact with them.[43] His emphasis on market-oriented book production ('print capitalism') was meant as an innovative hint at the close ties between national identification and the unfolding capitalist mentality, but was also interpreted as emphasizing the decisive role of book culture. Likewise his (not particularly original) hint at the importance of the Reformation for the evolvement of national languages was mainly connected to the intensification of social communication.[44] The relevance of conflicts of interest, especially in the social realm, was implicitly presupposed by Anderson, and he sought proof for it outside of Europe rather than inside it. That is why his argument appeared 'global' – he illustrates his theses with empirical data from all continents, which is detrimental to the credibility of his conclusions. Similar approaches can be found in the publications by Anthony Smith and Eric Hobsbawm.[45]

While Anderson marginalized the role of the state in nation-building, other authors put the state at the centre of their examinations. Here, interest in statehood was considered an interest in the ruling class – the bourgeoisie. Stein Rokkan, in cooperation with Charles Tilly, for instance, was concerned with this question as one of political science.[46] The relation to statehood, according to him, was decisive for the formation of the nations within the context of multi-ethnic empires. It was also relevant for the success of nation-building how much international prestige the respective empire had, how stable its institutions were and how strong the (remnants of) medieval institutions were to which the national movement reacted. National emancipation took place in the context of tensions between the periphery and the centre, these tensions comprising cultural, economic and political facets. Michael Mann placed the struggle for power at the centre of his attention, portraying not only internal, but also external conflicts and wars as nationally integrating.[47] In all of these cases, the nationally relevant conflict of interest is perceived as a nationally integrating force; nation formation was always part (and partially a product) of the new system of class and social conflicts and tensions, which accompanied the development of capitalist modernity.

Similarly, like Stein Rokkan, Immanuel Wallerstein did not make a clear distinction between the nation and the (national) state, but it was the state that was decisive for the development of the 'world system', to which he dedicated so many pages.[48] In his eyes, the state chronologically preceded the nation, while its internal class interests and conflicts defined the framework for the formation of national culture, of which language, religion, way of life were a part. In this respect, he agreed with Hobsbawm insofar as both considered national culture to be a construct ('invented tradition'), whose form and fate were shaped by the development of the global economy.

In Hobsbawm's synthesizing attempt, published in 1990, we can detect clear signs of his aversion to nationalism of any kind – and therefore also of his scepticism towards the nation (and the linguistic programme of the nation) as a vehicle of this nationalism.[49] In these anti-national views, he remained faithful to the tradition of the orthodox Marxist doctrine. His contribution first and foremost consists of the attempt to examine nation-building 'from below' – as a result of national movements of the lower middle classes. This foregrounded their interests in the broader sense of the word, meaning not only their material conditions, but also options to upward social mobility and a stringent democratization in the form of universal suffrage.

Conclusion

It is difficult – and rather ineffective – to assign labels to different authors and to sort them into 'Marxists', 'Constructivists', 'Perennialist' and so forth.

After Marxism as a political doctrine had been pushed into the background, the authors' self-identification and their explicit labelling also lost relevance. Even those among them who were markedly inspired by Marxism frequently display notable differences from each other. Given this reservation, let us summarize which fundamental concepts Marxist-inspired research has contributed to the elucidation and interpretation of nation formation, and possibly to nationalism. Of course, this does not preclude a critical appraisal of these authors' works.

- Especially in the context of European history, the nation is to be understood as a large social group, a decisive factor of whose development and existence was the widespread acceptance of a national identity by the different parts of the respective people. This is no eternally stable identity, but rather an identification with a community of equal citizens under the conditions of modern capitalist society.
- Nation formation is examined in a broad social context. First and foremost as a result of, or respectively a phenomenon parallel to, modernization, so as a consequence of the crisis of late feudal conditions and the formation of a capitalist social order. It is irrelevant in this context, whether individual authors choose to call this society modern, industrial, rather than 'capitalist'.
- National mobilization in Europe mainly flourished in the conditions of internal tensions and oppositions of interest, which gained national relevance for one reason or another. This role was taken not only by dichotomies of social status or class, but also by tensions between urban and rural settings, between centre and province, economy and politics. The more an understanding of the nation as a national state was consolidated, the more emphasis was put on the role and interests of the bourgeoisie.
- National mobilization was mainly caused by intense social communication, which in turn resulted from the onset of industrialization and increasingly strong relations to the market. The interconnection between the conditions of communication and interest can be assessed through concrete knowledge of the social structure of the national community and its protagonists.

Apart from these fruitful approaches that are counted among Marxist inspirations, there are also barren components which are mainly to be categorized as an heirloom of political Marxism. This concerns first and foremost the negative attitude, surviving from political doctrine, towards nationalism, whose role during the process of nation formation is overestimated. If a negatively connoted nationalism was the decisive reason for nation formation, then the legitimacy of national existence is put into question, as well. This often goes hand in hand with a rejection of the nation as an abstract community of cultural values. This paves the way for a concept of the nation as a cultural construct that can more or less be modified as required.[50]

In this context, one final sceptical question remains: Which of the above-mentioned methodological principles is to be categorized as authentically Marxist and how far do they overlap with historical materialism or structuralism? And what about political sympathizers? The term 'Marxist' still resonates with the connotations of a political programme, while historical materialism sounds rather neutral. But then, is it really that important which labels we use?

Notes

1 Translated from German by Vivian Strotmann.
2 This distinction is nothing new. It is not about juxtaposing the 'young' and the 'old' Marx. Rather, it is about the two sides of the 'fundamental internal contradiction in Marx's epistemology', as mentioned, for example, in Immanuel Wallerstein, 'To Each His Marx', in Etienne Balibar and Immanuel Wallerstein (eds), *Race, Nation, Class: Ambiguous Identities* (London and New York, 1991), pp. 125f.
3 Georg Wilhelm Friedrich Hegel, *Philosophy of Right* (German original 1820; Oxford, 1953), pp. 217ff.
4 See Friedrich Engels, 'The Democratic Panslavism', in *Marx Engels Collective Works,* vol. 8, pp. 362ff.; Karl Marx in his famous article on Panslavism and other articles in Eleanor Marx-Aveling (ed.), *Revolution and Counter Revolution* (London, 1971). See also Roman Rosdolsky, *Engels and the 'Nonhistoric' Peoples: The National Question in the Revolution of 1848* (Glasgow, 1987).
5 Systematic overview of Marx's opinions see Ian Cummings, *Marx, Engels and National Movements* (London, 1980); Charles C. Herod, *The Nation in the History of Marxian Thought* (The Hague, 1976); Ephraim. Nimni, *Marxism and Nationalism: Theoretical Origins of a Political Crisis* (London, 1994).
6 Marx's polemics in 1845 against Friedrich List's opinion, according to which the national market was a necessary and positive stage of development, is symptomatic. Roman Szporluk, *Communism and Nationalism: Karl Marx versus Friedrich List* (New York, 1988). See also Friedrich Lenz, *Friedrich List, der 'Vulgärökonome' und Karl Marx* (Jena, 1930).
7 Georg C. Iggers, *Historiography in the Twentieth Century: From Scientific Objectivity to Postmodern Challenge* (London, 1997), chapter 7.
8 Karl Kautsky, 'Die moderne Nationalität', *Die Neue Zeit. Revue des geistigen und öffentlichen Lebens* 5: 9 (1887), 402 f., 443ff. See also Nimni, *Marxism and Nationalism,* pp. 48f.
9 Rosa Luxemburg, 'The National Question and Autonomy', in Micheline Ishay and Omar Dahbour (eds), *The Nationalism Reader* (New Jersey, 1995), p. 202.

10 Rosa Luxemburg, 'The National Question and Autonomy', in Horace B. Davis (ed.), *The National Question* (New York, 1976). See also John P. Nettl, *Rosa Luxemburg* (Oxford, 1966).

11 Vladimir I. Lenin, *The Right of Nations to Self-Determination* (New York, 1970).

12 Nimni, *Marxism and Nationalism*, pp. 84ff.

13 Otto Bauer, *Die Nationalitätenfrage und die Sozialdemokratie* (1907; expanded second edition Vienna 1924). English translation: *The Question of Nationalities and Social Democracy* (Minneapolis, 2000).

14 Both Luxemburg and Lenin rejected this concept.

15 This vision bears a certain resemblance to Lenin's concept of national 'self-determination' after the October revolution, which later was reduced to a farce by Stalin's intervention.

16 Nimni, *Marxism and Nationalism*, pp. 127ff.

17 Otto Bauer, *Nationalitätenfrage*, pp. 112f., 126 (German original: 'die Gemeinschaft der durch Schicksalsgemeinschaft zu einer Charaktergemeinschaft verknüpften Menschen'; 'Schicksalsgemeinschaft'; 'nicht Unterwerfung unter gleiches Schicksal, sondern gemeinsames Erleben desselben Schicksals'; 'im dauerhaften Verkehr, fortwährender Wechselwirkung miteinander').

18 Bauer, *Nationalitätenfrage*, pp. 51ff.

19 Ibid., pp. 2f. (German original: 'Komplex körperlicher und geistiger Merkmale, durch die sich eine Nation von der anderen unterscheidet').

20 Ibid., pp. 124f.

21 Bauer, *The Question of Nationalities and Social Democracy*.

22 English translation in Josef Stalin, *Works*, Vol. 2 (Moscow, 1952).

23 Stalin, *Works*, Vol. 2, p. 307.

24 Stuart Hall, 'Gramsci's Relevance for the Study of Race and Ethnicity', in Stuart Hall (ed.), *Critical Dialogues in Cultural Studies* (London, 1996). Treated in a broader context by Nimni, *Marxism and Nationalism*, p. 110.

25 Georges Haupt, Claudie Weill and Michel Lowy, *Le Marxiste et la question nationale 1848–1914* (Paris, 1974).

26 Tom Nairn, 'The Modern Janus', *New Left Review* I/94 (1975), 2–29. Eric Hobsbawm's critique: 'Some Reflections on "The Break-Up of Britain"', *New Left Review* 1/105 (1977), 3–23.

27 Refer especially to the edited volume Eric J. Hobsbawm and Terence Ranger (eds), *The Invention of Tradition* (Cambridge, 1983).

28 Thus, for example, with Joseph R. Llobera, 'Modernization Theories of Nationalism', in Athena S. Leoussi (ed.), *Encyclopaedia of Nationalism* (New Brunswick, 2001), pp. 186ff.

29 Kenneth Minogue, 'Nationalism and Patriotism', in Athena S. Leoussi (ed.), *Encyclopaedia of Nationalism* (New Brunswick, 2001), pp. 230ff.

30 Eernest Renan, 'Qu'est-cequ'une nation?', in Eernest Renan (ed.), *Oeuvres Completes I* (Paris, 1947). Siegfried Weichlein, '"Qu'est-ce qu'une nation?", Stationen der deutschen Debatte um Nation und Nationalität in der Reichsgründungszeit', in Wolther von Kieseritzky and Klaus-Peter Sick, *Demokratie in Deutschland* (München, 1999), pp. 71ff.

31 Eric Hobsbawm, *Nations and Nationalism since 1789* (Cambridge, 1990), p. 10.
32 The *avant-garde* of this opinion was made up of Carlton J. Hayes. His influential modification in the form of a Western–Non-Western variant of nationalism was published by Hans Kohn at the end of the Second World War under the telling title 'The Idea of Nationalism'.
33 Tom Nairn, *The Break-Up of Britain: Crisis and Neo-Nationalism*, 2nd edn (London, 1981), p. 329.
34 Karl W. Deutsch, *Nationalism and Social Communication* (Cambridge, 1953). See also Hans Kohn, *The Idea of Nationalism: A Study of Its Origin and Background* (New York, 1944).
35 Karl W. Deutsch, 'Nation-Building and National Development', in Karl W. Deutsch and William J. Foltz (eds), *Nation-Building* (New York, 1966).
36 The book was published in German in 1968 and only later became available in English: Miroslav Hroch, *Social Preconditions of National Revival in Europe: A Comparative Analysis of the Social Composition of Patriotic Groups among the Smaller European Nations* (Cambridge, 1985).
37 Eric Hobsbawm, 'Some Reflections on Nationalism', in T. J. Nossiter, A. H. Hanson and Stein Rokkan (eds), *Imagination and Precision in Social Sciences* (London, 1972), pp. 385–406.
38 Ephraim Nairn, *The Break-Up of Britain*.
39 Michael Hechter, *Internal Colonialism: The Celtic Fringe in British National Development 1536–1966* (London, 1975). See also Michael Hechter, 'Internal Colonialism Revisited', in: Edward A. Tiryakian and Ronald Rogowski (eds), *New Nationalisms of the Developed West* (Boston, 1985), pp. 17–26.
40 A. W. Orridge, 'Uneven Development and Nationalism I & II', *Political Studies* 29:1 (1981), I, 1–15; II, 181–90.
41 Michael Hechter, 'Nationalism and Rationality', *Studies in Comparative International Development* 35 (2000), 3–19. This opinion was shared also by other authors, like for example, Russell Hardin, *One for All: The Logics of Group Conflict* (Princeton, 1995).
42 Benedict Anderson, *Imagined Communities. Reflections on the Origin and Spread of Nationalism* (London, 1983 [2nd edn, 1991]).
43 Cf. B. Anderson's comment in the second edition of his book.
44 Is it surprising or symptomatic that Anderson does not even name his predecessor K. W. Deutsch in the reference list?
45 Anthony D. Smith, *The Ethnic Origins of Nations* (Oxford, 1986); Anthony D. Smith, *National Identity* (New York, 1991); Eric Hobsbawm, *Nations and Nationalism* (Cambridge, 1989).
46 Stein Rokkan, 'Cities, States, Nations', in S. Eisenstadt and Stein Rokkan, *Building States and Nations*, vols 1–2 (Thousand Oaks, 1973–4); Stein Rokkan, 'Dimensions of State Formation and Nation-Building', in Charles Tilly (ed.), *The Formation of National States in Western Europa* (Princeton, 1975), pp. 347–80.
47 Michael Mann, *The Sources of Social Power II: The Rise of Classes and Nation-States, 1760–1914* (Cambridge, 1993).
48 Immanuel. Wallerstein, *The Modern World-System II* (New York, 1980); Immanuel Wallerstein and Étienne Balibar, *Race, Nation, Class: Ambiguous Identities II* (London, 1991).

49 Eric J. Hobsbawm, *Nations and Nationalism since 1780: Programme, Myth, Reality* (Cambridge, 1990).
50 See also the chapter by Wicke in this book.

Further reading

Anderson, B., *Imagined Communities: Reflections on the Origins and Spread of Nationalism*, 2nd edn. London, New York: Verso, 2006.

Bauer, O., *The Question of Nationalities and Social Democracy*. Minneapolis, London: University of Minnesota Press, 2000.

Davis, H. B., *Towards a Marxist Theory of Nationalism*. New York: Monthly Review Press, 1978.

Deutsch, K. W., *Nationalism and Social Communication*. Cambridge, MA: MIT Press, 1953.

Hobsbawm, E. J., *Nations and Nationalism since 1780: Programme, Myth, Reality*. Cambridge: Cambridge University Press 1990.

Hroch, M., *European Nations: Explaining their Formation*. London: Verso, 2015.

Nimni, E., *Marxism and Nationalism: Theoretical Origins of a Political Crisis*. London: Boulder Coll, 1991.

4

Modernism and writing the history of nationalism

John Breuilly

Introduction: The modernist view of nationalism

The modernist view of nationalism (henceforth modernism) can be summarized by two propositions.[1] First, nationalism is modern. The onset of the 'modern' for modernists can vary from about 1600, through the late eighteenth century into the mid-nineteenth century, depending on which aspect of modernity is highlighted. Second, nationalism arises from modernity, not from prior nations, even if pre-modern nations have existed in some form.

A history of any particular nationalism requires ideas about modernity which underpin the detailed presentation of that history. One also needs a clear view of what key terms mean.[2] Historians who regard nationalism as modern usually define it by criteria such as organization (e.g. political parties, pressure groups), explicit ideology, popular sentiment, and goals (e.g. to establish a sovereign nation state). Historians who assert the existence of nationalism in pre-modern societies – often called 'perennialists'[3] – usually focus on elite identities and loyalties and have less to say, if at all, on political ideology, organization or the drive to establish a nation state. These latter features appear marginal in pre-modern societies. As for nationalism having popular appeal, it is difficult to find historical evidence for this except in modern societies, although even that is often difficult. 'Arguments' about the modernity of nationalism often pass each other by because of these different approaches and definitions.[4] Generally historians, and even more social scientists concerned with the recent past and present, have tended to modernist positions.

While most historians have adopted the modernist position on nationalism, that is not so with the concept of nation. Many who see nationalism as modern also regard the nation as a necessary condition for its emergence. European history is often presented as having started to divide along national lines from the decline of the Roman Empire. Even historians opposed to nationalism make such assumptions, such as those who explain the disastrous course of modern German history in terms of a 'special path', a subject I address later. With the spread of the nation state as the 'normal' political unit across the world, the view that nationalism and nation states are built upon nations becomes 'common sense'. It is important to establish how far the modernist approach has persuaded historians to question this common sense and replace it with a different view.

To understand the initially counter-intuitive character of modernism I quote from the opening paragraph of Nationalism by Elie Kedourie:

> Nationalism is a doctrine invented in Europe at the beginning of the 19th century. . . . Briefly, the doctrine holds that humanity is naturally divided into nations, that nations are known by certain characteristics which can be ascertained, and that the only legitimate type of government is national self-government.[5]

Kedourie treats 'nation' as a term in the doctrine or ideology of nationalism, not as something existing prior and giving rise to that ideology. Kedourie argues that as this ideology acquires power it creates the very national identity it claims to express. Another modernist, Ernest Gellner, did not dispute that pre-modern national identity existed but argued this was different from modern national identity, not necessary for the rise of nationalism, and that nationalism often invented nations where they did not previously exist.[6]

Again, much depends on definitions. If by nation one means the use of words which connote nationality in some way or another in pre-modern historical sources (both general terms like *natio* and specific names like *Germania*), then nations clearly have a pre-modern existence. If one means a demonstrable sense of identity extending beyond elites to broader social strata, modernist arguments seem stronger.

Any modernist history of nationalism must go beyond definitions and narratives. One needs an argument about how modernity accounts for the emergence of nations and nationalism. This entails a theory of modernization. I first sketch the history of such theory before considering how it has shaped historical accounts of nationalism.

Modernization theory, nation and nationalism

Contrasts between ancient and modern to the benefit of the latter can be traced back to the eighteenth-century Enlightenment.[7] Scottish writers like Adam Smith, David Hume and Adam Ferguson outlined stages of 'progress' from primitive society, culminating in the recent achievement of 'commercial society' marked by global trade, capitalist agriculture and manufacturing, and arguing for the advantages of the free use of reason by individuals in pursuit of their interests. A century later emphasis was laid upon technologies which released new sources of energy (steam, electrical, chemical), enabling enormous increases in manufacturing and agricultural productivity, the speed and scale of transportation and communication, the military capacity of states, and the construction of global empires. Thinkers like Karl Marx, Max Weber and Emile Durkheim used various notions of modernity to understand the societal transformation involved. As yet nationalism was not identified as a general phenomenon which could be related to these notions.

After 1918 the two new world powers – the United States and the Soviet Union – proclaimed ideas of 'national self-determination' and 'national liberation' as alternatives to competing global empires. Meanwhile nationalism in its most aggressive forms – Fascism, Nazism, Japanese militarism – opposed the national aspirations of others and sought new empires. Their defeat in 1945 was widely equated with the defeat of nationalism, which was seen as reactionary and anti-modern.

Nevertheless, the post-1945 world was projected as one of nation states which both superpowers supported in the name of modernity and progress, even if these ideas were differently elaborated, indeed opposed to one another. In this Cold War period modernization theory was explicitly elaborated in the United States as an alternative to Soviet-style communism.[8] The two powers presented rival versions of modernity as models for the new nation states produced by the dismantling of overseas European empires. A distinction was made between the 'developed' world with stable national identity and nation states and the 'underdeveloped' world in which new states sought modernity through 'nation-building'. Nation-building was seen as very different from recently defeated and discredited 'nationalism'.

In the early 1980s modernism moved beyond 'classic' modernization theory with its distinctions between reactionary nationalism and progressive nation-building to a modernist theory of nationalism as a whole, leading to the first theoretical debates about nationalism. Since then there have been further developments. With the collapse of the Soviet Union, capitalist recession and endemic instability in many regions culminating in mass violence and social breakdown, ideas of modernity and progress have lost credibility. The dualist model of the modern advancing at the expense of the traditional or backward has long been rejected as simplistic. A related idea is that 'backwardness' was itself an aspect of how global capitalism had developed. The notion of modernity was further complicated by the concept of 'multiple modernities'.[9] Finally, postmodernists have doubted whether any concept of modernization works.

Three of the most influential modernist texts on nationalism were published in 1983, the *annus mirabilis* for theories of nationalism. These were the single-authored books by Ernest Gellner and Benedict Anderson, and one co-edited by Eric Hobsbawm and Terence Ranger.[10] Nothing is completely new and one can point to anticipations of the arguments of these books: before 1914, Otto Bauer and Karl Renner; after 1945, Karl Deutsch and Elie Kedourie.[11] There were also two general historical accounts of nationalism from the interwar period which were implicitly modernist, and less well-known works by German authors taking up modernist sociological, psychological and political positions.[12]

However, these earlier writers did not initiate a wave of scholarship or have as much impact on mainstream historical writing as those 1983 publications along with a cluster of others from the early 1980s.[13] One reason was that the widely accepted distinction between reactionary nationalism and progressive nation-building blocked the path to theories which unified these two forms.

National historiography in Europe took national identity for granted and linked it to nation state formation, although often distinguishing between 'state-nations' where the state preceded modern national identity (France, England/Britain Spain) and 'nation states' which reversed that sequence (Germany, Italy, Serbia, etc.). A division of labour formed between those who studied relations between states (military and diplomatic historians, international relations scholars) and those who studied the internal affairs of states (social and political historians, sociologists, anthropologists). The first group left unexamined the term 'nation' in 'nation state'. The second group equated nation with 'society' and explored internal differences such as class, occupation and region.

As for most of the non-European world, the focus was on how it could move from a little known and barely understood non-national past to becoming a modern nation. In a few cases (e.g. China and Japan) a similar approach was taken as towards the 'state-nations' of Europe.

To conclude: after 1945 nationalism was seen as archaic, reactionary and happily consigned to the past by defeat.[14] This contrasted with the settled national sentiment of developed nation states or the nation-building nationalism in new nation states. There was a strong moral implication: defeated nationalism was ethnic, exclusive and rooted in the past, while the nationalism of developed and modernizing nation states was civic, inclusive and forward looking. The modernist debate begun in the 1980s challenged these distinctions and sought to integrate these different forms of nationalism into an overall framework.

In the key texts from the early 1980s I distinguish between different concerns. First, there is 'nation formation' which addresses the question of how modern nations develop. A key study, published a few years earlier, is on French nation formation by Eugen Weber which I consider later. By nation is usually meant a 'whole society', comprising all major classes, with a shared sense of identity and located in a particular territory. Second, there is 'nationalism' by which is usually meant political movements pursuing national autonomy and justifying this with an ideology which makes the nation its central value. This was the focus of my own book.[15] Third, there is the 'nation state'. This does not lend itself to the same kind of comparative study as nation formation or nationalism. Being recognized as a 'nation state' by the United Nations tells us nothing about national identity or nationalism. The formation and recognition of such legal entities may or may not be accompanied by strong nationalism or mass national identity and may or may not successfully promote these once formed. Furthermore, nation state formation was a marginal issue before 1914, when the major question appeared to be which global empires would rise and which would fall. It was after 1918 that calls for 'national liberation' (Lenin) and 'national self-determination' (Woodrow Wilson) projected a vision of a world without empires. Modernism cannot easily address the contingencies associated with nation state formation and so modernist authors usually focus on nation formation and nationalism.[16]

What is it that makes a society 'modern' and how does modernity explain nation formation and nationalism? One can begin with economic, cultural or political explanations, though a full argument necessarily extends to all aspects of social change.[17] Those who stress economic modernity focus on class relationships or technology. Marx captured two different meanings of modernization with his distinction between 'relations of production' and 'forces of production'. Most Marxists concentrate upon 'relations', meaning how different 'modes of production' (e.g. slave, feudal, capitalist) are characterized by different class structures which determine the main lines of conflict and development. For many Marxist theorists and historians, there is a close relationship between the global development of capitalism, the formation of nations and nation states, and the rise of nationalism.[18] The difficulty has been to move from class interests, identities and ideologies ('bourgeois' liberalism, 'aristocratic' conservatism, 'working-class' socialism) to explaining mass national identity and nationalist commitment which transcend the 'real' solidarities of class.[19]

Ernest Gellner instead concentrated on the 'forces of production', arguing that economic modernity ('industrialism') explained the primacy of national over class identity.[20] Gellner sketched a universal human history of three stages: hunter-gatherers, sedentary agriculture and industrialism.[21] His lifelong concern was to understand modernity as a major break in human history which changed the nature of social being and knowledge. In *Nations and Nationalism* he applied his general arguments to nation formation and nationalism.

In fact, Gellner advanced two related theories: first, how industrialism forms nations; second, how the politics of resentment led by those who felt excluded, exploited and dominated by the industrializing nations produced nationalism.[22] His key argument is that industrialism generated unprecedented social mobility, whether 'up and down', geographically or through constant occupational transformation. People could no longer identify themselves in relation to fixed positions ascribed by criteria such as birth or privilege. This was replaced by the 'culture' people carried and shared as individuals. Gellner emphasized the importance of the organized learning of 'generic' knowledge and skills in industrial society which was only possible through universal, compulsory elementary schooling and the achievement of mass literacy. Culture became bound to a written vernacular instead of there being a separation between the local dialects of the non-literate majority and a written, often 'dead' language like Latin confined to elites. These written vernaculars became 'national' languages.

Gellner poses problems for historians. He is cavalier in his use of historical evidence. His one 'historical' chapter in *Nations and Nationalism* is a work of fiction! He imagines the province of Ruritania within the empire of Megalomania, the core of which has industrialized. Gellner then sketches how this generated Ruritanian nationalism. This seems to be a thinly disguised history of the late Habsburg Empire, if not the specific region which became Czechoslovakia (where Gellner was born and grew up). However, it is difficult to relate his ingenious and witty tale to historical particularity. This enabled him to escape confrontations with historians. However, in debate he conceded so many 'historical exceptions' that he left himself exposed to the charge that his theory had no serious historical grounding.[23]

Like Gellner, Anderson treats modernity as a profound transformation, changing even conceptions of time and space. His starting point of 'print capitalism' is a hybrid economic concept combining technology (mass production and circulation of printed literature) and organization (printing as capitalism). However, the argument swiftly becomes cultural. What interests Anderson is how the nation – like any large group – can only exist by being 'imagined' because its individual members can never all know each other directly. Modernity accordingly enables the particular style of imagining that is national. As individuals read newspapers and other literature as members of a national readership, they imagine that readership as their nation, a large group 'imagined as both inherently limited and sovereign'.[24]

Such imagining takes place in an increasingly distinct and autonomous 'public sphere'. As Gellner argued, mass literacy requires compulsory elementary education which places children in a specific institution: school. Modern industry and administration also require a cadre of highly educated people, hence modern universities and technical institutes. An expanded literate middle class and skilled working class supply the audiences for newspapers, theatres, museums, art galleries, parks, concert and music halls, which produce the professions which service these institutions, such as journalists, editors, curators, popular composers, artists and writers. Without this 'cultural sphere' one cannot imagine a Charles Dickens or Ludwig van Beethoven, a Louvre or British Museum. Increasingly these figures and institutions come to be identified as national.

Imagined Communities has had the biggest impact of any single book on nationalism studies measured by criteria like sales, editions, translations and citations.[25] Much is due to its range and brilliance, with short chapters on different kinds of national imagining and community across the world. As with Gellner there is a double focus on nation formation and nationalism, here framed in terms of imagination and community. The relationship between imagining and community is both closer and less clear-cut than between nation formation and nationalism in Gellner. Closer because Anderson connects them in historical examples; less clear-cut because imagining is a persuasive yet elusive idea, whereas industrialism is an explicit concept. It is also ambivalent. Most historians have concentrated attention on the agency of intellectuals, politicians and state officials: the social types Anderson describes as leading nationalism and making national communities. Cultural historians and theorists, in turn, have focused on processes and outcomes of 'national imagining', rather than individual or group agency.

Invented Traditions is another version of cultural modernism. This edited volume was not especially concerned with nation formation and nationalism. However, following the collapse of the Soviet Union, the rise of nationalist movements across the world and growing interest in the cultural aspects of politics, it was nationalism and those who 'invented' national traditions and rituals which came to be seen as the central subject of the book.

Historians have problems with notions of inventing or imagining. These are dramatic images rather than precise concepts. Furthermore, although often seen as interchangeable, they contain different, even opposed meanings. Inventing implies inventors as deliberate agents, something missing from the idea of imagining. In English usage the present participle which has become popular in book and book series titles on nationalism (inventing, imagining, writing, forging, etc.) does not allow the placing of a noun or pronoun – that is, a subject or agent – in front of it. The ambivalence between agency and structure, between nationalism as elite project and nation formation as unintended consequence of modernity, helps explain the extensive influence of these three books on very different, even conflicting views of nationalism.

While Anderson considers historical cases, this creates a different problem for historians. Historians can ignore or dismiss Gellner because of the absence of historical detail; with Anderson they can disagree in detailed ways. Many Latin American historians make Anderson prominent in their writing, but insist that his account is fundamentally flawed. Anderson put Latin America 'on the map' of a general readership, suggesting that nationalism started here. Historians of the region enjoy this pioneering role, but many go on to demolish the bold claims he makes.[26]

Political modernism also has two aspects, one of which is state modernization. In *Nationalism and the State* I argued that the modern state was a set of specialized institutions (bureaucracies, parliaments, courts, mass conscript armies) claiming rule over the inhabitants of an increasingly well-defined and policed territory.[27] Such political processes promote nation formation by creating a mass citizenry. The state's task is to represent the values and interests of those citizens: 'the nation'. The other aspect is the transformation of politics under modern conditions, such as mass mobilization through elections, parties, trades unions and professional associations, accompanied by a class of professional politicians who use nationalist language to engage popular support. As with Gellner's industrialism and resentment and Anderson's imagining and community, there is a double focus. One approach to nation formation and nationalism is concerned with institutions, elites and deliberate projects, while another is concerned with large-scale social processes and their unintended outcomes.

These different kinds of modernism are interlinked. Industrialism, print capitalism, state bureaucracy and mass conscript armies mutually condition each other. The most ambitious modernist theories seek to connect all these and, in so doing, present nation formation and nationalism as key outcomes of modernization. An outstanding synthesis is given in Michael Mann's monumental *Sources of Social Power*. Mann goes back to ancient civilizations in the first volume but volumes 2–4 consider the period after the mid-eighteenth century. That first volume which also outlines Mann's key concepts is another classic from the 1980s.[28]

Modernist arguments about nationalism 'as a whole' came in a cluster of publications in the early 1980s. Why did this happen as and when it did? With hindsight we can see that major global political changes were crucial. In the early to mid-1970s economic problems in the United States, compounded by the price hike organized by oil-exporting countries, led to the abandonment of the post-1945 financial settlement which included controlled exchange rates tied to the dollar. This presaged a shift away from Keynesian economic management with its goals of maintaining full employment and the welfare state, and an end to consensus between the major political parties on economic policy. With the elections of the British Conservative Prime Minister Margaret Thatcher and the American Republican President Ronald Reagan in 1979–80 the politics of the West became sharply polarized. The post-war period, once described as marking the 'end of ideology', was finished.

The accompanying global economic crises indirectly gave rise to the Iranian revolution, overt interventions by the United States in the internal affairs of many countries, the rise of separatist movements in Western Europe and national dissent in Eastern Europe. There was an increased emphasis on 'national identity' by many European historians.[29] Nationalism no longer appeared as something safely in the past, but here and now. Politics were no longer narrow disputes over how to run a mixed economy, but clashes of values in which claims about national identity played a central role. As economic crisis and ascendant neo-liberalism assaulted those institutions which had given substance after 1945 to what it meant to be a citizen of a nation state (trade unions, social housing, free university education and health care, decent pensions and unemployment benefit), there was an increased emphasis on 'identity' (gender, race, ethnicity and class, as well as nationality), almost as if offering a substitute for institutional forms of solidarity.[30]

One can trace this shift in the work of one scholar. Anthony Smith's first book on nationalism published in 1971 was indebted to his doctoral supervisor, Ernest Gellner, stressing the role of modern institutions such as state bureaucracies in shaping nationalism. In 1987 Smith published a book with a very different argument about the production and reproduction of national identity across generations.[31] Here Smith defined the modernist view of nationalism through his critique and proposed alternative. This provided the two necessary ingredients for a productive debate: opposed arguments taking place on common ground. Modernists and anti-modernists agreed that modern nationalism mattered as identity and ideology; they disagreed on its explanation.

At the time these publications were only straws in the wind. To illustrate with a personal anecdote: in 2015 a fellow modern German historian introduced a talk I was giving on nationalism by saying that he and other colleagues had been surprised to see me publish a book on so marginal a subject in 1982. Only after 1991 did they appreciate what a smart career move this was! Like almost everyone else, I had no premonition of the sudden collapse of the Soviet Union, though one had long been aware of its stagnation and corruption in the Brezhnev years. Like others, I had only been dimly aware of 'something in the air' which did not fit with assumptions that class mattered more than race, gender, ethnicity or nationality, and that international relations primarily revolved around the supranational interests and values of the Cold War.

It was only in the 1990s after the collapse of the Soviet Union and Yugoslavia, the re-emergence of war in parts of Europe, the revival of ethno-nationalist rhetoric, mass killings and genocide in Europe and beyond, the overthrow of apartheid in South Africa and much more that the trickle of publications on nationalism turned into a flood. The significance of those texts from the early 1980s was that they had established the terms of the debate about nationalism – modernist against non-modernist – which followed.

Modernist historical writing on nations and nationalism

It is impossible to survey comprehensively how modernism has shaped historical writing on nationalism. Instead I will focus on a few key texts, beginning with Weber's seminal *Peasants into Frenchmen* (1976).[32] The title makes clear the intent to connect nation formation to modernization. Weber draws on classical modernization literature, including Deutsch's *Nationalism and Social Communication*, which focused on 'nation-building' and ignored nationalism.[33] Concepts like integration and penetration were used to show how modernization forged a nation out of different classes and regions. In the first part, 'The way things were', Weber presents mid-nineteenth-century rural France as a series of isolated and backward regions, many of whose inhabitants did not speak French, were illiterate, were immured in a world of grinding work, poverty and superstition, and were without expectation of improvement. These people could not experience 'France' or 'being French' in the manner of townspeople and educated elites. To become French their world had to change.

The second part describes 'the agencies of change' which worked the crucial transformation between about 1880 and 1914. Extensive road building reduced physical isolation and permitted mass urban immigration. The expansion of elementary education spread the use of spoken French and increased literacy. Conscription of young men provided another national experience. Agricultural improvement raised living standards and expectations. All this increased social communication. Weber quotes Deutsch: 'A country is as large as the interdependence that it perceives.'[34] Or, as Anderson might put it: millions more inhabitants of France now came to imagine they were French. In the third part Weber summarizes the 'change and assimilation' which had taken place, concluding that the French nation was made through modernization.

Although concentrating entirely upon France, basing his account on primary sources such as reports by school inspectors and military commissions as well as testimonies of those affected, Weber regarded France as just one case. He compares how the French countryside became French with the ways France transformed its overseas colonies. Modernization theory after 1945 may have renounced military conquest as the way to spread modernity, but it saw modernity 'conquering' in other ways.

Weber's book had a major impact on non-French historiography.[35] Italian and Spanish historians read Weber as demonstrating the 'success' of French nation formation and contrasted it with 'failure' in their countries. German historians acknowledged that the Second Empire rapidly modernized, producing mass national identity by 1914. However, that very rapidity undermined significant elements of modernization such as liberalism. This 'partial modernization' stimulated the growth of mass but illiberal nationalism, with fateful consequences not only for Germany but also for the world. Thus the contrast between twentieth-century 'progressive' and 'reactionary' nationalism was connected to different kinds of nation formation in the nineteenth century. Weber's book influenced historical work on 'backward' European dynastic empires and their failure to turn peasants into Austrians, Russians or Ottomans. So his study was accepted as valid for France – 'successful' or 'full' modernization – but imitation of his methods led to the conclusion that elsewhere this was 'partial' or 'failed'.

However, the reception of Weber has been complicated by empirical critiques, which also question classical modernization theory. Weber's book is untheoretical. Modernization is not defined, but is a large fact – growth of towns, industry, improved agriculture, roads, schools, literacy, conscription, the French language, rising material living standards – which generates experiences of 'interdependence' and makes more and more inhabitants of France see themselves as modern and national. The two terms even appear interchangeable. As for 'explanation', these are the 'agencies of change'. Agency becomes agent: road building is the work of engineers, schools of teachers and educational reformers, conscription of army officers. There is a dualist model: modern agents work on unmodern peasants to turn them into modern Frenchmen. It is also unclear what happens to women.

This is not intended to deprecate the book. If Weber had entered into theory he almost certainly would not have written such a wonderful book. Nevertheless, it opened him to criticism. The initial critical reviews by British and American historians of France were empirical, not theoretical, insisting that there were extensive, even 'national' forms of peasant politics under the Restoration, the July Monarchy, in the 1848–9 revolutions and the resistance to Louis Napoleon's coup of December 1851. Weber's evidence – a mass of specific examples – was selected from the most backward parts of the most backward regions and failed to register the halting and varied nature of change across the whole country. Once the book was translated into French, French historians joined in such criticism while others defended his argument.

However, a second wave of criticism questioned classical modernism. Historians of France began to examine 'regionalism' as something other than resistance against or assimilation into the efforts from Paris and modernizing reformers.[36] The same critical responses began to inform non-French historiography. If France had not 'successfully' modernized as Weber had argued, perhaps other countries had not 'failed'. If French peasants 'negotiated' rather than rejecting or accepting change, and in complex, varied and halting ways, maybe that happened elsewhere too. If agencies of change included the Catholic Church and peasant cooperatives, should one see modernity exclusively as a project pushed by the modern-minded: rational schoolteachers, scientific engineers, nationalist officers, above all by a secular, anti-clerical, progressive-minded republican elite?[37]

These are powerful criticisms. However, they do not so much confront modernization theory head-on as complicate empirical history. Negotiation works better than domination, bottom-up change must be added to top-down change, interaction must replace dualism. Taken alone, such criticisms could encourage historians to go back into their national boxes, arguing over specific issues without relating these to general debates about either modernization or nationalism, and seeking to understand modern French history 'in its own terms', in short returning to methodological nationalism.

One possible way beyond can be found by distinguishing between modernization as project and as process. Weber's book is on nation formation, even if sometimes he calls this nationalism. His road and school builders and army recruiters are the equivalent of Gellner's industrialism. However, Gellner has a theory linking industrialism to nation formation; Weber does not. Can we introduce such a theory?

In quoting Deutsch, Weber helps us. What matters are not the schools, roads and armies themselves, but the common experiences they create. Common experience does not mean same experience but interdependency in the exchange of experience. This point undermines Weber's dualist model. As Weber himself notes, peasants must actively seize upon the new opportunities this scaling up of experience provides. If peasants see no point in school learning, their children will not learn. Roads must be travelled to take new-found literacy in search of better positions in towns. Conscripts will only be French if they do not experience the army as sheer compulsion and themselves as cannon-fodder. Resistance to 'national' events like the December 1851 coup might be extensive and use modern methods, such as print propaganda, but what matters is that these actions become embedded within the extended and specialized relationships of modernity. For that to happen they must become routine, not extraordinary episodes. The conscription of the first Napoleon was extraordinary, regionally patchy and resisted; it was not a 'national experience' in the manner of the Third Republic.

In other words, modernization as nation formation is not project but process. A few teachers, recruiting officers and road builders may be self-consciously 'nation-building', but most are just teaching the three R's, raising an army or trying to connect two places. It is how these actions are appropriated by the many which forms the nation.

Nation formation is not about political identities or motives but routinizing national exchanges of experience. We can see the force of this distinction by turning to another of Weber's books.[38] Weber's initial historical interests were in right-wing nationalism, in France before and after the First World War, elsewhere (especially Romania, the country of his birth) and inter-war fascism. His *The Nationalist Revival in France* is about the decline of one kind of nationalism and the rise of another. Right-wing nationalists like Charles Maurras and his organization *Action Française* vehemently opposed the values of the Republic, embracing regionalism against centralism, Catholicism against secularism. Such nationalism was parasitic on what it opposed. This right-wing nationalism lost support in France in the years up to 1914. The 'revival' to which Weber refers was closely associated with Jean Jaurès, a leading socialist. Yet he is seen as anti-nationalist, in line with a narrow definition of nationalism as reactionary. Maurras makes the 'nation' central to all his discourse, relating it to religion, tradition and locality; for Jaurès what is central are values about social justice framed in internationalist terms.

One could frame this difference as one between 'motivational' and 'structural' nationalism.[39] Motivational nationalism presents commitment to the nation as the sole or principal motive for action. Structural nationalism does not proclaim the nation or national identity as its core value, but other values such as social justice, democracy or individual liberty. However, socialist, radical democratic and liberal movements accept the nation state as the framework within which they must operate to realize their values. When that state's very existence appears threatened, as in France in August 1914, such movements prioritize its defence over their core values on the grounds that destruction of the nation state will also destroy the capacity to realize those values. It is difficult for historians to disentangle these elements and in crises people may become aware of values which previously seemed unimportant. Yet precisely such crises can help us understand how nation formation can give rise to different, even opposed kinds of nationalism. Given that it was pro-republican, socialist, 'structural' nationalism which eclipsed anti-republican, reactionary, 'motivational' nationalism in 1914, this suggests that the process of progressive, integrative nation formation Weber describes in *Peasants into Frenchmen* had achieved many positive results by 1914.

The German case raises other aspects of the relationship between modernization, nationalism and historical writing. It was as if the German equivalent of Maurras instead of Jaurés came to the fore by 1914 and then again in an extreme form in 1933. This interpretation of modern German history came to be known as the *Sonderweg* or special path. Historians like Hans-Ulrich Wehler who elaborated this account explicitly defended liberal democratic values in West Germany and saw it as their task to make clear where Germany had veered off the 'normal' path and to help it back on to that path. This position was substantively anti-nationalist, if by nationalism we mean an illiberal and authoritarian ideology. Methodologically it was nationalist because it saw German history as unique. These historians not only were indebted to modernization theory but argued that in the German case it was one crucial failure to modernize, namely the failure to develop liberal democracy, which meant that the power of modernity was harnessed to illiberalism.[40]

This interpretation was subject to a critique in another text of the early 1980s, by two British historians.[41] Why, they asked, should one assume that modernization 'normally' leads to liberal democracy? Modernization means industrial and urban growth, mass literacy and increased social mobility, but why cannot that be accompanied by new kinds of authoritarian or totalitarian rule as 'normally' as by parliamentary democracy? They thus questioned the orthodox Marxist argument that a rising capitalist class 'selects' parliamentary democracy as the form of government, which enables it best to dominate, and that the failure of liberal democracy is capitalist failure. Capitalists might feel threatened by liberal democracy in a society with a powerful and radical labour movement like pre-1914 Germany. They might find authoritarian nationalism more amenable.

Since then many modernizing societies have 'failed' to become liberal democracies. Classical modernization theory was linked to the Cold War and the need for the West to connect modernization to liberal democracy. The growing crisis of the liberal post-war order from the late 1970s led to arguments that illiberal nationalism was as much an aspect of modernity as liberal nationalism, and that modernization could take many different forms. The idea of 'multiple modernities' became increasingly popular in the 1990s.[42] It provided one possible conceptual support to historians who wanted to retain an overall notion of modernization, but detach it from the unilinear form of classic modernization theory.

Nationalism assumed new forms after 1914. The destruction of powerful empires and the prominence given to ideas of national self-determination meant that nationalist movements which previously had been unable to imagine, let alone pursue objectives beyond limited cultural and political autonomy, could now proclaim a sovereign nation state as their goal. Before 1914 one could only write 'national' history for the major Western powers and, to a more limited degree, for a few 'small' nations in the Balkans, as well as Japan which had asserted itself as a powerful nation state. Only after 1918 did nationalism appear to offer a global alternative to a world of empires.

However, the earlier assumption that nationalism was an outgrowth of national history continued. At the Paris Peace Conference nationalist claims were justified with reference to national history and identity. The US president Woodrow Wilson, though proud of his own 'new' and multi-ethnic nation, took ethnic nationality to be the leading principle for the organization of post-war Europe, and those seeking to exploit this assumption framed their demands accordingly. The Bolsheviks also defined nation as organic and objective, even if a world of nation states was not their ultimate aim. Historians such as Kohn and Hayes started to write about 'nationalism' as a general phenomenon while continuing to place it in that national frame.

However, the argument became increasingly strained with European decolonization. 'Ghana' or 'Indonesia' lacked the national credibility of even 'Yugoslavia' or 'Czechoslovakia'. Historians in part handled this by making a distinction between a Europe of long-established nations, including small ones which only recently had gained statehood, and non-European zones of imperial rule which had to build 'new nations'. Anderson in *Imagined Communities* shifted the focus away from Europe and from 'big' to 'small' nations.

One historian whose work inspired this shift was the Czech Miroslav Hroch.[43] His pioneering work on 'small nations' in Europe considered nation formation, nationalist ideology and politics. Both Marxist and presuming the pre-existent reality of national identity, Hroch's work made several innovations. It is systematic and comparative. His knowledge of a range of languages permitted comparison of many European cases. His three-stage theory of nationalism enabled Hroch to write in both an analytic and narrative form.

Stage one was the intellectual elaboration of national ideas. National identity had long existed, as with Czechs, but expressing that through standardized written vernaculars and dictionaries, presenting the national story in plays, novels, histories, visual art and music: these were modern achievements without which any national movement would be impossible. Stage two was the translation of such national ideas into political form by elites. Stage three was the shift from elite to popular politics. Hroch was clear that there was no inevitability about moving through these stages. An elite national movement might achieve statehood without having to mobilize mass support or might fail in the face of powerful opposition or the lack of conditions favourable for mass politics. But even if nationalism did not necessarily pass through all three stages, it followed this sequence.

The dual focus on nation formation and nationalism is present, with nation formation being seen as prior to nationalist ideas and dependent on economic change. Hroch traces the rise of national movements to regions of commercial agriculture and towns engaged in long-distance trade and manufacture and to the class interests these generate. National ideology is connected to the work of intellectual and political elites. This model became a standard way of writing the history of small nations and their national movements in modern Europe.

However, there are problems with this model.[44] It assumes national identity as prior to national movement but, given the many different and competing national claims in central Europe, does that help explain why some succeed and others fail, or account for the fact that some successful cases have the most exiguous forms of national consciousness before they succeed? Does a national movement need an elaborate national ideology before it achieves statehood? Serbia managed to become a nation state with very little in the way of modern conditions for nation formation and arguably it was the state which produced the nation.[45] Does the argument extend to 'big' nations where powerful states precede national movements?

Nevertheless, Hroch's work took the study of nationalism into a new area and has had a major impact on how national history is written. However, there are two historical fields where his work has had less influence: the appropriation of the key modernist texts of the 1980s in 'Western' historical writing and the writing of non-European history.[46]

The ideas that nationalism is modern and that the modernist texts of the early 1980s provide the key to understanding how modernity shapes nationalism became standard assumptions for many historians of the Western world, publishing views from the late 1990s. For example, every one of the six books published between 2000 and 2004 by Edward Arnold in the series 'Inventing the Nation' (including one on Germany by Stefan Berger) references some combination of Anderson, Gellner, Hobsbawm and Hobsbawm/Ranger, and does so usually within the first few pages. They often criticize an older historiography which connected nationalism to an assumed long-existing national identity and lay emphasis variously on print media, industrialism, modern warfare and mass politics.[47] It is difficult to trace more specific influences because the differences, even contradictions, between Anderson, Gellner and Hobsbawm are not so much registered as listed as a series of supporting positions and often linked to points going *against* what those authors argued. For example, some texts cite Anderson on imagined communities but argue that these have pre-modern roots, or shift implicitly from imagining nations as a societal process to inventing nations as an elite project. Typically historians do not systematically 'apply' a theory to their case or use their case to support a theory. More often the modernist view loosely underpins the history of the particular nationalism in question.

Modernism has also dominated much non-European history, with some exceptions where historians have been able to posit a pre-modern national history, such as with China and Japan. However, many historians of these cases make a sharp distinction between long-existing 'states' or 'civilizations' and modern nations, nationalism and even ethnicity.[48]

Although Anderson presented the novel argument that 'Creole nationalism' in British and especially Spanish America was the original form of nationalism which became a model for Europe, historians of these regions generally reject that argument, either on the grounds that some kind of nationalism pre-existed the independence movements against the Spanish or, more commonly, that nationalism only arose following the achievement of independence.[49] The arbitrary boundaries established by the imperial powers in the Americas, much of Africa, the Middle East and South and South-East Asia, as well as the failure to 'develop' these societies along the lines of classical modernity, have made it difficult for historians to construct long-run national narratives spanning precolonial, colonial and postcolonial history. For the most part the nations are described as 'new', along with nationalism. The classical modernization literature has seen such nationalism as the principal agent of 'nation-building'.

Once the optimism about nation-building had evaporated – also accelerating from the 1980s – historians could move in different directions. Some sought to maintain a national frame through the idea of 'ethnicity' as the key form of 'whole group' consciousness. Perennialists could argue that this was a precolonial heritage which cut across the 'artificial' boundaries imposed by imperial powers and which had formed the territorial framework for the new postcolonial states. Against this modernists have argued that tribes are a modern construct along the same lines as nations. Terry Ranger, co-editor of *Invention of Tradition*, has constantly revised his position on this as an historian of east-central Africa.[50]

Conclusion: End of the modernist paradigm?

I have been describing trends in the writing of the history of nationalism by professional historians. I want to finish by considering what impact this has had on popular understandings of national history and nationalism as well as the 'official' views projected by nation state regimes. I also want to ask how far the modernist paradigm continues to hold sway among professional historians.

While academics argue that nationalism and nation are modern phenomena, many regimes promote nationalist historiography as part of the effort to legitimize themselves. We see this, for example, in state-supported work on Chinese history where imperial and national history are systematically (con)fused.[51] The state has supported major archaeological excavations and recently loaned an impressive range of artefacts for a Royal Academy of Arts exhibition in London on the Qing dynasty.[52] The Turkish government did something similar for another Royal Academy exhibition. The catalogue had prefaces written by the then prime ministers, Blair and Erdogan. The nationalist message is made clear in the subtitle.[53]

This points to a divergence between 'official' views and the research and ideas of professional historians and social scientists. The resurgence of defensive nationalism in many parts of the world is buttressed by claims about long-run national history, whether this is the Han Empire or the Anglo-Saxons. New nation states, such as the former republics of Soviet Central Asia, manufacture ethno-national myths. Communal violence in India, Kenya, South Sudan or former Yugoslavia is blamed on 'ancient' ethnic enmities.[54] History textbooks tell long-run national stories in many countries, even if they require constant adaptation as one regime gives way to another.[55]

Yet at the same time professional historians argue that nations and tribes are 'imagined' or 'invented', the products of modern industrialism or capitalism or imperialism. Nationalism is interpreted as a transnational phenomenon which cannot be understood within a national context. Nationalist teleology is challenged by work on 'failed' forms of nationalism, such as the pan-nationalist movements which flourished in the late nineteenth and early twentieth centuries. Not only is there a divergence between 'official' and academic views of nationalism, with modernist ideas most influential among professional historians while teleological and primordial views prevail officially, but it also appears that the rise of defensive nationalism has increased the popular impact of such views.

Also weakening the influence of modernism has been its fragmentation and marginalization within academic circles. Modernization is either a distinct transformation which is now in the past and so can have little to tell us about nationalism in 'post-modern times'. Or modernity now takes secondary, derivative and multiple forms. A 'modern' education and medical system, along with legal sovereignty, can be achieved in 'colonial' societies entirely dependent on the export of primary commodities, such as Middle Eastern oil-producing countries. Developed economies can regress, as in some of the successor states to the Soviet Union. Identity politics has risen to prominence and makes a bewildering range of contradictory claims about the nation. The sheer variety of forms attributed both to nationalism and modernity can no longer be contained within the terms of the debate between modernist and non-modernist theories of nationalism which crystallized in those key texts in the 1980s, except possibly as an argument about the origins and emergence of nationalism. As one of the editors of the journal *Nations and Nationalism* I see that an increasing number of submissions simply bypass the issues raised by the modernist debate, focusing instead on subjects such as 'everyday' or 'banal' nationalism, identity claims, quantitative studies of the sources of support for populist nationalist movements and many other subjects. This is less true for historical studies which extend back into the twentieth century and earlier, but these themes also inform the choice of historical questions, such as about gender and nationalism. Whether a revised modernist paradigm can be developed and shape future historical study of nationalism and, even more important, whether it can challenge the revival of national myth-making at popular and official levels remains to be seen.[56]

Notes

1 I follow the usage established by Anthony D. Smith, *Nationalism and Modernism* (London, 1998).
2 For definitions see the web page *The Nationalism Project*, http://www. nationalismproject.org/what.htm: the section entitled 'What Is Nationalism'.
3 See chapter by Roshwald.
4 Oliver Zimmer and Len Scales (eds), *Power and Nation in European History* (Cambridge, 2005) represented an effort to effect a genuine dialogue. For more on different definitions see the debate on Aviel Roshwald's 'The Endurance of Nations', *Nations and Nationalism* 14:4 (2008), 637–63.
5 Elie Kedourie, *Nationalism* (London, 1960), p. 1.
6 Ernest Gellner, 'Do Nations Have Navels?' *Nations and Nationalism* 2:3 (1996), 366–70.

7 See the chapter by Berger.

8 Michael E. Latham, *Modernization as Ideology: American Social Science and 'Nation Building' in the Kennedy Era* (Chapel Hill, NC, 2000).

9 See two articles in *Daedalus* (2000), 129:1: Shmuel Eisenstadt, 'Multiple Modernities', pp. 1–29 and Björn Wittrock, 'Modernity: One, None, or Many? European Origins and Modernity as a Global Condition', pp. 31–60.

10 Ernest Gellner, *Nations and Nationalism* (Oxford, 1983); Benedict Anderson, *Imagined Communities: Reflection on the Origin and Spread of Nationalism* (London, 1983); Eric Hobsbawm and Terence Ranger (eds), *The Invention of Tradition* (Cambridge, 1983).

11 On Bauer and Renner see the chapter by Hroch. Karl Deutsch, *Nationalism and Social Communication* (New York, 1953), Kedourie, *Nationalism*.

12 Carlton Hayes, *The Historical Evolution of Nationalism* (New York, 1931); Hans Kohn, *The Idea of Nationalism* (New York, 1944; 2nd edn, 2005). Two outstanding German books were Eugen Lemberg, *Nationalismus* (2 vols, Munich, 1964), and Heinz Ziegler, *Der moderne Nation* (Tübingen, 1931).

13 See the preface to the second (1991) edition of Anderson, *Imagined Communities*. A fourth key modernist text published a little later is Eric Hobsbawm, *Nations and Nationalism since 1780* (Cambridge, 1990).

14 Kedourie prefaced his 1960 book with the comment that nationalism was now considered a strictly historical subject. Edward Hallett Carr entitled his immediate postwar book *Nationalism and After* (London, 1945).

15 John Breuilly, *Nationalism and the State* (Manchester, 1982).

16 For a pragmatic definition of the nation state see John Breuilly, 'Nationalism, National Self-Determination, and International Relations', in John Baylis, Steve Smith and Patricia Owens (eds), *The Globalization of World Politics*, 7th edn (Oxford, 2017), pp. 434–49 (437).

17 Michael Mann, *Sources of Social Power,* vol. I (Cambridge, 1986), chap. 1, who identified four kinds of power: military, administrative, economic and political. I prefer the triad of coercion, economics and culture; see Gianfranco Poggi, 'Political Power Un-Manned: A Defence of the Holy Trinity from Mann's Military Attack', in John A. Hall and Ralph Schroeder (eds), *An Anatomy of Power: The Social Theory of Michael Man* (Cambridge, 2006), pp. 135–49.

18 John Breuilly, 'Eric Hobsbawm: Nationalism and Revolution', *Nations and Nationalism* 21:4 (October, 2015), 630–57.

19 See chapter by Hroch.

20 Umut Ozkirimli, *Theories of Nationalism*, 3rd edn (Basingstoke, 2016). See also John Hall, *Ernest Gellner: An Intellectual Biography* (London, 2010).

21 Ernest Gellner, *Plough, Sword, Book* (London, 1988).

22 John Breuilly, 'Introduction', in Ernest Gellner, *Nations and Nationalism*, 2nd edn (Ithaca, 2006), pp. XIII–LI.

23 Gellner, 'Do Nations Have Navels?': 366–70.

24 Anderson, *Imagined Communities*, p. 15.

25 John Breuilly et al., 'Benedict Anderson's Imagined Communities: A Symposium', *Nations and Nationalism* 22:4 (October, 2016), 625–59.

26 See the chapters by Don H. Doyle, Eric Van Young and Nicola Miller in John Breuilly (ed.) *The Oxford Handbook of the History of Nationalism* (Oxford, 2013). I consider some of these criticisms later.

27 Breuilly, *Nationalism and the State.*
28 Michael Mann, *The Sources of Social Power* (Cambridge, 1986–2012), 4 volumes.
29 Ferdinand Braudel published his first books on the identity of France in 1986; Nairn, *The Break-Up of Britain* (London, 1977) sparked a sharp response from Eric Hobsbawm; the so-called *Historikerstreit* (dispute among the historians) on German history began in the mid-1980s; De Felice published 'positive' evaluations of Mussolini and Fascism in the late 1970s and 1980s.
30 See Bo Stråth, 'Identity and Social Solidarity: An Ignored Connection: A Historical Perspective on the State of Europe and Its Nations' *Nations and Nationalism* 23 (2017), 227–47.
31 Anthony D. Smith, *Theories of Nationalism* (London, 1971) and Anthony D. Smith, *The Ethnic Origins of Nations* (Oxford, 1987).
32 Eugen Weber, *Peasants into Frenchmen: The Modernization of Rural France, 1870–1914* (London, 1976).
33 See also Charles Tilly (ed.), *The Formation of National States in Western Europe* (Princeton, NJ, 1975).
34 Weber, *Peasants into Frenchmen*, p. 485.
35 Miguel Cabo and Fernando Molina, 'The Long and Winding Road of Nationalization: Eugen Weber's *Peasants into Frenchmen* in Modern European History (1976–2006)', *European History Quarterly* 39:2 (2009), 264–86.
36 See chapter by Storm.
37 Cabo and Molina, 'The Long and Winding Road'.
38 Eugen Weber, *The Nationalist Revival in France, 1905–1914* (Berkeley, CA, 1968).
39 John Breuilly, 'What Does It Mean to Say That Nationalism Is Popular?', in Maarten Van Ginderachter and Marnix Beyen (eds), *Nationhood from Below Continental Europe in the Long Nineteenth Century* (Basingstoke, 2012), pp. 23–43.
40 The literature on this is huge. For a collection of essays which both survey and critique the field, see Sven Oliver Müller and Cornelius Torp (eds), *Imperial Germany Revisited: Continuing Debates and Perspectives* (New York, 2011).
41 David Blackbourn and Geoff Eley, *The Peculiarities of German History: Bourgeois Society and Politics in Nineteenth-century Germany* (Oxford, 1984).
42 See note 9 for references.
43 His original texts from the 1960s first became available in English in Miroslav Hroch, *Social Preconditions of National Revival in Europe* (Cambridge, 1985). See also Miroslav Hroch, 'From National Movement to the Fully-Formed Nation: The Nation-Building Process in Europe', in Gopal Balakrishnan (ed.), *Mapping the Nation* (London, 1996), pp. 78–97 and *European Nations: Explaining Their Formation* (London, 2015).
44 John Breuilly, 'Constructing Nationalism as an Historical Subject', in Pavel Kolár and Miloš Rezník (eds), *Historische Nationsforschung im geteilten Europa 1945–1989* (Köln, 2012), pp. 15–27.

45 See Sinisa Malešević, 'The Mirage of Balkan Piedmont: State Formation and Serbian Nationalisms in the Nineteenth and Early Twentieth Century', *Nations and Nationalism* 23 (2017), 129–50.

46 See for the historical study of nationalism in communist societies and its legacy for post-communism Miroslav Hroch, *European Nations*; Sabine Rutar (ed.), *Beyond the Balkans: towards an Inclusive History of South-Eastern Europe* (Vienna, 2014) and Sabine Rutar, 'Nationalism in Southeastern Europe, 1970–2000', in *The Oxford Handbook of the History of Nationalism*, pp. 515–35.

47 John Breuilly, '*Imagined Communities* and Modern Historians', pp. 641–6. See note 21 for reference.

48 For example, Henrietta Harrison, *China: Inventing the Nation* (London, 2001). On ethnicity see Frank Dikotter, *The Discourse of Race in Modern China* (Hong Kong, 1992).

49 See Don Doyle and Eric Van Young, 'Independence and Nationalism in the Americas', in *The Oxford Handbook of the History of Nationalism*, pp. 97–126; Claudio Lomnitz, 'Nationalism as a Practical System: Benedict Anderson's Theory of Nationalism from the Vantage Point of Spanish America', in Miguel Angel Centeno and Fernando López-Alves (eds), *The Other Mirror: Grand Theory Through the Lens of Latin America* (New Jersey, 2001), pp. 329–49; Eric Van Young, 'A Nationalist Movement without Nationalism: the Limits of Imagined Community in Mexico, 1810–1821', in David Cahill and Bianca Tovias (eds), *New Worlds, First Nations: Native Peoples of Mesoamerica and the Andes under Colonial Rule* (Brighton, 2006), pp. 218–51.

50 Terence Ranger, 'The Invention of Tradition in Colonial Africa', in Terence Ranger and Eric Hobsbawm (eds), *The Invention of Tradition*, pp. 211–62; a revised view in Idem., 'The Invention of Tradition Revisited: the Case of Colonial Africa', in Terence Ranger and Olufemi Vaughan (eds), *Legitimacy and the State in Twentieth Century Africa* (Basingstoke, 1993), pp. 62–111. See also Gabrielle Lynch, *I Say to You: Ethnic Politics and the Kalenjin* (Chicago, 2011).

51 Joshua Fogel (ed.), *The Teleology of the Modern Nation-State: Japan and China* (Philadelphia, 2005); Lydia Liu, *The Clash of Empires: The Invention of China in Modern World Making* (Cambridge, MA, 2004).

52 Evelyn Rawski and Jessica Rawson (eds), *China: The Three Emperors, 1662–1795* (London, 2005).

53 David Roxburgh (ed.), *Turks: A Journey of a Thousand Years, 60–1600* (London, 2005).

54 David Laitin, *Nations, States and Violence* (Oxford, 2007).

55 For a good recent study of 'Western' states, see Rachel Hutchins, *National and History Education: Curricula and Textbooks in the United States and France* (New York, 2016).

56 For a more extended consideration of whether the 'modernist paradigm' has had its day, see Umut Ozkirimli, *Theories of Nationalism: A Critical Introduction*, 3rd edn (Basingstoke, 2017), especially chap. 7, 'Nationalism: Theory and Practice'. I have argued for the use of explicit modernization theory to understand nationalism in 'Modernisation and Nationalist Ideology', *Archiv für Sozialgeschichte* 57 (2017), 131–54.

Further reading

Baycroft, Timothy and M. Hewitson (eds), *What Is a Nation? Europe, 1789–1914*.
    Oxford: Oxford University Press, 2006.
Breuilly, John (ed.), *The Oxford Handbook of the History of Nationalism*.
    Oxford: Oxford University Press, 2013.
Hayes, Carlton. *The Historical Evolution of Nationalism*. New York: Smith, 1931.
Hroch, Miroslav. *Social Preconditions of National Revival in Europe*.
    Cambridge: Cambridge University Press, 1985.
Kohn, Hans. *The Idea of Nationalism*. New York: Macmillan, 1944;
    2nd edn, 2005.
Weber, Eugen. *Peasants into Frenchmen: The Modernization of Rural France,
    1870–1914*. London: Stanford University Press, 1976.
Zimmer, Oliver and L. Scales (eds), *Power and Nation in European History*.
    Cambridge: Cambridge University Press, 2005.

5

Nations are (occasionally) forever: Alternatives to the modernist perspective

Aviel Roshwald

Introduction

Writing in the 1860s, Lord Acton expressed his deep concern over a continental European phenomenon that struck him as both novel and dangerous – 'the theory of nationality'. All too presciently, he argued that the unconditional and exclusive attribution of legitimate political sovereignty to communities of race or culture threatened to elevate collective authority over individual liberties, majority interests over minority rights and state power over civic freedoms.[1]

On their face, Acton's words would seem to place him in the category of what has come to be known as the modernist camp in nationalism studies. (If so, he would have to be counted as being among its founding parents, given that his analysis predated that of Ernest Renan by a couple of decades.) Yet a double take is in order, for no sooner did he characterize 'the theory of nationality' as an unprecedented ideological construct, than he went on to charge that, paradoxically, the repression and intolerance likely unleashed by any attempted institutionalization of nationalist principles were such as to make those principles 'the greatest adversary of the rights of nationality'.[2] In other words, it was the nationalist claim that every nation must be coterminous with a sovereign state that Acton decried as a new-fangled and pernicious phenomenon. Nations as such, he clearly assumed, had long played roles on the historical stage as bearers of cultural traditions and distinctive values.

Moreover, he was convinced that nations did have a productive political role to play as constituent elements of larger states that recognized in them 'an essential, but not a supreme element in determining the forms of the State'.[3] It was precisely in their capacity as historically rooted communities, Acton argued, that nations were able to interact autonomously within the framework of multi- or supranational entities such as the United Kingdom and the Habsburg monarchy in ways that checked the very ability of the state to exercise unfettered, centralized power in the name of a sovereign people. It was through this dialectical interaction of nations with one another and with the state in the framework of supranational polities that the principle of 'political nationality' (what we might term civic nationalism) would come to prevail over what he saw as the more ancient and primitive qualities of nationhood as defined by purely ascriptive characteristics (such as shared genealogical or geographical origin).[4] One way or the other, Acton anticipated that the contradictions inherent in 'the theory of nationality' would ultimately 'contribute . . . to obtain that which in theory it condemns – the liberty of different nationalities as members of one sovereign community'.[5] As a liberal Catholic critic of the modern trend towards the centralization of power in the hands of the state (be it in the name of monarchic absolutism or – even more dangerously in his view – of popular sovereignty), Acton saw the historic, sociocultural community of the nation as having the potential, along with religious conscience, of serving as a barrier against the very tyranny of the majority that he believed inhered in the idea of the nation *state*.[6]

Such fine distinctions have often been lost amidst the turbulent currents of debate over nationalism in the century-and-a-half since the publication of Acton's essay. These debates have been profoundly shaped by the transformative and often violent struggles over fundamental issues of sovereignty, identity and self-determination that have periodically convulsed the world in the course of modern history. On the one hand, ideologues, public intellectuals, partisan historians, politicians and governments caught up in struggles to propagate and legitimize nationalist political agendas have tended to indulge in what might be termed reductionist and theoretically unreflective forms of perennialism, strongly associated with a proclivity for essentialism. That is, they have grounded their political claims in dogmatic assertions about the perennial, inherent and essentially unchanging identity and character of the nation in whose name they claim to speak. As Anthony Smith has pointed out, from at least as early as the nineteenth century, it was common for nationalist ideologues to depict the people whose freedom they espoused as having once – in ancient times – enjoyed a golden age of political liberty, social cohesion and cultural distinctiveness and accomplishment, only to have fallen into a protracted, centuries- or millennia-long era of decline and dormancy as a result of internal division, foreign conquest and oppression, or both.[7] It was nationalists' task, drawing inspiration from this romanticized past, to awaken the nation from its deep sleep and rouse it to claim its birthright.

Thus, nineteenth-century advocates of German national unification and aggrandizement fashioned a cult of Arminius (Hermann) – the Germanic chieftain who had cut a Roman army to pieces in the Teutoburg Forest in the year 9 CE[8] (see Figure 5.1). Nineteenth- and early-twentieth-century

FIGURE 5.1 *The* Hermannsdenkmal *(Hermann (Arminius) Monument) in the Teutoburger Wald. Completed in 1875 by Ernst von Bandel (1800–1876). North Rhine-Westphalia, Germany.*

Czech nationalists harkened back to the Hussite tradition of resistance to Habsburg and Roman Catholic authoritarianism as the expression of the indomitable spirit of their people; the triumph of the forces of the Habsburg Counter-Reformation at the 1621 Battle of the White Mountain marked the beginning of an age of darkness for the Czechs from which they had to be redeemed.[9] The political revolution of the 1860s that set Japan on the path to centralization and modernization under the aegis of the Meiji emperor was packaged as a restoration of traditional imperial authority, and in subsequent decades, Japanese nationalists and militarists mobilized support for their expansionist ambitions by invoking the allegedly timeless qualities of the Japanese national character (the 'Yamato spirit').[10] Many among the late-nineteenth-century precursors of Arab nationalism and their twentieth-century successors depicted the spiritual, political and cultural achievements of early Islam as expressions of an underlying Arab national genius that had fallen under the shadow of first Ottoman and then European military and material power.[11] Reflexively reductionist forms of perennialism continue to play a significant role in nationalist discourse to this day: the identification of one's own people with the virtues and sacrifices of their forebears and of rival communities with ancient enemies has been a common and familiar phenomenon in recent years among warring parties in the former Yugoslavia and Northern Ireland, to name just two of many possible examples.

On the other hand, the often shrilly doctrinaire tone of what might be termed the propagandist version of perennialism, along with the grandiose political claims and violent conflicts it has often spawned and validated, has long provoked critics of nationalism into questioning perennialist claims in any shape or form. As early as the 1880s, the French philosopher of religion and society Ernest Renan implicitly countered the newly unified Germany's annexation of the province of Alsace (which German nationalists justified in the face of local dissent among the province's population by making claims about that population's German ethnocultural ancestry and heritage) by questioning the very notion of ascribing national belonging to any group of people based on anything other than their own self-ascribed identity (what he termed the 'daily plebiscite').[12]

The various schools of modernism, from those rooted in the nineteenth-century Marxist tradition to the post-Cold War social constructivists inspired by Ernest Renan have, like Acton, called into question the political and ethical legitimacy of attributing exclusive territorial-sovereignty rights to groups defined by ascriptive qualities. But, in their eagerness to debunk and unmask the fallacies of crudely perennialist forms of nationalist chauvinism, many of them have gone on to question whether national identity in anything but the most passive and apolitical form – let alone any politically significant form of nationalism – predated the onset of modernity (however dated and defined – whether by the onset of the Industrial Revolution, the outbreak of the French Revolution or the invention of the printing press). For many modernist scholars, be they traditional Marxists like Eric Hobsbawm, anti-Marxist structuralists like Ernest Gellner or post-modernist/Marxisant hybrids like Benedict Anderson, any assertion about the pre-modern origins of national identity is – at best – based on such tiny grains of truth as to be interchangeable with national historical narratives fabricated out of thin air.[13] Integral nationalism's association with pseudo-scientific racism and its culmination in the ethnic cleansings and genocides of the twentieth century undoubtedly served to reinforce the radical scepticism among post-1945 progressive academics about any historical claims that might have even the potential of contributing to essentialist understandings of national identity. Conversely, late-twentieth-century anticipation of the decline of the nation state and nationalism in the face of globalization seemed to further buttress the view that the very concept of the nation and role of the nation state were transitional historical phenomena.

Yet the apparent triumph of modernist interpretations of nationalism among late-twentieth-century academics did not go unchallenged. The Achilles' heel shared in common by the various modernist schools of thought was their failure satisfactorily to explain the powerful emotional grip nationalism is capable of exerting on people. If nationalism was merely the functional outgrowth and cultural/ideological by-product of certain socio-economic processes associated with modernization, why did it seem to strike such a deeply resonant chord with so many people? Could it be connected to some profound attribute of human nature or to some forms of social identity that predated and contributed to shaping modern conceptions of popular sovereignty and self-determination?

In the pages that follow, we shall begin by surveying some of the major theoretical counterpoints to modernism, go on to consider challenges rooted in empirical historical scholarship and conclude by briefly touching on the implications for this field of recent academic critiques of the very concept of modernity as a radical break in human experience.

Theoretical challenges to modernism

One theoretical line of attack on modernist purism was developed almost four decades ago by the anthropologist Pierre van den Berghe in his short yet powerful essay on the sociobiological foundations of race and ethnicity.[14] Van den Berghe gave systematic expression to a perception of nationalism that Anthony Smith dubbed 'primordialist': the view of nationalism as a manifestation of innate human characteristics rooted in our very evolutionary origins as social animals. According to the sociobiological model, the social construction of, and identification with, ethnocultural communities is one of several ways in which humans have succeeded in modifying their genetic predisposition to reserve altruistic behaviour for kin by latching onto shared cultural and physiognomic traits to create the wider circles of 'virtual kin' needed to sustain comparative advantage in a world that has grown ever more intensely competitive and complex since the onset of the agricultural revolution.

In his recent book on the 'long history' of nations, the political scientist Azar Gat has built on van den Berghe's insights to construct one of the most sustained and uncompromising cases for the perennial importance of political ethnicity and nationalism across the *longue durée* of recorded human history.[15] Gat sees nationalism as the politicization of ethnicity in the context of the state – be it the pre-modern or the modern state. And he contends that 'ethnicity in general, as opposed to any specific ethnos, is primordial in the sense that it has always been a defining feature of our species'.[16] He explains this by suggesting that shared culture very likely was strongly correlated with genetic closeness among the hunter-gatherer groups who constituted the overwhelming majority of the global human population prior to the agricultural revolution. Hence, the tendency to feel a sense of kinship with people who share one's cultural traits is itself likely to have been selected for genetically in the course of human evolution. In Gat's view, this helps explain why ethno-national solidarities have tended to trump other, ostensibly more rational, factors, such as individual self-interest and class interest, during moments of crisis such as the outbreak of the First World War. He hastens to add that recognizing the prehistoric, sociobiological roots of human behaviour does not serve to validate it normatively. People still have ethical choices to make, and those choices can and often should challenge some of our genetically ingrained predispositions. But his point is that it is folly to deny the power of that heritage.[17]

As Gat himself points out, although van den Berghe is routinely cited, his theory does not seem to substantively influence many historical treatments of nationalism other than Gat's own. This is undoubtedly in part because scholars have, since the racist abominations of the Second World War, shied away from anything smacking of a biologically deterministic understanding of human behaviour. But it may also reflect the fact that sociobiological theories are inherently very generic, broad and sweeping. Reading van den Berghe may well reinforce and lend scientific legitimacy to a pre-existing intuition that nationalism stems from traits that are deeply rooted in humanity as a species. Yet historians are generally more interested in explaining how shifting environments, contexts and contingencies shape *variations* in human culture and identity across populations and over time. One may readily grant that humans have a strong, biologically ingrained proclivity to think of their in-groups as virtual kin and of out-groups as alien, but this merely begs the question why this tendency manifests itself in any particular one of an infinity of possible combinations of ethnic, national, religious, ideological and/or other forms at any given time or place.

The late historical sociologist, Anthony D. Smith, developed a much more influential and sustained critique of modernism, proposing instead a concept that he termed 'ethno-symbolism.' It is noteworthy that Smith began his academic career as a student of the famed modernist theorist, Ernest

Gellner. Intellectually brilliant as Gellner's approach was,[18] Smith had, by the 1980s, concluded that it was premised on too radical a break between pre-modern and modern structures of society and culture. Smith would have been the first to agree that modernization in all its multifarious senses has profoundly transformed the human experience. He did not take issue with the claim that nationalism as an explicitly articulated, widely disseminated political program is a fundamentally modern phenomenon. In fact, he was at pains to distinguish his perspective from 'perennialists' – a term he used to denote not just nationalist propagandists but also historians and others who may unreflectively assume that nationalism (be it of an existing group or associated with long-vanished peoples) has been a perennial feature of human history from time immemorial. What he did insist on was that humans have coped with the challenges of modernization and modernity in part by adapting elements of pre-modern ethnocultural traditions and identities to the conditions of a rapidly changing world; those traditions and identities have, in turn, contributed to shaping the modern world of nation states. More specifically, what Smith's theory of 'ethno-symbolism' suggests is that, while national*ism* (in the sense of a mass political movement devoted to the attainment of national sovereignty) is modern, where and in what form it takes root is powerfully influenced by pre-modern patterns of ethnic identity and sociocultural history.[19]

That is to say, whereas most modernists see nationalism as (counter-intuitively) preceding the nation, Smith argued that what he termed (using the French term for ethnic community) the *ethnie* – a community held together by a myth of shared ancestry as manifested in, and reinforced by, shared cultural symbols and practices, and an attachment to a defined territory – precedes nationalism.[20] The successful mobilization of social masses around a nationalist agenda, Smith contended, is contingent on an ideological vanguard's selection, manipulation and/or reinterpretation of a set of symbols and myths associated with a pre-existing *ethnie*. In the famous debate at Warwick University in 1995, Ernest Gellner caricaturized Smith's concern with the pre-modern antecedents of modern nations as analogous to medieval theologians' preoccupation with whether Adam, not being born of woman, did or did not have a navel. But in his calm, steady voice, Smith insisted that, in the absence of a pre-modern ethno-communal substratum, the seeds of latter-day nationalist endeavour are unlikely to strike root.[21]

His erstwhile mentor's playful jabs notwithstanding, over the course of his prolific career Smith shifted ever so incrementally towards a slightly more perennialist position. This was not an ahistorical, reductionist form of perennialism; no serious academic historian or social scientist today would claim that every contemporary nation can trace its origins to an ancient nation from which it derives certain immutable qualities. Rather, what Smith suggested was the possibility that recognizable forms of nationhood – the association of ethnicity with a shared public culture and the 'occupation and development' of an ancestral homeland – may have manifested themselves in a number of notable cases centuries or even millennia before the seventeenth and eighteenth centuries. The ancient Jews and ancient Egyptians were among the examples he pointed to. Such forms of national identity may have been largely restricted to political and cultural elites, Smith emphasized; in the absence of modern infrastructures and technologies for the mass diffusion of political ideas, full-blown nationalism in the form of an ideological agenda embraced by a significant, mass following was not yet possible according to him. Yet he came to think that in some of these pre-modern cases we could speak of nations, in the sense of large communities among whom at least a passive perception may have existed of a link between shared ethnocultural identity and legitimate political-territorial authority.[22]

The evolution of Anthony Smith's ideas was in part influenced by a burgeoning literature of historical case studies and comparative studies, many of which have themselves been shaped by Smith's path-breaking scholarship. Whereas most historians have followed the modernist school's assumptions, a notable minority have embraced varieties of what might be termed empirical perennialism: that is, in looking at the primary sources left behind by various pre-modern societies, they find compelling evidence that national identity in some form played a significant role in a number of those societies; some have concluded that one can even speak of pre-modern forms of nationalism (in the sense of active political claims articulated in the name of national identity).[23]

The interpretation of this evidence is, of course, highly contested. There are plenty of early modernists and medievalists who insist that any similarities between pre-modern and modern vocabularies of political community and ethnocultural belonging belie profound differences in context, meaning and mentality, and that modern conceptions of nationhood and nationalism have little in common with their apparent pre-modern antecedents.[24]

Yet, partly in response to the crescendo of theorizing by modernists during the last years of the Cold War, in light of the resurgence of ethnic nationalism in post-Communist Eastern Europe as well as other parts of the world following the end of the Cold War, and amidst the worldwide nationalist backlash against economic and cultural globalization, a growing number of historians have in recent years questioned the notion that nationalism is exclusively bound up with a particular phase of socio-economic, cultural and political modernity.

Europeanist historians critical of modernism

In his collection of historical case studies of national-identity formation, based on his 1996 Wiles Lectures at Queen's University Belfast, the theologian and historian of religion Adrian Hastings threw down the gauntlet to modernists by arguing that nationalism (in the sense of a particularistic assertion of political sovereignty claims based on the cohesion and distinctness of an existing polity's ethnocultural identity) had played a formative role in the history of late-medieval England. As a paradigmatic success story, Hastings argued, the medieval and early-modern English nation state, in turn, exerted influence on the later development of nationalism in other countries in Europe and beyond.[25] By the same token, Hastings contended, both early English nationalism and its emulators were strongly influenced by a far more ancient example: that of the Hebrew Bible's narratives and teachings about the Chosen People.

Hastings was not alone in this insight. An entire field known as Hebraic Political Studies has burgeoned over the past two decades, focusing on the role of the Hebrew scriptures as a source of sacred narratives and of ethnopolitical theology which a variety of early modern elites adopted and adapted to legitimize their own political undertakings. A journal by the name of *Hebraic Political Studies* was published between 2005 and 2009, and a number of scholarly works apart from the journal's contents have systematically explored the theme over recent years. The Dutch Republic, England/Britain and the Puritan settlement in New England during the eras of Reformation and Counter-Reformation are among the most commonly cited examples of national or proto-national societies of the sixteenth, seventeenth, and eighteenth centuries that imagined themselves to be latter-day counterparts to the Israelites of old. Espousing a covenantal theology that became part and parcel of their Protestant religious faith, a significant cross section of each of these societies conceived of their nation as a new Chosen People whose attainment and/or preservation of political self-governance was both a condition of and heavenly reward for its pursuit of Christian religious purity.[26]

Note that the identification of these ideologies as national – and even nationalist – does not simplistically conflate modern with pre-modern forms of national identity. It acknowledges that the secularizing trends of late European modernity shifted many nationalist master narratives away from these earlier, explicitly religious sources of legitimization and inspiration. But it emphasizes the evolutionary connections between pre-modern and modern versions of nationalism, rather than rejecting outright the very idea of nationalism in any form prior to industrial and political modernity. Moreover, it reflects the recognition that religious ideas and identities continue to shape a variety of contemporary nationalisms: the significant part played by Catholicism in sustaining and shaping Poland's Solidarity movement of the 1980s, the influence of Evangelical Protestantism on right-wing conceptions of national identity in the United States, and the rising profile of religious Zionism in Israel since the 1967 Six-Day War are just a few of many possible examples. Are these phenomena to be considered something other than nationalist or something other than modern simply because they fail to conform to a particular secular, natural-rights-based conception of popular sovereignty and self-determination associated with the legacy of the Enlightenment and the American and French revolutions?

The widespread acknowledgement of the seminal role played by Biblical concepts of nationhood in shaping early modern forms of European nationalism begs an obvious question: what role did national identity in fact play among the ancient Hebrews themselves? Modernists and literary deconstructionists may be quick to reject the very question as based on a misplaced literalism; the early modern European nation-builders may, after all, have simply been projecting their own agendas onto ancient texts which were universally accepted as sacred in their societies. But a number of authors have insisted on taking scriptural and archaeological evidence of ancient Jewish national identity as a matter for serious evaluation rather than facile dismissal. Notable here is the work of Steven Grosby, who has published a series of erudite and influential articles on various aspects of this phenomenon (as well as on the influence of the Hebraic paradigm on modern national myths and identities).[27] Like Smith, Grosby is careful to draw distinctions between modern nationalism and pre-modern national identities, while at the same time emphasizing the crucial importance of the latter to any fundamental understanding of the forces underlying modern nationhood and nationalism. In Grosby's eyes, there is strong textual evidence for the crystallization of ancient Israel as a nation as early as the late First Temple era (i.e. the seventh or sixth centuries BCE), when the crucial idea of the covenant between God and people gained coherence and centrality in the Judean ethno-religious tradition.[28]

In my own writing, I have (like Grosby) conceded that Jewish ideas of national distinctiveness may have been back-projected onto early Israelite times – but a convergence of Jewish, Hellenistic and Roman literary, archaeological and numismatic evidence strongly suggests that this tradition of back-projection began no later than the second or first centuries BCE.[29] To the objection that any such imagined sense of community would have been the preserve of a tiny literate elite, Grosby has pointed to the work of William Schniedewind on the evidence for relatively widespread literacy among the Judean population as early as the late First Temple era.[30] As historians working on many different pre-modern societies have also pointed out, the dissemination of standardized, official or otherwise elite-fashioned information is not necessarily limited to the literate in societies where sacred texts, royal pronouncements and the like may be read out to audiences (as in the Jewish tradition of weekly readings from the Pentateuch in the synagogue).

Other ancient societies have also been cited as examples of pre-modern national communities. Grosby has explored evidence for the existence of a shared ethno-geographic identity falling just short of nationhood among politically fragmented, first-millennium BCE Aramean communities.[31] He has also noted the propagandist use of myths about past ethno-religious conquests and cleansings by Sinhalese-Buddhist historians in strife-torn, mid-first-millennium CE Sri Lanka.[32] Edward Cohen has made the case for ancient Athens as a *polis* that imagined itself as a nation, even as it claimed pride of place among competing city-states that all recognized one another as part of a broader Hellenic world.[33]

It may be relatively easy to find recognizable (yet distinctive to their own time and place) instances of national identity and even nationalist politics in the Reformation-era Euro-Atlantic world on the one hand and among some of the smaller, more cohesive (and in fifth-century BCE Athens' case, even democratic) polities of the ancient/classical Mediterranean world on the other. But what of medieval and Renaissance Europe? Here, the hodgepodge of overlapping imperial and local authorities, the bewilderingly complex structures and almost caste-like divisions of feudalism, and the apparent predominance of universalistic religious idioms over explicitly particularistic political claims conspire to make national identity seem an irrelevant and anachronistic point of reference. Indeed, it seems likely that it is the stark contrast drawn by eighteenth-, nineteenth-, and twentieth-century political thinkers between the modern ideal of the territorially and demographically uniform application of state sovereignty on the one hand, and the seeming anarcho-irrationalism of the medieval political world on the other, that contributed to the equally sharp contradistinction between modern nationalism and the radically different patterns of identity formation attributed to all pre-modern 'agro-literate societies', as Ernest Gellner dubbed them.[34]

Nonetheless, as seen above, Adrian Hastings challenged orthodoxy by asserting the nationalist qualities of late-medieval English public culture. A mounting chorus of other, similarly dissenting voices has since emerged among historians, asserting the existence of a variety of national frames of reference in Europe of the late Middle Ages and Renaissance. This historiographical trend may in part be inspired – or at least find indirect and unintended validation – in the cultural turn within the modernist school of nationalism studies itself. To the extent that Marxist and Gellnerian conceptions of nations as materially structured communities have given way to Andersonian (or neo-Renanesque) emphases on the 'imagined' character of nations,[35] it becomes easier to detect national proclivities in societies that antedate the invention of the printing press (which plays such a central role in Anderson's ingenious attempt to merge Marxist and post-structuralist modes of analysis through the concept of 'print capitalism').[36] Thus, Caspar Hirschi attributes a seminal role in the very genesis of nationalism-as-an-idea to the politically ambitious, yet frustrated publicists and propagandists of Renaissance-era Humanism: 'The same utopian energy that enabled the imagination of an independent scholarly community transcending all political boundaries also made possible the fashioning of the nation as an autonomous community, engaging in an intensive competition of honour with other nations. In this sense, modern internationalism and modern nationalism have their origins in the same cultural setting, the humanist literary sphere constructed as a political stage'.[37]

For her part, *pace* Hastings and his claims of primacy for English nationalism, Colette Beaune makes a strong case for the powerful role national identity had to play in another pre-Reformation, Roman Catholic monarchy – late-medieval France. She demonstrates how the very universalism of Catholicism was leveraged into claims of chosenness articulated on behalf of the 'most Christian' kingdom of France.[38] 'The term "most Christian" was applied without distinction to the French king, the people, and the territory'.[39] Conceptions of nationhood in fifteenth-century France were bound up with symbols and images of Church, monarchy and social hierarchy that obviously made them radically different from the latter-day, republican conception of a nation of citizens. But Beaune insists that those symbols and images (more important than the written text in an age of widespread illiteracy) were disseminated far and wide among the populace through vectors such as coinage and church decorations, while parish sermons could literally be used to spread the word about the chosenness of France, its kings and its people – all this well over a century before the rise of classical political Hebraism in Protestant Western Europe. Thus propagated, the idea of nationhood played a significant role in facilitating and sustaining French political cohesion in the face of internal challenges and of the gruelling Hundred Years' War with England. The zeal of the peasant girl Joan of Arc in rallying support for the King of France against his English enemies did not spring forth out of nowhere, nor was it an anachronistic anomaly, Beaune suggests.[40]

Susan Reynolds has articulated a more systematic claim about the compatibility of medieval feudalism and monarchy with national identity. Her point is that precisely because medieval conceptions of authority and community were understood in such multi-layered terms as to defy modern conceptions of loyalty-monopolizing national communities, modern historians have failed to recognize the important place that idealized notions of kingdoms-as-communities occupied (alongside local, religious and other forms of social solidarity) in medieval imaginations. In her early work, Reynolds chose to eschew the term 'national' in describing the medieval idea of kingdoms as 'units of government which were perceived as peoples', simply for fear of creating semantic confusion with reductionist modern understandings of the term.[41] But as she emphasized in a 2005 essay, 'when I decided to use the word "regnal" instead of "national" in discussing medieval loyalties it was not, as Smith thought, because I thought medieval kingdoms were "not nations in the modern sense", but because the word "national" seems to make others focus on the modern "nation-states", with their modern boundaries'. She goes on to state flatly her view that 'medieval kingdoms were quite often perceived as something very like "nations in the modern sense"'. Reynolds' fundamental point is that, within the borders and configurations of their time, medieval Europeans were generally inclined to conceive of their kingdoms as 'not just . . . the territories that happened to belong to kings, but as territories that also belonged to the collective or corporate groups of their peoples'.[42]

In the same volume, edited by Scales and Zimmer, Patrick Wormald ups the ante over Adrian Hastings, contending that 'before 1066 as for centuries afterwards, the key to the English realm's operation was the mutual dependence of the king and a decidedly broad political nation'.[43] Even in central Europe, Len Scales argues, the very political fragmentation of the Holy Roman Empire of the German Nation was an impetus to the imagination of a geographically diverse range of late-medieval writers – many of them stemming from relatively humble socio-economic backgrounds – who articulated a vision of German political identity which, Scales insists, lent impetus to the idea of German cultural nationhood, rather than vice versa.[44]

Even if some of these scholars concede that it is hard to know whether or not a majority of the population of medieval and early modern West European societies would have thought to identify themselves as French, English, German, and so on,[45] their point remains that references and appeals to the idea of nationhood played significant roles in the propagandist and self-validating rhetoric of various literate strata in medieval and early modern Europe.[46] To the extent that the written word had a disproportionately important role to play in shaping the history of European societies, it can be argued, expressions of national identity in this historical context should not be dismissed as incidental curiosities merely because they shared, or contested control of, the political stage with religious, socio-hierarchical, local/regionalist and other sources of personal and communal identity.

Asianists critical of modernism

Criticisms of modernism have not been restricted to Europeanists. Some Asianists have also discussed the possibility that precursors of modern nationalism can be discerned in the precolonial, pre-modern antecedents of a number of contemporary Asian countries. Now, it is true that some of the harshest critiques of nationhood as a substantive analytical category have come from scholars of Asian history. These sceptics have suggested that nationalism in postcolonial societies may itself constitute an artefact of imperial structures of categorization and domination (as adopted and exploited by Westernized postcolonial elites). Partha Chatterjee and other scholars associated with the school of Subaltern Studies have contended that the academic world's preoccupation with the triumphalist narrative of South Asian nationalism has blinded it to the diverse and complex experiences, perspectives and identities – defying neat ethno-national pigeonholing – of hundreds of millions of peasants and other sociocultural 'subalterns'.[47]

But a more recent academic trend has been to try and find ways of 'rescuing' the very idea of modernity from its association with the alleged primacy of Euro-Atlantic civilization and the legacy of Western imperialism. What some scholars have sought to document instead is the existence of diverse historical paths to socio-economic, cultural and political modernity and, indeed, of multiple modernities. One aspect of this approach has been to suggest that non-Western nationalisms may be more than contrived replicas of Western forms of political legitimacy and identity. Rather, some of these nationalisms might have indigenous, precolonial historical roots of their own. C. A. Bayly acknowledged that many nineteenth- and twentieth-century non-Western nationalist movements arose in direct response to European imperialism. Yet he also suggested some among these movements drew on what he termed older forms of territorial patriotism. In cases 'such as northern Vietnam, Korea, Japan, and Ethiopia', he argued, 'if nations had indeed been "constructed," it had been over a very long period' antedating the direct challenge of Western imperialism.[48]

In his massive, two-volume comparative study of the historical trajectories of Southeast Asia and Europe, Victor Lieberman argues along somewhat similar lines that what he terms 'politicized ethnicity' had a significant role to play in the legitimization of political authority among a number of Southeast Asian states as early as the fifteenth century. He traces the origins of a few of these polities (e.g. Burma and Vietnam) as far back as the ninth century (to Pagan and Dai Viet, respectively) and argues for a continuity of historical memory and cultural tradition at least from the fifteenth century onwards that lent itself, over the course of centuries, to the periodic recreation (following interregna of political breakdown) in this region of ever more centralized and culturally assimilationist states. These polities, he contends, were configured along territorial lines roughly comparable to those of their predecessors, and marked by certain religious-linguistic continuities with them. What he finds striking about this pattern are its parallels and convergences with (rather than conditioning by) the trajectories leading to the consolidation of cultural-political authority in what became the major European nation states.[49] By the same token, within the vast imperial domain of China under the Qing dynasty (1644–1911), the political and social significance of ethnic identity was recognized and carefully manipulated by the country's ethnic-Manchu rulers, as Mark Elliott has shown.[50]

Finally, Prasenjit Duara, a historian of China, has called into question the radical break with past forms of political and sociocultural identity that modernists ascribe to latter-day nationalism:

In privileging modern society as the only social form capable of generating political self-awareness, Gellner and Anderson regard national identity as a distinctly modern mode of consciousness. . . . The empirical record does not furnish the basis for such a strong statement about the polarity between the modern and the premodern. . . . Whether in India or China, people historically identified with different representations of communities, and when these identifications became politicized, they came to resemble what is called modern 'national identities'.[51]

The neo-imperial turn and the questioning of conventional periodization

Such questioning of the Eurocentric assumptions about modernity that underlie modernist interpretations of nationalism may, somewhat paradoxically, be reinforced by what I would term 'the neo-imperial turn', the recent renewal of historians' interest in empires as no-less important and viable engines of modernization than nation states. This turn may partly be occasioned by frustration over the failure of post-imperial national and international institutions to fulfil their promise and partly by the perception that informal versions of imperialism continue to play more structurally significant roles in the post-1945 and post-Cold War world than might once have been imagined. Historians of both territorially contiguous and overseas empires have variously suggested that the inevitability of empires dissolving into nation states has been greatly exaggerated, that the twentieth century's world wars played vital roles as exogenous forces that precipitated the break-up of empires that might otherwise have continued to evolve rather than disintegrate, and that the very concept of decolonization is an ex post facto invention designed to induce the uncritical acceptance of imperial collapse as a historically progressive inevitability rather than the product of a highly contingent and morally ambiguous (because of its sharpening of the boundaries and objective inequalities between former rulers and ruled, European and non-Europeans) set of choices.[52]

At one level, this historiographic trend has, unsurprisingly, gone hand-in-hand with a deep scepticism over nationalist claims to authenticity and antiquity. But suggesting that empires can be seen as having been powerful engines of modernity and active shapers and manipulators of ethnopolitical identities, rather than as doomed dinosaurs vainly struggling to adapt to the onset of a mammalian age of nation states, may also at least indirectly raise the question of whether national identity, for its part, is an exclusively modern phenomenon. Empires have risen and fallen throughout history, and their era may not be altogether behind us; perhaps nations should also be seen as gelling and melting, coming in and out of existence, across the course of history, rather than portrayed as the exclusive and inevitable products of a narrowly conceived modernity. Philipp Ther points out that the non-linear trajectories of nationalist mobilization and national consciousness over the course of the past few centuries (and, one might add, decades) speak to a weakness of the modernist school of nationalism studies: it is based on teleological assumptions that may not be empirically grounded. I would suggest that calling into question the *inherence* of nationalism in modernity serves, at least indirectly, to cast doubt on whether nationalism is *necessarily* modern.[53]

Such interpretive issues have arisen in tandem with broader trends (perhaps partly inspired by the rise of religious fundamentalism, the crises of the European Union, global financial and economic instability, and the failure of liberal internationalism to take hold globally in the aftermath of the Cold War) questioning teleological narratives about the rise of the West, the triumph of secularism, the success of civic forms of political identity – in brief the very idea of modernity as a sharp and irreversible break from past forms and norms of human existence. A recent article in the flagship journal of the American Historical Association called for the 'removal of key elements of the grammar of modernity from our analysis' of history.[54] This may go too far for some of us, but there is certainly a case to be made for exploring modernity in its aspect as merely the most recently accreted layer of human history – incomprehensible without seeing it against the background of all the earlier experiences that continue to be reflected in social and political structures, perceptions and identities, and that continue to shape the development of modernity itself. In light of this broader debate, the modernist school of nationalism studies, which pioneered the critique of essentialist understandings of nationhood, may prove vulnerable to accusations of essentialist sins of its own. As Anthony Smith has argued, even if one concedes that 'the "*modern* nation" is a mass phenomenon, this is no more than an interesting tautology, unless of course we claim *a priori* that the only kind of "nation" is the "modern nation". If we do not accept this equation, then, presumably, we would have to concede that in pre-modern epochs there was a type of nation that was more of an elite phenomenon'.[55]

Conclusion

How, then, do we escape the overly deterministic and potentially ahistorical pitfall of insisting on national identity as exclusively and necessarily a feature of modernity, without falling into the reductionist quicksand of an overly simplistic perennialist or primordialist position? As suggested above, perhaps there is room for what might be termed 'punctuated perennialism' – a view of national sentiment as a fluctuating phenomenon that may be catalysed and energized under some circumstances, while waning under others. A similar notion is conveyed by Anthony Smith's concept of 'recurrent perennialism'.[56] Derek Sayer's study of Czech national identity is a perfect example of such a dynamic. He documents the development of a pre-modern Czech national consciousness that clearly enjoyed popular roots and became politically influential during the era of the Hussite revolts of the fifteenth century, and persisted into the seventeenth century, only to decline and disappear altogether under the impact of the Habsburg suppression of religious reformism and secessionist elites in Bohemia following the Battle of the White Mountain in 1620.[57] Having made a bold and unapologetic case for a pre-modern Czech national identity, Sayer goes on to insist that the rise of Czech nationalism in the nineteenth century should not be understood as the resurfacing of a submerged yet still vital undercurrent of popular consciousness, as romantic nationalists liked to claim. Rather, Czech nationhood had effectively disappeared in the intervening centuries. What took place under the impact of changing economic and political conditions in the nineteenth century, he argues, was the coming into being of a new national movement that drew (among other sources) on the symbols, myths, traditions and precedents of the Hussite era to construct a sense of Czechness that resonated with its intended audience because it was plausibly connected to an ancestral past. Could the Czech case as depicted by Sayer serve as a more broadly applicable model for exploring continuities and disjunctures in the history of national sentiment?

Having said all that, it is also worth reminding ourselves that most scholars do not wish to throw the modernist baby out with the bath water. To say that modern nationalism is best understood within a capacious historical frame of reference that includes pre-modern forms of national identity need not suggest that there are no developmental trajectories at all to be considered. Uriel Abulof has usefully distinguished between what he sees as the 'negative nationalism' (in the form of opposition to alien rule) of pre-modern eras and modern 'positive nationalism' (rooted in claims about self-determination and popular sovereignty, 'which legitimate polity and authority, respectively').[58] From the perspective of a 'punctuated perennialism,' the critical feature of modernity that transformed national identity into a dominant, globally pervasive source of legitimation for territorial sovereignty claims was not industrialization per se, but rather the doctrine of popular sovereignty (itself a by-product, to be sure, of a variety of convergent socio-economic, ideological and geo-political transformations). Transferring a notionally indivisible sovereignty from the organically unitary body of a monarch to millions of subjects-turned-citizens unavoidably poses the question of what it is that lends (or can lend) those millions of bodies an organic cohesion – what is it that makes their sovereign whole greater than their individual parts? The answer unavoidably lies in some form of collective identity that transcends any internal divisions. And the preponderance of historical evidence suggests that such collective identities cannot readily be invented out of thin air; as Anthony Smith has argued, they are most likely to gain traction when they are plausibly connected to a pre-existing set of identities, symbols, cultural commonalities and historical precedents.

The very principles of self-determination and representative government thus force the issue of national identity upon a society, as Lord Acton's more secularly minded, fellow liberal thinker John Stuart Mill pointed out: 'One hardly knows what any division of the human race should be free to do if not to determine with which of the various collective bodies of human beings they choose to associate themselves.' Mill went on to claim that 'free institutions are next to impossible in a country made up of different nationalities'.[59] It was precisely this view that Lord Acton, with whom we began this essay, took issue. The dangers Acton pointed to were all too real. But the alternatives – other than trying to recreate polities based on arbitrary authority and institutionalized hierarchy and inequality – are far from obvious.

Notes

1 John Emerich Edward Dalberg-Acton (Lord Acton), 'Nationality' (1862) in John Emerich Edward Dalberg-Acton, *The History of Freedom and Other Essays* (London, 1919), pp. 270–300.

2 Ibid., 297.

3 Ibid., 289.

4 Ibid., pp. 291–2.

5 Ibid., p. 298.

6 Gertrude Himmelfarb, *Lord Acton: A Study in Conscience and Politics* (1952; Grand Rapids, 2015).

7 Anthony Smith, 'The "Golden Age" and National Renewal', in Geoffrey Hosking and George Schöpflin (eds), *Myths and Nationhood* (New York, 1997).

8 See Roland Vogt and Chong Li, 'German National Identity: Moving Beyond Guilt?', in Roland Vogt, Wayne Cristaudio and Andreas Leutzsch (eds), *European National Identities: Elements, Transitions, Conflicts* (New Brunswick, NJ, 2014), p. 77.

9 Derek Sayer, *The Coasts of Bohemia: A Czech History* (Princeton, 1998), pp. 127–53.

10 Kenneth J. Ruoff, *Imperial Japan at Its Zenith: The Wartime Celebration of the Empire's 2,600th Anniversary* (Ithaca, 2010), chapter 1 and p. 81; Owen Griffiths, 'Japanese Children and the Culture of Death, January-August 1945', in James Marten (ed.), *Children and War: A Historical Anthology* (New York, 2002).

11 Albert Hourani, *Arabic Thought in the Liberal Age, 1798–1939* (Oxford, 1962), chapters 6, 9, and 11.

12 Ernest Renan, 'What Is a Nation? (March 1882)', in Geoff Eley and Ronald Grigor Suny (eds), *Becoming National: A Reader* (New York, 1996), pp. 41–55.

13 Eric Hobsbawm, *Nations and Nationalism since 1780: Programme, Myth, Reality* (Cambridge, 1990); Ernest Gellner, *Nations and Nationalism* (Ithaca, 1983); Benedict Anderson, *Imagined Communities: Reflections on the Origin and Spread of Nationalism* (rev. edn, London and New York, 1991; 1983).

14 Pierre L. van den Berghe, 'Race and Ethnicity: A Sociobiological Perspective', *Ethnic and Racial Studies* 1:4 (October 1978), 401–11.

15 Azar Gat with Alexander Yakobson, *Nations: The Long History and Deep Roots of Political Ethnicity and Nationalism* (Cambridge, 2013), chapter 2.

16 Ibid., p. 42.
17 Ibid., chapter 2.
18 See chapter by Breuilly.
19 Smith's scheme of categorization is more differentiated and refined than I can do justice to here. Cf. Anthony D. Smith, *Nationalism and Modernism: A Critical Survey of Recent Theories of Nations and Nationalism* (London, 1998), chapters 7–8.
20 Anthony D. Smith, *The Ethnic Origins of Nations* (Oxford: Blackwell, 1986), pp. 21–32. Cf. also Anthony D. Smith, *Ethno-Symbolism and Nationalism: A Cultural Approach* (Abingdon, 2009).
21 Anthony D. Smith, 'Nations and Their Past' and Ernest Gellner, 'Do Nations Have Navels?', in Anthony D. Smith and Ernest Gellner, 'The Nation: Real or Imagined? The Warwick Debates on Nationalism', *Nations and Nationalism* 2:3 (1996), 357–70.
22 Anthony D. Smith, *The Antiquity of Nations* (Cambridge, 2004).
23 My thanks to John Breuilly for suggesting the contrast between the empiricist quality of historiographical perennialism and the theoretical formulations typical of the various schools of modernism as well as of ethno-symbolism.
24 See, for instance, Patrick Geary, *The Myth of Nations: The Medieval Origins of Europe* (Princeton, 2003).
25 Adrian Hastings, *The Construction of Nationhood: Ethnicity, Religion and Nationalism* (Cambridge, 1997), chapters 1–2 and *passim*.
26 Simon Schama, *The Embarrassment of Riches: An Interpretation of Dutch Culture in the Golden Age* (New York, 1987), chapter 2; Philip S. Gorski, 'The Mosaic Moment: An Early Modernist Critique of Modernist Theories of Nationalism', *American Journal of Sociology* 105:5 (March 2000), 1428–68; Adam Sutcliffe, *Judaism and Enlightenment* (Cambridge, 2003), chapter 2; Diana Muir Applebaum, 'Biblical Nationalism and the Sixteenth-Century States', *National Identities* 15:4 (2013), 317–32; Anthony D. Smith, 'Biblical Beliefs in the Shaping of Modern Nations', *Nations and Nationalism* 21:3 (2015), 403–22.
27 A number of these essays are collected in Steven Grosby, *Biblical Ideas of Nationality: Ancient and Modern* (Winona Lake, 2002).
28 Ibid., *Biblical Ideas*, chapters 1–2. See also David Goodblatt, *Elements of Ancient Jewish Nationalism* (New York, 2006).
29 Aviel Roshwald, *The Endurance of Nationalism: Ancient Roots and Modern Dilemmas* (Cambridge, 2006), pp. 14–22.
30 William M. Schniedewind, *How the Bible Became a Book* (Cambridge, 2004). William M. Schniedewind, *A Social History of Hebrew: Its Origins through the Rabbinic Period* (New Haven, 2013).
31 Grosby, *Biblical Ideas of Nationality*, chapter 6.
32 Steven Grosby, *Nationalism: A Very Short Introduction* (Oxford, 2005), pp. 60–1.
33 Edward E. Cohen, *The Athenian Nation* (Princeton, 2000). See also Roshwald, *The Endurance of Nationalism*, pp. 22–30.
34 Ernest Gellner, *Nations and Nationalism* (1983; Ithaca, 2008), chapter 2.
35 Anderson, *Imagined Communities*.
36 Anthony Smith makes this point about what he terms the 'double-edged' quality of Anderson's argument in *Nationalism and Modernism*, p. 142.

37 Caspar Hirschi, *The Origins of Nationalism: An Alternative History from Ancient Rome to Early Modern Germany* (Cambridge, 2012), p. 141.
38 Colette Beaune, *The Birth of an Ideology: Myths and Symbols of Nation in Late-Medieval France* (1986 [orig. French edn]; trans. Susan Ross Huston, Berkeley and Los Angeles, 1991), chapter 6.
39 Ibid., p. 192.
40 Beaune, *Birth of an Ideology*, pp. 193 and 320–25.
41 Susan Reynolds, *Kingdoms and Communities in Western Europe, 900–1300* (Oxford 1984), chapter 8; quotation from p. 331.
42 Susan Reynolds, 'The Idea of the Kingdom as a Political Community', in Len Scales and Oliver Zimmer (eds), *Power and the Nation in European History* (Cambridge, 2005), p. 56.
43 Patrick Wormald, 'Germanic Power Structures: The Early English Experience', in Len Scales and Oliver Zimmer (eds), *Power and the Nation*, p. 118.
44 Len Scales, 'Late Medieval Germany: An Under-Stated Nation?', Len Scales and Oliver Zimmer (eds), *Power and the Nation*, pp. 152–79.
45 Cf. Len Scales, *The Shaping of German Identity: Authority and Crisis, 1245–1414* (Cambridge, 2012), p. 537.
46 Cf. also the Introduction and some of the essays in Lotte Jensen, *The Roots of Nationalism: National Identity Formation in Early Modern Europe, 1600–1815* (Amsterdam, 2016).
47 Partha Chatterjee, *The Nation and its Fragments: Colonial and Postcolonial Histories* (Princeton, 1993). See also chapter by Seth.
48 C. A. Bayly, *The Birth of the Modern World 1780–1914: Global Connections and Comparisons* (Oxford, 2004), p. 218.
49 Victor Lieberman, *Strange Parallels: Southeast Asia in Global Context, c 800–1830, Vol. 2: Mainland Mirrors: Europe, Japan, China, South Asia and the Islands* (New York, 2009), chapter 1.
50 Mark Elliott, *The Manchu Way: The Eight Banners and Ethnic Identity in Late Imperial China* (Stanford, 2001).
51 Prasenjit Duara, *Rescuing History from the Nation: Questioning Narratives of Modern China* (Chicago, 1995), p. 54.
52 See, e.g., Pieter Judson, *Guardians of the Nation: Activists on the Language Frontiers of Imperial Austria* (Cambridge, 2006); Jeremy King, *Budweisers into Czechs and Germans: A Local History of Bohemian Politics, 1848–1948* (Princeton, 2002); Tara Zahra, *Kidnapped Souls: National Indifference and the Battle for Children in the Bohemian Lands, 1900–1948* (Ithaca, 2008); Karen Barkey, *Empire of Difference: The Ottomans in Comparative Perspective* (Cambridge, 2008); Todd Shepard, *The Invention of Decolonization: The Algerian War and the Remaking of France* (Ithaca, 2006); Frederick Cooper, *Citizenship between Empire and Nation: Remaking France and West Africa, 1945–1960* (Princeton, 2014).
53 Philipp Ther, '"Imperial Nationalism" as a Challenge for the Study of Nationalism', in Stefan Berger and Alexei Miller (eds), *Nationalizing Empires* (Budapest, 2015), p. 580.
54 Daniel Lord Smail and Andrew Shyrock, 'History and the "Pre"', *American Historical Review* 118:3 (June 2013), 709–37.
55 Smith, *Nationalism and Modernism*, p. 164.

56 Smith, *Nationalism and Modernism*, pp. 167 and 190. See also John A.
    Armstrong, *Nations before Nationalism* (Chapel Hill, 1982), p. 4; John
    Hutchinson, *The Dynamics of Cultural Nationalism: The Gaelic Revival and
    the Invention of the Irish Nation-State* (London, 1987), Introduction.
57 Sayer, *Coasts of Bohemia*.
58 Uriel Abulof, *The Mortality and Morality of Nations* (New York, 2015), p. 20.
59 John Stuart Mill, *Considerations on Representative Government* (1861)
    in Mill, *Utilitarianism, On Liberty,* and *Considerations on Representative
    Government*, ed. H. B. Acton (London, 1972), 361. Mill did acknowledge
    a variety of exceptions in practice, and his embrace of 'nationality' was
    predicated upon his concern with the viability of liberal polities rather than
    upon any sort of sympathy for chauvinism. Cf. Georgios Varouxakis, *Mill on
    Nationality* (London, 2002), *passim*.

Further reading

van den Berghe, Pierre L. 'Race and Ethnicity: A Sociobiological Perspective',
    Ethnic and Racial Studies 1:4 (October 1978), 401–11.
Gat, Azar with Alexander Yakobson, *Nations: The Long History and Deep Roots
    of Political Ethnicity and Nationalism*. Cambridge: Cambridge University
    Press, 2013.
Grosby, Steven, *Biblical Ideas of Nationality: Ancient and Modern*. Winona Lake,
    IN: Eisenbrauns, 2002.
Hastings, Adrian, *The Construction of Nationhood: Ethnicity, Religion and
    Nationalism*. Cambridge: Cambridge University Press, 1997.
Hirschi, Caspar, *The Origins of Nationalism: An Alternative History from
    Ancient Rome to Early Modern Germany*. Cambridge: Cambridge University
    Press, 2012.
Roshwald, Aviel, 'On Nationalism', in J. R. McNeill and Kenneth Pomeranz
    (eds), *The Cambridge World History*, Vol. VII, *Production, Connection, and
    Destruction, 1750 – Present,* Part 1: *Structures, Spaces, and Boundary Making*.
    Cambridge: Cambridge University Press, 2015, pp. 306–30.
Scales, Len and O. Zimmer (eds), *Power and the Nation in European History*.
    Cambridge: Cambridge University Press, 2005.
Smith, Anthony D., *The Ethnic Origins of Nations*. Oxford: Blackwell, 1986.

6

Cognitive and psychoanalytic approaches to nationalism

Steven J. Mock

Introduction: Nations in the brain

Of the terms crucial to discussing the history of nations and nationalism, 'identity' must be among the most problematic. Originating in the field of psychology, it refers by definition to what makes a person distinct: to the perception of an autonomous self, separate from the outside world. But when examining nationalism, it tends to be used in a seemingly opposite sense: to refer to properties that define the national group into which the individual is subsumed. These two senses of the term may not be as opposed as they seem. It is natural for a person trying to find her unique place in the world to turn to her social environment as a point of reference. The question 'who am I?' must be answered in large part through the question 'who are we?' Still, without a clear sense of how individual and group identity interact and relate to one another, the conflation of these concepts can cause confusion.

Early efforts to write the histories of nations and nationalism tended to make frequent use of terms like 'national honour', 'national character' or 'national spirit', treating nations as entities with personality and agency. It was developments in the field of psychology, specifically the rise of behaviourism and its influence on the social sciences in the decades after the Second World War, that caused such anthropomorphic language to fall out of favour. The effort to apply objective quantitative methods to the study of history and politics led to a dismissal of notions that implied that groups could think and feel as collective persons. Nations do not have minds, only the minds of the individuals that compose them. Hence, they cannot have their own attitudes, thoughts and feelings. And to the extent that the attitudes, thoughts and feelings of individuals could be documented and measured, they proved too varied and fragmented for talk that treated nations as collective agents to be anything more than metaphor. Lutz Niethammer has argued that the very concept of collective identity is a creature of modernity, a collective exercise of embracing arbitrary signifiers of essential commonality so as to obscure the reality of vast difference between members of a community, in a way that was not necessary at a time when community was justified by more stable religious or traditional norms and affiliations.[1]

Fear of such reductionism has led scholars to avoid psychological explanations for group phenomena in favour of a focus on structures and institutions. Even those who acknowledge the importance of shared ideas and emotions are reluctant to theorize as to what goes on in the minds of large numbers of diverse people as these usually prove to be vast generalizations. But it would be wrong to disregard a crucial factor due to the difficulties involved in documenting and measuring it. It is impossible to understand the human capacity for collective behaviour, how and why people put aside individual needs and interests to mobilize as a group, without some reference to shared concepts like culture, identity and ideology. Scholars of nationalism have long acknowledged that the phenomenon can hardly be explained without addressing the emotions at the heart of national mobilization. Gregory Jusdanis, for instance, writes: 'References to sentiments, attitude, and loyalty underscore the very visceral dimensions of identity. Nationalism works through people's hearts, nerves and gut. It is an expression of culture through the body.'[2] Ernest Renan, in describing the nation as a 'daily plebiscite' during his 1882 lecture 'What is a Nation?' explained that nations could not exist without a 'clearly expressed desire to continue a common life'.[3] Decades later, parsing the essential units of sociological analysis, Max Weber spoke of the nation as an abstract 'sentiment of solidarity'[4] in contrast to the tangible instrumentalities of the state. Benedict Anderson described the nation as a form of 'imagined community'[5] while Eric Hobsbawm preferred to speak of the 'invention of tradition',[6] in contrast to Anthony Smith who claimed that the nation depends on an authentic matrix of ethnic myths and memories.[7]

Desire, sentiment, imagination, invention and memory are ultimately properties of the mind. Whether we like it or not, all of us who deal with the subject of nations and nationalism do so with at least an implicit theory of mind. If we do not examine those theories deliberately, critically and openly, we run the risk of inviting incorrect or at least unexamined assumptions.

This is not to suggest that one can explain nationalism solely with reference to individual psychology. The nation is an emergent social phenomenon, more than the minds and bodies that compose it; therefore, social structural and systemic factors are crucial to the equation. But whatever else might go into building a national community or discourse, the one element that is essential without which no nation could exist is human minds that perceive themselves as part of such a group. For this reason, it is vital we address the question of how the relationship between the mind and the nation is best understood, as well as examine what theories of mind may have implicitly informed past approaches to the history of nations and nationalism.

Nationalism and its discontents

Any engagement with psychoanalytic theory must start at its origin: the framework developed by Sigmund Freud for understanding personality and behaviour. Psychoanalysis was one of several cultural and intellectual paradigms embedded in the *fin de siècle* era that grappled with the alienation arising from rapid economic growth and social transformation, which according to some modernist theorists of nationalism such as Ernest Gellner was also the crucible from which the construct of nation itself came to fruition. But like his contemporaries in the nascent disciplines of sociology and anthropology, Freud never set out to develop a theory of nationalism as such. Principles relevant to understanding nationalism can however be drawn from his observations on related phenomena like religion, ideology, war, ethnocentrism and prejudice. In particular, Freud cited nations as illustrative examples of his theories on the wider phenomenon of group formation. And while these theories may leave much to criticize, they provide a language that has served as the point of departure for a rich subsequent literature of psychoanalytic theory.

Two particular insights attributable to the psychoanalytic revolution are now so widely accepted we rarely think of them as controversial anymore. The first is the unconscious, the principle that many of the mental processes most significant to personality and behaviour occur beyond our awareness and agency. The second, related insight is that the bulk of the human personality is formed through the development, early in life, of mechanisms for resolving the inevitable conflict between the organism's innate biological drives and the need to behave as part of a group.

This development is represented by Freud in the Oedipal complex. The human infant enters the world physically aware of his survival needs, but helpless to perform even the most basic tasks, remaining in this state for a long time compared to other species. We begin life entirely dependent on the care and goodwill of our parents. In particular, the mother appears as the most immediate source of satisfaction of bodily needs, thus as the first object of the infant's nascent desire. But this places the infant in apparent competition for the mother's affection with the other dominant parental figure, the father. As the father is more powerful, dominant and self-sufficient, the child self-defensively adopts the father as model as well as competitor, in order to appease him and ameliorate the perceived threat he poses, as well as in the hope of being found worthy to share in his otherwise exclusive relationship with the mother.

The father thus becomes the first object of *identification*, a model from which the seemingly arbitrary rules as to how one may or may not go about fulfilling one's biological needs and drives are adopted. This identification will always be ambivalent. The father is on the one hand loved and needed as the source of order without which the infant would be lost. On the other hand, he and his rules are despised as obstacles to the unconstrained fulfilment of its needs: a frustration that manifests in castration anxiety, a repressed fear of the father's uncompromising determination to constrain the fulfilment of the son's desires.

Due to this inner conflict, identification is always incomplete; the identity it generates is perpetually ambivalent. As the individual develops the means to communicate and enter more fully into society he craves new objects as means to more stable fulfilment, first those provided by the parents then drawn from the wider community, and experiences new frustrations at the limits these objects impose. Through this process the individual develops the three interactive components that make for personality according to the psychoanalytic model: the perception of a conscious, rational self or *ego* that mediates between the biological/instinctual drives of the *id* and the demands of the *ego-ideal* or *superego* which serve as the moral conscience, internalizing the norms of society learned from objects of identification. 'Like a garrison in a conquered city', the superego takes the place of parental authority to reward and punish, limiting instinctual drives and aggressions to what is socially acceptable instead through mechanisms of guilt and shame.[8]

In *Totem and Taboo* (1913), Freud spun a tale as to how this system defined the origins of human history.[9] Connecting Darwin's theory of evolution with Durkheim's studies of primitive religion, he hypothesized humanity's starting point as the 'primal horde': a pack dominated by a jealous male who kept the females to himself driving away competitors, his sons, by means of brute force. His rule would end only when he was killed and replaced by a younger, stronger competitor. At some point in human evolution the sons developed the ability to cooperate in their mutual interest to kill the father, accomplishing together what they were unable to do individually. The goal was to be free of the restrictions his presence placed over the satisfaction of their own desires; in effect, to become like him. But it was impossible for all of the brothers to act like the father, following their desires and jealousies without constraint. If any of them did so it could only be at the expense of the others, introducing the problem all over again. In order for the 'brotherhood' of society to remain stable, they had to reintroduce the image of the father as the symbolic head of the clan: a mythic, god-figure who could continue to enforce his will so long as the community believed in him, allowing the community to maintain itself with equal rights guaranteed to all.[10] This was the origin of religion: where the ability to identify in common with a mythical image replaced brute force as the means by which our aggressive instincts are held in check in the interests of cooperative behaviour.

A large, impersonal group thereby comes into being when its members, raised according to similar patterns in a similar cultural environment, are directed to internalize a common object as part of their superego, identifying first of all with this object and secondarily through it with each other.[11] The key point with relevance to nationalism is that national identity is therefore not a given result of birth into a pre-existing nation with essential characteristics, nor can it be reduced to a rational choice to affiliate with a national ideology or community for instrumental reasons. The nation, as with any group, is ultimately an emotional tie; an investment of libido, a kind of energy, hypothesized by Freud as quantifiable in principle if not measurable in practice, originating in the primary sexual drive, but that can be diverted into other forms of love directed at other kinds of objects such as a leader, idea or symbol.[12] It is this shared investment of energy in a common object that gives otherwise unrelated individuals the means and motivation to act together as a group.

The point that must be stressed is that this emotional attachment is nothing abstract or ephemeral. Our species' ability to form groups is a bodily response derived from a process endemic to the human condition. The trauma the infant experiences that triggers this process is real and tangible, with lasting impact through formative periods of later life. Even before babies are capable of abstract thought, able to conceive of their sense of self, they are aware of their needs and the discomfort those needs generate when they are hungry, wet or frightened; of the security they feel having their needs filled through direct contact with seemingly omnipotent parental figures, and the anxiety they experience when that contact is lost.[13]

The implications of this basic experience to the construction of identity were considered to some extent by Freud, but more so by subsequent theorists applying his framework. For a being that spends years of its early life dependent on others, development of a personality acceptable to the social environment is imperative for survival. Being good, adhering to parental demands and received cultural norms, however arbitrary they may seem, means being safe and secure; it means life. Violating the imperatives of identification, doing something that earns the rebuke of parents or is at odds with cultural norms threatens the sense of security previously provided by proximity and affection, which means feelings of insecurity and anxiety, which means death.[14] And though this pattern of association between a secure sense of identity and the gratification of primary needs is established during those early years, as Erik Erikson later stressed, the emotions engendered persist throughout life as identifications are made with more diffuse models, ideologies, myths and symbols associated with the community on to which our feelings of dependence are transferred.[15]

This is why individuals are driven to bolster and defend shared symbols crucial to their identity. This drive is not an innate, biological trait, though it can manifest as aggressively as the gratification of hunger or sexual instinct. Nor is it a rational, instrumental calculation, though it has its origins as a means to improved needs-gratification. It is, rather, a psychological dynamic derived from the innate biological need to adapt to the social environment. The symbol system that amounts to the nation is not something we are born with, nor is it merely a social contrivance imposed on our unformed minds. Our species is driven by a need to crave, create and cling to symbols as a means of survival in a complex human environment. When we consider that this process may occur differently, and attach to different objects of identification between different regions or cultures, we find at least a rudimentary methodological basis for the notion of national character.[16]

The nationalist personality

Theodor Adorno and the Frankfurt School of critical social theory developed such an argument applying Freud's method as a means to explain the contemporary rise of Fascism and Nazism in Europe, culminating in the Second World War and the Holocaust. The idea behind *The Authoritarian Personality* was that individuals subjected to an overly harsh and punitive early upbringing will experience exaggerated castration anxiety.[17] Blocked from the usual outlets for expressing their natural hostility to the rules and limits represented by their parents, they will be unable to move on to internalize the wider diversity of identifications, beyond infantile parental attachment, that characterize the healthy superego of a well-rounded identity. Such people will then be inclined to seek and identify strongly with external symbols, especially leaders, to compensate for the lack of internalized ego-ideals. They will believe firmly in their group's innate superiority, displacing any aggression and hostility they are unable to express towards its strictures on to safe, external targets such as ethnic minorities. They will idolize strong and arrogant authority figures, shunning compromise and revelling in images of power and force. A culture characterized by strict modes of child-rearing could be expected to have a disproportionate number of such people drawn to authoritarian nationalist movements.

Adorno, in effect, understood nationalism in terms similar to the way Freud explained religion: as a kind of delusion tracing back to infantile helplessness and need for the father's protection. But while Freud saw this need as being mitigated in the modern era of scientific rationalism,[18] Adorno, drawing from a Marxian critique of modernity,[19] thought it all the more acute given the fragmentation of identity under modern industrial capitalism. By this reading, the rise of nationalism is modernity's inevitable downside. With the discrediting of the more deeply internalized ideals of traditional religion, obsessive identification with the leader or the group, involving excessive elevation of its power and complementary denigration of others, is left as the only means of closure and stability.[20] Constructivist theories of nationalism have explained the nation as a form of identity suited to the norms and structures of modernity.[21] Psychoanalysis, as adapted by the Frankfurt School, suggests this causal process works the other way, whereby modernity produces a certain type of individual with a psychology predisposed to attach to national myths and symbols.

Adorno's theory has been criticized as relying on too narrow and literal a reading of Freud that can tend towards psychological reductionism where whole societies are treated as a collective patient on the couch, all their members suffering from the same diagnosable disorder. Concerned primarily with explaining the appeal of fascism, Adorno bundled traits characteristic of fascist ideology into a single 'F-scale' used as a measure of authoritarianism: fixation on rank and status, submission to authority, preoccupation with power and toughness, rigidity of opinion, belief in traditional values, rigid us–them distinctions and ethnocentric hostility to out-groups. One could question whether such traits always cohere together, whether they all are equally integral to authoritarian nationalism, whether harsh parenting explains them all or, for that matter, whether harsh parenting will always produce such personalities. Even in the paradigmatic case of Nazism, it is unlikely that all active Nazis had an identical personality profile in each of these particulars, caused by identical modes of harsh upbringing.

But Adorno's notion of a distinct authoritarian personality does have merit, at least as an explanation for outbreaks of extreme nationalism. Approaches that attribute nationalist sentiment to personality type can benefit from more recent research in social psychology and cognitive science on the links between personality and political ideology; in particular, approaches that draw from the 'Five Factor Model' where extensive survey data have shown personality to be reducible to a limited set of essential traits: energy, agreeableness, conscientiousness, emotional stability and openness.[22] Drawing from a thorough review of literature in anthropology and evolutionary psychology, Jonathan Haidt identified five corresponding 'moral foundations', with the individuals' political value-system being the product of where she is located on each of the dimensions of *harm/ care, fairness/reciprocity, in-group/loyalty, authority/respect* and *purity/ sanctity*.[23] Endeavoring to explain escalating political polarization in America and elsewhere during the early twenty-first century, he observed that cosmopolitan liberals tend to be overly developed in the first two of these dimensions, whereas conservatives balance all five, and hence might be expected to be more inclined towards nationalist sentiment with greater concern for in-group loyalty and respect for authority. However, it should be stressed that the in-group loyalty and authority respect dimensions could also be separated, as is arguably the case with American libertarians who are both strongly nationalist and anti-authoritarian. Haidt also observed the extent to which feelings of disgust are triggered by violations of group norms and symbols, suggesting a crucial role for the purity–sanctity dimension in reproducing national identity.

But it has also been suggested that efforts to attribute nationalism to a particular political ideology or personality type obscure the pervasiveness of the nation in the modern world. From a Freudian perspective, one might even venture that such theories act themselves as a form of repression. They allow liberal-minded academics to relegate nationalism to the exotic or peripheral: to less advanced cultures, or less sophisticated elements of our culture, spreading into the general population only under exceptional circumstances such as war, thereby denying its significance to our own constructions of identity. Freud, like many early social theorists, seemed to treat the nation simply as a type of group formation among many; if anything, a more rational form of group identification than the superstitious attachments to mythic father-gods characteristic of pre-modern times. Even if mass psychology had the character of shared delusion, nations at least had the sense to worship themselves openly through the conduit of a tangible, visible leader.[24] Adorno's tendency was the opposite; to focus on nationalism in its extreme and violent manifestations, treating it as an exceptional product of dysfunctional development on a mass scale.

Both tendencies, to either 'naturalize' or 'pathologize' nationalism, have the same ultimate effect of downplaying the pervasiveness of nationalism and significance of nations to the modern world. The former views the historical development of identity teleologically, leading inexorably towards a more scientific, less neurotic future. Such assumptions take a world of nations for granted, neglecting to explore just what processes the construction of such a world is contingent upon. The latter tendency, by equating nationalism with only its most extreme manifestations, projects it to the margins of society, neglecting to explore how it shapes modern society at its very core, as part of the essential reservoir of language and knowledge on which all people draw to construct their sense of community and identity. As social-psychologist Michael Billig noted through his concept of 'banal nationalism', extreme manifestations of nationalism during war or crisis are only possible where the nation is continuously reproduced as the natural and acceptable background condition of ordinary life.[25]

The national pathology of everyday life

The plausibility of Freud's model depends on how literally you insist on taking it. Does the infant really desire sexual union with his mother, or is this a metaphor for direct unconstrained fulfilment of needs? Does he fear literal castration by his father, or does this represent frustration at the need to submit to a rule of law and limits? Did the murder of the primal father really have to happen? There is every indication that Freud meant for his theories to be taken quite literally indeed, treating acknowledgement of the primacy of the sexual drive and the incest impulse as litmus tests for membership to the psychoanalytic discipline. And certainly there is insight to be found here. Sexuality is no doubt a powerful driver of human personality and behaviour, and studies that draw from his framework to theorize on the role of sexuality in mechanisms of nationalist mobilization should not be dismissed out of hand. In 1974, Richard Koenigsberg developed the concept of 'psychoanalytic sociology' around the case of Nazi ideology as articulated in the speeches and writings of Hitler, identifying nationalism as the overarching framework whereby Hitler projected the image of his mother dying of cancer into the image of a national body beset by disease and disintegration in the form of Jews and foreign enemies, with anti-Semitism and sacrifice in war the heroic cures required to secure national life and purity.[26] Klaus Theweleit has examined narratives of the Freikorps, the right-wing militias that formed in Germany after the First World War that were precursors to Nazi paramilitaries, arguing that a distorted sexuality led these soldiers to find perverse satisfaction and common cause in acts of collective violence driven ultimately by misogyny.[27]

But while Freud may be credited for shedding light on such dynamics in the face of the mores of his time, his insistence on the sexual drive as the primary force behind personality development, itself innate and independent of cause, could be called into question. Subsequent theory and research in human psychology and cognition suggest the drives that contribute to identity are considerably more complex. Our species' capacity for abstract symbolic thought – the ability to form and manipulate images in our minds that stand for things in the world – sets us apart from nature in many ways. It gives us our sense of self as subject, distinct from the external world, locatable in time, able to reflect on a past and anticipate the future. But one of the first things we become aware of as we develop this power is just how embedded in nature we inescapably are. Once able to observe our bodies with their cravings and excretions, we rapidly infer that we are little more than leaky bags of meat stuck on a rock in space, no more enduring or significant in the long run than an insect or vegetable. We are the only species able to reflect on being alive. But knowing that one is alive, being able to anticipate the future, to observe the fate of objects in our environment and to reason by analogy, inevitably produces the terrifying awareness not only that one's own death is inevitable, but that it could happen at any time for reasons that can never be fully predicted or controlled.[28] This awareness is integral to the anxiety of helplessness impressed on us in early childhood. Psychotherapist Irvin Yalom observed that death anxiety can develop in children as early as age 3, alongside concepts and language. 'Children's concerns about death are pervasive and exert far reaching influence on their experiential worlds. Death is a great enigma to them, and one of their major developmental tasks is to deal with fears of helplessness and obliteration.'[29]

Drawing from the frameworks of Freud and Otto Rank, in 1973 Ernest Becker argued that the core function of the personality that develops at this time is to protect us from this budding awareness enough to allow us to get on with the business of living productive and fulfilling lives.[30] Identification with a cultural worldview is the means by which this is achieved by locating us in a system where we are beings of enduring significance. Culture can manage this in two ways.[31] The first, which most humans prefer, is through a promise of literal immortality. This is the appeal of the dualistic belief systems that pervade religion and philosophy across cultures, built around the idea that the human individual, as natural and animal as he seems to be, is nonetheless formed around an immortal spiritual core reflecting our capacity for abstract symbolic thought that endures the death of the natural body. But in absence of such a belief, or perhaps in tandem with it, culture can also offer symbolic immortality: the notion that even if the body must someday die, taking the transcendent conscious self down with it, our lives will still have meaning as part of something greater and more enduring. To that end, we are driven to participate in culturally sanctioned 'hero projects', collective endeavours that will live on after us and to which the higher faculties of our individual selves can contribute, whether by creating lasting works of art, breaking an Olympic record, passing our genes, inheritance and values on to our children, or furthering knowledge by writing brilliant book chapters on psychoanalytic approaches to nationalism.

The nation could be understood as such a hero project,[32] especially suitable to the modern era. With the rise of rational empiricism during the Enlightenment, along with increased contact between and consequent relativization of previously universal religious belief systems, the promises of literal immortality associated with traditional religions lost their vitality. Human communities compensated through the symbolic immortality that the nation could offer. Of course, I am not the first to suggest this. Benedict Anderson noted that the appeal of the nation lay in large part in its ability to take on the role of religion in 'transforming fatality into continuity'.[33] Perennialist and ethno-symbolist theorists of nationalism argue that continuity with long-lasting ethnic communities of pre-modern origin is closely associated with the strength and stability of nationalist sentiment in the present. But one must look to individual psychology to understand why this is so. If the nation can present itself as coming from a distant past, it is more plausible that it will continue to endure into the indefinite future. If it has outlived its founders and past members, it should outlive us as well, in which case our biological, physical and intellectual contributions to this collective endeavour will continue to have meaning after we are gone. Indeed, it becomes our responsibility to previous generations to continue the mission of national mobilization to ensure that their contributions were not in vain, and to pass on that responsibility in the expectation that future generations will preserve ours as well. As Anthony Smith put it, the nation can 'confer on mortals a sense of immortality through the judgment of posterity, rather than through divine judgment in an afterlife'.[34]

Becker's argument has since been given a fair amount of empirical grounding by the proponents of Terror Management Theory. Explaining the rise of religious terrorism and how citizens of Western nations have confronted it since 9/11, they have shown that 'mortality primes', signals that direct the subject's attention to the prospect of death, increase defensive responses against perceived challenges to one's national community, along with heightened expressions of in-group solidarity and out-group hostility.[35] But while this theory makes a compelling argument as to how and why threats to the abstraction of the nation can trigger existential passions, it is unlikely that this is the whole story. Culture and identity do more than divert us from our fear of death; they have a very practical role in forestalling it, enabling cooperative social behaviours that vastly enhance not just our sense of place in relation to the world, but our material comfort and security as well, with the effect of improving and extending our lives beyond what would be possible were we but solitary beings reliant on instinct alone. Systems Justification Theory holds that people are driven to support, defend and justify the status quo of prevailing social, economic and political arrangements.[36] The need for stability and order can extend even to the point where members of groups disadvantaged by a social system will persist in behaviours that maintain the hierarchy of that system, rationalizing their status by adopting beliefs about their own inferiority. This might be seen as a kind of psychological instrumentalism: attachment to national symbols is a factor of our attachment to the social system they represent, adherence to which is in the material interest of system stability, whether we are conscious of this motivation or not. But it also resonates with the approach of constructivists such as Gellner, whereby the effectiveness of the nation as a construct of identity is a factor of its compatibility with the functioning of modern industrial society.[37] More recently, Uriel Abulof has applied some of these approaches, reinterpreting the histories of certain 'small nations' – which is to say, nations compelled by nature and circumstance to constantly confront their collective mortality – as shifting bundles of hero projects that ebbed and flowed according to their relative ability to provide their adherents both epistemic and ontological security.[38]

Nationalism: Enjoying the Real Thing

Even without taking the Oedipal complex literally, one can still acknowledge that the terror that accompanies the infant's realization of its own helplessness, and the consequent need to adapt to an external social world perceived as predictable and orderly, has a lasting impact on personality. The helpless infant rapidly learns that to whatever extent she can attain control of her environment and the instruments of needs-gratification, this must be achieved through language. Screams and cries attract the attention of parents, enabling the infant to articulate need and linking her to external objects of its satisfaction.[39] As the child learns and develops, each new means of controlling her environment through observation and imitation demands more sophisticated mechanisms of language and representation. But entering into a world mediated through language means losing the world of direct, unmediated experience. According to theorists such as Slavoj Žižek, Julia Kristeva and Yannis Stavrakakis influenced by the broader, symbolic interpretation of Freud found in the earlier work of Jacques Lacan from the 1960s and 1970s, it is this, and not the incest prohibition itself, that is the crisis that produces identity.

As we acquire language and throughout our lives as we learn and relearn the rules of how to function in society, we become increasingly aware that the social world we inhabit is very different from the world that would be if our animal instincts were left to their devices. We want to inhabit that social world; we are happier, safer and can live longer in that social world. The essence of community is that all members sacrifice their aggressive instincts and restrain their prospects for satisfaction, instead submitting in common to the rule of law so that none are left at the mercy of brute force. For society to function, no individual may be above this principle.[40] But a part of us cannot help resenting the sacrifices we are required to make every day to live in that world through the continuous need to suppress our instinctual desires and aggressions.

As René Girard noted in the early 1970s in his critique of Freud, the real problem illuminated by the Oedipal complex is not that the child wishes to destroy the father, but rather that he wants to be the father, or at least what the father represents; and in all ways, not just in his relationship with the mother.[41] He wants to experience the complete autonomy of action the father seems to enjoy. Similarly, the problem introduced into civilization by the murder of the primal father is not the guilt we collectively feel over the act. Until Freud came along, no one even knew that it happened, and tracing a psychological mechanism back to a single act of prehistoric murder stretches credulity. The problem is the guilt we feel over the secret desire we all harbour, on an ongoing basis, to take the symbolic primal father's place: to follow instinct unrestrained, to make rather than submit to the rules of society. This desire must be repressed in all of us if society is to function as a theoretical 'brotherhood of equals'; we all must surrender our individual capacities for violence to a common symbol that represents the community, which in return offers us protection.

We use our ability for abstract representational thought to justify and explain this loss by telling ourselves stories. And though these stories may differ in significant ways between individuals and cultures, they follow a characteristic pattern since they satisfy a universal need. To begin with, the 'mother' should not be equated with the individual's actual mother. Rather, the mother represents the Real, our experience of the world before that experience was mediated by language, the most tangible experience of which is the direct fulfilment of need that the mother provides the newborn infant. Similarly, the father is not equal to the individual's actual father. The 'image of the father' rather stands at the forefront of a network of symbols that construct and enforce a world fundamentally different from the natural order, a world of human society represented by concepts and constrained by laws, all of the things that stand as obstacles to direct unmediated enjoyment (*jouissance*) of the Real.

This is what castration means on a symbolic level. Entering a world of symbols means the loss of direct unmediated fulfilment. Instead, we are forced to experience the world through the filter of language and concepts. Once we are alienated from the Real, this most intimate part of our selves is lost forever. Its sacrifice having been demanded by the symbolic father, it becomes an external, unreachable object, prohibited under the new order. Its loss permits the emergence of Desire, and it is our craving for the lost *jouissance* of direct experience, rather than drive to sexual union as such, that is the true source of the energy Freud called libido.[42] This is why our feelings towards the symbol of the father, to all of the identifications that constitute that symbol and to the world of social order it represents, are ambivalent. The capacity for abstract representational thought that alienates us from the Real, from our *jouissance*, is also the only means at our disposal for constructing a sense of self and identity that allows us to at least partially approach and recapture it.[43] By definition, the Real cannot be described or represented. Language and symbols can never fully express it. Yet language and symbols are the only tools we have to approach it, through the production of Fantasy.

Fantasy is the system of representations that fuels the energy of the libido, by offering the promise of fulfilment. Yet because representation is the very thing that alienates us from the Real, this promise is ultimately impossible. Each identification internalized leaves us short of the Real, therefore driven to seek the next object outside of ourselves; the *object petit a*.[44] No word or symbol can tell the whole truth; it leads us only to another word or symbol. For such an impossible system to coalesce into any remotely stable identity it must be anchored to some fixed point, the *point de capiton*. The symbol that serves this nodal function, though necessary to the system, does not and cannot have any intrinsic meaning in and of itself. As its sole purpose is to represent the organization of a system of otherwise heterogeneous and unrelated signifiers, its placement and content is contingent and arbitrary. Its only important trait is that it must be uncontested. Stavrakakis compared this metaphorically to the historical appointment of a given point of latitude as the Prime Meridian. There is no natural logic to either, any line of latitude or nodal symbol could serve just as well, as their only purpose is to function as points of reference, to provide a structural order necessary to ensure stability.[45]

What, then, does all this abstract theorizing have to do with nationalism? By way of illustration, consider national flags: pieces of cloth with an arbitrary collection of shapes and colours that mean nothing in themselves until their patterns are understood as pointing to a whole system of myths, ideas and values. But it is not the flag, as such, that is the *point de capiton* in a nationalist Fantasy. A flag, after all, is a tangible object. As a symbol it points to something else: the nation, which is itself the quintessential *point de capiton*:[46] a concept that means nothing except as a nodal point in the organization of a system of other concepts. 'America' is not a group of people, or a territory, or a system of government. It is a concept that links these and many other images – leaders, historical figures, myths, laws, institutions, abstract political principles, landmarks, foods, songs and so on – any or all of which can serve as *objects petit a* of identification in the individual's quest for meaning, but none of which would provide any measure of meaning unless they were related to one another. In a monograph published in 1999, Carolyn Marvin and David Ingle have specifically examined how the symbol of the American flag has structured American nationalism through its association with the succession of violent sacrifices made to preserve and regenerate national unity.[47]

A quote often cited to illustrate this concept is John Major's speech to the Conservative Group for Europe in April of 1993, in which he argued that integration into the European Union would not harm Britain's distinctive identity: 'Fifty years on from now, Britain will still be the country of long shadows on cricket grounds, warm beer, invincible green suburbs, dog lovers and pools fillers' and, as George Orwell said, 'old maids bicycling to holy communion through the morning mist' and, if we get our way, Shakespeare will still be read even in school.'[48] This assortment of images, which are not strictly visual but also evoke sounds, tastes, sensations, language and history, have no inherent connection to one another. Yet even to those members of the group who might never experience these images themselves (they reflect a distinctly masculine, Christian, middle-class and English experience), they conjure an emotion of being associated with some underlying reality called Britain. Žižek referred to this underlying felt reality that ties together otherwise disparate images into a mystical national totality as the Thing.

It is not the sum total of these images and activities that makes up the national Thing. It is rather the sense that there is more to these images and activities than would be apparent on the surface, a connection to a larger unifying principle. Indeed, the Thing is felt as not just underlying these images, but in fact producing them; it is a force of mystical will and agency that maintains the consistency and order of the group identity. If there is a standard term in nationalist rhetoric that points to the Thing it would be 'our way of life'. Though if asked to explain exactly what this way of life amounted to, we would be unable to do more than list certain of its more visible features, activities that members of our group characteristically perform with our bodies and minds: official and unofficial traditions, mating rituals, initiation ceremonies, culinary preferences and various other assorted myths and symbols. In other words, all of the tangible ways the community organizes and enacts its unique *jouissance*.[49]

It is this element of *jouissance* that sets the Lacanian psychoanalytic approach apart from constructivism, by insisting that national identity must be more than a social construct, a 'discourse' that dwells in the ether of social communication to be absorbed by pliant individuals. There is rather a real substance behind it; the assortment of myths, symbols and rituals that amount to a nation would not hold together if they did not derive from some real, material, non-discursive core. The Thing that is the nation is not just the unique set of properties that make up a particular national mythology or 'way of life'. These features are merely a manifestation. The core derives from the body. By participating in the rituals of the nation, by reproducing its myths, members signal their belief in this underlying reality, and their belief in the belief of other members, enabling the affective links that bind the community.[50] 'A nation *exists* only as long as its specific *enjoyment* continues to be materialized in a set of social practices and transmitted through national myths that structure those practices.'[51]

But since the Fantasy of primordial fullness of enjoyment is ultimately impossible, the experience of *jouissance* is always only partial, the mobilization of nationalist energies revolves around a constant and unfulfilled striving for it, as well as the omnipresent fear of its loss if elements of 'our way of life' stand threatened. This is why the politics of nationalism characteristically involves images of a utopian past which we are called on to restore in the indefinite future. This belief in a lost state of harmony that in fact never existed and can never be realized masks the fact that the real national project lies not in this goal as destination, but the journey of striving towards it. Our desire, and with it our drive to continue identifying with national objects – leaders, myths, rituals and so on – is driven by our ability to go through limited experiences that allow us to approach and taste *jouissance* through bodily participation in celebrations, festivals, consumption rituals and so on, as well as in the reproduction of various myths and symbols of national destiny through official and informal channels. But every national victory in war or sport, or every national ceremony or election, however dramatic or impressive these may be, offers only partial and momentary enjoyment, leaving us short of the promise of absolute fulfilment, fuelling further need and dissatisfaction, leading to further activity in a perpetual cycle. The drive to recapture our lost/impossible *jouissance* provides the Fantasy support that fuels the nation as a political project, maintaining the solidarity of the community, grounding national identity and animating desire, even, indeed especially when it inevitably fails to deliver the fullness it promises.[52]

It is important to stress that this is not the case only for essentialist, blood-and-soil types of nationalism. The fantasy that makes up 'our way of life' can contain principles of civic culture like freedom, or democracy, or institutions like constitutional government such as are integral to the notion of 'the American way of life'. Nor is it necessarily an elite construction, but can include popular or working-class elements such as in the original quote from Orwell to which John Major referred, where 'the clatter of clogs in the Lancashire mill towns, the to-and-fro of the lorries on the Great North Road, the queues outside the Labour Exchanges, the rattle of pin-tables in the Soho pubs' preceded the 'old maids *hiking* to Holy Communion through the mists of the autumn morning' (emphasis added) as emotively English images.

The approaches of the Lacanian theorists arose and flourished along with the counterculture movement of the 1960s and 1970s, and were influential in the development of critical theory and poststructuralism. Contrary to proponents of the Authoritarian Personality thesis, attachment to one's national 'way of life' was not viewed as a feature only of an extreme or dysfunctional personality. Though nationalism is relegated to the notion of Fantasy, axiomatically impossible to achieve, it is not thereby understood pejoratively as a delusion to be cured. It is a constructive, even crucial component of a stable identity, necessary to maintaining the cooperative energies of the community. It is only by finding common cause through identification with the national Thing, a shared means by which members of a given nation organize their collective enjoyment through national myths, that social differences are levelled and a democratic conception of citizenship tolerant of ideological and cultural diversity becomes possible.[53] 'National pride is comparable, from a psychological standpoint, to the *good narcissistic image* that the child gets from its mother and proceeds, through the intersecting play of identification demands emanating from both parents, to elaborate into an ego ideal.'[54] It is therefore not inherently racist or authoritarian, but rather natural for a national community to want to maintain closure of its way of life. Extremism results rather from challenges to this closure. 'By not being aware of, underestimating, or degrading such a narcissistic image or ego ideal, one humiliates or lays subject or group open to *depression*',[55] the signs of which are either apathy and inability to participate in the collective project, or paranoid, exaggerated counter-reaction.

Selves and Others

So national identity is good for you, then. Even if from the standpoint of individual psychology it could justly be described as a form of delusion, it is a healthy, even necessary delusion: a way to channel aggressive instincts and enable cooperative behaviour; a way to make peace with one's mortality and find meaning in life. Perhaps. But that does not mean its dark side is ever far from the surface. That channel has to go somewhere; that sense of meaning is always at risk. If true *jouissance* is always out of reach, the utopia of complete fulfilment impossible to achieve, one of the inevitable features of any group Fantasy must be a ready explanation for its continual failure, one that nonetheless maintains the credibility of the national project. That means attributing this failure to the agency of something external to the group; an Other, an outsider or, in terms familiar to nationalist rhetoric, a foreigner.

To some extent, the Other is built into any conception of a bounded community. Nationalism, as Michael Billig reminds us, is an ideology of the 'first person plural'[56] but there can be no *us* without a corresponding *them*, 'no positive sense of identity can be separated from its condition of possibility, difference'.[57] According to Social Identity Theory, associated with Henri Tajfel, any psychological process of group categorization must divide as much as it unites. Individuals seek to join or remain in groups, placing emotional value in group membership, if such belonging has a positive impact on their self-esteem.[58] This naturally leads to the generation of positive in-group and, by extension, negative out-group stereotypes, even if the initial basis of the division into groups is trivial or arbitrary.[59]

But the need for an Other goes deeper than the inevitable flipside of positive in-group stereotyping. The belief system that organizes our enjoyment, mitigates our terror and ratifies our social arrangements must seem natural or inevitable if it is to be effective.[60] If culturally constructed beliefs are our means of denying death and finding meaning in life, then the mere existence of people with alternate conceptions of reality threatens to expose the contingent nature of our own, compromising their death denying function. 'Encountering people with different beliefs and accepting the possible validity of their conceptions of reality necessarily undermines (implicitly or explicitly) the confidence with which people subscribe to their own death-denying conceptions, and, in so doing, threatens to unleash the overwhelming terror normally mitigated by the secure possession of one's existing beliefs.'[61]

One might argue that the strength of nationalism in the modern era lies in part in its ability to deal with this problem more effectively than religious belief systems with universal pretensions. Living in a world of nations with defined boundaries allows for the continued plausibility of one's own hero project while tolerating the persistence of alternative hero projects next door. If I believe in a universal truth, and someone else believes in a different universal truth, one of us must be wrong. But if my meaning system is felt to be applicable to my group only, the existence of others outside those boundaries should not provoke anxiety. This is true enough, and indeed individuals and groups with very different belief systems and cultural practices do live peacefully next to each other or even together within the same national community more often than not. The problem is that our nations never bring us perfect satisfaction. This is impossible, as no symbol system can bring us complete *jouissance* and no cultural construction can entirely eliminate or compensate for our death anxiety. Literal immortality beliefs may not be able to tolerate challenge as well as symbolic ones. But the trade-off is that the comfort provided by hero projects is always only partial. Residual anxiety that is repressed must be projected on to something, typically a group of outsiders who serve as scapegoats. Targeting this group, participating in a heroic struggle against evil in so doing, becomes another means of restoring our feelings of safety and security.[62]

As Žižek puts it, Fantasy 'constructs a scene in which the *jouissance* we are deprived of is concentrated in the Other who stole it from us'.[63] When frustration and anxiety arise in times of crisis, the presence of these Others, appearing to enjoy their own alternative, excessive, perverse *jouissance*, is offensive to us; we perceive them as the cause of our frustration and fear.[64] We are bothered by the peculiar way the Other organizes his enjoyment; the different tastes, smells, sounds, symbols and values. We attribute malicious intent to the Other, a seemingly motiveless desire to interfere with our way of life, to steal our national Thing. We imagine that everything would be fine if only the Other were not there to disrupt our enjoyment.[65] 'What we conceal by imputing to the Other the theft of enjoyment is the traumatic fact that *we never possessed what was allegedly stolen from us*',[66] but the notion that it was stolen explains its absence, satisfying our need to believe that it exists and might someday be (re)possessed. Because the nation only purports to lie in the utopian fantasy of a perfectly functioning, stable society, when in fact it is located in the permanent striving towards this unreachable goal, we need the Other to provide a perpetual alibi to explain its failure and deny its unreachable character.[67]

This purpose is not served by the mere existence of outsiders with beliefs and practices different from our own. We are compelled to designate 'Significant Others' as integral parts of the national mythology: negative principles to serve as scapegoats for the failure of our *jouissance*, for the threat to our way of life, as channels for the aggression we must disavow and project away from the community. The Significant Other may be a group with which the nation has a genuine conflict of interest or values. The United States experienced a real threat from the Soviet Union during the Cold War, as it does from terrorist groups like Al Qaeda today, yet notions that they 'menace our way of life' or 'hate our freedom' nonetheless add a visceral measure of Fantasy to the perception of that threat. But the need for Others to make sense of our national identity is such that if they are not readily available, our symbol-craving minds will invent them. Any group will do for whom a plausible story can be told as to how they threaten our identity or independence. It is often observed, for example, that Jews do not necessarily have to live in or near a national community for anti-Semitic conspiracy theories blaming them for that community's ills to gain traction.[68] It is not the reality of threat or difference that causes ethnic conflict, so much as the psychological need for communities to channel their own repressed antagonism outward. Freud himself observed that 'it is always possible to bind together a considerable number of people in love, so long as there are other people left over to receive the manifestations of their aggressiveness'.[69] If civilization is built on the frustration of instinct, the renunciation of drives, it generates a reservoir of hostility towards itself within its member individuals.[70] Girard argued that the safest way to deal with these excess aggressions is to attribute them to the agencies of an outsider, channelling this violence unanimously against a symbolic 'surrogate victim', such that the energies that constantly threaten to unravel the community instead function to unite it.[71]

If the reality of our bounded group is of such existential significance to us, then the Other is not a threat to our world-view, but a necessary reinforcer. This is especially true for a modern nation, which, at its best, is a large group of anonymous and diverse fellow members which must therefore rely on relatively trivial or even invented signifiers to maintain its boundaries, such as a dialect or line on a map. This is why the significance of these boundary mechanisms is frequently exaggerated, a phenomenon Freud called the narcissism of minor difference. While stereotypes ostensibly disparage what is different in the Other, their real function is to obscure his similarity, which is the real source of our insecurity as it calls into question the reality of the group. The reason we fear that the Other will rob us of *jouissance*, take our national Thing, is because, perhaps through no fault or intention of his own, he can, if his failure to be a sufficiently hostile, foreign and exotic target of our animosities, calls the reality and efficacy of our own national project into question. Stereotypes, as a means of distinguishing them from us, contribute to the force of our claims of unique identity.[72]

From a psychoanalytic perspective, then, the drive to despise and eliminate faceless Others is the inevitable flipside of the drive to love and cooperate with anonymous insiders, necessary to maintaining any form of functioning society. In studying the role of the nation in history, one can choose to focus on the former and view nationalism as delusional and pathological or focus on the latter and see it as natural and constructive. In fact, it is always both. All that historians can do to manage these contradictions, in the best tradition of psychoanalytic therapy, is expose them to the light of conscious thought. By recognizing that the Fantasy of complete fulfilment of national destiny has not been thwarted by a malicious Other, it was never achievable, though our community exists and remains productive through the never-ending striving for it.[73] By recognizing that we are all ultimately outsiders, alienated from the core of our enjoyment, reaching towards it by voluntarily opting in to identification with a shared national Thing, that what we fear or despise in the foreigner is ultimately a projection of we ourselves lack, that the Other is in fact us.[74] And by recognizing that the nation, as an empty signifier, is not and can never be the fulfilment of utopia; rather, at its best, it serves as a container in which competing utopian visions can safely contend with one another within a framework of shared rules, this being the outcome of a functioning democratic politics,[75] an idea that resonates with John Hutchinson's conception of nations as 'zones of conflict'.[76]

Conclusion: Unravelling the national mind

While the Lacanians had significant impact in the areas of linguistics and critical literary theory, their work has had little influence to date on the study of history, outside of their own speculations as to how their theories apply to historical and contemporary political events. Žižek, for instance, has done so for the fall of Communism, the Iraq War and the European

Union.[77] This is largely because the objects of their observations are notoriously difficult to document using the standard methods and sources of empirical historical inquiry. But in principle there is no reason why this need remain so. Symbols, ideas and fantasies are ultimately brain processes, objects in nature rather than ephemeral abstractions. Like all objects in nature, they are objects of history; not mystically created givens, but temporal products of processes of causation that require the historical discipline to unpack.

One example is the recent revival of interest in emotions as legitimate subjects of historical inquiry. Previously dismissed as irrational and therefore unfathomable drivers of human behaviour, impossible to document or predict, the social sciences are starting to follow the cognitive sciences in recognizing emotions as crucial to any rational decision-making process.[78] Drawing in part from the work of sociologists such as Norbert Elias who already in 1939 argued that the palate of human emotion has changed significantly between eras of civilization,[79] historians like Ute Frevert have explored how different social expectations, such as between genders, classes and nations, can affect not just how feelings are perceived but what is actually felt.[80] The ability to reconstruct the emotional repertoire characteristic of a subject group, time or place therefore becomes crucial to understanding behaviours that lead to events.

It may help to visualize the nation as consisting of two distinct but related elements, one of which is smaller and the other larger than the human individual. It is easy enough to see the nation as larger than the individual; as thousands or millions of individuals, along with the objects they identify with, the stories they tell and the norms and institutions they construct between them. But on the cognitive level, the nation is smaller than the individual; it is the subset of mental representations – concepts, symbols, beliefs, values – through which the individual perceives herself to be part of the national group. The nation cannot exist without both of these conditions: a collection of individuals linked by networks of social communication, and a cognitive construct common to the minds of member individuals according to which the nation is conceived and defined. Neither condition can exist without the other; neither is prior to the other. The nation is the product of multidirectional feedback between these two systems. Networks of social communication are required to create the cognitive construct of the group in the minds of member individuals; yet those networks are themselves generated through the presence and content of the cognitive construct.[81]

Cognitive and psychoanalytic approaches can help us to better understand the structure of the system of mental representations that make up the nation in the mind. They encourage us to isolate this element, disentangle its components, map its connections and track its changes. What are the key objects of identification associated with the national Thing: the images, words, stories, songs, smells, sensations, rituals and values felt to be part of the nation's distinctive 'way of life'? How do they connect to one another, forming a coherent system? How has this system changed over time in response to changes in the social environment, and how have those changes shaped the social environment in turn? And how do they function to deal with the psychological needs at the core of any social identity, which include (but may not be limited to) the organization of enjoyment, the mitigation of terror, the maintenance of social stability and the channelling of aggression to the community's exterior?

Understanding the nation as the product of interaction between systems at two different levels of analysis, cognitive and social, can help to illuminate the dramatic upheavals characteristic of the history of nations and the politics of nationalism; why relatively small changes to people's beliefs can have dramatic significance to how they organize and mobilize as a community, while events that seem minor at the time can have unpredictable effects on their beliefs. It offers us the means to treat different social-level explanations of nationalism less as rival theories that challenge each other and more like a set of tools, each of which may be useful in the right situation. They may seem contradictory as social theories: the nation cannot at the same time be both a wholly modern construct and continuous with pre-modern ethnicities; its terms of membership cannot be civic/voluntary and ethnic/ascriptive all at once. But at the level of individual psychology, the human mind is constantly tasked to reconcile contradictions stemming from conflicting drives and diverse identifications. The needs of terror management might call for a primordial and unchanging national 'hero project', while the need for system justification demands the rationalization of modern social norms radically different from those characteristic of that project's history. The ideal, important to self-esteem and social stability, that the nation should be a voluntary civic community of equal and diverse citizens may be confounded by the reality that mobility in a modern society and the cohesion of a modern community require conformity to at least some common cultural traits as well as attachment to symbols of common destiny. The most important national myths and symbols, the ones that are the focus of the most intense emotional investment, may be those that function to maintain the coherence of the national Thing in the face of these and other precarious contradictions.

And while this network of myths and symbols will likely also contain a myth of its own permanence and closure, the ultimate contradiction is that it can never be fully closed. As no symbol system can ever achieve its goal of expressing the Real, the nation in the mind will always be a place of dynamism, reflecting the nation in the social world that will always remain a container for political conflict. Like the mythic Ouroboros eternally chasing its own tail, it is a moving target, circling but never touching the void at the core of human experience, blissfully oblivious that its pursuit of this hopeless goal is the very energy that sustains it.

Notes

1   Lutz Niethammer, 'The infancy of Tarzan', *New Left Review* 19 (2003), 79.
2   Gregory Jusdanis, *The Necessary Nation* (Princeton, 2001), p. 31.
3   Quoted in Michael Billig, *Banal Nationalism* (London, 1995), p. 95.
4   Max Weber, *From Max Weber: Essays in Sociology* (Oxford, 1946), p. 176.
5   Benedict Anderson, *Imagined Communities: Reflections on the Origin and Spread of Nationalism* (New York, 1991).
6   Eric Hobsbawm and Terence Ranger (eds), *The Invention of Tradition* (Cambridge, 1983).
7   Anthony D. Smith, *Myths and Memories of the Nation* (Oxford, 1999).
8   Sigmund Freud, 'Group Psychology and the Analysis of the Ego', in Sigmund Freud (ed.), *Civilization, Society and Religion: Group Psychology, Civilization and its Discontents and Other Works*, translated by James Strachey and edited by Albert Dickson (London,1991 [1921]), p. 139; Sigmund Freud, 'Civilization and Its Discontents', in Sigmund Freud (ed.), *Civilization, Society and Religion*, pp. 253–55, 316–17.
9   Sigmund Freud, *Totem and Taboo: Resemblances between the Psychic Lives of Savages and Neurotics*, translated by Abraham A. Brill (New York, 1946).
10 Sigmund Freud, 'Group Psychology and the Analysis of the Ego', in Sigmund Freud (ed.), *Civilization, Society and Religion*, p. 168.
11 Ibid., pp. 124–5.
12 Ibid., pp. 119, 171.
13 Ibid., pp. 149–51.
14 Tom Pyszczynski, Sheldon Solomon and Jeff Greenberg, *In the Wake of 9/11: Rising above the Terror* (Washington,DC, 2003), pp. 24–6.
15 Erik H. Erikson, *Identity and the Life Cycle* (New York, 1959).
16 William Bloom, *Personal Identity, National Identity and International Relations* (Cambridge, 1990) pp. 17–18, 33.
17 Theodor W. Adorno, Daniel Levinson, Else Frenkel-Brunswik and Nevitt Sanford, *The Authoritarian Personality* (New York, 1950).
18 Freud, 'Civilization and its Discontents', pp. 260–1.
19 See chapter by Hroch.
20 Alan Finlayson, 'Psychology, Psychoanalysis and Theories of Nationalism', *Nations and Nationalism* 4:2 (1998), 151–3.
21 See chapter by Wicke.
22 Gian-Vittorio Caprara, Claudio Barbaranelli, Laura Borgogni and Marco Perugini, 'The "Big Five Questionnaire": A New Questionnaire to Assess the Five Factor Model', *Personality and Individual Differences* 15:3 (1993), 281–8.
23 Jonathan Haidt, 'The Emotional Dog and Its Rational Tail – A Social Intuitionist Approach to Moral Judgment', *Psychological Review* 108:4 (2001), 814–34; Jonathan Haidt, 'The New Synthesis in Moral Psychology', *Science* 316:5827 (2007), 998–1002. A sixth dimension of *liberty/oppression* was added in his later work, Jonathan Haidt, *The Righteous Mind: Why Good People Are Divided by Politics and Religion* (New York, 2012).
24 As Gellner, adapting Durkheim, would later point out; Ernest Gellner, *Nations and Nationalism* (Ithaca, 1983); Emile Durkheim, *The Elementary Forms of the Religious Life* (New York, 1971).

25 Michael Billig, *Banal nationalism*.
26 Richard A. Koenigsberg, *Hitler's Ideology: A Study in Psychoanalytic Sociology* (New York, 1975).
27 Klaus Theweleit, *Male Fantasies* (Minneapolis, 1987).
28 Pyszczynski, Solomon and Greenberg, *In the Wake of 9/11*, pp. 15–17.
29 Irvin D. Yalom, *Existential Psychotherapy* (New York, 1980).
30 Ernst Becker, *The Denial of Death* (New York, 1973).
31 Robert J. Lifton, *The Broken Connection: On Death and the Continuity of Life* (New York, 1979).
32 Pyszczynski, Solomon and Greenberg, *In the Wake of 9/11*, p. 50.
33 Benedict Anderson, *Imagined Communities*, p. 19; see also Liah Greenfeld, *Nationalism and the Mind: Essays on Modern Culture* (Oxford, 2006), p. 95.
34 Anthony D. Smith, *Nations and Nationalism in a Global Era* (Oxford, 1995), p. 158.
35 Pyszczynski, Solomon and Greenberg, *In the Wake of 9/11*, p. 9; Jeff Greenberg, Tom Pyszczynski, Sheldon Solomon, Deborah Lyon and Abram Rosenblatt, 'Evidence for Terror Management Theory II: The Effects of Mortality Salience on Reactions to Those Who Threaten or Bolster the Cultural Worldview', *Journal of Personality and Social Psychology* 58:2 (1990), 308–18.
36 John T. Jost, Mahzarin R. Banaji and Brian A. Nosek, 'A Decade of System Justification Theory: Accumulated Evidence of Conscious and Unconscious Bolstering of the Status Quo', *Political Psychology* 25:6 (2004), 881–919.
37 Gellner, E. (1983), *Nations and Nationalism*, Cornell University Press.
38 Uriel Abulof, *The Mortality and Morality of Nations* (Cambridge 2015).
39 Pyszczynski, Solomon and Greenberg, *In the Wake of 9/11*, p. 24.
40 Freud, *Civilization and Its Discontents*, p. 284.
41 René Girard, *Violence and the Sacred*, translated by Patrick Gregory (Baltimore, 1977).
42 Yannis Stavrakakis, *Lacan and the Political* (London, 1999), pp. 42, 52–53.
43 Stavrakakis, *Lacan and the Political*, pp. 31–4; Slavoj Žižek, *Tarrying with the Negative: Kant, Hegel, and the Critique of Ideology* (Durham, 1993), p. 3.
44 Stavrakakis, *Lacan and the Political*, pp. 35–6, 49.
45 Stavrakakis, *Lacan and the Political*, pp. 60–1, 78–81; Slavoj Žižek, *The Sublime Object of Ideology* (London, 1989), p. 87.
46 Stavrakakis, *Lacan and the Political*, p. 80.
47 Carolyn Marvin and David W. Ingle, *Blood Sacrifice and the Nation: Totem Rituals and the American Flag* (Cambridge, 1999).
48 Guardian, 23 April 1993; cited, for example, by Michael Billig, *Banal nationalism*, p. 102 and Alan Finlayson, 'Psychology, Psychoanalysis and Theories of Nationalism', pp. 154–5.
49 Yannis Stavrakakis, *The Lacanian Left: Psychoanalysis, Theory, Politics* (New York, 2007), pp. 204–5; see also Slavoj Žižek, *Tarrying with the Negative*, p. 201.
50 Finlayson, 'Psychology, Psychoanalysis and Theories of Nationalism', p. 154.
51 Žižek, *Tarrying with the Negative*, p. 202.
52 Stavrakakis, *The Lacanian Left: Psychoanalysis, Theory, Politics*, pp. 196–9.

53   Slavoj Žižek, *Looking Awry: An Introduction to Jacques Lacan through Popular Culture* (Massachusetts, 1992), p. 165; see also Žižek, *Tarrying with the Negative*, p. 215.
54   Julia Kristeva, *Nations without Nationalism* (New York, 1993), p. 52.
55   Ibid.
56   Billig, *Banal Nationalism*, p. 70.
57   Stavrakakis, *The Lacanian Left: Psychoanalysis, Theory, Politics*, p. 195.
58   Henri Tajfel, *Human Groups and Social Categories: Studies in Social Psychology* (Cambridge, 1981).
59   Henri Tajfel, Michael Billig, Robert P. Bundy and Claude Flament, 'Social Categorization and Intergroup Behaviour', *European Journal of Social Psychology* 1:2 (1971), 149–78.
60   Billig, *Banal Nationalism*, pp. 15, 37.
61   Pyszczynski, Solomon and Greenberg, *In the Wake of 9/11*, p. 29.
62   Ibid., p. 30.
63   Slavoj Žižek, *The Plague of Fantasies* (New York, 1997), p. 32.
64   Žižek, *Looking Awry*, p. 165.
65   Alan Finlayson, 'Psychology, Psychoanalysis and Theories of Nationalism', p. 155.
66   Žižek, *Tarrying with the Negative*, p. 203.
67   Stavrakakis, *Lacan and the Political*, p. 100; Stavrakakis, *The Lacanian Left*, pp. 197–8.
68   Žižek, *Tarrying with the Negative*, p. 205.
69   Freud, *Civilization and its Discontents*, p. 305.
70   Ibid., p. 286.
71   Girard, *Violence and the Sacred*.
72   Billig, *Banal Nationalism*, p. 81.
73   Žižek, *Tarrying with the Negative*.
74   Kristeva, *Nations without Nationalism*, pp. 50–1; see also Julia Kristeva, *Strangers to Ourselves* (New York, 1991).
75   Stavrakakis, *Lacan and the Political*, pp. 136–37.
76   John Hutchinson, *Nations as Zones of Conflict* (Thousand Oaks, 2005).
77   Slavoj Žižek, *Iraq: The Borrowed Kettle* (New York, 2003); Slavoj Žižek, *Living in the End Times* (New York, 2010); Slavoj Žižek, and Srećko Horvat, *What Does Europe Want?* (New York, 2015).
78   António R. Damasio, *Descartes' Error: Emotion, Reason, and the Human Brain* (New York, 1994).
79   Norbert Elias, *The Civilizing Process* (Hoboken, 2000).
80   Ute Frevert, *Emotions in History: Lost and Found* (Budapest, 2011).
81   Manjana Milkoreit and Steven Mock, 'The Networked Mind: Collective Identities as the Key to Understanding Conflict', Chapter 8 in Anthony J. Masys (ed.), *Networks and Network Analysis for Defense and Security* (Berlin, 2014).

Further reading

Abulof, U., *The Mortality and Morality of Nations*. New York: Cambridge University Press, 2015.

Adorno, T. W., E. Frenkel-Brunswik, D. J. Levinson and R. N. Sanford, *The Authoritarian Personality*. Oxford: Harpers, 1950.

Becker, E., *The Denial of Death*. New York: The Free Press, 1973.

Billig, M., *Banal Nationalism*. Los Angeles, London, New Delhi, Singapore, Washington DC: Sage Publications, 1995.

Freud, S. (1930). 'Civilization and Its Discontents', in S. Freud (ed.), *Civilization, Society and Religion: Group Psychology, Civilization and Its Discontents and Other Works*. London: Penguin, 1991.

Frevert, U., *Emotions in History: Lost and Found*. Budapest, New York: Central European University Press, 2011.

Haidt, J., *The Righteous Mind: Why Good People Are Divided by Politics and Religion*. New York: Pantheon Books, 2012.

Kristeva, J., *Nations without Nationalism*. New York: Columbia University Press, 1993.

Marvin, C. and D. Ingle, *Blood Sacrifice and the Nation: Totem Rituals and the American Flag*. Cambridge: Cambridge University Press, 1999.

Pyszczynski, T., S. Solomon and J. Greenberg, *In the Wake of 9/11: Rising above the Terror*. Washington, DC: American Psychological Association, 2003.

Stavrakakis, Y., *The Lacanian Left: Psychoanalysis, Theory, Politics*. Edinburgh: Edinburgh University Press, 2007.

7

Constructivism in the history of nationalism since 1945

Christian Wicke*

Introduction

Constructivism, which holds that truth, knowledge and reality are socially constructed, has sought to disenchant national mythology in questioning the 'obvious' and the apparently 'normal'. In the decades following the Second World War, the history of nations and nationalism attracted an increasing number of critical scholars, while from the 1960s social constructivism became a leading perspective in social sciences and humanities. Since the early 1980s, the idea that national traditions had been 'invented'[1] and national communities 'imagined'[2] became dominant. Social constructivists thus, to some extent, have undermined the apparent authenticity of nations, which have become such an important part of everyday and political cultures around the globe.[3]

This chapter will discuss the importance of social constructivism for the study of the history of nations and nationalism. Deep-cutting transnational events, that is, predominantly the effects of Nazism, but also to some degree de-colonization movements and the ethnic-nationalist revival after the end of the Cold War, profoundly shaped constructivist theory and the historiography of nationalism. Scholars argued that nations should not be regarded as static cultural units in history, but rather as fluid and manipulable categories articulated through nationalist narratives and symbols in politics and society. The rise of nationalism studies, this interdisciplinary sub-discipline, from the early 1980s happened largely thanks to constructivist thinking that was critically applied to the history of nations and nationalism during the transition from pre-modern to modern society. The modernist perspectives on nationalism[4] were intrinsically constructivist, as they questioned the legitimacy of teleologically constructed national histories and the histories of nations as unitary and fixed objects in time and space, and thus the existence of nations as a regularity of the human condition. Interestingly, over recent decades historical studies of pre-modern formations of nations have also employed constructivist methods and perspectives. And while most authors have focused on the role of states and elites 'from above', some historical studies have started exploring ways to better understand the construction (and reception) of nations and nationalism among ordinary people in the past.

The disenchantment of national identity in the twentieth century

In many ways, Ernest Renan's famous speech from 1882 at the Sorbonne, *Qu'est-ce qu'une nation?* already questioned – or deconstructed – the assumption of nations' eternity and their foundation on supposedly 'objective' categories such as race, language, religion, economic interests and geographic boundaries. Renan found that nations relied on a constructed past – myths, remembering and also forgetting the great and not so great episodes of the past. According to Renan ultimately it was a 'daily plebiscite' that was required to form a nation, which to him was primarily a 'community of will'. Alsace, which had been annexed by the new German Empire in 1871, could thus happily become either French or German, if the inhabitants wished so. Renan, however, did not critically engage with the question of how this willingness was constructed; rather, he took for granted the imagination as well as the essential satisfaction of nationals in their somewhat fictitious world of nations. Whether he would therefore qualify as a constructivist historian remains doubtful. However, he did problematize the romantic assumption that nations were secure objects in the chaos of history.

Arguably it was nationalism's growing 'dark side' in the twentieth century that attracted more critical constructivist perspectives. Already during the interwar period the Catholic historian Carleton Hayes described nationalism as a dangerous pseudo-religion that had emerged during the modern processes of secularization.[5] From the 1940s, 'critical theory' transcended its dissatisfaction with both the problems of the American capitalist model as well as German Nazism into a general critique of 'rationalization' in Western society since the Enlightenment, a process that itself was producing new myths, as Horkheimer and Adorno, the founding fathers of the Frankfurt School and its critical theory, argued.[6]

In response to the experiences of the Second World War and the Holocaust scholars began to study the deeper causes of the catastrophe, including the history of nationalism. The historian Hans Kohn, for example, who migrated from Prague to the United States because of his Jewish background, argued that nationalism was foremost a modern 'state of mind'; in some nations it could take a 'good', civic and liberal path, but in others it could also pervert into a 'bad', ethnic and illiberal form, as it had been the case in Germany.[7] Germany in many ways can be seen as a paradigmatic case in nationalism studies. Nazi Germany's triggering of the Second World War, and the subsequent crimes against humanity committed by Germans in Europe, were driven by extreme nationalist motifs. Kohn and others traced the roots of Nazism through German intellectual history back to the early romantics and Protestant traditions (Germany's cultural *Sonderweg*). German historiography thus became strongly contested. It was no longer only a self-congratulatory, but increasingly, a self-reflective narrative of the national past. The history of the nation hence became, at least to some degree, liberated from the tradition of glorifying the nation and its past.

Brutal episodes in the (post)colonial world, such as the Algerian War, underpinned such critical approaches to nationalism in the West. The postcolonial experiences of the post-war era inspired scholars, such as Edward Said and Jacques Derrida, to further 'de-construct' the history, language and thinking of Western civilization, and thus its domineering place in the world.[8] Roland Barthes, another influential French thinker, exposed the ongoing role of myths in the everyday life of modern society,[9] while Michel Foucault questioned historically grown hegemonial relations within and between societies. These authors argued that 'truth' was constantly changing rather than absolute.[10] Foucault, for example, criticized the role of states in institutionalizing absurd ideas of racial purity.[11]

Many scholars argued that nationalism was a condition of modernity, though not one that would be beneficial, or strictly necessary, to maintain modern society. The Prague-born political scientist Karl Deutsch saw social communication and social mobility as the basic requirement for the construction of national identities. Industrialization and the world's snowballing urbanization required increasing mobilization and communication, and thus allowed for the nation formation of the modern world. However, Deutsch did not perceive this as an inescapable condition, but instead encouraged humankind to find alternatives to a world divided into nation states.[12]

'Social constructivism', as a defined method or intellectual tradition, only took shape after Peter L. Berger and Thomas Luckmann published a hugely influential book entitled *The Social Construction of Reality* in 1966. Berger, who was born in Vienna, had escaped the Holocaust via Palestine to the United States. Luckmann, who studied the sociology of religion, was born in the Kingdom of Yugoslavia to parents of different ethnic backgrounds. In their book they pointed to the construction of social reality, that is, the institutionalization of beliefs and symbols. Their way of thinking put pressure on established norms and values that had legitimized political institutions and collective identities. And they arguably paved the ground for critical accounts of the history of nation states, which often have been perceived as constituting a historical and incontestable condition in our everyday life. Berger and Luckmann saw meaning and knowledge as constructed discursively over time through interaction in the social sphere, rather than as something given and static. Society's understanding of the world should be seen as a product of our perceptions of each other and thus of ourselves. The institutionalization of such perceptions secures the formation of what we often think of as normal. Think of education and a graduation ceremony, of love and marriage, ideas of race and apartheid, or of human gender relations in different cultures. Social reality is not unreal, but largely constructed and thus not to be taken for granted. Similarly, nations are both real and imagined, not static constructs that remain the same over time, as society's institutions and imaginations change over time.

One should be aware, however, that constructivism can mean many things. And every constructivist thinks differently. One way of identifying whether a text about the origins and history of nations and nationalism is written from a constructivist perspective is to look at its terminology. A combination of words such as 'myth', 'fiction', 'imagination', 'narration', 'invention', 'fabrication' or 'construction' may indicate the author is taking a constructivist stance. Constructivists usually believe that the supposedly homogenous entities of nations were discursively produced rather than deriving from any kind of fixed entity in history, and that these discursive processes had intensified at a time of socio-economic, intellectual and political transition. As this major shift is often associated with the making of modern society, it may be difficult to clearly differentiate historical constructivism from the modernist perspective on the origin of nations. However, not all constructivists have been modernists.

Constructivist scholars of national identities disenchant established myths about the past by exposing the 'unnatural' in the history of nations. Constructivism thus has the potential of undermining the legitimacy of ethnic conflict, territorial claims and wars between nations. It questions the inevitability of one of the most pivotal ideologies of today – nationalism.[13] Culture, for example, for the constructivist, is nothing given or essential to the nation, even though it feels so familiar to us. Some constructivists hold that national cultures have been built by dominant groups in society who have been able to impose their own culture onto others.[14] Others study the production of national identities through institutions, transport, communication, art, literature, rites and symbols, for example. By carefully tracing the origins and changing meanings of these elements over time, constructivist historians de-construct the apparently 'obvious' and 'normal'.

Two relatively early examples of social constructivist scholarship in the history of nationalism are Eugen Weber's *Peasants into Frenchmen* and George Mosse's *The Nationalization of the Masses*, both published in the 1970s. The first work questioned the widespread existence of French national identity around the time of the 'national' revolutions of 1789 and 1848. Weber argued that the population of France at that time could not actually be considered as a singular nation. When G.-E. Haussmann (1809–1891) wrote in his memoirs that 'our country, [is] the most "one" in the world', Weber thought that '[t]he myth was stronger than reality'.[15] Weber was born in multicultural Romania, educated in England and served in the British Army, studied in France and eventually migrated to the United States. His transnational experiences supported his aversion to the xenophobic turn nationalism had taken towards the twentieth century. Weber was especially concerned with the nationalist revival before the First World War as represented by *Action française*. In his book, the historian informed his readers that the construction of the French nation predominantly was a Parisian project. It was not until a century after the French Revolution that encompassing modernization processes took place, and rural France was thoroughly nationalized, meaning that peasants adopted the French language and 'thought'. Weber studied the spread of a national culture, for example, through the building, transport and communication networks that led to a more interconnected economic system, which closed the gaps between the developed and underdeveloped parts of the state. He also looked at the institutionalization of national culture through educational reforms, the judicial system and, in particular, the military service which promoted the spread of the French language, values and culture among the rural communities. In Weber's view, it was only this dynamic process that had turned 'peasants into Frenchmen'. By the time of the First World War the French government could count on millions of loyal French patriots being able to sing the national anthem; eventually the nation was fully constructed.

The second important monograph of that time focused on the aesthetics of politics in the age of nationalism. Mosse, who, because of his Jewish origin, emigrated from his hometown Berlin via England to the United Stated, traced the roots of German nationalism and the Nazi dictatorship to a new style of politics that had spread from France during the Napoleonic wars. Mosse, however, did not present Nazi Germany as exceptional but rather as an extreme example, historically following a similar development towards mass democracy and popular sovereignty as other nations in the making. Nationalism had become a 'secular religion', overshadowing rational discourse in the modern age. This process involved nationalist aesthetics which can be studied through liturgy, symbols, forms and myths which have nationalized the masses and thus legitimized existing political regimes. Think of national monuments and architecture, festivals and holidays, songs and poems. Mosse showed that the new national symbolism had been endorsed by a large variety of civil society groups, ranging from labour organizations to gymnastic clubs, choral societies and shooting associations.[16]

1983: *Annus mirabilis* and its consequences in nationalism studies

It is sometimes overlooked that Ernest Gellner's well-known modernist and functionalist theory of nationalism, which can be read as a critique of the way modern nationalism has destroyed traditional forms of multiculturalism in Central Europe, was already published in 1964. In *Thought and Change* Gellner held: 'Nationalism is not the awakening of nations to self-consciousness. It invents nations where they do not exist.'[17] Only his *Nations and Nationalism* from 1983, however, would be considered a foundational text for the new sub-discipline of Nationalism Studies that was formed towards the 1990s. Gellner's caricatural reconstruction of the fictional nation of Ruritania, as based on Anthony Hope's books from the 1890s,[18] was a highly influential exercise worth pursuing by any student of nationalism interested in constructivist perspectives.

Dissimilar to most nationalists, for Gellner the multicultural past appeared much more natural than the nationalized present. He was of Jewish-Bohemian origin, spoke German at home and was brought up in cosmopolitan Prague. Gellner's Ruritarians were originally low-ranking peasants in a multi-ethnic empire, speaking different dialects and not a single language, inhabiting patches of a very loosely connected territory, and following a diversity of churches with different liturgies. A common national identity was strange to them, and was only created during the course of industrialization through mass education and cultural policies. This identity construction ultimately led to stark ethnic divisions within the 'Megalomanian Empire'. Modern nationalism became the new normality. Gellner saw this as an extremely destructive as well as deceptive development, as he made the ironic remark: 'A man must have a nationality as he must have a nose and two ears; a deficiency in any of these particulars is not inconceivable and does from time to time occur, but only as a result of some disaster, and it is itself a disaster of a kind.'[19]

Eric Hobsbawm strongly sympathized with Gellner's definition and rejection of nationalism. Hobsbawm's own family background was culturally mixed and his upbringing cosmopolitan. Before he migrated to London in 1933 (the year when Hitler came to power), he had spent his childhood and youth in Vienna and Berlin. Hobsbawm's introduction to the concept of 'invented tradition' was published in the same year as Gellner's *Nations and Nationalism*. Following a conference sponsored by the critical journal *Past & Present*, Hobsbawm and Terence Ranger edited a collection of essays illustrating the 'break in continuity' societies had witnessed as nations under construction during the transition to modernity. The invention of tradition that was booming during this transition, Hobsbawm argued, should be seen as distinct from the customs of traditional societies. The new traditions were designed to respond through 'ritualized practice' to a new superstructure, that is, nationalism.[20] To Hobsbawm the manufacturing of a suitable past had been an existential need of modern nationalism since the late nineteenth century. It is worth noting that he was even critical of his own profession in serving the construction of nations.[21] As nationalism cannot operate without historical narratives, Hobsbawm would later express that he saw both danger and responsibility in the social and political function of historians and historiography as related to nationalism:[22] 'Historians are to nationalism what poppy-growers in Pakistan are to heroin-addicts: we supply the essential raw material for the market.'[23]

Hobsbawm argued that the production of historic symbolism increased in times of rapid change, that is, when previous traditions no longer suited the emerging social and political patterns.[24] At such times, both the 'demand and supply side' for invented tradition became greater. Under conditions of modernity, important institutions – such as armies, universities and the churches – were forced to operate in a radically new social and political context and thus reinvented their symbolic representation. More importantly, as legitimacy seemed to inhere to anything that bore 'history', new traditions were then constructed of supposedly 'ancient material' from an immemorial past which often was recycled and reassembled in order to serve the 'novel purposes' of the cultural and political elites in mass society:

> Invented tradition is taken to mean a set of practices, normally governed by overtly or tacitly accepted rules and of a ritual or symbolic nature, which seek to inculcate certain values and norms of behaviour by repetition, which automatically implies continuity with the past. In fact, where possible, they normally attempt to establish continuity with a suitable historic past.[25]

The new symbols suggested authenticity, and they were usually aimed at triggering national sentiment and ensuring loyalty to the institutions and elites that represented the nation. Hobsbawm referred to a 'brilliant' study by ethnologist Rudolf Braun,[26] who exposed how traditional folk song in Switzerland was re-composed by educators to nationalize schoolchildren. As much as ancient heroes, who themselves had no idea of nationhood, suddenly became represented as national heroes, old melodies acquired completely new meaning. In numerous instances, however, tradition had to be made entirely fresh; when no material that bore continuity could be retrieved from the limited identity repertoire. National flags, anthems and code of arms in many countries thus were totally new inventions. To Hobsbawm these were foremost symbols suggesting membership: membership of a club that had never existed as such.

In Europe between 1870 and 1914, numerous 'mass-producing traditions' were invented 'officially and unofficially'.[27] For example, '[o]fficial new public holidays, ceremonies, heroes or symbols, which commanded the growing armies of the state's employees and the growing captive public of schoolchildren' were invented in the new German nation state. The mushrooming of Bismarck towers across the country in response to the death of the Iron Chancellor in 1898 contributed to the nationalization of Germany's historical culture.

Britain, where parallel nation-building processes have taken place, has also provided the invention-of-tradition thesis with a rich number of historical examples. It showed how modern symbols often came to suggest pre-modern continuities. Think of the romantic narrations of the Scottish highland culture from the eighteenth century, or the kilt and the bagpipe, which only in the nineteenth century became typical symbols of the Scottish nation. It is also worth remembering that the invention of tradition was in fact an imperial method in the British world. For example, during the colonial rush into Africa, the European rulers assumed the existence of a native aristocracy and African monarchies that they sought to quarter into the Empire: 'Since so few connections could be made between British and African political, social and legal systems, British administrators set about inventing African traditions for Africans.'[28] Traditional tribal Africa largely was a product of European imagination, ethnicities were constructed in an attempt to create order in a complex network of loyalties and identities. New traditions of monarchy would eventually radically transform the political and military culture of Colonial Africa and the emerging national movements in the following century were able to heavily draw from the ideology and symbols implanted by their colonizers.

What Hobsbawm perhaps did not see clearly enough was that constructivist historians, including himself, did not necessarily contribute to the nationalist production system by supplying society with nationalized narratives of the past. Historians also have been able to contest established histories of nations, or to de-nationalize history by highlighting global entanglements. Not all history is 'raw material' for the national 'market'. Benedict Anderson, for example, published his famous book on nationalism in the same year. Like Hobsbawm, he was struck by the 'objective modernity of nations to the historian's eye vs. their subjective antiquity in the eyes of nationalists'.[29] Anderson, like Gellner, emphasized the anonymity of modern society, which required some cultural homogeneity. The political community of the nation would therefore have to be primarily 'imagined'. His work still reads as extremely critical of nationalism and should count as a prime example of constructivist literature in this field. It is therefore highly interesting to note that Anderson always sought to distinguish himself from the constructivist rhetoric of Ernest Gellner: 'Gellner is so anxious to show that nationalism masquerades under false pretences that he assimilates "invention" to "fabrication" and "falsity", rather than to "imagining" and "creation".'[30] Gellner had implied that there were authentic communities and that nations were fundamentally different to them, whereas Anderson was not willing to restrict his constructivism to national communities per se: 'In fact, all communities larger than primordial face-to-face contact (and perhaps even these) are imagined.' He would later state in an interview: 'I must be the only one writing about nationalism who doesn't think it ugly. If you think about researchers such as Gellner and Hobsbawm, they have quite a hostile attitude to nationalism. I actually think that nationalism can be an attractive ideology. I like its Utopian elements.'[31] The nation was, in Anderson's view, 'imagined as a *community*, because, regardless of the actual inequality and exploitation that may prevail in each, the nation is always conceived as a deep, horizontal comradeship'. The problem, however, is that 'it is this fraternity that makes it possible, over the past two centuries, for so many millions of people, not so much to kill, as willingly to die for such limited imaginings'.[32]

Anderson was different to many other foundational scholars in nationalism studies. Unlike Kohn, Hobsbawm and Gellner, for example, he did not have Jewish and Central European family connections, or any sense of a homeland lost to nationalism. But his upbringing, too, was very cosmopolitan which allowed him to look at nations and nationalism as an outsider. He spoke many languages and his work was strongly interdisciplinary. His anthropological interest in Southeast Asia led him to a rather abstract perspective on the world of nations and their histories, drawing heavily from the colonial experiences in this region. Anderson illuminated transnational connections in the construction of nations and the habitual 'forgetting' of these connections in the national memory cultures.[33]

As the Enlightenment worldview had questioned traditional authority and religion, and promoted ideals of egalitarianism, the tombs of Unknown Soldiers around the world came to epitomize this essential meaning of nations in the modern world.[34] Anderson thus also took the religious features of modern nationalism very seriously.[35] The horizontal and vertical transcendence, across society and time, he perceived as a vital characteristic of the national imagination. Like Hobsbawm, he was aware of the irony that 'nation states are widely conceded to be "new" and "historical"', but 'the nations to which they give political expression always loom out of an immemorial past'.[36] Modern nations' distant past and origin were in his view always dependent on discursive constructions through the exchange of literature, creating a new mythology that could be shared among anonymous individuals in mass societies.

Anderson perceived nations' construction being spurred not only by the spread of affordable books and newspapers in the age of print capitalism but often also from above by monarchies whose legitimacy was declining. Resonant to the boom of 'invented tradition' during the transformation of monarchies, Anderson dedicated a section of his book to 'official nationalism':[37] when faced with nationalist thinking and national movements from below, the European dynasties were forced to 'naturalize' themselves and present themselves as representative of the nation. The rulers thus sought to promote a nationalism from above that would re-legitimize the *ancien régime* by bringing it out in a new fashion. Anderson's monograph is rich in historical examples of official nationalism around the world. Both Anderson and Hobsbawm thus attached great agency to the traditional monarchies in the history of nationalism. Nevertheless, it would prove often difficult to maintain the compatibility of empire and nation: 'The First World War brought the age of high dynasticism to an end.'[38] However, Anderson attributed this shift towards the nation state not only to the rationalization of politics and religion, but more profoundly to a new conception of time that people acquired during the transition to modernity. Anderson observed that modern society was connected through an awareness of simultaneity: individuals who never actually met began to share the same information, which they internalized from novels and newspapers. Their horizon was thus broadened, and they were beginning to imagine the wider social context in which they lived. The fictional world and the real world would eventually merge. Like Gellner, Anderson thus focused on processes of cultural homogenization and on the making of new 'high cultures' that would shape the individual lives of all social strata. Similar to Hobsbawm, Anderson also emphasized the importance of new traditions that became possible in mass society due to the new organization of time, such as public ceremonies that have been repeated annually. Instead of the daily morning prayer, national holidays had to be 'historically clocked' in the calendar.

From Anderson's narrative of this transition in time (and space) conceptions the student of nationalism barely gets the sense of any 'abrupt' construction of nationhood in mass society. The decline of divine languages and script, of monarchies and religious authority, and the modern 'conception of temporality' did not occur overnight.[39] Print-capitalism in conjunction with long-term processes of colonization and decolonization, the Reformation and the bureaucratization of states created an internally homogenous and externally diverse landscape of proto-national language groups. This suggests that a constructivist history of nationalism could also be written from a not-so-strictly modernist perspective. As Anderson concludes, unlike individual biographies, the biographies of nations 'have no clearly identifiable births, and their deaths, if they ever happen, are never natural'.[40]

Thanks largely to Gellner, Hobsbawm and Anderson, constructivist accounts on the transition to the age of nations would from then onwards inspire an incredible amount of critical scholarship, both empirical and theoretical. In 1988, for example, Immanuel Wallerstein and Etienne Balibar pointed to the problems in historical categorizations of groups in different cultural and legal systems. Wallerstein wrote that 'race', 'ethnicity' and 'nation' had been subject to such inconsistency from place to place and time to time that it was puzzling how they were able to maintain their naturalizing effect in social, political and intellectual practice.[41] Balibar reasoned this was mainly due to the way such diverse categories had been narrated as a continuous project. This historical tradition of fabricating myths of nationhood had emerged in the West, which served as a model, and spread from the 'old' nations across the colonial world into the 'young' nations. The ideal nation had thus been constructed as a 'fictive ethnicity'. Further, to Balibar this 'nationalization of society' was not an organic process from below, but was possible only thanks to the hegemony of the bourgeoisie. Nationalism was a process from above, dependent on social hierarchies.

One of the most outstanding examples in historical scholarship that closely applied both Hobsbawm's concept of invented tradition as well as Anderson's reflections on 'official nationalism' was Selim Deringil's work, which illustrated the construction of Turkish nationhood from above in the declining Ottoman Empire, years before Atatürk would become 'father' of the Turkish Republic. By analysing administrative processes, Deringil demonstrated how in the second half of the nineteenth century the monarchical system felt threatened by nationalist movements from below and related changes in the relations with the European powers, and sought to re-legitimize its political power through the development of a nationalism from above. Deringil critically examined official language, education and stereotypes constructed during the reign of Sultan Abdul Hamid II from 1876 to 1909. The state symbols Deringil analysed comprised music, ceremonies, architecture and decorations. An Italian artist, for example, was invited to invent a European type coat of arms for the Sultan, assembling religious, philosophical, military and national symbols. The state increasingly interfered into public and private affairs. Religious proselytization served imperial interest as Islam was re-interpreted by state officials with the invention of the caliphate. While the Hamidian administration took efforts to present the Empire as a European nation state (which were predominantly Christian), it felt threatened by subjects and external forces that were not following the Islamic religion.[42]

The relationship between religion and the invention of ethnic identity during emergence of nationalism in the Ottoman Empire is also a strong theme in Ussama Makdisi's work on the conflict between the ethno-religious group of the Druzes and the Christian Maronites of Mount Lebanon. He argued that 'European imagination invented the tribes of Lebanon' (p. 23), which did not simply rise in the form of a primordial reaction to modern imperialism. The invention of opposing sects Makdisi found to be a brainchild of a dynamic process of elite interests, both domestic and international. Prior to external influence in the modern period, Druze and Maronite communities had enjoyed peaceful coexistence. Ethnographic 'knowledge', teleological conceptions of history and orientalist imaginations of tribal differences in the 'East' then derived from European countries, such as France and Britain, and shaped a nationalist discourse with terribly violent consequences. This process of 'othering' occurred as a reaction to *Tanzimat* reforms in the Ottoman Empire, which sought to re-legitimize itself as a secularized Islamic state with all groups as direct subjects of the Sultan. The colonial attitude in Europe followed a civilizing mission, which presented Christians as suppressed in the East. As part of a 'gentle crusade' local elites gained material support from outside and therefore realized the modern construction of sectarian identities.[43] Their modern construction should thus not only be seen as an endogenous process but also be placed into a complex geopolitical context in which nationalism would become increasingly important.

In more recent times, the sudden end of the Cold War and ethnic revival in Eurasia assisted nationalists again in suggesting that nations and ethnicity were natural (rather than constructed) categories which only had been suppressed by communist ideology, before they could thrive organically to regain their place in the world of nations. The emergence of new nation states was associated with the victory of liberal democracy as history's happy ending. Nationalism and ethnicity, then, appeared as something real, just and stronger than any (other) ideology that had sought to overwhelm it. Nationalism was perceived by some as promoting human rights, participation and solidarity, even though the nationalist revival led to a lot of bloodshed in Eurasia. And as nationalism during this period mattered so much it would attract some serious scholarship in political theory. Scholars of nationalism, such as David Miller, accepted the constructedness of nations and yet they found national mythology helpful to produce a more inclusive society: the constructedness of nations should be accepted as something rationally valid for the viability of democracy.[44] Others, and most prominently Jürgen Habermas, felt that the re-nationalization of society should be prevented, as liberal societies could well do without nationalism.[45]

As the early 1990s indeed demonstrated that nationalism remained a powerful and frequently violent ideology, the constructed relationship between the fluid categories of ethnicity and nation remained worth further study.[46] The 'fall of communism' had perhaps brought more democracy, but democracy itself could not prevent violent conflicts between ethnic groups claiming national sovereignty. Rogers Brubaker in *Nationalism Reframed* reflected on the national revival of the new Europe after the end of the Cold War, and reminded the world of the fluidity of national identities. Similar to Wallerstein and Balibar, to Brubaker the nation was a 'contingent event' but at the same time a strongly institutionalized social practice, articulated through 'idioms, practices and possibilities'. To him it was foremost a cognitive category as our general way of thinking and communication reifies nations as 'real' objects. We talk of peoples as unitary entities and therefore, in some way, turn them into what they are not, that is, homogenous nations with supposedly legitimate claims to statehood.

Brubaker saw three ideal-types of nationalism operating especially strongly in interwar Europe: nationalizing nationalism, transborder nationalism and minority nationalism. As territorial borders have been redrawn over time, new states promoted a nationalization of the domestic society (nationalizing nationalism), while often also claiming 'homeland' outside of the state territory (transborder nationalism). Similarly, minority nationalisms claimed nationality status often across more than one nationalizing state. Representing their groups as nations, rather than ethnic groups, and claiming the right to an own state, political and cultural elites thus propagated the idea that they were forced to live in mismatched territories. To Brubaker, however, these national groups were socially – and politically – constructed as well as historically fluid. They should not be understood as static entities. Their origins, development and territorial claims should therefore be assessed very carefully.[47] Inspired by this work, historian Alexander Maxwell demonstrated in *Choosing Slovakia* that Brubaker's theory of contingency has remained a useful tool for historians of nationalism: national identities of ethnic groups have occasionally been dual, that is, loyal to more but one nation (e.g. Czech, Hungarian and/or Slovak), and they have practically shifted over time reflecting geopolitical changes that 'accidentally' affect ideological and legal frameworks in which the nationalist claims nationality.[48]

The history of nationalism remains a hot topic. And Europe, arguably the birthplace of modern nationalism, still is a strongly contested and transformative political landscape shaped by nationalisms of various kinds. Joep Leerssen in his relatively recent *National Thought in Europe* also refused to study nationalism as a static 'thing', but interpreted it rather as a dynamic worldview, historical process and cultural phenomenon, 'taking shape in the constant back-and-forth between material and political developments on the one hand, and intellectual and poetical reflection on the other'. He assumed that his object of study in fact had been formed by historically manifested but false assumptions: (a) that humanity is naturally divided into nations and therefore deserved primary loyalty; (b) that loyalty to the state derives logically from national (including cultural, linguistic, ethnic) sovereignty; and (c) that the ideal political structure of the globe should be based on the congruency of state and nation.[49] In his article from 2006, 'Nationalism and the cultivation of culture' he called for a transnational approach to the history of nationalism, which emerged in Europe very much thanks to the interactive agency of cross-border networks among cultural elites.[50]

This point was also made very strongly by Anne-Marie Thiesse, whose *La création des identités nationales* is an outstanding overview of the rise of nationalism in Europe from the late eighteenth century until the present. Her modernist account focuses on the cultural, emotional and aesthetic construction of national identities. In her view the official histories of nations go further back in time than the 'real' histories of modern nations, which were recent constructions dependent on conscious action and the transnational nationalist ideology that grew in nineteenth-century Europe. The creative idea of the nation came before the reality of the nation. Thiesse established that all nations, while representing themselves as unique, have followed similar construction plans. They all required the authentication (i.e. nationalization) of heroes, folklore, holidays, educations, monuments, geneses, iconographies, languages, visual arts, landscapes, music and so on. What is fascinating about Thiesse's transnational account on the popularization of national cultures is that intellectuals and artists actively engaged in the construction of foreign nationhood. The construction of nations was a pan-European project. The elites interacted, met physically in the cultural capitals and copied from each in their nation-building acts. Nationalism in modern Europe was very much a product of cultural transfer. International scholars such as philosophers, historians, archaeologists and philologists provided the 'proofs' for political claims in the name of the nation, not only for their own but also for others.[51]

Pre-modern constructivism?

Such modernist-constructivist approaches have been supplemented by a constructivism in the history of nations that goes further back in time, as a good number of authors felt unsettled with the idea that nationalism had taken off only in the modern Transatlantic sphere from the late eighteenth century. In a work published in 1986, entitled *The Ethnic Origins of Nations*, Gellner's former student Anthony Smith countered the assumption that the material used to construct the modern nation was essentially modern. Instead he argued that nations usually require a pre-existing identity repertoire offered by ethnic groups of which some has the capacity to serve their construction. Ancient mythology could thus be reconstructed in the modern age and in the name of the nation. Smith would become the most prominent representative of what he called the ethnosymbolist approach to nationalism.[52] Adrian Hastings also challenged the modernist view of nationalism in arguing that nationhood has been constructed from the medieval age. He found that the state should be seen as the primary agent in this social construction, and that pre-modern England could be studied as the prototype of the nation state.[53]

It is impossible to provide an extensive overview, but there are a good number of fascinating historical studies of nations and nationalism that could perhaps be labelled as 'pre-modern constructivist'. Some of them have gone very far back in time. Edward Cohen, for example, suggested that more than two thousand years ago Athens – unlike other, smaller poleis in the classical Greek world – could be already considered a nation. Cohen based his argument on Anderson's concept of the imagined community, in which an anonymous group needed 'the creation and perpetuation of "myths" set in historical fabrications that establish or reinforce this group's claims to cohesiveness, uniqueness, self-determination, and/or aggrandizement'.[54] In Cohen's view, classical Athens during the transition towards an imagined community, similar to modern nationalisms, experienced exactly such 'nation-building tales', claiming a common history as bound to territory. As such mythology of common origin became so engrained in Athens' culture, its relatively heterogeneous migrant society could imagine itself as being of autochthonous descend from Attic soil. In defence of his motherland Socrates found in the fourth century AD that such 'noble lies' were serving communal interests and should therefore be respected.

Victor Lieberman, in his two-volume opus *Strange Parallels,* also pointed to constructions of ethnic nationalism in Southeast Asia before Europe's so-called modern era, and warned of overstating the differences between the two regions: also in Southeast Asian states national identities had been constructed through 'written histories, folk tales, pilgrimage traditions, puppet shows, and national cults devoted to protective deities'.[55] Lieberman saw, from a nationalism point of view, more similarities in the cultural integration of post-1500 Burma, Siam, Vietnam, Russia and France than in, for example, Japan, where local identities had been more dominant.[56] Nevertheless, Lieberman explained that early representations of nationhood in Southeast Asia were more strongly constructed from above by the rulers and lacked the egalitarian visions found in European-style nationalism. He thus saw this form of hierarchical nationalism rather as what he calls 'politicized ethnicity',[57] which over centuries had genocidal and assimilatory consequences. For example, by the late eighteenth/early nineteenth century in Burma, ethnic minorities concealed themselves by wearing Burmese dresses and using the Burmese language in order to escape repression.[58] Lieberman thus reminded his readers that the cultural and symbolic dimension in the construction of nations should not be seen as disconnected from ethnic and political violence.

Similarly, Mark Elliot in his work on the making of the Chinese nation and the complex ethnic relations of the Qing era (1644–1912) took Smith's concept of 'myths of restoration' as inspiration: such myths connect present generations with a shared noble origin in the distant past, for the sake of community building and often to legitimize territorial and political claims. To Elliot ethnicity was a way of 'constructing identity (i.e. "selfness") whenever and wherever human groups come into contact'.[59] While the social construction of ethnicity for him, thus, had always existed, specific ethnic identities nevertheless were historically contingent and highly malleable categories. Elliot observed that in the second half of the twentieth century the Manchu population in China grew to such an extent that only its (re)construction as a national minority, rather than any natural rate of reproduction, could serve as a plausible explanation. And he wondered if a similar social-constructivist process had not already happened in the seventeenth century when the Manchus seized power over the Chinese empire: 'To find out who the Manchus were we must trace the ways in which the category "Manchu" was shaped historically, how the boundaries that delimited it from other ethnic categories were made, how they were guarded, and how they were changed over time.'[60] During the Qing dynasty this ruling minority was very careful in maintaining its distinctive identity against other groups, while at the same time taking efforts to assimilate in order to stay in power. Elliot argued that this ethnic identity from the early seventeenth century was fostered through relatively flexible military, social, economic and political institutions, and therefore survived the following centuries. Further, there was always a notion of what *the* Manchu was and this notion had been conveyed through historical foundation myths, which were not about accuracy but about the idea that contemporary customs and beliefs had ancient roots, and that there was some kind of common birthplace of the nation/ethnicity. Even though the Manchus readily integrated non-Manchus, Emperor Yongzheng (1678–1735), for example, insisted that all Manchus ultimately descended from the same four ancestors.[61] Elliot's work on the Manchus thus suggests that the mechanisms of constructing nations had already existed in China at least from the seventeenth century, even if rivalling identity projects would ultimately succeed in the making of modern China.

Philip Gorski also found that modern nationalism has not been that fundamentally different to early modern nationalism, as he sought to demonstrate in an article on the history of the national movement in the Netherlands from the sixteenth century. Gorski analysed two myths that he saw as fundamental to the legitimacy of the Dutch republic. Both became part of the official symbolism and public ritual, supported by republican activists and intellectuals. In the early modern Netherlands nationalists represented the Dutch as a chosen people or New Israel, above other nations and blessed by God as long as they followed His commands. At the same time, there was a strong imagination of being the continuation of the 'ancient Batavians', a freedom-loving people that had resisted the Romans and Spaniards. Gorski showed that during the Dutch Revolt, when the Protestant Provinces in the North resisted the Spanish-Catholic rule, a 'Hebraic Nationalism' was invented. A powerful example was the 1577 celebration of the liberation from Spanish dominion, when William of Orange was rowed down the river Scheldt in Brussels. Followed by several floats, which each portrayed a different symbolic imagery, William was presented in line with (a) David, who had besieged Goliath (i.e. the mighty King of Spain, Philip II), (b) Moses, who had liberated the children of Israel from Egyptian bondage (i.e. the domination of Habsburg Spain) and (c) Joseph who had freed Jacob and his linage, reunited the tribes and created national unity (i.e. the 1576 Pacification of Ghent). The key agents in Hebraic Nationalism, Gorski explained, were Dutch Calvinists, but also more moderate Protestants and even Catholics promoted this myth. Gorski used a great diversity of symbolic items, including memorial pennies carrying

Hebraic-nationalist imagery. One inscription, glorifying the Spanish siege of the city of Leiden and thereby referring to the Assyrian campaign seven centuries AD said: 'Like Senach'erib in Jerusalem, the Spaniards fled Leiden by night.'[62]

Parallel to Hebraic Nationalism, the secular myth of Batavian Nationalism was invented and, according to Gorski, found appeal in the seventeenth century among the average Netherlander. Grotius' *Treatise on the Antiquity of the Batavian Republic* (originally written in 1601), which became a bestseller, proudly claimed that the Dutch ancestors, the Batavians, had never been controlled by a monarchical system but always by a 'government of the best'. Gorski explained how this myth, tracing back the revolutionary spirit of the republic to ancient times, became part of the official nationalism in the Dutch republic: 'In 1612, for example . . . the burgomasters of The Hague bought a series of 36 etchings depicting the Batavian rebellion against Rome. And the following year, the States of Holland commissioned a series of 12 paintings on the same subject, which they then hung in their meeting rooms.'

The German historian Stefan Berger recently studied the construction of national identities through history writing, which often entailed nationalist ideas before the manifestation of the modern nation state. He thus moved from a modernist perspective to one that also took pre-modern constructions of nationhood seriously. In *Germany* Berger demonstrated how many different concepts of Germany have existed in the past and thus deconstructed the idea that a unitary German identity had existed over the last centuries. In *The Search for Normality* he carefully pointed to the nationalist traditions in German historiography, showing that historians have traditionally followed ideological motifs and seeking to construct a positive and continuous history for a German nation with a relatively short lived nation state (1871–1945, and again since 1990). He deepened and widened this constructivist approach in a transnational study on the relationship between the history of nationalism and the history of historiography, entitled *The Past as History*. There, he found that in Europe from the Middle Ages professional historians have written narratives of *national* pasts. The professionalization of history increasingly endowed the producers of the past, historians, with hegemonial authority in society allowing them to significantly contribute to the nationalization of the past. History, and its methodological nationalism, became a respectable and incontestable 'science'. Berger, thus, argued that nationalist historiography had already existed prior to the age of the nation state, often in service of monarchs and states that they sought to historically legitimize. This academic tradition paved the ground to a more encompassing development, which took place from around 1850 towards the First World War. During this period, the 'scientificity' of history writing paralleled the rise of nationalism as a dominant and globalizing ideology. The institutionalization of the historical profession became evident through the mushrooming of museums, universities, journals and historical associations.[63]

Constructivism 'from below'

The modern and pre-modern constructivism applied in many studies suggested that nations and nationalism were predominantly produced by political, cultural and intellectual elites. Over recent years, however, scholars of nationalism have increasingly explored avenues to study the construction of nationhood 'from below', that is, from within ordinary society. This can be a challenging exercise for students of nationalism, as the data collection might not always be easy: the speeches of Mr President can often be downloaded online, whereas the collection of Average Joe's conversations in the pub is not as accessible.

In the early 1990s, Thomas Hylland Eriksen called for a 'life-world approach' that would make visible the meaning of national identity to individual actors in society.[64] Correspondingly, Michael Billig reacted to the fact that nationalism in the industrialized West was studied only at the periphery of time and space – in the past or in crisis areas – but not in the centre of established societies. Reminiscent of the 'ritualized practices' explored in *The Invention of Tradition*, he therefore began focusing more on the everyday consumption of nationalism; the continuous and unreflexive internalization of national symbolism (as 'banal' as the American flag) that he found central to the continuous existence of nationalism in the industrialized West where nations appear as natural.[65]

Billig's everyday-constructivist approach, which itself takes a top-down approach focussing on state symbols, has remained influential in recent nationalism research that suggests bottom-up perspectives.[66] Most impressively, the sociological research on national identities in Cluj-Napoca, a Transylvanian town in Romania, by Rogers Brubaker, Margit Feischmidt, Jon Fox and Liana Grancea called for more research that takes constructivism seriously: the constructivist consensus hardly ever engaged with the question of *how* nations as cultural, social and political categories are actually constructed. They felt a great need to look more closely at the local level to see how the making of nationalism actually works among ordinary people; how did they respond to efforts of nationalization from above? And how have ordinary people themselves acted as agents in the history of nationalism? The authors analysed the nationalist claims and counter-claims over time in the politics over the ethnically diverse city, which has been populated predominantly by groups identifying as Romanian, Hungarian, German and Jewish, and witnessed a number of significant regime changes. Focusing primarily at the relations between Romanian and Hungarian nationalisms, they first studied the institutionalization of nationalism through territorial boundaries, centralist policies, nationalist parties and organizations, and education. But the second half of the book provides some detailed ethnographic research on the 'everyday ethnicity' among the population, how nationalism was perceived and enacted in, for example, private conversation, the use of languages, regular encounters between individuals of different ethnic groups and moments of mixing of groups. Nationalism and ethnicity then become discursive categories that people 'do' or 'not do', and not which people 'have' or 'not have'. A similar approach has also been adopted for more distant periods by Tara Zahra, Pieter Judson and Jeremy King.[67]

Maarten van Ginderachter and Marnix Beyen pointed out that identity projects, as envisaged by the state and elites, do not necessarily work out the way intended. Rather the contingency of nationalization can only be grasped if the articulation of national identities among ordinary people in the past becomes apparent. In their influential volume, *Nationhood from below*, they sought to find out what the nation in nineteenth-century Europe meant at the grassroots level, how 'nationalism from above' was received in society and how popular ideas of nationhood were among social groups. The authors of the volume discussed how economic cycles affect people's nationalism, when and why national loyalties have changed, how patriotic villagers were, how ethnic politics were performed at the very local level and different identities (e.g. gender, class, regional, religious) were blended.[68]

Studying nationalism in the history of everyday life remains a challenging and important exercise to understand the fine distinctions within nations and nationalism. Glenda Sluga, for example, distinguished between female and male forms of citizenship. More practically, she explored how gender roles within the middle-class family of the nineteenth century had affected the image of nationhood that was dominated by men. In her view, the changing idea of the human body in the history of nationalism had always had an impact on the way national communities were imagined and legitimized.[69] Jonathan Hearn more recently spoke of 'the ecology of identity', suggesting that national and historical narratives have offered individuals a sense of logical order and future orientation. Deriving from his ethnographic research on the history of Scottish identity, Hearn asserted that individuals identify their own person with protagonists in national history, and that national narratives mobilize individuals to take particular actions. Biographical studies of ordinary nationalists will be very helpful to better understand the dynamics of personal nationalism within the individual's social and political context, and the interactive constructions between nationalism from above and below.[70]

Concluding reflections

It has been impossible to mention all the many wonderful contributions of constructivist scholarship on the history of nations and nationalism that have been influenced by – or remind us of – the key texts from 1983. And there has been no clearly identifiable constructivist school in nationalism studies. In the second half of the twentieth century the constructivist approach emerged with the critical enquiry into the history of nations and nationalism, which persisted after the horrific experiences of the Second World War. Postcolonial perspectives underpinned the critique of the West and its role in exporting nationalism. The history of nation states was no longer written only to construct national identity but also to contest it. Scholarship thus challenged established worldviews holding that nations were natural units of human life. The idea that nations had been socially constructed as part of a process of modernization in Europe and the Transatlantic sphere became the dominant view towards the end of the twentieth century, including important contributions suggesting that efforts to construct nations and nationalism had already been existent in pre-modern times. Most constructivist studies have taken a predominantly elitist perspective on the way nations and national identities have been created. In recent years, there has been a strong call in nationalism studies to further investigate the construction of national identities at the popular level.

The sudden geopolitical changes around 1990 curbed the hope for a postnational future. Constructing the past for the sake of the nation remains a popular exercise, within and outside of academia. Prasenjit Duara's plea to rescue history from nationalism remains topical.[71] Nevertheless, recent ethnic conflicts associated with the making of new nation states also further stimulated the writing of critical histories that continue to challenge the global normality of nationalism. It will remain important for historians in the twenty-first century not only to critically historicize 'the dark side of democracy'[72] but also to be reflective of their own role in constructing the domain of nations. We should also be wary of the instrumentalization of constructivism by denialist and conservative claims against the critics of nationalism. In the so-called History Wars, for example, critical historians who pointed to the genocidal elements (against the Aboriginals) in Australian history were attacked by nationalists that they were 'fabricating' history.[73] Nationalism, as constructivist scholarship has suggested, is a dynamic and somewhat contingent process, which is not primarily about historical truth but is a discourse shaped by changing constellations of belief and authority.

Notes

* I am very grateful for the extensive feedback from Jon Fox, the useful suggestions by Aviel Roshwald and the stimulating comments from the editors.

1 Eric Hobsbawm, 'Introduction: Inventing Traditions', in Eric Hobsbawm and Terence Ranger (eds), *The Invention of Tradition* (Cambridge, 1983).

2 Benedict Anderson, *Imagined Communities: Reflections on the Origin and Spread of Nationalism* (revised and extended edn) (London, 1991 [1983]), pp. 6–7.

3 One should perhaps note that one of the most notorious advocates of the constructivist approach to nationalism, Umut Özkirimli, uses the term 'constructionism'. See Umut Özkirimli, *Contemporary Debates on Nationalism: A Critical Engagement* (Basingstoke, 2005), p. 162. It might also be worth noting that some refer to a *de*-constructivist approach to describe the modernist and constructivist heyday in nationalism studies in the 1980s/1990s. See Christian Jansen and Henning Borggräfe, *Nation – Nationalität – Nationalismus* (Frankfurt/M, 2007), p. 14.

4 See chapter by Breuilly.

5 Carlton Hayes, *Essays on Nationalism* (New York, 1926).

6 Max Horkheimer and Theodor W. Adorno, *Dialectic of Enlightenment: Philosophical Fragments* (trans. E. Jephcott) (Stanford, 2002 [1944]). See also Thorsten Mense, *Kritik des Nationalismus* (Stuttgart, 2016).

7 Hans Kohn, *The Idea of Nationalism: A Study in Its Origins and Background* (New York, 1944). See, e.g., Liah Greenfeld, *Nationalism: Five Roads to Modernity* (Cambridge, 1992).

8 Jacques Derrida, *De la Grammatologie* (Paris, 1967); Edward Said, *Orientalism* (New York, 1978).

9 Roland Barthes, *Mythologies* (Paris, 1957).

10 See, e.g., Michel Foucault, *Histoire de la folie à l'âge classique: Folie et déraison* (Paris, 1961); Michel Foucault, *Les mots et les choses: Une archéologie des sciences humaines* (Paris, 1966).

11 Michel Foucault, *Society Must be Defended* (trans. D Macey) (London, 2003 [1976]).

12 Karl W. Deutsch, *Nationalism and Social Communication: An Inquiry into the Foundations of Nationality* (Cambridge, 1953); Karl W. Deutsch and W. J. Foltz (eds), *Nation-Building* (New York, 1966); Karl W. Deutsch, *Nationalism and Its Alternatives* (New York, 1969).

13 Sandra Fullerton Joireman, *Nationalism and Political Identity* (London/New York, 2003), pp. 54–70.

14 See, e.g., Jonas Frykman and Orvar Löfgren, *Culture Builders: A Historical Anthropology of Middle Class Life* (New Brunswick, 1987).

15 Eugen Weber, *Peasants into Frenchmen: The Modernization of Rural France, 1870–1914* (Stanford, 1976), p. 9. See also chapter by Breuilly.

16 George L. Mosse, *The Nationalization of the Masses: Political Symbolism and Mass Movements in Germany, from the Napoleonic Wars Through the Third Reich* (New York, 2001 [1975]).

17 Gellner, *Thought and Change*, p. 11.

18 See Anthony Hope's *The Prisoner of Zenda* (1894), *The Heart of Princess Osra* (1896) and *Rupert of Hentzau* (1898)

19 Gellner, *Nations and Nationalism*, p. 6. See also the chapter by Breuilly.

20 Hobsbawm, 'Introduction: Inventing Traditions', p. 2.

21 Ibid., pp. 12–13.

22 Eric Hobsbawm, *On History* (London, 2007 [1997]), p. 356.

23 Eric Hobsbawm, 'Ethnicity and Nationalism in Europe Today', *Anthropology Today* 8:1, 3.

24 Eric Hobsbawm, 'Introduction: Inventing Traditions', pp. 4–5.

25 Ibid., p. 3.

26 See Rudolf Braun, *Sozialer und kultureller Wandel in einem ländlichen Industriegebiet im 19. Und 20. Jahrhundert* (Zürich, 1965), ch. 6.
27 Eric Hobsbawm, 'Mass-Producing Traditions: Europe, 1870–1914', in Eric Hobsbawm and Ranger (chapter 7), p. 263.
28 Ibid., p. 212.
29 Anderson, *Imagined Communities*, p. 5.
30 Ibid., p. 6.
31 https://www.uio.no/english/research/interfaculty-research-areas/culcom/news/2005/anderson.html (last accessed on 4 August 2016).
32 Anderson, *Imagined Communities*, p. 7.
33 Anderson, *Imagined Communities*, ch. 11; see also Benedict Anderson, *Under Three Flags: Anarchism and the Anti-Colonial Imagination* (London, 2007).
34 Ibid., p. 9, and pp. 11–19.
35 Ibid., p. 10.
36 Ibid., p. 11.
37 A concept he had borrowed from Hugh Seton-Watson's work on the origins of nations published only a few years before: Hugh Seton-Watson, *Nations and States: An Enquiry into the Origins of Nations and the Politics of Nationalism* (York, 1977).
38 Anderson, *Imagined Communities*, see especially Chapters 6 and 7.
39 Ibid., p. 36.
40 Ibid., p. 205.
41 Immanuel Wallerstein, 'The Construction of Peoplehood: Racism, Nationalism, Ethnicity', in Immanuel Wallerstein and Etienne Balibar (trans. Chris Turner), *Race, Nation, Class: Ambiguous Identities* (London, 1991 [originally published in French, 1988]), pp. 71–85.
42 Selim Deringil, *The Well-Protected Domains: Ideology and the Legitimation of Power in the Ottoman Empire, 1876–1909* (London, 1998).
43 Ussama Makdisi, *The Culture of Sectarianism Community, History, and Violence in Nineteenth-Century Ottoman Lebanon* (Oakland, 2000), p. 23.
44 David Miller, *On Nationality* (Oxford, 1995).
45 Jürgen Habermas, *The Postnational Constellation: Political Essays* (Cambridge MA, 1998).
46 Craig Calhoun, 'Nationalism and Ethnicity', *American Review of Sociology* 19 (1993), 211–39; Thomas Hylland Eriksen, *Ethnicity and Nationalism: Anthropological Perspectives* (London, 1993).
47 Rogers Brubaker, *Nationalism Reframed: Nationhood and the National Question in the New Europe* (Cambridge, 1996).
48 Alexander Maxwell, *Choosing Slovakia: Slavic Hungary: The Czechoslovak Language and Accidental Nationalism* (London, 2009), p. 69.
49 Joep Leersen, *National Thought in Europe: A Cultural History* (Amsterdam, 2006).
50 Joep Leerssen 'Nationalism and the Cultivation of Culture', *Nations and Nationalism*, 12:4 (2006), 559–78; see also *Encyclopedia of Romantic Nationalism in Europe*, online at: http://ernie.uva.nl/viewer.p/21.
51 Anne-Marie Thiesse, *La Création des identités nationales Europe: XVIIIe-XXe siècle* (Montrouge, 1999).
52 Anthony D. Smith, *The Ethnic Origins of Nations* (Hoboken, 1986). See also the chapter by Roshvald.

53 Adrian Hastings, *The Construction of Nationhood: Ethnicity, Religion and Nationalism* (Cambridge, 1996).

54 Edward E. Cohen, *The Athenian Nation* (Princeton, 2004), p. 4.

55 Victor Lieberman, *Strange Parallels: Southeast Asia in Global Context, 800–1830*, vol. 1 (Cambridge, 2003), pp. 202ff.

56 Victor Lieberman, *Strange Parallels: Southeast Asia in Global Context, 800–1830*, vol. 2 (Cambridge, 2009), p. 490.

57 Lieberman, *Strange Parallels*, vol. 2, p. 41; Victor Lieberman, *Strange Parrallels*, vol. 1, pp. 202ff.

58 Lieberman, *Strange Parallels*, vol. 1, pp. 204–5.

59 Mark Elliot, *The Manchu Way: The Eight Banners and Ethnic Identity in Late Imperial China* (Stanford, 2001), p. 19.

60 Ibid., p. 44.

61 Ibid., p. 65.

62 Philip S. Gorski, 'The Mosaic Moment: An Early Modernist Critique of Modernist Theories of Nationalism', *American Journal of Sociology* 105:5 (2000), 1428–68.

63 Stefan Berger, *Germany* (Inventing the Nation) (London, 2004); Stefan Berger, *The Search for Normality: National Identity and Historical Consciousness in Germany since 1900* (New York, 1996); Stefan Berger, *The Past as History: National Identity and Historical Consciousness in Modern Europe* (Basingstoke, 2015).

64 Thomas H Eriksen, 'Ethnicity vs. Nationalism', *Journal of Peace Research* 28:3 (1992), 263–78.

65 Michael Billig, *Banal Nationalism* (London, 1995).

66 See, e.g., Rogers Brubaker, Margit Feischmidt, Jon Fox and Liana Grancea, *Nationalist Politics and Everyday Ethnicity in a Transylvanian Town* (Princeton, 2007) and J. Paul Goode and David R. Stroup, 'Everyday Nationalism: Constructivism for the Masses', *Social Science Quarterly* 96:3 (2015), 717–39.

67 See chapter by Storm.

68 See, e.g., Maarten Van Ginderachter and Marnix Beyen (eds), *Nationhood from Below: Europe in the Long Nineteenth Century* (Basingstoke, 2012).

69 Glenda Sluga, 'Identity, Gender, and the History of European Nations and Nationalisms', *Nations and Nationalism* 4:1 (1998), 87–111.

70 Jonathan Hearn, 'Nationalism, Biography and the Ecology of Identity', *Humanities Research* 19:1 (2013), 5–22.

71 Prasenjit Duara, *Rescuing History from the Nation: Questioning Narratives of Modern China* (Chicago, 1995).

72 Michael Mann, *The Dark side of Democracy: Explaining Ethnic Cleansing* (Cambridge, 2005).

73 Stuart Macintyre and Anna Clark, *The History Wars* (Melbourne, 2004).

Further reading

Berger, Stefan, *The Past as History: National Identity and Historical Consciousness in Modern Europe*. Basingstoke: Palgrave Macmillan, 2015.

Billig, Michael, *Banal Nationalism*. London: Sage, 1995.

Brubaker, Rogers, M. Feischmidt, J. Fox and L. Grancea, *Nationalist Politics and Everyday Ethnicity in a Transylvanian Town*. Princeton: Princeton University Press, 2007.

Deringil, Selim, *The Well-Protected Domains: Ideology and the Legitimation of Power in the Ottoman Empire, 1876–1909*. London: I.B. Tauris, 1998.

Duara, Prasenjit, *Rescuing History from the Nation: Questioning Narratives of Modern China*. Chicago: University of Chicago Press, 1995.

Leersen, Joep, *National Thought in Europe: A Cultural History*. Amsterdam: Amsterdam University Press, 2006.

Mosse, George L., *The Nationalization of the Masses: Political Symbolism and Mass Movements in Germany, from the Napoleonic Wars Through the Third Reich*. New York: Howard Fertig, 2001 [1975].

Van Ginderachter, Maarten and M. Beyen (eds), *Nationhood from Below: Europe in the Long Nineteenth Century*. Basingstoke: Palgrave Macmillan, 2012.

8

Deconstructing nationalism: The cultural turn and poststructuralism

Gabriella Elgenius

Introduction

This chapter explores perspectives that set out to deconstruct central discourses associated with nations and nationalism. The critical assessment (deconstruction) of underlying assumptions, concepts and ways in which we write and talk (discourses) about nations, directs us to nationalist claims about social solidarity, ethnic homogeneity and national unity. The nation relies on such claims and the appropriation of history for its political legitimacy and authority. This chapter focus on some central contributions made by the cultural turn and the poststructuralist school and suitably bridges the previous chapter on constructivism with the subsequent one on postcolonialism. A brief outline is provided about the 'turns' towards culture and poststructuralism, the relationship between culture and power, after which we turn towards nationalism and its associated rhetoric, narration, symbolic repertoires, and supporting discourses of social solidarity, unity and earned membership.

The cultural turn and the shift towards culture

The 'cultural turn' in the social sciences denotes both the era from the 1970s onwards and the series of theoretical impulses within a number of disciplines to problematize history and culture. The term 'cultural turn' appeared in

Jeffrey Alexander's chapter on 'The New Theoretical Movement' in the 1988 *Handbook of Sociology*,[1] highlighting the subjective meanings and social structural constraints of culture. The substantial shift towards culture, its expressions, dimensions and unequal conditions, has had a profound impact of how we understand culture and history as socially constructed, as supportive of existing power structures and as interconnected with knowledge, meaning and subjectivity.[2] Cultural processes are therefore reinterpreted as 'systems of signification', that is, value-coded differences expressed through binary concepts such as insider–outsider or majority–minority. Since culture is integral to all social spheres and saturated with cultural images of historical processes, norms and values are 'consumed throughout daily life'.[3] Culture hereby represents and conveys meanings integral to the production of knowledge, socio-historical narratives and social change.[4] It is therefore essential to understand how culture works as a system of signification, in terms of constituting a politics of culture or cultural politics. Michel Foucault's use of 'politics' and 'power' is therefore a good starting point to assess ways in which culture impacts social life and practices. Culture, according to Foucault, is constitutive and forming a central part of power relations and the social identities that provide the actual 'site of politics'[5] since 'power is everywhere':[6]

> Power is plural: it is exercised from innumerable points, rather than from a single political centre, as the possession of an elite or the logic of bureaucratic institutions, and it is not governed by a single over-arching project.[7]

The analytical shift towards culture and cultural images had implications for the study of nationalism and encouraged the study of culturally constructed practices and representations of culture as an instrument of state policy and ideological battles.[8] The cultural turn wished to move beyond explanations that placed the nation state at the centre of the social order – as a single over-arching project – and towards culture as central to the production and experience of the social order.[9] Culture within advanced capitalist societies has therefore been increasingly approached as fragmented, unstable and constantly changing,[10] rather than unified or unitary, and best studied through its intersections of disadvantage based on class, ethnicity, gender, race and sexuality. The relationship between culture and power is therefore central to the deconstruction of national discourses and exposes the intimate power relations of knowledge creation in the context of nationalism and national history. It is the discourse of nationalism that turns culture into politics and power through its systematic support of dominant assumptions about nations. Established meanings also turn individuals and groups into either subjects (actors) or objects (the acted upon). Thus, discourses are much more than spoken or written words: they control objects through its 'power-knowledge' and rules of exclusion.[11] We must therefore ask a few central questions: Under which circumstances do subjects speak or write about objects and why? Who has the right to speak and about who? Or, in the case of nations, whose imagined community are we speaking or writing about?

The cultural turn has explored culture theoretically by analysing its constitutive roles not only in the forming of social relations and identities but also in its historical foundation in relation to social change. The former, the epistemological direction, has been linked to poststructuralist thought and discourse analysis, whereas the latter, the historical direction, has provided a basis for postmodern thought.[12]

The 'poststructuralist turn' and the deconstruction of privileged identity

Poststructuralism emerged as a post-perspective in the 1960s onwards[13] with the turn from structuralism dating from the early to the mid-twentieth century. A main critique against structuralism was its use of self-sufficient binary opposites (subject–object) that denoted a signifier and a signified exemplified by, for example, civilized–savage, modern–primitive, male–female, public–private, written–unwritten. Dichotomies such as these illuminate knowledge construction based on hierarchies and biases conveyed through everyday language, cultural and historical images. The supremacy of the West and the nation states of modern Europe were established on the basis of such opposites and binary dichotomies. By deconstructing the concept of the 'West' we may study how Europe wrote itself into the core of history, promoted at the expense of the unnamed 'Rest'.[14]

The boundaries between structuralism and poststructuralism are blurred: Michel Foucault, Roland Barthes and Jacques Lacan are associated with both structuralism and poststructuralism whereas Jacques Derrida,[15] Gilles Deleuze and Julia Kristeva[16] are named as proponents of poststructuralism. Jacques Derrida is referred to as the founder of deconstruction in view of his critical appraisal of Western culture and philosophy and his pursuit to democratize intellectual thought. Derrida challenged established meanings of historical texts by exposing concealed conflicts, hidden inner meanings or misrepresentations by critically assessing the relationship between the surface and the subtext. Derrida argues:

> These concealments and contextualizations might be viewed as the assumptions that every text makes in presuming that it will be understood. But these assumptions are suppressed, and thus the reader's attention is diverted from them.[17]

For Derrida, understanding the significance of difference (differential significance) is crucial to deconstruct and reveal the privilege of one binary over the other. It is on the basis of difference that hierarchical models (supported through binary concepts, dualisms, opposites or contradictions) are created out of reference points or contrasts to something that is allegedly absent. Thus, the deconstruction of 'the privileging of identity' is integral to understand the (re)production of knowledge.[18] The concept of the 'West' legitimizes an authorized relationship as do various other terms used to narrate its supremacy as 'the Centre' in contrast to 'the Periphery'.[19] Thus, the privileging of one binary justifies not only privilege but also inequality and exploitation of the other. Derrida therefore challenges, re-conceptualizes and deconstructs difference[20] and the perceived subservience and otherness that contribute to perpetuate privilege and hierarchical relations.[21]

Postcolonial studies about political domination and economic exploitation draw heavily upon concepts and analyses developed by the poststructuralist school and the two are closely associated.[22] Philip Leonard argues that the overall aim of both poststructuralism and postcolonialism is rethinking the colonial legacy, postcolonial resistance and globalization's impact on national identity,[23] which requires the deconstruction of the culturally constructed 'Eurocentric software'.[24] These two schools do not arrive at one explanatory model of culture and history but probe into the uneven and unequal processes of differentiation, globalization and nationalism and the exclusive political circumstances that once led Partha Chatterjee to respond to Benedict Anderson's definition of the nation as an imagined community by asking: 'Whose imagined community?'[25] European history is hereby challenged as a history of the 'discrepancy between Enlightenment ideals upholding liberty and democracy for a common humanity and the reality of such ideals being reserved for Europe and withheld from its colonies'.[26]

> One of the most crucial contributions made by the [poststructuralist and postcolonial] theorists considered here is the argument that these discourses of national identity need to be challenged, but without ignoring the singularities of geographical, cultural, and historical location, or routinely dismissing national identification as a uniform operation of phobic differentiation. For them, national identity – even nationalism – is not necessarily an affliction that needs to be overcome in order to arrive at an even distribution of wealth and power: different groups engage in, respond to, and rewrite Western narratives of national specificity and, as a result, cultural theory needs to develop more complex analyses of the nation-state and its transfiguration.[27]

By highlighting conflict, resistance and discrimination as part of national identity, poststructuralist perspectives dispute that globalization constitutes a force for democratization and multiculturalism a movement for the free flow of peoples and ideas. In doing so, poststructuralists set out to explain the relationship between agency and structure, power, culture and difference in the construction of sociopolitical identities.[28]

Nationalism as rhetoric, narration and symbolic repertoire

With the above in mind we turn to some approaches to nationalism that critically engage with its discursive claims and build on, or relate to, deconstruction or discourse analysis. The following assumptions about nationalism and history are useful to keep in mind: National history is partially defined by the events deemed as memorable and significant and can be restricted to particular periods without due attention to historical antecedents. Political elites have a say about how events are selected, narrated and remembered, all central features of self-definition (who we are) and classifications of others (who we are not).[29] The narration and remembrance of national events contribute towards perceiving the nation in the singular – as one nation, one community and one identity – and explains why traditionally marginalized groups often are omitted from national history. The exclusive nature of nations and nationalist claims are discussed below through ideological habits, narrations, symbolic repertoires and rhetoric and support for discursive claims about nationalism as social solidarity, ethnic homogeneity and earned membership.

Michael Billig compares nationalism to an ideology of the 'first person plural' (we) in *Banal Nationalism* (1995) and as closely associated with the 'existing ideological foundations', the rhetoric of familiar images and clichés, practices and beliefs, through which the nation is being reproduced in invisible yet effective ways.[30] Billig argues that nationalism should not primarily be associated with war, conflict, separatism or right-wing movements and so forth. Instead, we ought to turn our attention to the ideological habits that sustain the taken-for-granted reproduction of nations through harmless references to 'we', 'us', 'ours' and 'here'. For instance, take the implied 'we', togetherness and solidarity reported by the national press by its references to 'the' prime minister, 'the' weather, 'our' team or 'domestic' news (as opposed to international news). National claims are also discursively supported by the implicit references to 'we' and 'us' through the use of national symbols, the national flags hanging outside cultural, social and political institutions (museums, educational or parliamentary buildings) or use of flags and national anthems in sporting competitions, national festivities or commemoration events. Such boundaries are also drawn with the help of national passports and national currency.

Ultimately, it is 'banal nationalism' such as these ideological habits that turns the abstract nation into an objective reality[31] quietly and invisibly and allows nations to mobilize. The rhetoric of nations contributes towards the internalization of 'us' (and of our shared territory, history and beliefs) and enables the exclusion of non-members by turning other peoples' beliefs into 'foreign' ones.[32] Taken-for-granted phrases, rhetorical references, images, clichés and symbols of nations are therefore far from innocent. On the contrary, they facilitate the reproduction of 'our' nation without receiving much critical attention.

The nation can also be approached and deconstructed as a narration that resembles the story of a novel or film and depend on narrators in similar ways as novels and films depend on writers and directors. According to Homi Bhabha in *Nation and Narration* (1990), national history is actively constructed on behalf of narrators whose strategy is to create a master narrative of political authority. This means that some historical events are emphasized over others and that the national discourse therefore contains a certain ambivalence about claims to a unified and a unitary culture. Bhabha understands the nation as an 'ambivalent narration that holds culture at its most productive position' and as a force for subordination. Thus, quite contrary to official narrations, nations are 'internally marked by cultural difference and the heterogeneous histories of contending peoples, antagonistic authorities, and tense cultural locations'.[33] Moreover, nations are 'Janus-faced' and characterized by hybridity, contestation and antagonism,[34] formed on the basis of intersections of identifications (and disadvantage) bound to location, generation, gender, race and class. Yet, such complexities are buried in official history narration that tends to produce a linear story of a unified history and unitary culture. National narration does not allow for contradictions that jeopardize the coherence of the master narrative or the ethos of solidarity and unity. Contradictions and deviations raised by, for example, repressed issues or marginalized groups or identities are therefore excluded.

Bhabha argues forcefully that nations are characterized by ambivalence in view of the cultural difference, diversity and internal contestation that characterizes these, and stand in sharp contrast to the certainty by which 'facts' are presented about their origins, master narratives and unified histories. The ambivalence is particularly evident in the colonial discourse of metropolitan centres', their codes of discrimination and recognition of authority.[35] The certainty by which the narrations of nations are presented can be challenged from a number of angles and by highlighting the changing, diverse and complex nature of the 'locality' in which one lives (as opposed to the narrated unitary culture). Bhabha writes:

This locality is more *around* temporality than *about* historicity: a form of living that is more complex than 'community'; more symbolic than 'society'; more connotative than 'country'; less patriotic than *patrie;* more rhetorical than the reason of state; more mythological than ideology; less homogeneous than hegemony; less centered than the citizen; more collective than 'the subject'; more psychic than civility; more hybrid in the articulation of cultural differences and identifications – gender, race or class – than can be represented in any hierarchical or binary structuring of social antagonism.[36]

In short, the reality of the locality points towards contestation, hybridity, 'us' in 'them' and 'them' in 'us' rather than towards unity and homogeneity. The nation is therefore best defined by its ambivalence, hybridity and 'splitness'[37] and as a narrative strategy of political authority.[38] 'The "other" is never outside or beyond us; it emerges forcefully, within cultural discourse, when we think we speak most intimately and indigenously "between ourselves".'[39] In order to deconstruct domineering narratives and expose biases through textual analysis, the narrator must be decentred.[40] By decentering, we deconstruct the production of knowledge in relation to the social structure of which the narrator is part. Hereby, we may assess the potential discrepancies between 'the language of those who write it' and 'those who live it'.[41] An implication of decentering the narrator is the critical assessment of university curricula and the awareness of bias towards Western scholars. For instance, students and faculty at the University of Cambridge recently called for 'broadening the English curriculum to be more inclusive of literature from the global south' on the grounds of the inequality of knowledge production.[42]

Discursive information about nations can also be deconstructed through the claim-making of its symbolic repertoires. According to Lyn Spillman, symbols express meanings and values and make claims to political authority and national identity. Spillman argues convincingly in *Nation and Commemoration* (1997):[43]

National identities are understood as repertoires of symbols contingently mobilized in claims-making. These repertoires are distinguishable from and shaped by an underlying and persistent discursive field constituting nationality, a field that makes particular symbolic claims 'national' (rather than, for instance, regional or ethnic) by situating them in relation to issues of internal integration, international standing, or both.[44]

The mobilization of claims-making is studied by Spillman through a comparison of the centennial celebrations of the American Revolution (4 July, 1776) in 1876 and the settlement in Australia (26 January, 1788) in 1888 (today Australia Day) and their bicentennial counterparts in 1976 and 1988. As two relatively young 'settler nations', based on migration and diversity, it is interesting to learn that their discursive routes ended up with divergent images of nationality, visions of history and diversity, and place of the nation in the world.[45]

Symbolic repertoires are analytically interesting as they stake out identity claims and reproduce official norms and values. Spillman also demonstrates that the production of cultural meanings and norms is an uneven and nationalized process, by developing Shil's distinction of norm-producing centres and norm-receiving peripheries.[46] Norms, values and meanings are promoted and produced by cultural centres and structure activities, roles, networks whereas the periphery receives values and norms through commemorations such as those above rather than producing these themselves.

The fiftieth anniversary of independence in more than a dozen countries in Africa, celebrated in 2010, must be understood from a perspective of rebelling against norm-producing centres and reclaiming centre position. The celebration of Independence Day in India from the British (15 August 1947) also has much to tell us about breaking away from colonialism and the strategic role of the dramatization of the national identity discourse on national days, in the case of the latter in a post-colonial context with deep-seated ethno-religious divisions post-partition.

On the subject of symbolic repertoires, Gabriella Elgenius analyses national symbols and ceremonies as markers of official nation building in *Symbols of Nations and Nationalism: Celebrating Nationhood* (2011). National symbols are far from arbitrarily chosen and the adoption of flags, anthems and national days constitutes claims to political authority, sovereignty and identity.[47] Exploring nations as regimes of symbolism, symbolic regimes, help us trace nation building through the adoption (modification or abolishment) of national symbols during pivotal times of nations' history. The symbolic-regime approach also provides a framework for comparative studies of national symbols aided by a focus on 'rival clusters', that is rival national claims made through national symbols. For example, rival claims to history, territory and nationality may be traced by the establishment of, for example, national flags, celebrations of national days or the establishment of national museums in Britain (England, Northern Ireland, Scotland and Wales), Spain (e.g. the Basque Country, Catalonia and Madrid), in Scandinavia (Denmark, Finland, Iceland, Norway and Sweden) or in Cyprus, Greece and Turkey.[48] The Spanish flag or national day, for example, do not tell the whole truth and has yielded protests by way of counter-flags and counter-days and so forth. Thus, official symbolism is analytically interesting as part of strategic unity narration and power-scripts of the dominant identity. For instance, the national days in Europe have typically supported official myths about the one national origin, a golden age (saints, patrons and heroes), the forming of a republic, confederation and constitution, or liberation and independence.

The distinction between centre and periphery, mentioned above, is useful also to understand the representativeness of historical narration and inclusivity of national ceremonies.[49] Historically speaking, the working classes, women and ethnic groups gained access to national ceremonies at an even later stage than to other social institutions in Europe.[50] Thus, attention must be paid to the design of celebrations. The design and choreography of national day celebrations for instance expose nation-building strategies and identity claims that enforce the image of commonality and equality (classlessness). National day design is a lens into the larger social processes of democratization and inclusion.[51]

In short, the taken-for-granted nature of national symbols and ceremonies is analytically relevant in the deconstruction of national discourses from a number of angles: identity claims, the (re)production of meaning and norms, the enactment of some narratives over others, as indicators of social inclusion, existing hierarchies and power relations, and as identity tools to help reinforce nationalism as a discourse of social solidarity.

Craig Calhoun writes in *Nations Matter* (2007) that the nation cannot exist without nationalism and nationalism not without the discourse of social solidarity. Arguably, the concept of the 'nation' existed long before the eighteenth century and the modern nation, and became a powerful building block of social life as the discourse of social solidarity was linked to the principles of self-determination, popular sovereignty and citizenship. Thus, the nation exists discursively before it exists 'objectively' and national history is reconstructed retrospectively as the key framework for modern history writing and sociopolitical context.[52]

According to Calhoun, the rhetoric of the nation is centred around three clusters of national claims: The first cluster of rhetoric relates to the nation's boundaries, a geographical territory, a corresponding population to the sovereignty of the self-sufficient state (or state to be). The second cluster evolves around claims about a special relationship to a territory and a common ethnic or racial descent linking the population throughout generations through a common culture, language, and beliefs. The third cluster of national rhetoric capitalizes on political membership and participation, equality in citizenship, people's engagement and popular participation in national affairs in accordance with the ascending notion of legitimacy, that is, a legitimate government supported by the popular will. The discursive formation about nations, the assumptions we make and concepts we think with, shape everyday nationalism or methodological nationalism, that is, the practices that organize belonging into particular nations and states and that leads historians to organize history as stories of nations and social scientists to approach comparative research through data sets of national units.[53] The discourse of nationalism as social solidarity is therefore continually 'implicated in the widespread if problematic treatment of societies as bounded, integral, wholes with distinctive identities, cultures, and institutions'.[54] The collective self-representations of the social solidarity discourse are supported by the rhetoric of the nation as a community and produced with help of the rhetoric about the nation's boundaries and the special relationship of its people. Calhoun aptly highlights that it is a mistake to equate the artificial and constructed nature of nations with it 'not being real':

> Traditions may be no less real for being invented, however, or even for incorporating falsehoods. It is a sociological misunderstanding to think that the reality of nations depends on the accuracy of their collective self-representations.[55]

The pluralism of local experiences is also analysed by Gurminder Bhambra in *Connected Sociologies* (2014).[56] Her analysis of the terminology 'left behind' during the Brexit campaign in the United Kingdom is of special relevance for this chapter. The structured inequality embedded in nation-making and nationalism, the dominance of some groups over others, are manifest in the discursive divisions of this terminology.[57] The referendum in the United Kingdom in 2016 was fought between two campaigns to leave or stay in the European Union with a subsequent win for the Leave campaign. Fractions within the Leave Campaign became associated with the rhetoric of earned citizenship suggesting to 'take our country back' from the undeserving. The discourse of the 'left behind' made it into the public referring to the less educated, the poor, the disenfranchised and disadvantaged groups left behind or cut out from the opportunities of globalization. In the context of the left behind, the working class was reported to be a 'white British working class' or a 'white English working class' being tricked out of their rights.[58] Undoubtedly, the British working class had suffered economic hardship that worsened during and in the aftermath of the economic slump of 2008 with ensuing austerity politics and welfare cuts.[59] However, the discourse of the left behind of the Brexit campaign supported the discursive divisions between the deserving and the undeserving through racialization. Thus, ethnic groups were blamed for inequalities increasingly shared by the working classes regardless of skin colour. Further, according to Bhambra, the discursive information about 'those who perceive themselves as *left behind*' were pitted against the '*left out*',[60] many of whom were British citizens now demoted to 'migrants'. The 'racialization of socio-economic inequalities'[61] took place within anti-migrant discourses,[62] as the racialization of class was supported through claims about earned membership. The structure of discursive binary divisions, discussed earlier, constituted an essential part of the rhetoric pitting insider (native, citizen, member) against outsider (foreigner, migrant) and testifies to the ongoing imaginings of the nations as sovereign and homogenous. This rhetoric echoed, in part, the ethnicity-based nationalism found elsewhere in Europe within which the nation is framed as an ethnically homogenous community betrayed by metropolitan and international elites.[63]

Conclusion and discussion: Relevance and critique

This chapter has explored some of the deconstructive approaches that wish to move beyond the subjectively formed knowledge produced by discourses of nationalism and of particular cultures and historical periods. The wish to move 'beyond' the subjectivity of nations has generated criticisms against these perspectives. Smith,[64] for instance, argues they lack historical depth and underestimate the objective factors that bind people together and are ultimately unable to explain the appeal of nationhood. Arguably, most theories of nationalism are in need of further analyses of the mechanisms of nation building and why nations matter. With regard to the discourse of nationalism, Hechter[65] argues for a focus on the conditions under which such a discourse becomes powerful. Moreover, theoretical concepts associated with deconstruction have created 'a productive ambiguity' and need further precision.[66] Although the cultural turn has rejuvenated many fields with new theoretical impulses its many outcomes have met criticism with reference to the imprecise application of the concept of culture and ways in which culture shapes individuals and groups, exaggeration of the cultural predispositions of actors at the expense of other socio-economic structures.[67]

In closing, the purpose of this chapter has been to discuss some of the ways in which the deconstruction of discourses may enable analysis of nationalist claims. At the surface, such discourses may appear harmless, but when translated into exclusive discursive information about lost sovereignty (within and without nations), lost homogeneity within or calls for exclusion of those less deserving, they are not. In sum, analytical perspectives proposed by the cultural turn and poststructuralist explanations are valuable to challenge the alleged unity and homogeneity of nations and cultures. They do so by highlighting the diversity and hybridity of national narratives and the constructed supremacy of the West through privileged identities and the signification of difference. Thus, the deconstruction of discourses fulfils an important role for theories of nationalism to critically assess the role of history in nationalist discourse and to acknowledge marginalized histories and identities.

Notes

1 Jeffrey Alexander, 'The New Theoretical Movement', in N. J. Smelser (ed.), *Handbook of Sociology* (Beverly Hills, 1988).
2 David Chaney, *The Cultural Turn: Scene Setting Essays on Contemporary Cultural History* (London, 2002).
3 Fredric Jameson, *The Cultural Turn: Selected Writings on the Postmodern, 1983–1998* (Brooklyn, 2009), p. 111.
4 Mark Jacobs and Lyn Spillman, 'Cultural Sociology at the Crossroads of the Discipline', *Poetics* 33 (2005), 1–14.
5 Michel Foucault, 'The Subject of Power', *Critical Inquiry* 8:4 (1982), 777–95. See also Kate Nash, 'The "Cultural Turn" in Social Theory: Towards a Theory of Cultural Politics', *Sociology* 35:1 (2001), 77–92.
6 Michel Foucault, *The History of Sexuality: An Introduction* (Harmondsworth, 1984).
7 Nash, 'The "Cultural Turn" in Social Theory', p. 82.
8 Peter Jackson, 'Pierre Bourdieu, the "Cultural Turn" and the Practice of International History', *Review of International Studies* (2008), 155–81.

9 Raymond Williams, *The Sociology of Culture* (Chicago, 1981).
10 Nash, 'The "Cultural Turn" in Social Theory'; Kate Nash, *Contemporary Political Sociology: Globalization, Politics and Power*, 2nd edn (Chichester, 2010).
11 Michel Foucault, 'Truth and Power', in Colin Gordon (ed.), *Power/ Knowledge: Selected Interviews and Other Writings 1972–77* (Brighton, 1980); Foucault, 'The Subject of Power'.
12 Nash, *Contemporary Political Sociology*.
13 Caroline Rooney, 'From Liberation Theory to Postcolonial Theory: The Poststructuralist Turn', in Benoît Dillet, Iain MacKenzie and Robert Porter (eds), *The Edinburg Companion to Poststructuralism* (Edinburg, 2003), pp. 471–88; David Howarth. *Poststructuralism and After: Structure, Subjectivity and Power* (Basingstoke, 2013).
14 Bill Ashcroft, Gareth Griffiths and Helen Tiffin, *Post-Colonial Studies: The Key Concepts* (Abingdon, 2007).
15 Jacques Derrida, *Structure, Sign and Play in the Discourse of Human Sciences* (Baltimore, 1966). See also Jacques Derrida, *Writing and Difference* (Chicago, 1967).
16 See chapter by Stephen Mock.
17 Ben Agger, 'Critical Theory, Poststructuralism, Postmodernism: Their Sociological Relevance', *Annual Review of Sociology* 17 (1991), 105–31 (quotation on page 112).
18 Caroline Rooney, 'From Liberation Theory to Postcolonial Theory: The Poststructuralist Turn', pp. 471–88.
19 Jacques Derrida, 'Structure, Sign, and Play in the Discourse of the Human Sciences' (Chicago, 1978), p. 353. Also produced in the edited volume by Joyce Oldham Appleby et al. *Knowledge and Postmodernism in Historical Perspective* (London, 1996), p. 438.
20 Jacques Derrida, *Of Grammatology* (Baltimore, 2016).
21 Jacques Derrida, 'Structure, Sign, and Play', in Jacques Derrida, *Writing and Difference* (Chicago, 1978).
22 Ben Agger, 'Critical Theory, Poststructuralism, Postmodernism: Their Sociological Relevance', pp. 105–31 (quotation on page 106).
23 Philip Leonard, *Nationality between Poststructuralism and Postcolonialism: A New Cosmopolitanism* (Basingstoke, 2005), p. 154.
24 Peter Jackson, 'Pierre Bourdieu, the "Cultural Turn" and the Practice of International History', pp. 155–81.
25 Partha Chatterjee, 'Whose Imagined Community?' in Partha Chatterjee, *The Politics of the Governed: Reflections on Popular Politics in Most of the World* (New York, 2004); See also Partha Chatterjee, *Nationalist Thought and the Colonial World: A Derivative Discourse?* (Oxford, 1986).
26 Caroline Rooney, 'From Liberation Theory to Postcolonial Theory: The Poststructuralist Turn', pp. 471–88.
27 Philip Leonard, *Nationality between Poststructuralism and Postcolonialism*, p. 154.
28 Howarth, *Poststructuralism and After*.
29 Edwin Arderner, 'The Construction of History: "Vestiges of Creation"', in Elizabeth Tonkin, Maryon McDonald, Malcolm K. Chapman (eds), *History and Ethnicity* (ASA Monograhs 27) (New York, 1989), pp. 24–32.

30 Michael Billig, *Banal Nationalism* (London, 1995), p. 70.
31 Billig, *Banal Nationalism*, pp. 5–17.
32 Julia Kristeva, *Nations without Nationalism* (New York, 1993), pp. 38–9.
33 Homi Bhabha, 'DissemiNation: Time, Narrative, and the Margins of the Modern Nation', in Homi Bhabha, *Nation and Narration* (London, 1990), pp. 291–322 (quotation on page 310).
34 Bhabha, *Nation and Narration*, p. 3.
35 Leonard, *Nationality between Poststructuralism and Postcolonialism*, p. 128.
36 Bhabha, 'DissemiNation: Time, Narrative, and the Margins of the Modern Nation', pp. 291–322 (quotation on page 292).
37 Peter Herman (ed.), *Historicizing Theory* (New York, 2004).
38 John Scott, *Fifty Key Sociologists – The Contemporary Theorists* (London, 2006).
39 Bhabha, *Nation and Narration*, p. 4.
40 Bhabha deconstructs the 'excess' of syntactic properties by exploring meanings beyond the words and the hidden meanings given by formal grammatical rules and arrangement of words and signs and their relationships in sentences (rather than their stated content).
41 Bhabha, *Nation and Narration*, p. 1.
42 Maev Kennedy, 'Cambridge academics seek to 'decolonise' English syllabus', *The Guardian* 25 October 2017, Available at: https://www.theguardian.com/education/2017/oct/25/cambridge-academics-seek-to-decolonise-english-syllabus.
43 Lyn Spillman, *Nation and Commemoration: Creating National Identities in the United States and Australia* (Cambridge, 1997).
44 Lyn Spillman and Russell Faeges, 'Nations', in Julia Adams, Elisabeth S. Clemens and Ann Shola Orloff (eds), *The Making and Unmaking of Modernity: Politics and Processes in Historical Sociology* (Durham, NC, 2005), pp. 409–37, quotation page 432.
45 Lyn Spillman, *Nation and Commemoration*.
46 Edward Shils, 'Center and Periphery: An Idea and Its Career, 1935–1987', in Liah Greenfeld and Michel Martin (eds), *Center: Ideas and Institutions* (Chicago, 1988).
47 Gabriella Elgenius, *Symbols of Nations and Nationalism* (Basingstoke, 2011).
48 Gabriella Elgenius, 'National Museums as National Symbols: A Survey of Strategic Nationbuilding; Nations as Symbolic Regimes', in Gabriella Elgenius and Peter Aronsson (eds), *National Museums and Nation-Building in Europe 1750–2010: Mobilization and Legitimacy, Continuity and Change* (Basingstoke, 2015), pp. 145–66.
49 Gabriella Elgenius, 'The Principles and Products of the Identity Market: Identity, Inequality and Rivalry', in Gunnar Olofsson, Sven Hort and Robin Blackburn (eds), *Class, Sex and Revolutions: Göran Therborn, a Critical Appraisal* (Stockholm, 2016), pp. 337–54.
50 See also Paul Connerton, *How Societies Remember* (Cambridge, 1989); John R. Gillis (ed.), *Commemorations: The Politics of National Identity* (New Jersey, 1996).
51 Gabriella Elgenius, 'The Politics of Recognition: Symbols, Nation-building and Rival Nationalism', *Nations & Nationalism* 17:2 (2011), 396–418; Gabriella Elgenius, 'A Formula for Successful National Day Design' ('Varför

är 17e maj fortfarande så populär? En formel för lyckat nationaldagsfirande.')
Bibliotheca Nova 1 (2014), 92–107. Available at: http://www.nb.no/Om-NB/
Publikasjoner/Skriftserien-Bibliotheca-Nova.

52 Stefan Berger, *The Past as History: National Identity and Historical
Consciousness in Modern Europe* (Basingstoke, 2014).

53 Craig Calhoun, *Nations Matter: Culture, History and the Cosmopolitan
Dream* (London, 2007), p. 27.

54 Ibid., p. 40.

55 Ibid., p. 41.

56 Gurminder K. Bhambra, *Connected Sociologies* (London, 2014).

57 Gurminder K. Bhambra, 'Class Analysis in the Age of Trump (and
Brexit): The Pernicious New Politics of Identity' (2016). Available
at: https://www.thesociologicalreview.com/blog/class-analysis-in-the-age-
of-trump-and-brexit-the-pernicious-new-politics-of-identity.html 2016];
Gurminder K. Bhambra, *Viewpoint: Brexit, Class and British 'National'
Identity* (2016) Available at: http://discoversociety.org/2016/07/05/
viewpoint-brexit-class-and-british-national-identity/.

58 Gurminder Bhambra, 'Locating Brexit in the Pragmatics of Race, Citizenship
and Empire', in William Outhwaite, *Brexit: Sociological Responses* (London,
2017), p. 91.

59 Gabriella Elgenius, 'Social Division and Resentment in the Aftermath of the
Economic Slump', in Shana Cohen, Christina Fuhr and Jan-Jonathan Bock
(eds), *Austerity, Community Action, and the Future of Citizenship in Europe*
(Bristol, 2017).

60 Gurminder K. Bhambra, *Class Analysis in the Age of Trump* (and Brexit).

61 Gurminder K. Bhambra, *Viewpoint: Brexit, Class and British 'National'
Identity*.

62 Gabriella Elgenius, 'Ethnic Bonding and Homing Desires: The Polish Diaspora
and Civil Society Making', in Kerstin Jacobsson and Elżbieta Korolczuk (eds),
Civil Society Revisited: Lessons from Poland (Oxford, 2017).

63 Gabriella Elgenius and Jens Rydgren, 'Frames of Nostalgia and Belonging: The
Resurgence of Reactionary Ethno-Nationalism in Sweden', *European Societies*
https://doi.org/10.1080/14616696.2018.1494297; Gabriella Elgenius and
Jens Rydgren, 'The Sweden Democrats and the Ethno-Nationalist Rhetoric of
Decay and Betrayal', *Journal of Sociological Research, Sociologisk forskning*
54:4 (2017), 353–58.

64 Anthony D. Smith, *Nationalism and Modernism: A Critical Survey of Recent
Theories of Nations and Nationalism* (London, 1998); Anthony D. Smith,
Ethno-Symbolism and Nationalism: A Cultural Approach (Abingdon, 2009).

65 Michael Hechter, *Internal Colonialism: The Celtic Fringe in British National
Development* (New Brunswick, 1999).

66 Mark Jacobs and Lyn Spillman, 'Cultural Sociology at the Crossroads of the
Discipline', *Poetics* 33 (2005), 1–14.

67 P. Jackson, 'Pierre Bourdieu, the "Cultural Turn" and the Practice of
International History', *Review of International Studies* 34:1 (2008), 155–81.

Further reading

Bhabha, Homi (ed.), *Nation and Narration*. London: Routledge, 1993.

Billig, Michael, *Banal Nationalism*. London: Sage, 1995.

Calhoun, Craig, *Nations Matter: Culture, History and the Cosmopolitan Dream*. London: Routledge, 2007.

Chaney, David, *The Cultural Turn: Scene Setting Essays on Contemporary Cultural History*. London: Routledge, 2002.

Howarth, David, *Poststructuralism and After: Structure, Subjectivity and Power*. Basingstoke: Palgrave, 2013.

Leonard, Philip, *Nationality Between Poststructuralism and Postcolonialism: A New Cosmopolitanism*. Basingstoke: Palgrave, 2005.

Nash, Kate, *Contemporary Political Sociology: Globalization, Politics and Power*. 2nd edn. Chichester, United Kingdom: Wiley-Blackwell, 2010.

Spillman, Lyn, *Nation and Commemoration: Creating National Identities in the United States and Australia*. Cambridge: Cambridge University Press, 1997.

9

Postcolonialism and the history of anti-colonial nationalism

Sanjay Seth

Introduction

Postcolonialism is the name sometimes given to a set of analytical tools, questions and more generally a style of thought that places colonialism at the centre of its concerns. Since this interdisciplinary theory is relatively new, and not as well known as some of the other approaches surveyed in this volume, I will begin with a brief account of postcolonialism.[1] This chapter will then focus upon *Subaltern Studies*, a historiographical project on Indian history that has been a very important current in postcolonial theorizing, especially when it comes to analyses of nationalism.

Postcolonialism is in one important respect a misleading term, for the 'post' does not indicate a periodization according to which colonialism now lies behind us and is only of historical interest. The 'post' in postcolonialism in fact aggressively makes the opposite claim: that colonialism was central to the shaping of the entire period after it, and – like the Industrial Revolution, the spread of capitalism and the Enlightenment – it has shaped the economy, politics, culture and intellectual life of the modern world. It transformed not only the colonized but also the colonizer, not only by providing the loot, raw materials and markets that fuelled the Industrial Revolution but also by shaping the very sense of self of both colonizer and colonized, of West and East, as well as by structuring the categories through which the world came to be known and understood.

The grosser forms of political domination and economic exploitation characterizing colonialism have been the subject of enquiry for a long time, and hardly need a new term and approach. Where postcolonialism adds something to our understanding – and here it is a theoretical as well as a historical claim – is in drawing attention to the fact that the colonial encounter was also one with enduring effects in other domains, including culture and knowledge; and that precisely because colonialism was a relationship of power, these other domains were not the 'outside' or 'remainder' of a relationship of power (which is how we usually think of culture and knowledge), but were themselves permeated with power and inequality. In connecting knowledge and culture with power, postcolonialism draws upon, and is indebted to, concepts and analyses developed by post-structuralism.[2]

This can be seen in one of its early and seminal texts, Edward Said's *Orientalism* (1978). Said draws upon two insights from the work of Michel Foucault: that knowledge and discourse do not just 'represent' things, but have real effects (they do not merely describe, but also shape what is described); and that knowledge and power are inseparable. He puts this to service, characterizing Orientalism – that vast body of writings and other representations concerned with the Arab and Asian worlds – as 'a style of thought based upon an ontological and epistemological distinction made between "the Orient" and (most of the time) "the Occident"'.[3] These ways of knowing and representing the Orient were not simply *enabled* by the power relations that defined colonialism, they were one of the forms of this power, one of the modes by which it was exercised and reproduced. The dense network of representations and knowledges that Said calls Orientalism was a way of 'dealing with [the Orient] . . . by making statements about it, authorizing views of it, describing it, by teaching it, settling it, ruling over it. . . . Orientalism [was/is] a Western style for dominating, restructuring and having authority over the Orient.'[4] While there were of course considerable variations in how the Orient was represented and understood, these were not unlimited – 'no one', writes Said, 'writing, thinking, or acting on the Orient could do so without taking account of the limitations on thought and action imposed by Orientalism',[5] limits beginning with the presumption that the West and the East were fundamentally different.

Western representations and knowledges of the Orient, according to this claim – one that has been central to postcolonialism – presupposed colonial domination, and were themselves a form of power. This was not principally due to 'arrogance' – the modern West did not have a monopoly on arrogance, and other cultures, including non-Western ones, have assumed that they were 'right' and others 'wrong' – but rather due to two other factors. First, Europe in the era of colonialism was able to insist that the knowledges it championed were the only true ones, because it alone had the power to enforce its claims. Second, the Enlightenment claim that it had discovered a new, scientific and universal form of knowledge was qualitatively different to any previous or competing claims. For unlike other knowledges and cultures, which were rooted in culturally and historically specific communities and their attendant practices and beliefs, post-Enlightenment knowledge was claimed to have been deduced from nothing less than Reason itself, uncontaminated by any specificities of history or culture. A knowledge conceived to be grounded in the purity of a Reason uncontaminated by history was one that was particularly blind to the relations of knowledge with history and power, and yet obstinately insistent on its own incontrovertible character. Other knowledges and cultures were always *someone's* knowledge claims and *someone's* morality and culture, whereas the colonizer's knowledge presented itself as knowledge 'as such', unaffected by historical, empirical 'impurities'.

Postcolonialism thus foregrounds the connections between knowledge and culture on the one hand, and power on the other. In insisting that all knowledges, cultures and moralities are products of specific histories and cultures – including the knowledges and the culture of the modern West, now part of our globalized modernity – it also draws attention to the ways in which knowledges and forms of life mutually constitute each other. That this has implications for how one understands nationalism will be immediately apparent. For anti-colonial nationalism was at once a challenge to the dominance of the West, and yet inasmuch as the sovereign statehood and the modernity that anti-colonial nationalism sought was intimately tied to the knowledge and culture of the West, it also reproduced that dominance.

The most sustained investigations into nationalism under the aegis of postcolonial theory were those undertaken by the historians of the Subaltern Studies group, who collaboratively produced twelve edited volumes of (mostly) historical essays on India from 1982 to 2005. However, the *Subaltern Studies* volumes, and the monographs and other writings of the members of the group, were not an application of a pre-existing postcolonialism to Indian history. Indeed, in its beginnings Subaltern Studies was not postcolonial, but rather a version – if an original and provocative one – of Marxism. But it subsequently became one of the sites where a distinctively 'postcolonial' mode of theorizing developed, and did so with specific reference to the Indian past and Indian nationalism: hence the focus on it in this chapter.

Subaltern Studies

The first volume of *Subaltern Studies* began with a programmatic statement by Ranajit Guha (the editor of the first six volumes of the series, and a major intellectual force within it), which declared, 'The historiography of Indian nationalism has for a long time been dominated by elitism – colonialist elitism and bourgeois-nationalist elitism', both of which shared 'the prejudice that the making of the Indian nation and the development of the consciousness – nationalism – which informed this process were exclusively or predominantly elite achievements'.[6] For colonialist historiography – the British histories produced during the colonial period, and also the contemporary 'Cambridge school' of Indian history-writing,[7] which Guha characterized and condemned as colonialist – Indian nationalism was best understood as a 'learning process', one in which 'the native elite became involved in politics by trying to negotiate the maze of institutions and the corresponding cultural complex introduced by the colonial authorities'. By contrast, elitist historiography of the nationalist variety presented Indian nationalism as a venture 'in which the indigenous elite led the people from subjugation to freedom', and the history of Indian nationalism was 'written up as a sort of spiritual biography of the Indian elite'.

The obvious opposition between these two kinds of history could not obscure the fact that neither acknowledged nor could make sense of 'the contribution made by the people *on their own*, that is, *independently of the elite* to the making and development of this nationalism'; and in particular, could not adequately explain those moments of mass upsurge when popular initiative asserted itself 'in defiance or absence of elite control'. In short, what neither could account for was 'the politics of the people'; for parallel to elite politics was 'another domain of Indian politics in which the principal actors were not the dominant groups of the indigenous society or the colonial authorities but the subaltern classes and groups constituting the mass of the labouring population . . . that is, the people. This was an *autonomous* domain, for it neither originated from elite politics nor did its existence depend on the latter.' The most striking form of this popular politics was the peasant uprising, the subject of Guha's brilliant *Elementary Aspects of Peasant Insurgency in Colonial India*. But while this peasant politics was 'traditional' in that it was rooted in structures and a sensibility that were not that of the colonial-modern, it was so 'only in so far as its roots could be traced back to pre-colonial times, but it was by no means archaic in the sense of being outmoded'. Indeed, while Guha's *Elementary Aspects* sought to document and retrieve the rebel consciousness that informed peasant insurgency up to 1900, he concluded his book by suggesting that 'the actual career of this consciousness extends well beyond the nineteenth century', and that peasant insurgency and the autonomous consciousness that informed it were to be found in the nationalist and communist mobilizations of the twentieth century.[8]

In Guha's view, elitist historiography in both its varieties overlooked the existence of subaltern politics. But it was very much there in Indian nationalism as an independent form of politics that elite nationalism had not succeeded in bringing under its sway, testifying to 'the failure of the Indian bourgeoisie to speak for the nation'. Conversely, the failure of subaltern consciousness and politics to rise above localism to become a national liberation movement explained the shortcomings, and the insufficient radicalism, of a nationalist struggle that succeeded in winning political independence for India in 1947, but without any corresponding social transformation, nor a total break with imperialism.

In its early volumes, *Subaltern Studies* was a recognizable, if unconventional and innovative, species of Marxist historiography.[9] It was explicitly indebted to the works of the Italian Marxist theorist and communist leader Antonio Gramsci, from whom it borrowed the term 'subaltern', as well as other concepts and critical tools ('hegemony' being one of these). Its emphasis on the peasantry, and on the semi-feudal relations and modes of power that characterized many aspects of Indian society, owed an obvious debt to Maoism. And at least some its arguments, such as that bourgeois nationalism had sought to appropriate peasant and worker radicalism while keeping it within certain bounds, so that it threatened British rule without calling into question relations of exploitation and dominance between Indian elites and the lower classes of Indian society, had been anticipated by earlier generations of Indian Marxists.[10] And it had many affinities with the 'history from below', pioneered by Christopher Hill, George Rude, Eric Hobsbawm and E. P. Thompson, that immediately preceded it, not least in its innovative use of historical sources.

However, *Subaltern Studies* was also critical of most Marxist history writing on Indian nationalism, accusing it of a shortcoming very similar to that which characterized colonialist and bourgeois history writing: namely, that it failed to register the consciousness that informed subaltern revolt. According to the subalternists, colonialist historiography treated the peasant rebel as if he had no rational consciousness at all, and his rebellion was a spontaneous and undirected expression of rage. Bourgeois nationalist historiography read an elite consciousness into rebellion, as if the rebel, lacking consciousness or will of his own, could only follow his elite leaders. The Marxist historian, according to Guha, could not come to terms with the fact that rebel consciousness was usually religious rather than secular, and was sometimes also sectarian: 'Unable to grasp religiosity as the central modality of peasant consciousness in colonial India . . . [h]e is obliged to therefore rationalize the ambiguities of rebel politics', by converting the rebel into 'an *abstraction* called Worker-and-Peasant, *an ideal rather than the real historical personality of the insurgent*', the result of a 'shallow radicalism' that has abdicated the responsibility 'of exploring and describing the consciousness specific to . . . rebellion'.[11]

From Marxism to postcolonialism

But even if initially Subaltern Studies appeared as a (creative and innovative) form of Marxist historiography, there were already features, and tensions, that anticipated its subsequent development in a postcolonial direction. The insistence on an elite/subaltern divide was ambiguous, allowing for two interpretations of what was entailed in this claim, and what its consequences for the study of Indian history might be. If taken to be an empirical claim about the existence of two distinct social entities, it followed that a central aim of the Subaltern Studies project was to verify or prove that there was an autonomous subaltern nationalist politics, not subsumed by, and separate from, elite politics. And a number of contributors undertook studies which showed, in Guha's later summary, that 'in region after region the initiative of such [nationalist] campaigns passed from elite leaderships [of the Indian National Congress] to the mass of subaltern participants, who defied high command . . . to make these struggles their own by framing them in codes specific to traditions of popular resistance and phrasing them in idioms derived from the communitarian experience of living and working together'.[12] Valuable as these studies were, and important as the point about a subaltern politics was, many otherwise sympathetic critics felt uneasy with the insistence on 'autonomy'. In a society where elite and subaltern classes shared social and economic space, was the claim to an 'autonomous' subaltern domain plausible?

Moreover, this insistence on autonomy was at odds with the other interpretation that could be placed on this claim, namely that it was designed to draw attention to the fact that the elite–subaltern relation was principally one of power, rather than one that derived from differential size of landholdings and wealth. In 'semi-feudal' India, inequality was related to but not reducible to land ownership; domination and subordination were also inscribed in dress, language, body language and so on. By contrast, in a bourgeois society where certain notions of formal equality have taken root, inequality stems from differences in ownership of the means of production – you do not have to be very well dressed to eat in an expensive restaurant, as long as you have the money to pay for your meal. It was this difference in forms of inequality and power, between bourgeois societies such as Britain or the United States, and India, that constituted the great divide between elites and subalterns in the subcontinent. But this was a relational understanding of power, and sat ill with an insistence on separateness and autonomy. Nor was there any suggestion that this was simply a function of 'backwardness' and was destined to disappear as India became more capitalist and 'modern'. On the contrary, the point being made, as Dipesh Chakrabarty later put it, was that 'the global history of capitalism need not reproduce everywhere the same history of power. In the calculus of modernity, power is not a dependable variable and capital an independent one. Capital and power can be treated as analytically separable categories.'[13] The peculiar workings of power in India – peculiar from a point of view which takes the working of bourgeois society as its norm – stemmed from the fact that non-Western societies had been incorporated into the global circuits of capital, but 'without effecting or requiring any thoroughgoing democratic transformation in social relationships of power and authority'.[14]

These two accounts of the elite/subaltern divide were both present in the early volumes of *Subaltern Studies*, but they pulled in different directions. The first took the form of a general proposition that was then to be verified by empirical research; the latter was a theoretical argument that enjoined research that would remain attentive to the ways in which relations between different strata in Indian society were shaped and permeated by relations of power, relations that were not reducible to the economic disparities emphasized by certain types of Marxism and were inexplicable in the terms we are accustomed to in societies where power, even though it exists, exists in the midst of formal equality. The former emphasizes that social groups were distinct, even if they interlaced; the latter's emphasis on power logically entailed an insistence upon relationality, for power was here understood as a relation, not a 'possession' (it is not that landlords had power and peasants did not, but that power defined the relations and the differences between them, making one a landlord and the other a peasant).[15] The emphasis, however, shifted towards the latter, and this led to conceptualizations of community, and analyses of nationalism, that became important landmarks in postcolonial theory.

There was also a tension, and at times an outright contradiction, in the early volumes of *Subaltern Studies* between an attempt to 'recover' the (subaltern) subject and restore to him the subjectivity that was his own, and an incipient critique of the category of 'the subject' as a misleading humanist fiction. It is clear from what has been said above that *Subaltern Studies* presented itself in part as a recuperative project – one that sought to unearth and restore a subaltern consciousness, one overlooked or assimilated to another consciousness in elite historiography. Yet this was at odds with the structuralist and anti-humanist theoretical referents that informed the work of some of the leading contributors to the *Subaltern Studies* volumes, according to which the subject and his/her consciousness were not the 'ground' and cause that give rise to everything else but rather the 'effect' of certain institutions and practices. These institutions and practices came into being during the modern history of the West, and were closely connected to the emergence of modern bourgeois society. The subject was thus neither transhistorical nor generalizable to all times and places.

The tension was widely noted by sympathetic interlocutors of Subaltern Studies: Rosalind O'Hanlon noted that 'there appears a persistent wavering or slipping between the two positions',[16] and Gayatri Spivak, writing in volume IV of *Subaltern Studies*, observed that the subalternists 'fall back upon notions of consciousness-as-agent, totality, and upon a culturalism, that are discontinuous with the critique of humanism',[17] a critique which was otherwise present in their insistence that identity and consciousness were not givens, not part of the furniture of the world, but were rather produced, and constructed through contrasts and oppositions. Since the subject was not 'some *thing* that can be disclosed'[18] as the ground and cause of politics, ideology and language, but was rather the product or effect of 'strands that may be termed politics, ideology, economics, history, sexuality, language and so on',[19] it followed that 'Subaltern consciousness . . . is never fully recoverable',[20] indeed, that it is 'a theoretical fiction'.[21] In her appreciative overview and critique, Spivak expressed the desire that the subalternists overcome this tension by self-consciously embracing post-structuralism/deconstruction. Some members of the group did so, and as they did, *Subaltern Studies* moved away from its self-declared ambition to recover subaltern subjectivity and consciousness, and began its trajectory as a postcolonial project.

While *Subaltern Studies* was from its beginnings critical rather than celebratory in its approach to Indian nationalism, it was not always clear whether this critical attitude was towards only the 'elite' nationalism of the Indian National Congress, or whether it extended to nationalism as such. As earlier observed, Mao's writings – and the Indian Maoist-led insurgency of the late 1960s and early 1970s – was a strong influence on the early volumes of *Subaltern Studies*,[22] and this influence could be seen in the implication that a 'proper' or full nationalism would have been one led by subaltern classes, culminating in a 'people's democracy'. However, as the series progressed it increasingly became a critique, not of an insufficiently radical nationalism, but one that was sceptical of nationalism more generally: in its postcolonial avatar, *Subaltern Studies* came to be marked by its critical deconstruction of nationalist claims to unitary identity.

As *Subaltern Studies* proceeded, these tensions or contradictions did not disappear, but the claim to the autonomy of subaltern consciousness and politics increasingly gave way to an emphasis on the centrality of power and thus on relationality rather than autonomy. The criticisms/suggestions of Spivak and others were taken on board by some of the members of the collective, and poststructuralist or deconstructionist understandings of the subject and consciousness became increasingly prominent. And the Subaltern Studies project increasingly became a postnationalist one, critical of all national essentialisms.

Naturally, this was not true of all members of the group. One of its senior members, the distinguished Indian historian Sumit Sarkar, became a public critic of the direction which the series took, castigating it for its rejection of Marxism and its embrace of Said's ideas, and more generally, for its postmodern and postcolonial turn.[23] But as a collective enterprise *Subaltern Studies* did take a postcolonial turn, and one important aspect and effect of this was to produce a distinctive historiography of nationalism, as exemplified in the works of Partha Chatterjee, the member of the group who most directly and sustainedly addressed the issue of nationalism.

Subaltern Studies and the history of anti-colonial nationalism

One of the striking features of postcolonial histories of nationalism is their emphasis on nationalism as a body of ideas or a discourse, rather than as a phenomenon to be explained by reference to its social or material 'causes'. Chatterjee's important book *Nationalist Thought and the Colonial World: A Derivative Discourse?* (1986) asks, 'What does nationalist discourse presuppose? Where is it located in relation to other discourses? What are the cracks on its surface, the points of tension in its structure, the contrary forces, the contradictions? What does it reveal and what does it suppress?' These, Chatterjee declares, 'are the types of questions with which I propose to conduct this study, not with a positive sociological theory'.[24] The centrality accorded to discourse and the rejection of 'sociological' explanations of nationalism – meaning explanations in which nationalism is taken to be something best understood and explained by looking for its underlying social or material 'causes' – reflect the insistence in both post-structuralist and postcolonial scholarship that social and material phenomena do not exist independently of our descriptions of them. To designate something as social or material is already an act of cognition, a form of organizing the phenomena of the world, rather than a passive 'recognition'. Even material phenomena are discursively constituted; this does not mean that they do not exist outside of our analytical and descriptive categories, but it does mean that they are only accessible to us through these categories, and not independently of them. This is true even of knowledge of the natural world, that is, of the natural sciences, as Thomas Kuhn argued long ago,[25] and it is especially so of those phenomenon that are human creations, and that already have human purposes and meanings built into them.

According to this approach, 'class', 'gender' and 'nationalism', for example, are not 'things' that already exist in the world, and that our analyses simply reveal or unveil, but rather exist in the way that they do because of our modes of apprehending and characterizing them. There is thus no escaping discourse by getting 'behind' or 'under' it to what is 'really' driving things. Discourses structure the way in which an object/phenomenon presents itself to us, and frame the field of possibilities of what can be thought and said about it – as Said sought to show with reference to the discourse of Orientalism.

This general and abstract point is especially pertinent to studies of nationalism, because nationalism is very much embodied in ideas, consciousness and discourse. Of course, these ideas exist in social contexts, and are embodied in movements, parties and the like, and often proceed hand in hand with changes in economic and social institutions, and practices. Thus the study of nationalism cannot be simply a history of ideas, in the way that the history of philosophy, perhaps, can be. But nor can economic or social changes 'explain' nationalism for us. The emergence of a middle class is only part of the history of nationalism to the degree that this class thought of itself as belonging to a nation and voiced nationalist demands; otherwise, this 'fact' is part of another history (of capitalism, for instance). What characterizes the 'sociological' histories of nationalism that Chatterjee rejects is that they are marked by a circularity. The identification/ selection of what is part of the story of nationalism necessarily occurs at the level of ideas and discourse; but this consciousness and discourse has then to be situated and is often explained, in terms of the social forms and practices in which it was embodied. To continue the example raised above, it is only when a middle class, or a section of it, raises nationalist demands, organizes or joins political parties and movements seeking a nation state, that all this becomes part of the story of nationalism. In telling this story, histories of nationalism (because they are historical narratives, wedded to certain notions of explanation and causality) ask 'why' this sentiment or idea emerged; they then frequently, and retrospectively as it were, provide a 'material' or social explanation for the rise of nationalism precisely in terms of the rise of the middle class.[26]

Chatterjee does not think classes, economic changes and the like are not important; but he thinks that they are part of the story of nationalism, not what is 'behind' or 'underneath' it, and therefore that which explains nationalism. To understand nationalism we need to attend to nationalist discourse, in all its variety and complexity, including, as the quote from Chatterjee above emphasizes, its tensions and contradictions. The single most important of these, which Chatterjee suggests runs through Indian nationalism in all its varieties and phases, and which he argues characterizes anti-colonial nationalisms more generally, is a tension or contradiction which he describes as follows: 'Nationalist thought, in agreeing to become "modern", accepts the claim to universality of this 'modern' framework of knowledge. Yes it also asserts the autonomous identity of a national culture. It thus simultaneously rejects and accepts the dominance, both epistemic and oral, of an alien culture.'[27] At first glance this does not sound dissimilar to a point made, in different ways, by a number of scholars, including John Plamenatz, Elie Kedourie, and Tom Nairn:[28] namely, that the nationalism of 'latecomers' is animated by a desire to be 'like' others while yet insisting upon an absolute, irreducible (national) 'difference', and is thus marked by a simultaneous acceptance and rejection of the standards of the 'advanced' or dominant nations.

However, while there is a similarity, Chatterjee is saying something more than this. Indeed, he declares that the theoretical problem he is drawing attention to is one that cannot be posed

> within the ambit of bourgeois-rationalist thought. . . . For to pose it is to place thought itself, including thought that is supposedly rational and scientific, within a discourse of *power*. It is to question the very universality, the 'givenness', the sovereignty of that thought, to go to its roots and thus radically to criticize it. It is to raise the possibility that it is not just military might or industrial strength, but thought itself, which can dominate and subjugate. It is to approach the field of discourse, historical, philosophical and scientific, as a battleground of political power.[29]

The influences of Foucault and Said are apparent here. The scientific, rational thought of modernity, which first arose in the West, is not treated as the 'discovery' of what the truths of the world are, but is approached agnostically, as the organizing beliefs of a particular culture at a certain historical period. That nature is devoid of meaning and purpose and simply subject to blind physical laws, and conversely that there is an object or domain of 'culture' which is wholly the domain of meanings and purposes and desires; that the individual is the most basic reality of the social realm; that gods are matters of 'belief' but not objects of knowledge, let alone actors in the world; these are all treated as culturally and historically specific ways of construing and inhabiting the world, rather than as the 'discovery' of transhistorical and transcultural 'truths'. Nationalism, as a project seeking sovereignty, citizenship and usually 'development', 'democracy' and the like, accepts this knowledge and uses it to 'think' and justify its own project. But in doing so, it adopts a goal and uses procedures of justification that may not accord well with the moral and epistemological standards of the community in question, a community which may not, for instance, regard nature as disenchanted, the community as composed of individuals and so on. Inasmuch as it accepts this knowledge as its horizon and uses it to legitimate its project, then this dilemma and contradiction will mark all nationalist thought.

The ways in which this dilemma is negotiated vary greatly between different historical moments of nationalism, and different strands or varieties of it. Much of Chatterjee's book is taken up with a study of Bankimchandra Chatterjee, Mohandas Karamchand Gandhi and Jawaharlal Nehru, three of the most prominent leaders or thinkers of Indian nationalism, and of the various (and different) ways in which this contradiction marks their nationalist thought. But these important differences notwithstanding, Chatterjee insists that inasmuch as anti-colonial nationalism 'reasons within a framework of knowledge whose representational structure corresponds to the very structure of power nationalist thought repudiates', this contradiction 'signifies, in the domain of thought, the theoretical insolubility of the national question in a colonial country . . . within a strictly nationalist framework'.[30] For even where anti-colonial nationalism triumphs, as it did in India with the end of colonialism and the achievement of independence in 1947, this victory was a partial and contradictory one; the 'difference' in the name of which nationalism spoke was harnessed to modes of thinking, and to a form of polity, that undercut this difference, and/or remade it to fit the categories and institutions of Western modernity. In short, the triumph of anti-colonial nationalism may at the same time mark a continuing, even intensified, subordination to the epistemic categories and the institutions of western capitalist modernity.

The argument is developed – and changes emphasis – in Chatterjee's subsequent book, *The Nation and its Fragments: Colonial and Postcolonial Histories* (1993). Taking issue with Benedict Anderson's immensely influential *Imagined Communities*, Chatterjee argues that it is not the case that the various models or types for 'imagining' the nation came into being in Europe and then in the Americas, such that all that was left for Asia and Africa to do was to adopt one of the existing models. He objects to this argument not, he says, for 'sentimental reasons', but because the evidence shows that 'the most creative results of the nationalist imagination in Asia and Africa are posited not on an identity but rather on a *difference* with the "modular" forms of the national society propagated by the modern West'.[31] This has been overlooked (and not only by Anderson) because scholars have concentrated on nationalism as a political movement, and on its aspiration to found a sovereign state. If we focus only on this, Asian and African nationalisms are indeed modelled upon European precedents, and the independent postcolonial states of Asia and Africa very much resemble their European and American counterparts. Here there is indeed little evidence that the nation was 'imagined' in ways that had not already been anticipated.

However, this is to overlook precisely what was distinctive about anti-colonial nationalism: that it operated at two levels, of which the political level, where it imitated precedents, was only one. For anti-colonial nationalism divided the social world into two domains, the material and the spiritual, the 'outside' and the 'inside'. The material was the domain of the institutions and practices which enabled the West to conquer and colonize – including science and technology, economy and statecraft – and these had to be imitated if the colonizer was to be overthrown. The 'spiritual' or 'inside' domain – which encompassed language and literature, music, theatre and the arts, and gender and family relations – was where the essence of cultural identity was declared to lie, and here there was to be no imitation: indeed, 'the greater one's success in imitating Western skills in the material domain . . . the greater the need to preserve the distinctiveness of one's spiritual culture'.[32] The 'spiritual' or 'inner' domain was where Westernization must *not* occur, and anti-colonial nationalism proclaimed sovereignty over this domain, asserting, even before political sovereignty was sought, that the colonial state had no right to interfere here.

Here as elsewhere, Chatterjee's arguments are developed with reference to Indian materials, but his claim is that the spiritual/material distinction is true of all anti-colonial nationalisms. And it is certainly the case that many countries that were colonized by the West, or were in danger of being so, sought to imitate Western science, technology and bureaucratic/state organization while zealously insisting that institutions and practices deemed to be marks of national cultural identity must be retained and protected. Thus in nineteenth-century China, reformers urging changes that would allow China to resist Western depredations made a distinction between 'essence' and 'utility' (*ti-yong*); Chinese essence was to be preserved, while 'useful' knowledges and practices from the West needed to be learned and freely borrowed. In Japan, seeking to 'modernize' during the Meiji Restoration, and thereby avoid the fate of India or China, the slogan of *wakan yôsai* (Japanese spirit, Western technique) was a similar endeavour to acquire Western techniques, not in order to 'become' Western (and thereby lose 'Japaneseness'), but rather precisely as a means to preserve that which was deemed to be at the very heart of Japanese identity.

The material/spiritual or outer/inner divide was not the same as the public/private distinction characteristic of bourgeois society. Culture and the arts are not 'private' for instance, yet in anti-colonial nationalism, these were treated as belonging to the 'inner' domain. Nor is the inner/outer or spiritual/material distinction the same as the modern/traditional distinction. For the 'spiritual' domain was not one of an unchanging tradition which anti-colonial nationalism sought to 'preserve'. On the contrary, it was in this domain, writes Chatterjee, that 'nationalism launches its most powerful, creative, and historically significant project: to fashion a "modern" national culture that is nevertheless not Western'.[33] It was this difficult, sometimes contradictory project that characterized anti-colonial nationalism: the desire to become modern and yet remain different; as one Indian nationalist pithily put it, 'we do not want to be English or German or American or Japanese . . . we want to be Indians, but modern, up-to-date, progressive Indians'.[34]

This can be seen, for example, in nationalist projects for the refashioning of women. The 'woman question' became a much debated one with the rise of nationalism, for the material/spiritual and inner/outer distinctions came to be 'mapped onto' women. Nationalists treated women as one of the most essential repositories and signifiers of national identity, and yet at the same time, saw them as 'backward' and insufficiently modern, and as thus contributing to the backwardness that prevented the nation from shaking off colonial rule. There is now a body of work (some of it influenced by Chatterjee) which explores the centrality the 'woman question' came to assume in nationalist debates, and charts the tensions which marked the attempts to make women modern, while ensuring that they would also function as embodiments of the national culture and essence. Deniz Kandiyoti, Lila Abu-Lughod, Margot Badran and Beth Baron have published important works investigating how the relation between women and the nation was imagined and debated in the Middle East.[35] There is a significant literature on this theme with reference to the Republican and communist movements and revolutions in China, and a growing number of such studies for Japan.[36] A considerable body of such work exists for colonial India,[37] and there are also some more general or comparative enquiries.[38]

Chatterjee's claim is that nationalism *did* create new forms of community, and was thus not derivative and imitative of Western nationalism. Non-Western cultures and forms of community were different from those in the West, and this difference was not erased in the course of anti-colonial struggles, but – despite contradictions and tensions – creatively reconfigured. Chatterjee's historical account of nationalism is in some ways more appreciative here, than in his earlier *Nationalist Thought*. However, his point is that this creative aspect of nationalist imaginings is easy to overlook precisely because as a political project, nationalism harnessed these creative imaginings to the goal of founding an independent sovereign state, with all the panoply of flags, anthems and the like. Anti-colonial nationalism thus often created new forms of community, but subsumed these under the 'old' forms of the state. As Chatterjee elegiacally puts it, 'autonomous forms of imagination of the community were, and continue to be, overwhelmed and swamped by the history of the postcolonial state. Here lies the root of our postcolonial misery: not in our inability to think out new forms of community, but in our surrender to old forms of the modern state.'[39] Or as Sanjay Seth, another postcolonial theorist, puts it,

> the nation-state presupposes (and helps to create) certain relations between authority and the people, between custom and law, knowledge and practice; presupposes certain forms of selfhood and community . . . it is not an empty container into which anything can be poured; it already has a content . . . [and thus] cannot serve as a vehicle for expressing those aspirations which do not already accord with or 'fit' the frame of nation, state and modernity; and indeed, it may ill-serve as the vehicle for recovering and expressing what is autochthonous, rather than Western and derivative, about a political community and culture.[40]

Conclusion: The impact of postcolonialism

Subaltern Studies was to have an important effect on the world of scholarship, including on studies of nationalism. What began as an intervention into Indian history became, especially following the publication of a selection of essays from the first five volumes in the United States in 1988, 'hugely influential in the US academy'.[41] Its impact extended far beyond Indian specialists, and was especially influential in Latin American Studies, where, inspired by the Indian group, in 1993 a group of scholars of Latin America founded 'a similar project dedicated to studying the subaltern in Latin America',[42] and Florencia Mallon offered a new reading of popular nationalism in Peru and Mexico in that spirit.[43] Some other scholars of Latin America insisted that the specificities of Latin America and of the colonial-modern could not be attended to within the framework of postcolonialism: Sara Castro-Klaren writes, 'the inception point of the modern/colonial as a world system must be set back to the time of the Spanish conquest of Amerindian societies' and not, as postcolonialism wrongly assumes, to the Enlightenment and the eighteenth- and nineteenth-century colonial conquest of Asia and Africa.[44] Decolonial theory, as it has come to be known, has been a major current in scholarship on Latin America, drawing upon some of the same anti-Eurocentric critical energies as postcolonial theory, but distinguishing itself from it.[45]

Postcolonial theory has not made great impact in scholarship on China or Japan, though Prasenjit Duara's *Rescuing History from the Nation: Questioning Narratives of Modern China*, which challenges the reduction of history to a biography of the nation state, is an important exception.[46] In African studies postcolonial theory has had a significant impact upon studies of contemporary Africa, rather than studies of decolonization and nationalism. This includes the important work of John and Jean Comaroff, who have argued that contemporary Africa and the postcolony should not be seen as lagging 'behind' the West, but rather as prefiguring the future of the West: 'Contrary to the received Euromodernist narrative of the last two centuries – which has the global south tracking behind the curve of Universal History, always in deficit, always playing catch-up – there is good reason to think the opposite: that, given the unpredictable, under-determined dialectic of capitalism-and-modernity in the here and now, it is the south that often is the first to feel the effects of world-historical forces . . . thus to prefigure the future of the global north.'[47]

As far as histories of nationalism go, the impact of *Subaltern Studies*, and perhaps of postcolonialism more generally, is now less evident than it once was. Writings on anti-colonial nationalism in the 2000s do not reprise the themes that once dominated debates on Indian nationalism in the 1980s and 1990s. However, it is a measure of the impact of *Subaltern Studies* and postcolonialism that certain themes and analyses, once relatively novel, now exert influence well beyond the ranks of avowedly postcolonial scholars. Three such analyses may be singled out.

First, the study of nationalism is today much less likely to search for 'underlying' economic and social causes of nationalism, thus treating nationalist ideas and discourse as secondary. This is the outcome of many intellectual influences, but postcolonialism has been one of these influences. Second, and perhaps most important of all, the 'difference' of the non-Western world, including of its nationalism, is now more widely acknowledged and explored. It is true, of course, that the non-West has for a very long time – at least since the beginnings of the colonial era – been regarded as different. But the 'difference' postcolonial scholarship has drawn attention to is not an essentialist, ontological and in essence racist difference – 'East is East and West is West, and never the twain shall meet.' And nor is it the 'difference' recognized by stagist theories of historical development, according to which the non-Western world is at an earlier and lesser stage of 'modernization' and Enlightenment. For a long time this modernist view dominated historiography,[48] and writing the history of the non-West was a search for its 'lacks' and its shortcomings, and descriptions of how far it had proceeded in its 'transition' to where the West had already arrived, all this in keeping with the premise that what had first happened in the West would eventually reshape the Rest. There seemed to be two choices – to regard the non-West as 'ontologically' different (and lesser) or to regard it as in principle similar, but historically 'behind' the West, needing to 'catch up'.

One of the contributions of postcolonial theory has been to suggest that these two unpalatable choices may not exhaust our intellectual options. Postcolonial scholarship has sought to show that the non-West is not different because it is 'not yet' modern and fully rational, but that the globalization of capital and modernity has not effaced difference, and that what we have taken to be Reason is but a historically and culturally specific way of conceiving of, understanding and inhabiting the world, rather than the 'correct' way finally discovered. The spread of capitalism, for which colonialism was one of the main mechanisms, did indeed transform the non-Western world in many ways: but forms of thinking, living and conceiving of collective life that do not accord with Western modernity have not always been consigned to the dustbin of history. It is necessary, then, to study the non-West not as an earlier form of what the West was, nor as something 'on its way' to becoming like the West, but rather as something that embodies ways of life and thought that are part of the modern but without necessarily being like the Western forms of modernity. This includes anti-colonial nationalisms, which successfully challenged the more obvious and racist forms of regarding and treating non-Western peoples as lesser versions of the West, but did so without fully emancipating themselves from the epistemic and moral assumptions of Western modernity.

Third and finally, if there are important ways in which non-Western countries may be 'different' from the West, and if furthermore what we take to be Reason is not the truth discovered, but a culturally and historically situated way of 'knowing', then it would seem to follow that the analytic categories through which we seek to understand the non-Western world may not always be adequate to their object. A great deal of the more recent postcolonial theorizing has been concerned with exploring this possibility – for instance, not just with asking why the non-West seems to have peculiar and even dysfunctional forms of 'civil society', and seems to lack individuals who seek to optimize their self-interest, but going further to ask whether these categories of analysis are helpful at all in understanding non-Western societies. One of the most important such recent works is by Dipesh Chakrabarty, a member of the Subaltern Studies group, who seeks to 'explore the capacities and limitations of certain European social and political categories in conceptualizing political modernity in the context of European life-worlds',[49] concluding that many of the central categories of the human sciences arise out of a European history and experience, and cannot always be generalized and applied to non-European historical contexts. Achille Mbembe has argued similarly: 'by defining itself both as an accurate portrayal of Western modernity – that is, by starting from conventions that are purely local- and as universal grammar, social theory has condemned itself always to make generalizations from idioms of a provincialism . . . [thus for social theory] it proves extremely difficult to understand non-Western objects'.[50] Such questioning has extended to the discipline of history itself – some recent works have asked, given that modern historiography is a Western product, whether it is adequate and useful as a way of understanding Indian pasts.[51] In this regard, postcolonial theorizing has come full circle. What began as an attempt to write history differently has become, in part, a critical interrogation of historiography.

Notes

1   See also Leela Gandhi, *Postcolonial Theory: A Critical Introduction* (Edinburgh, 1998); Robert J. C. Young, *Postcolonialism: An Historical Introduction* (Hoboken, 2016) and Robert J. C. Young, *Postcolonialism: A Very Short Introduction* (Oxford, 2003); Ania Loomba, *Colonialism/ Postcolonialism*, 3rd edn (London/New York, 2015).
2   See chapter by Elgenius.
3   Edward Said, *Orientalism* (London, 2003 [1978]), p. 2.
4   Ibid., p. 3.
5   Ibid.
6   Ranajit Guha, 'On Some Aspects of the Historiography of Colonial India', in Ranajit Guha (ed.), *Subaltern Studies I* (Delhi, 1982), pp. 1–8.
7   See for instance Anil Seal, *The Emergence of Indian Nationalism: Competition and Collaboration in the Later Nineteenth Century* (Cambridge, 1968) and John Gallagher, Gordon Johnson and Anil Seal (eds), *Locality, Province and Nation: Essays on Indian Politics 1870 to 1940* (Cambridge, 1973).
8   Ranajit Guha, *Elementary Aspects of Peasant Insurgency in Colonial India* (Delhi, 1983), p. 334.
9   See also chapter by Hroch.
10 These included M. N. Roy and R. P. Dutt – see Sanjay Seth, *Marxist Theory and Nationalist Politics: The Case of Colonial India* (New Delhi, 1995).
11 Ranajit Guha, 'The Prose of Counter-Insurgency', in Ranajit Guha (ed.), *Subaltern Studies II* (Delhi, 1983), quotes from pp. 33–8.
12 Ranajit Guha, 'Introduction', in Ranajit Guha (ed.), *A Subaltern Studies Reader, 1986–1995* (Minneapolis, 1997), p. xviii.
13 Dipesh Chakrabarty, 'A Small History of Subaltern Studies', in Dipesh Chakrabarty, *Habitations of Modernity: Essays in the Wake of Subaltern Studies* (Chicago, 2002), p. 13.
14 Chakrabarty, 'A Small History of Subaltern Studies', p. 13.
15 See Rosalind O'Hanlon, 'Recovering the Subject: Subaltern Studies and Histories of Resistance in Colonial South Asia' [first published in *Modern Asian Studies* in 1988], reproduced in Vinayak Chaturvedi (ed.), *Mapping Subaltern Studies and the Postcolonial* (London, 2000), pp. 84–5.
16 Ibid., p. 81.
17 Gayatri Chakravorty Spivak, 'Subaltern Studies: Deconstructing Historiography', in Guha (ed.), *Subaltern Studies IV* (Delhi, 1985), p. 337.
18 Ibid., p. 338.

19 Ibid., p. 341.

20 Ibid.

21 Ibid., p. 340. See also Spivak, 'Can the Subaltern Speak?', in Cary Nelson and Lawrence Grossberg (eds), *Marxism and the Interpretation of Culture* (Urbana and Chicago, 1988).

22 On this see Sanjay Seth, 'Revolution and History: Maoism and Subaltern Studies', *Storia della Storiografia* 62:2 (2012), 131–49.

23 Sumit Sarkar, 'The Decline of the Subaltern in Subaltern Studies', in Sumit Sarkar (ed.), *Writing Social History* (New Delhi, 1997).

24 Partha Chatterjee, *Nationalist Thought and the Colonial World: A Derivative Discourse?* (Delhi, 1986), p. 42.

25 Thomas Kuhn, *The Structure of Scientific Revolutions*, 2nd enlarged edn (Chicago, 1962).

26 This point is developed in greater detail in Sanjay Seth, 'Rewriting Histories of Nationalism: The Politics of "Moderate Nationalism" in India, 1870–1905', *The American Historical Review* 104:1 (February 1999), 95–7.

27 Chatterjee, *Nationalist Thought and the Colonial World*, p. 11.

28 See John Plamenatz, 'Two Types of Nationalism', in Eugene Kamenka (ed.), *Nationalism: The Nature and Evolution of an Idea* (London: Edward Arnold, 1976); Elie Kedourie, *Nationalism* (London: Hutchinson, 1960); and Tom Nairn, 'The Modern Janus', in Tom Nairn (ed.), *The Break-Up of Britain*, 2nd expanded edn (London, 1981), pp. 329–63.

29 Chatterjee, *Nationalist Thought and the Colonial World*, p. 11.

30 Ibid., pp. 38, 39.

31 Partha Chatterjee, *The Nation and its Fragments: Colonial and Postcolonial Histories* (Princeton, 1993), p. 5.

32 Chatterjee, *The Nation and Its Fragments*, p. 6.

33 Ibid.

34 Lajpat Rai, *The Problem of National Education in India* (London, 1920), p. 75.

35 Beth Baron, *Egypt as a Woman: Nationalism, Gender and Politics* (Berkeley, 2005); Deniz Kandiyoti (ed.), *Gendering the Middle East: Alternative Perspectives* (New York, 1996); Lila Abu-Lughod (ed.), *Remaking Women: Feminism and Modernity in the Middle East* (Princeton, 1998); Margot Badran, *Feminists, Islam and Nation: Gender and the Making of Modern Egypt* (Princeton, 1995).

36 Joan Judge, *The Precious Raft of History: The Past, the West, and the Woman Question in China* (Stanford, 2008); Christina Gilmartin, *Engendering the Chinese Revolution* (Berkeley, 1995); Gail Hershatter, *Women in China's Long Twentieth Century* (Berkeley, 2007); Mara Patessio, *Women and Public Life in Early Meiji Japan: The Development of the Feminist Movement* (Ann Arbor, 2011); Andrea Germer, Vera Mackie and Ulricke Wohr (eds), *Gender, Nation and State in Modern Japan* (London/New York, 2014).

37 Kumkum Sangari and Sudesh Vaid (eds), *Recasting Women* (New Brunswick, 1990); Mrinalini Sinha, *Specters of Mother India: The Global Restructuring of an Empire* (Durham, 2007); Sumit Sarkar and Tanika Sarkar (eds), *Women and Social Reform in Modern India: A Reader* (Bloomington, 2008); Tanika Sarkar, *Hindu Wife, Hindu Nation* (Bloomington, 2001).

38 Including Deniz Kandiyoti, 'Identity and Its Discontents: Women and the Nation', in Patrick Williams and Laura Chrisman (eds), *Colonial Discourse*

and Postcolonial Theory: A Reader (New York, 1994); Antoinette Burton (ed.), *Gender, Sexuality and Colonial Modernities* (New Brunswick, 1999); and Sanjay Seth, 'Nationalism, Modernity, and the "Woman Question" in India and China', *Journal of Asian Studies* 72:2 (May 2013), 273–97.

39 Chatterjee, *The Nation and Its Fragments: Colonial and Postcolonial Histories*, p. 11.

40 Sanjay Seth, 'A "Postcolonial World"?', in Greg Fry and Jacinta O'Hagan (eds), *Contending Images of World Politics* (London, 2000), p. 221.

41 Vinayak Chaturvedi, 'Introduction', in Vinayak Chaturvedi (ed.), *Mapping Subaltern Studies and the Postcolonial*, p. xii; *Selected Subaltern Studies*, edited by Ranajit Guha and Gayatri Chakravorty Spivak (Oxford, 1988); Ranajit Guha (ed.), *A Subaltern Studies Reader: 1986–1995* (Minneapolis, 1997).

42 'Founding Statement: Latin American Subaltern Studies Group', *boundary 2* 20:3 (1993). See also *Dispositio*, special issue on 'Subaltern Studies in the Americas' 19:46 (1994); F. E. Mallon, 'The Promise and Dilemma of Subaltern Studies: Perspectives from Latin American History', *The American Historical Review* 99:5 (December 1994), 1491–515; and Ileana Rodriguez (ed.), *The Latin American Subaltern Studies Reader* (Durham, 2001).

43 Florencia E. Mallon, *Peasant and Nation: The Making of Postcolonial Mexico and Peru* (Berkeley, 1995).

44 Sara Castro-Klaren, 'Posting Letters: Writing in the Andes and the Paradoxes of the Postcolonial Debate', in Mabel Morana, Enrique Dussel and Carlos Jauregui (eds), *Coloniality at Large: Latin America and the Postcolonial Debate* (Durham, 2008).

45 The volume cited in the preceding footnote collects some of the important writings of decolonial theorists. See also Walter D. Mignolo, *The Darker Side of the Renaissance: Literacy, Territoriality, and Colonization*, 2nd edn (Ann Arbor, 2003) and *Local Histories/Global Designs: Coloniality, Subaltern Knowledges, and Border Thinking* (Princeton, 2000).

46 Prasenjit Duara, *Rescuing History from the Nation: Questioning Narratives of Modern China* (Chicago, 1995), chapter 7. See also Sanjay Seth, 'Nationalism, Modernity, and the "Woman Question"', pp. 288–93.

47 Jean Comaroff and John L. Comaroff, *Theory from the South: Or, How Euro-America Is Evolving toward Africa* (Boulder and London, 2012), p. 12; Jean Comaroff and John L. Comaroff (eds), *Law and Disorder in the Postcolony* (Chicago, 2006) and Achille Mbembe, *On the Postcolony* (Berkeley, 2001). See also Pal Ahluwalia, *Out of Africa: Post-structuralism's Colonial Roots* (London/New York, 2010).

48 See the chapter by Breuilly.

49 Dipesh Chakrabarty, *Provincializing Europe: Postcolonial Thought and Historical Difference* (Princeton, 2000), p. 20. See also Sanjay Seth, *Subject Lessons: The Western Education of Colonial India* (Durham, 2007).

50 Mbembe, *On the Postcolony*, p. 11.

51 See for instance Dipesh Chakrabarty, 'Minority Histories, Subaltern Pasts', *Postcolonial Studies* 1:1 (1998); and Sanjay Seth, 'Reason or Reasoning?: Clio or Siva', *Social Text* 78 (Spring 2004); and the special issue of *Postcolonial Studies* on 'Historiography and non-Western Pasts', 11:2 (June 2008).

Further reading

Chakrabarty, Dipesh, *Habitations of Modernity: Essays in the Wake of Subaltern Studies*. Chicago: University of Chicago Press, 2002.

Chakrabarty, Dipesh, *Provincializing Europe: Postcolonial Thought and Historical Difference*. Princeton: Princeton University Press, 2000.

Chatterjee, Partha, *Nationalist Thought and the Colonial World: A Derivative Discourse?* Delhi: Oxford University Press, 1986.

Chatterjee, Partha, *The Nation and Its Fragments: Colonial and Postcolonial Histories*. Princeton: Princeton University Press, 1993.

Chaturvedi, Vinayak (ed.), *Mapping Subaltern Studies and the Postcolonial*. London: Verso, 2000.

Gandhi, Leela, *Postcolonial Theory: A Critical Introduction*. Edinburgh: Edinburgh University Press, 1998.

Majumdar, Rochana, *Writing Postcolonial History*. London: Bloomsbury Academic, 2010.

Said, Edward, *Orientalism*, 1978. London: Penguin, 2003.

Young, Robert J. C., *Postcolonialism: An Historical Introduction*. Chichester & Malden: Wiley-Blackwell, 2016.

10

Gender approaches to the history of nationalism

Elizabeth Vlossak

Introduction

The woodcut of Guido Schmitt's 1890 painting (see Figure 10.1), which was mass-produced in Germany, is an allegorical depiction of the forging of the German nation. Otto von Bismarck, the 'Iron Chancellor' and the father of unification, is portrayed as a blacksmith. Sleeves rolled up, clad in a leather apron and standing at his anvil, he holds his hammer in his right hand, and from his left passes a newly forged sword to Germania, the embodiment of the German nation, who stands above him on her pedestal of stone. At first glance, this image may not seem especially unusual or significant. Nations have generally been depicted as women, just as the ancient Greeks and Romans relied on the female form to represent abstract concepts such as justice and liberty. Germania was commonly used to depict the nation. What makes Schmitt's painting particularly interesting, however, is that the feminine, largely passive Germania stands in direct contrast to the masculine, active Bismarck. Despite her helmet and armour, Germania, pale and blond, appears far too soft, gentle and modest to be a mighty warrior. Bismarck, on the other hand, is sweaty, steely-eyed and determined. Germania may represent the nation, but, as a woman, she is ornamentation, an abstraction, an idea. Bismarck instead is a real, flesh-and-blood man, embodying dynamism, power and agency. These rather explicit differences between Germania and Bismarck are telling: they reveal that traditional gender ideals played an instrumental role not only in how the German

FIGURE 10.1 The Blacksmith of German Unity – *Bismarck handing Germania the sword 'Unitas'. Woodcut, c.1895, after painting, 1890, by Guido Schmitt (1834–1922).*

Photo credit: akg-images

nation was understood and imagined, but also that gender affected how the nation was created, maintained, and experienced.

Not all historians look at this image and draw the same conclusions. My interpretation of Schmitt's image uses gender as a category of analysis, an approach that emerged in the late 1980s and continues to be employed by scholars in numerous disciplines, including sociology, literary criticism, international relations, as well as history. As a contested concept, gender has been defined in many different ways. We could group these definitions into three main categories. The first can be called 'biological essentialism', according to which gender is simply an extension of unchanging biological realities. The second, and arguably most widely adopted approach, distinguishes between sex and gender: sex is biological and typically unchanging, while gender is socially and culturally constructed. As the existentialist philosopher Simone de Beauvoir stated in 1949, 'one is not born, but rather becomes a woman'.[1] There is nonetheless variation within this category regarding the extent to which gender is consciously or unconsciously 'performed'. While the philosopher and gender theorist Judith Butler is most well-known for her notion of the 'performativity' of gender, she actually supports the third, and perhaps most controversial definition of gender.[2] Without denying that biology exists, it argues that the *category* of sex is no less socially constructed than gender practices. Practically speaking, we cannot think of the sex/gender relation without the (socially constructed) category of sex. In doing so, however, the popular sex/gender distinction made by the second approach breaks down because the dualism of biology/social construction (or nature/nurture) no longer holds.

It was Joan Scott, in her 1986 article in the *American Historical Review*, who first called on historians to focus their attention on gender, which she defined as 'a constitutive element of social relationships based on perceived differences between the sexes', as well as 'a primary way of signifying relationships of power'.[3] Scott was in part responding to the current state of women's history, a field that had emerged in the late 1960s and early 1970s, and which, according to some, had remained 'ghettoized'. Women's history, which had grown out of social history and second-wave feminism, sought to uncover the past of the 'second sex' and write women back into textbooks. By focusing on the 'forgotten history' of women, it also tended to highlight women's oppression and their attempts to fight for equality. Yet it had become clear to some historians that women's experiences could not be properly understood if they were not studied alongside those of men.[4] French historian Michelle Perrot demanded that we 'change the direction of historical attention by posing the question of the relationship between the sexes as central'.[5] But another shortcoming of women's history was that it took for granted the binary of 'man' and 'woman' without questioning how sexual differences were themselves rooted in historical processes and changing notions of gender.[6] Feminist scholars could no longer regard gender as a fixed identity, but rather as created for specific purposes at particular historical moments.

Because of its genesis and its association with the feminist movement, gender history is often understood as synonymous with women's history. It is true that many studies that take a gender approach have focused primarily on women's roles and experiences, and how power structures rooted in gender expectations affected them specifically. But just as femininity is bound by time and culture, so too is masculinity. Historians Michael Roper and John Tosh in their work on nineteenth-century British masculinity argued that we must distinguish between 'imagined and lived masculine identities'.[7]

Within the gender order, the construction of a 'hegemonic masculinity' that maintained patriarchy led to a hierarchy in which some men were considered more 'manly' than others, thus affecting their relationship to each other and to power.[8] Gender identity was in fact contingent on other factors, most notably class, race, ethnicity and religion, and gender historians have recognized the importance of including these in their studies.[9]

By the early 1990s, the lens of gender was being used to study nations and nationalism. At the time, the collapse of the Soviet Union, the resurgence of racial nationalism, the horrors of ethnic cleansing in the former Yugoslavia and Rwanda, as well as the growing field of postcolonial studies had led to renewed academic interest in nationalism, especially how it affected women differently to men.[10] But the theories of nations and nationalism and methodological frameworks that had recently emerged – in particular post-structuralism and the linguistic turn – were also of crucial importance: as German historian Karen Hagemann, a pioneer in the field who remains one of its leading experts, explained, gender and nation have to be understood and studied in relation to one another since both are sociocultural constructions.[11] Gender was, and in many ways continues to be understood by governments and societies as an 'unchallenged system of cultural knowledge and cultural representations' which not only informed the creation of national symbols, myths and rituals, but also affected individuals' relationship to national movements and the nation state. Ultimately, gender was central in shaping national identity: because men and women had different roles to play as members of the nation, their gender identity directly affected their understanding of and sense of belonging within the national community. From the conception of the nation to the lived experiences of those who constitute it, gender is a pervasive feature of life which hierarchically structures and organizes the nation. Moreover, as Anne McClintock argues, nationalism is itself 'constituted from the very beginning as a gendered discourse, and cannot be understood without a theory of gender'.[12]

Hagemann's own research trajectory reflects both the broader shift from women's to gender history, as well as the impact that gender approaches have made to the study of nations and nationalism. Her early work focused on women workers in Weimar Germany. But through her studies of working-class gender relations, Hagemann began to theorize more explicitly about the relationship between gender and nation, eventually shifting her attention to Prussia's early nineteenth century and the birth of modern German nationalism, and in particular on the relationship between gender, nation and war. As we will see in this chapter, gender approaches like Hagemann's have challenged and redefined our understanding of the history of nationalism. Through nation-specific case studies as well as comparative, transnational and 'transversal' research, historians have demonstrated how citizenship and state formation, the 'invention' of traditions, myths and symbols, the experience of war, imperialism and postcolonial struggles, as well as memory and the writing of national histories have all been shaped by gender order.[13] Moreover, taking a gender approach to the study of nationalism has also highlighted some of the shortcomings of many theories of nationalism, most of which fail to recognize that most nationalist projects were rooted in gender assumptions and expectations, thus affecting men and women differently. As we shall see, gender roles over time and cultures were certainly fluid, but nations and nationalisms were never gender-neutral.

State, citizenship and national belonging

One of the first works to explore the relationship between nationalism and gender was not a feminist historian at all, but the German-American historian George Mosse. In his groundbreaking 1985 work on nationalism and sexuality, Mosse noted that the emergence of normative bourgeois social values, aesthetics, sexual mores and gender distinctions not only paralleled the rise of European nation states but was also the direct result of nationalist movements.[14] Mosse later argued that positive middle-class stereotypes of ideal masculinity and femininity established a set of rules and codes of conduct governing men's and women's morality and behaviour, which would in turn maintain order and national cohesion.[15] Historians of France and Germany, in particular, began to explore how men, as soldiers and citizens, were expected to embody the nation by exhibiting the qualities of strength, discipline, order and progress.[16] They argued that masculinity also defined itself against stereotypes, including femininity, which in turn affected women's prescribed roles within the nation. As mothers and wives, women were expected to be passive, submissive and nurturing, as well as provide a link to traditions and the past. Ultimately, the nation was to be understood as a family, with men engaging in public life, and women restricted to the private sphere. Nationalist discourse may have centred itself on an ideal of masculinity, but it certainly did not completely ignore the existence of women, and in fact placed great importance on the maintenance of a feminine ideal. As a result, men and women had very specific roles to play in the nation: politics would be the preserve of men, while women were tied to culture. But despite the polarization of gender roles and expectations, how and to what extent were these distinctions actually maintained?

Although excluded from the public domain of formal politics, women were nonetheless political beings, and feminist scholars have largely dismantled the public/private binary that became so entrenched in political discourse.[17] Moreover, they have demonstrated that while women may not have been expected to fulfil the same roles and have the same responsibilities as men within the national community, this did not mean that women were or even felt excluded from nationalist programmes. Sociologists Nira Yuval-Davis and Floya Anthias helped shatter the long-held perception that women's involvement in the nationalist project was restricted to the private sphere, demonstrating instead that the relationship between woman and nation is complex. Yuval-Davis and Anthias list women as biological reproducers of members of the nation, as reproducers of national boundaries, as reproducers and transmitters of national culture, as symbols of national differences and as active participants in national struggles.[18] Women's roles were both passive *and* active, and were of central importance in the construction, maintenance and reproduction of nations and national identity. This list continues to be a useful starting point for historians interested in taking a gender approach to the study of nationalism, although it has been critiqued. Sylvia Walby, for example, has argued that it fails to acknowledge the gendered division of labour, and does not emphasize the fact that 'conflict, and the maintenance of boundaries, between ethnic/national groups is also a conflict between different forms of social hierarchies, not only different cultures'.[19] Gender historians have since demonstrated that not all women (or men) played the same role within the nation, nor did they all internalize their understanding of the nation in the same way or at the same time, since their own identities were affected by class, religion, language and ethnicity.

What Mosse and others have demonstrated is that the concept and rhetoric of citizenship are themselves gendered. In the nineteenth century, citizenship was associated with qualities and characteristics seen as intrinsically masculine (strength, honour, discipline, reason), and this remains the case in many parts of the world today.[20] This was in large part due to the fact that citizenship was associated with war and military service, from which women have traditionally been excluded.[21] Yet historically women have engaged in nationalist struggles and consequently expected certain rights and protections from the state in exchange for their loyalty. Linda Colley has shown that British women became increasingly involved in civic life during the Napoleonic Wars. But women's activism prompted widespread anxiety, and the traditional social order was consequently further entrenched. As Colley observes, 'if British women were being urged to remain at home more stridently in this period than ever before, it was largely because so many of them were finding an increasing amount to do outside the home'.[22] Women saw their legal, political and civic rights severely limited, although through their prescribed private roles as mothers and wives they paradoxically became public heroines of domestic virtue and guardians of the nation's morality. Hagemann reveals a similar development at the same time in Prussia which had a profound impact on the very nature of German nationalism.[23] Meanwhile in France, Napoleon's *Code Civil* prevented French women from becoming full citizens despite (or, rather, in response to) their participation in political life during the revolution.

Throughout the Western world, women were denied, among other things, the right to vote and hold public office. If a woman married a foreigner, she would automatically take the nationality of her husband and, despite the fact that women were seen as transmitters of national culture, she could not confer her nationality on her children. This practice continued in many countries long after women had been enfranchised.[24] Studies of more recent historical developments have demonstrated how the welfare state, a cornerstone of post-war nationhood, was itself constructed based on concepts of traditional gender roles. What we see, then, is that gender affects the 'nationalization of the masses' and that this process happens at different times for men and women, in what has been termed 'rounds of restructuring'.[25]

Yet nationalism could also provide women with the opportunity to disrupt gender order. Some nationalist movements provided women with a platform on which to demand full citizenship, and most notably suffrage. For example, between 1909 and 1921 feminists were active in the Polish independence movement since 'they perceived the reconstructed Polish state as a vehicle for improving the conditions of women'.[26] Some scholars have argued that feminism and nationalism cannot coexist because they are ideologically incompatible.[27] However, European feminists often relied on nationalist rhetoric and demanded rights on the basis that it was for the good of the nation.[28] If we move beyond Europe, we see numerous examples of women who became involved in national liberation and self-determination movements as a means of also fighting for sexual emancipation.[29] In India, Hindu and Muslim women played a vital part in the struggle for independence, although they were unable to and actively prevented from capitalizing on this political space after independence had been achieved.[30]

It is indeed in the field of postcolonial studies and the history of empire that gender approaches to the history of nationalism have yielded the richest and most diverse literature.[31] Imperialism had a profound impact on national identity formation, both in the metropole and in the colonial territories themselves.[32] European men and women actively supported their nation's imperialist campaigns and internalized their sense of nationhood in relation to their perception of the colonial 'other'. But imperial identities were also informed by gender. Prior to the First World War, German women created and funded imperial societies, and even sought employment in the colonies as a means of demonstrating their own racial superiority by civilizing the 'natives' through domesticity.[33] The empire, as an integral part of the nation, thus offered women of all classes and colonizing nations an opportunity to 'cast their gaze more broadly', even if women tended to restrict their roles to those of mother and housewife. British feminists concerned themselves with the condition of women in Indian society, focusing their attention on issues such as child marriage. On the one hand, feminists viewed Hindu women's inferior status as a sign that India was uncivilized. But as Antoinette Burton has revealed, they also saw the relatively high legal status of Indian Muslim women as a beacon of hope, and a means through which to improve their own legal rights when it came to property ownership, for example.[34]

Nationalist discourse was gendered, and nations perceived as being feminine or 'less masculine' tended to be denigrated, both beyond and within their own borders. The British described Indian men, and in particular the

Bengalis, as effeminate and therefore unfit for self-rule.[35] The discourse of imperialism and conquest also relied on gendered language: Africa, as a continent that needed to be penetrated, was thus feminized, and many orientalist tropes grew out of European perceptions of an exotic femininity. Mrinali Sinha argues that the emerging dynamics between colonial and nationalist politics 'is best captured in the logic of colonial masculinity'.[36] As Anne McClintock explored in her seminal work, *Imperial Leather*, gender discourse intersected with race (as well as with class), informing perceptions of the other as well as restricting both women's and men's access to citizenship.[37] But political theorist Partha Chatterjee has called attention to the fact that Indian nationalism, because it was seen as spiritual and 'internal' rather than material and 'external' like British nationalism, was coded as being feminine not only by the British but by early Indian nationalist thinkers too.[38] Thus Indian nationalists embraced the 'femininity' of their own nationalism as a means of contrasting it to the foreign, European version.

Accusing nations of being feminine, as the British for example did against the French during the Napoleonic Wars,[39] could help strengthen national belonging, especially during times of conflict, instability and change. Political leaders would question their rivals' manhood,[40] thereby appealing to culturally constructed notions of masculine legitimacy and superiority to stir up and mobilize public opinion. But hegemonic masculinity and the masculine discourse of citizenship also excluded whole categories of men.[41] This could be based on race, class, ethnicity, sexuality and even political allegiance. Simply having a male body did not necessarily guarantee rights and privileges. Moreover, men often had to earn their citizenship by proving their manliness. While we may assume that the masculine ideal centred on men's military service, it could also include gainful employment and fatherhood. Indeed, just as gender historians have challenged assumptions that women's roles in the nation were restricted to the private sphere, so too have they questioned the degree to which middle-class masculinity was predicated solely on men's public roles. By placing such importance on domestic life, nationalists in fact politicized the home. The private was public. Thus women's and men's roles in the nation could not simply be described as either cultural or political, just as we cannot describe nationalism as either purely ethnic or civic.

Symbols, myths and traditions

The gendering of nations and nationalism is most obvious when we look at national symbols. Nations have traditionally been depicted as women, as we have already seen. Symbols, as well as myths and traditions were part of a new 'nationalist aesthetics' crucial to the process of nationalizing the masses.[42] If the nation was an 'imagined community', then individuals required means through which to internalize their understanding of nationhood. National allegories gave the abstraction of the nation a more tangible existence. But if nationalists celebrated masculine strength and political agency, why was the nation itself usually depicted as a woman? Rather than take the allegories for granted, historians such as Marina Warner began to focus on their meaning, their construction, as well as their evolution over time.[43] Allegories that relied on the female form were not only shaped by gender stereotypes, but they in turn reinforced these stereotypes.

Some historians have pointed to the fact that female national allegories 'were usually pictured seated to indicate stability and passivity',[44] feminine qualities celebrated by bourgeois nationalists. These female forms thus reflected and ensured the subordination of women while strengthening masculine political agency.[45] Moreover, the prominent image of woman in nationalist aesthetics was not restricted to allegory but was in fact used in the construction of national identity itself.[46] The nation was not only symbolized by a woman's body, but citizens were also to imagine the nation as a woman.[47] National sentiment and loyalty were to mimic emotions felt for a mother, daughter, sister or lover.[48] But a closer look at national symbols reveals a much more complicated interaction between gender, iconography and national identity. Nations, as portrayed through the female form, were not static. Marianne, symbol of French republicanism, was depicted in many different ways in official paintings and sculptures, as well as in caricatures and political satire.[49] Republicans depicted her as a loving mother or a desirable mistress, while monarchists and socialists critical of the Republic cast her either as a sexually depraved whore or an old hag. The fact that she was a woman made her a potential object of love and affection, as well as an easy target for criticism. During the Second World War, Marianne was replaced by Joan of Arc as the embodiment of the French nation under Pétain's Vichy regime.[50] Anti-English and devoutly Catholic, Joan was nonetheless problematic since, as a childless warrior who had led an army, she did not necessarily reflect the virtues that the regime aimed to inculcate in young girls. The Joan of Vichy France, depicted in school textbooks as loving children and domestic chores, was thus carefully reinvented in order to adhere to and strengthen traditional gender roles while also remaining a potent symbol of French nationalism.

Gender historians have shown that female personifications of the nation acted as a 'meeting point between gender/normative roles and the processes of the state'.[51] While Britannia tended to be depicted as a weeping mother, a vulnerable virgin, an overbearing nanny or a warlike Athena, she was sometimes portrayed in the guise of a 'modern woman' struggling to be heard during debates about whether women should be granted the right to vote. Germania was used by political commentators and social critics in a similar fashion, and in some cases served as a tool to challenge the status quo. Yet by and large these depictions were primarily the product of male artists, architects and statesmen, and thus 'remained an instrument of masculine renderings of the nation'.[52] Women may have played powerful roles as symbols of the nation, but their actual power and status often remained limited.[53]

Women's symbolic role was not simply through artistic renderings of the nation. Women's actual bodies could take on national meaning, as they did in the twentieth-century Indian nationalist movement.[54] Egyptian nationalism, too, relied on women as 'symbols on which to rally male support'.[55] The nation was a family, and since family honour was contingent on female sexual purity, women's bodies needed to be protected in order to safeguard national honour. Although Safiya, the wife of Egyptian revolutionary and later Prime Minister Saad Zaghloul (1859–1927), became the metaphoric mother of the nation, she remained restricted to traditional gender roles that in many ways reaffirmed the patriarchal structure of Egyptian society.

Women's symbolism, both in national iconography and in real life, could be codified in the way she was dressed. As maintainers of tradition, women were often encouraged to wear traditional peasant clothes. These costumes were carefully constructed to provide both a link to the past, as well as to reflect the nationalist aims of the present,[56] in contrast to the modern, rational suit or military uniform worn by men. The political significance of what men and women wore was especially important in non-Western nations and former colonies. In Republican China, the new rulers wore uniforms to promote a more military model of the masculine citizen-soldier that would counter Western perceptions of Chinese men as weak and effeminate.[57] This in many ways was a continuation of earlier efforts by the late Qing government, which in 1907 had banned the traditional male hairstyle known as the queue. But the government had also banned the foot-binding of Chinese women based on the belief that raising the status of women through the rejection of outdated traditions would strengthen the nation.[58] In contrast, in the 1960s Indonesian president Suharto tried to proscribe Western trousers for men, while women were to wear an uncomfortable, impractical and highly stylized version of the traditional peasant dress.[59] The relationship between nation, citizenship and clothing could also shift over time. In colonial-era Philippines, men tended to wear American-style suits as a symbol of modernity, while women kept their traditional dress. However, upon achieving independence from the United States in 1946 men became the 'bearers and wearers of tradition' and donned the national outfits, which then became less frequently worn by women. Today, Philippine women involved in formal politics are more likely to wear the national dress, perhaps 'as a strategy to negotiate citizenship, while still proclaiming difference'.[60] Some scholars have drawn similar conclusions when exploring the role that the veil and other Muslim women's clothing have played in the construction of femininity and nationalism in Islamic countries as well as in the West.[61]

Although female historical figures such as Joan of Arc were also used at various moments in time, most national heroes or founders of the nation were men. The Germans built statues to Arminius, Bismarck and, after the

Great War, Hindenburg. But some nationalists sought to locate or even create male symbols of the nation, and Britain's John Bull, the United States' Uncle Sam and the German Michel became popular representations. In Mexico, the *charro*, or Mexican cowboy, functioned as a symbol of the Mexican nation, and the *gaucho* played a similar role in Argentina.

Symbols, myths and traditions were invented, but once created they did not remain static. Their meanings changed over time, constantly contested and re-contested, and refashioned often in gendered terms. Joane Nagel maintains that it is masculine interests, ideology and what she terms 'microcultures' that have dominated nationalist movements.[62] In some nations, the rites and rituals associated with the masculine microcultures of sport and drinking, for example, remain linked to national belonging. In Canada the corporate promotion of beer and ice hockey as the central tenets of Canadian identity has been criticized by those who see this advertising as perpetuating a conservative, outdated nationalism based on white, heteronormative masculinity.[63] Yet women, as mothers of the nation, were responsible for passing songs, stories, and folklore down to future generations. The traditions that helped forge and solidify national belonging could in fact be distinctly feminine: as Nancy Reagin has argued, the belief that German women were endowed with superior domestic skills created a national community of 'imagined *Hausfrauen*'.[64] Moreover, the nationalization of cuisine was largely done by middle-class housewives and female authors of cookbooks. Thus women, far from being absent from the nation-building project, were instrumental in developing the 'banal nationalism' that ultimately proved so crucial for nationalizing the masses.[65]

Sexuality and the reproduction of the nation

If the nation has been understood as a family in which men and women fulfil specific roles and responsibilities to maintain order and protect national honour, then it is not surprising that historians have demonstrated that modern nationalism has been 'concerned with sexual control and restraint from the start'.[66] Nation states needed sexuality to be regulated not only because it determined a nation's respectability and morality, but also because it marked others for exclusion from the national community and was the basis for reproduction of the national body. Sex was no longer a private matter, but instead subject to state intervention and public scrutiny.

The regulation of sexuality applied primarily to women, the biological and cultural reproducers of the nation. Nation states passed laws controlling women's bodies, and nationalism celebrated women who were 'good mothers' and vilified those who transgressed appropriate gender roles. The regulation of prostitution was in part a response to moral panic related to the stresses of modernity, as prostitutes became the embodiment of perceived decay, degeneracy and disease. To many they also presented a direct threat to the sanctity of the family, to middle-class respectability and by extension to the health and strength of the nation.[67] But controlling women's sexuality was also a means of protecting men's bodies. Men needed to remain healthy and virile, and their physical fitness was a sign of national strength. Contagious diseases acts were more about protecting soldiers from the ravages of venereal disease than they were about keeping women safe. 'Abnormal' sexuality, especially among men, was also seen as a direct threat to the nation. Homosexuality was criminalized throughout the Western World, including the German Reich. Paragraph 175 of the Criminal Code declared homosexuality illegal and punishable as an unnatural sexual act, in contrast to the comparatively liberal laws that had governed many German states prior to unification.[68] Crimes against respectability were crimes against the nation, as sexual immorality and perceived abnormal sexual practices were believed to lead to the degeneration of the nation.

Nationalist policies of population control were not all the same, but were instead influenced by what Nira Yuval-Davis has distinguished as three specific 'discourses of reproduction': the people-as-power discourse, the eugenics discourse and the Malthusian discourse.[69] Historians, sociologists and political scientists have explored how each has had a very specific effect on women's relationship to the nation, and how the consequences of the policies are also gendered. The people-as-power discourse is predicated on the belief that a nation's wealth and power rest on the size of its population which must therefore increase indefinitely. Women are encouraged to have as many children as possible and childless women are viewed as having failed in their national duty. The eugenics discourse focuses instead on quality, rather than quantity, with the nation state determining which women should reproduce, and which should not, usually along lines of race and class, but also physical and mental health. Nation states that subscribe to the Malthusian discourse restrict the growth of their population to a bare minimum. The most obvious example is China, where the one-child policy not only controlled women's fertility but led to a gender imbalance, as the preference for male children led to a rise in abortions and infanticides directed at female children.

But research into these reproduction policies reveals that nation states subscribed to different discourses at specific historical moments. Tensions rose when population policy came into direct conflict with nationalist discourse. During the First World War, for example, the mass rapes of French women by invading German soldiers prompted widespread debates about what to do with the 'children of the barbarian' that had been born out of these acts of violence.[70] Because of the symbolic role women's bodies play as boundaries and markers of national difference, these children could act as a shameful reminder that French men had failed to protect their women and, by extension, their nation. But suggestions that these children should be aborted or cast away were rejected by French pro-natalists who feared that France's population was in steep decline, especially in comparison to Germany's. They argued that these children, raised by patriotic French mothers, would become future French citizens and soldiers.

This was a far cry from the discourse of sexuality constructed in the nineteenth century by European politicians, poets, writers and musicians, which encouraged women to find a partner of the same nationality. A so-called 'endogamous' relationship would be characterized by fidelity, love and sexual pleasure.[71] Men, on the other hand, were allowed to engage in exogamy since it was suggested that patriotic men would be able to nationalize foreign women through sexual conquest. This national sexual double standard encouraged men to cross national boundaries, which would cement strategic national/sexual alliances, denationalize foreign women and restrict the sexuality of their 'own' women.

Endogamy was especially stressed in ethnic nations, none more so than Nazi Germany. Nazis were concerned with reproduction and their policies explicitly targeted women. However, there were two competing population control discourses at work. The Nazis did not uphold all women as child bearers, housewives and mothers. As Gisela Bock argued, the Nazis excluded many women from bearing and rearing children, using sterilization as their principal deterrent.[72] According to Bock, Nazi policies subjected German women to 'sexist racism' or 'racist sexism'. Claudia Koonz, however, countered that female consent and behaviour were in fact essential in legitimizing and strengthening the Nazi state.[73] German women enthusiastically voted for Hitler, joined Nazi organizations, saw themselves as racially superior, supported the war effort and were complicit in Nazi atrocities. Heated debates prompted by these two interpretations led to the so-called '*Historikerinnenstreit*' (women historians' dispute) which generated even more research on the relationship between gender, race and National Socialism. Nazi racial policies did focus to a great extent on women's reproductive role, but they were also directed at men and sought to control male sexuality, as the growing literature on the persecution of homosexuals during the Third Reich has revealed.

The emergence of what today is called the 'alt-right' reinforces the reality that women are never absent from ethno-nationalist projects, even when these groups threaten women's autonomy and reproductive rights amid fears of 'race suicide' and 'white genocide'. In 2016, up to 20 per cent of the American 'alt-right' were women.[74] Yet this is part of a much longer tradition, as white American women have supported white nationalist movements since the late nineteenth century. In her groundbreaking study of women in the Ku Klux Klan (KKK), historian Kathleen Blee revealed that KKK women's activities may have been less public than those of their male counterparts, but were nonetheless extensive and deadly.[75] Despite the male-oriented agendas of organized racism, women members have reconciled these with their own gendered self-interests.[76] But just like men, women's support for these groups was and continues to be driven in large part by 'aggrieved entitlement' and 'status threat' which they can feel themselves and on behalf of men who they think are being prevented from realizing the kind of lives they have come to expect.[77] Although rooted in misogyny and anti-feminism, like Nazism and other fascist movements, the 'alt-right' ultimately relies on the support of women in order for it to present itself as socially acceptable and less exclusionary.[78]

War, militarism and violence

Catherine Hall has argued that 'the masculinization of war and of citizenship are intimately connected, and the exclusion of women from the military has been a key aspect of their exclusion from citizenship'.[79] Women have traditionally not been involved in military conflict, which affects their relationship to the state, their role within the nation as well as the ways in which they internalize their own sense of national belonging. Specifically, feminist scholars have suggested that women are more willing to engage in local and supranational projects, and that certain boundaries other than national ones have more salience for women, such as region and religion.[80] These scholars often cite Virginia Woolf's adage from *Three Guineas* (1938) that 'as a woman, I have no country'. There are certainly many examples across time and space of women rejecting war, or engaging in cooperation in places of deadly national enmity.[81] Nonetheless, gender historians have also shown that not all women have a 'natural' affinity to internationalism and pacifism, just as men are not all warmongers.

War could offer women new opportunities to transgress traditional gender roles, consequently allowing them to develop a new relationship to the nation. This could include performing 'men's work' on the home front while the male population was away fighting, as well as being actively engaged in violent conflict. During the Second World War, women throughout Nazi-occupied Europe joined resistance and partisan movements, and some even found themselves in leadership positions. They engaged in acts of sabotage and armed confrontations. Women's expected roles as mothers, wives and caregivers often limited their opportunities to participate fully in resistance activities, prompting them to take on responsibilities that could be incorporated into their domestic duties. This included holding meetings in their homes, providing food and lodging to escaped prisoners or, like Czech women, maintaining national identity through cooking traditional dishes.[82]

But historians have also shown that as women took on new types of work in wartime so, too, did men. Ultimately, men's contribution to the nation continued to be valued more highly than women's. Historians Margaret and Patrice Higonnet have described this relationship between war and gender as a 'double helix'.[83] Wartime roles, however much they changed, remained fixed within the existing gender framework, something we see perhaps most explicitly in the fact that women's wartime roles are rarely celebrated in peacetime, while the sacrifices of men tend to be those that are officially commemorated.[84] What is more, many of the changes women did experience in times of war were short-lived, as gender relations tended to revert back to the antebellum status quo as a means of re-establishing post-war normality. Such was the case not only in European nations after the two world wars, but in many former colonies after they had achieved independence.

Men and women who engaged in armed conflict often relied on certain gender assumptions, using them to their advantage. The film *The Battle of Algiers* (1966) famously depicts Algerian women helping the FLN move weapons and bombs in their prams, and flirting with French soldiers to clear checkpoints unhindered.[85] Gender stereotypes afforded women a degree of mobility that men did not have. The Mau Mau guerrillas would enlist attractive young women to seduce British soldiers at nightclubs. The women would get the soldiers drunk, take them back to their lodgings or even the soldiers' barracks and steal weapons and ammunition when the soldier had fallen asleep or was unconscious.[86] Women could be called on to use their sexuality to help defeat the enemy. But during times of war, women have often been the victims of sexual violence.[87] Scholars from a variety of disciplines have studied how rape is used by armies as a weapon of psychological deterrence.[88] Rape seeks to emasculate the enemy by dishonouring its women and by blurring national and racial borders. But rape can also be used to strengthen soldiers' *esprit de corps* and thus acts as a form of male bonding.[89]

Wartime propaganda employed imagery that tapped into fears of mass rapes and national humiliation. Men were called on to protect their women and their nation. Those who did not enlist were publically shamed, and their manliness was called into question. During the First World War, British women singled out young men not dressed in uniform by handing them a white feather, the symbol of cowardice.[90] Conscientious objectors were accused of shirking their duty, and in some cases imprisoned. The British press ridiculed them, depicting them as small and slight, weak-kneed and limp-wristed. The stereotype of the conscientious objector resembled that of the homosexual. Refusing to fight was a sign of effeminacy or sexual abnormality, neither of which were acceptable within military ranks. On the battlefield, men were expected to embody the manly qualities of the nation. The crime of desertion was most severely punished not just because it was an act of treason, but because it was dishonourable, cowardly and a sign of moral weakness.

Historians have nonetheless shown that war destabilizes masculinity and can alter the relationship between men and nationalism. Joanna Bourke, in her groundbreaking work on British working-class soldiers, argues, among other things, that during the First World War men's bodies went from being agents of action to being objects of destruction and contemplation.[91] In the United States, conscientious objectors may have been considered feminine, cowardly 'slackers', but according to Timothy Stewart-Winter the 1940 draft actually 'masculinized' the peace movement by making prestigious martyrs of all those men who were sent to prison in a refusal to obey the draft or alternative work forces.[92] Similarly, conscientious objectors tried to invent belligerent forms of peace activism that could stand up to the cultural expectations which made soldiering the pinnacle of manhood. Finally, although there is evidence to suggest that soldiers condemned their comrades who had deserted, there was also a surprising amount of sympathy for those who had lost the will to fight.[93] The act of desertion could be viewed in some circumstances as an act of courage, defiance and political agency.

We may agree that 'nationalism has typically sprung from masculinized memory, masculinized humiliation and masculinized hope'.[94] But the growing literature on men and masculinity has revealed that even in times of war there were multiple competing masculinities, and so we must also question which memory, humiliation and hope became embedded in a particular nationalist project, the reasons this took place at specific moments in time and who was consequently excluded from the national community. While gender could be renegotiated in times of war, specific gender roles and ideals that embodied a politically expedient national identity were reinforced in an effort to help differentiate a nation from its enemies. For example, American scholars have explored how the framing of gender and nationalism affected wartime domestic and foreign policies. Support for traditional gender roles for women and men during the Cold War was part of a policy of 'domestic containment',[95] which later influenced American policies in the 'War on Terror'.[96] The emphasis on traditional gender roles also informed treatment of LGBTQ military personnel, who found themselves excluded from the nationalist post-war project following wartime service.[97] In this way, the deployment of gender norms varied considerably in times of war and peace, but both could be used to deny men and women full rights and national belonging on account of their gender or sexuality.[98]

Conclusion

In 2010, when revisiting her 1986 article, Joan Scott argued that gender 'is the study of the vexed relationship (around sexuality) between the normative and the psychic, the attempt at once to collectivize fantasy and to use it for some political or social end, whether that end is nation-building or family structure'.[99] Scott reminds us that since gender is not fixed, the term needs to be historicized, and its 'meanings . . . need to be teased out of the materials we examine'. Gender remains a useful category of historical analysis only when we acknowledge that 'gender is an open question about how these meanings are established, what they signify, and in what contexts'. Gender continues to be useful because it is critical.

As we have seen in this chapter, since the 1990s scholars in a wide range of academic disciplines have used the lens of gender to study the history of nationalism, and have made rich contributions to our understanding of how nations and nationalist discourse are constructed, how citizenship is negotiated and how individuals 'become national'. Gender approaches have allowed scholars to re-evaluate theories of nationalism, to explore more fully the relationship between nation and empire, to offer fresh insight into how national belonging intersects with other forms of identity and to understand how memory and national commemoration are negotiated.[100] Rather than being simply a fad, gender as a category of analysis has shown remarkable resilience, and this is no doubt in part due to its malleability. The field has indeed evolved in response to the various other methodologies that have emerged over the last twenty-five years, most notably postcolonialism, the spatial turn and the transnational turn. It is in these areas that we see some of the most exciting research currently taking place.

Despite these successes and Scott's assertion that gender remains an important category of analysis, the discipline is not without controversy. There has been some concern among feminist historians that too much work now focuses on men and masculinity, and that this has undermined the political and activist goals originally set out with the development of gender history.[101] While many historians have acknowledged the immense contribution that the study of gender has made to our understanding of nations and nationalism,[102] it is arguably still underutilized. One challenge is the persistent reluctance to incorporate gender into national histories and grand narratives.[103] Yet some of the most important and influential works on gender and nationalism have come from scholars who are neither feminist historians, nor historians of gender, most notably George Mosse and Linda Colley. This raises the question of whether a gender approach should remain distinct from other methodologies, or if it should instead be embedded in all historical analysis. Does gender history run the risk of being 'ghettoized', as women's history was several decades ago, and thus being ignored by other historians? Or will it lose its political teeth if it becomes too 'mainstream'? I would argue that the lens of gender is at its most exciting and, indeed, critical, when the reader is not expecting it.[104] Yet broader studies of nations and nationalism that have attempted to address the question of gender, while certainly valuable, tend to suffer from conceptual confusion, and the implications of gender remain underdeveloped.[105] I would also question the degree to which gender as a subject of concern has actually achieved mainstream status. One test is whether or not it is mentioned in each of the chapters of this book as a matter of course, or whether it remains something that is a necessary inclusion but exists in a silo.

Notes

1 Simone de Beauvoir, *The Second Sex* (New York, 1973), p. 301.
2 Judith Butler, 'Performative Acts and Gender Constitution: An Essay in Phenomenology and Feminist Theory', *Theatre Journal* 40:4 (1988), 519–31.

3 Joan W. Scott, 'Gender: A Useful Category of Analysis', *The American Historical Review* 91:5 (1986), 1067.

4 For an overview of the shift from women's history to gender history, see Laura Lee Downs, 'From Women's History to Gender History', in Stefan Berger, Heiko Feldner and Kevin Passmore (eds), *Writing History: Theory and Practice* (London, 2003), pp. 261–81.

5 Michelle Perrot, 'Introduction', in Michelle Perrot (ed.), *Writing Women's History* (Oxford, 1992), p. 8.

6 Gisela Bock, 'Women's History and Gender History: Aspects of an International Debate' *Gender & History* 1:1 (1989), 10.

7 Michael Roper and John Tosh, *Manful Assertions: Masculinities in Britain since 1800* (New York, 1991), p. 4.

8 John Tosh, 'Hegemonic Masculinity and the History of Gender', in Stefan Dudink, Karen Hagemann and Josh Tosh (eds), *Masculinities in Politics and War: Gendering Modern History* (Manchester, 2004), pp. 41–60.

9 This is also referred to as 'intersectionality'.

10 Sita Ranchod-Nilsson and Mary Ann Tétrault (eds), *Women, States and Nationalism: At Home in the Nation?* (London and New York, 2000).

11 Karen Hagemann, *'Männlicher Muth und Teutsche Ehre:' Nation Militär und Geschlecht zur Zeit der Antinapoleonischen Kriege Preussens* (Paderborn, Munich, Vienna and Zurich, 2002), p. 58. See also Ida Blom, Karen Hagemann and Catherine Hall (eds), *Gendered Nations: Nationalisms and Gender Order in the Long Nineteenth Century* (Oxford and New York, 2000).

12 Anne McClintock, 'Family Feuds: Gender, Nationalism and the Family', *Feminist Review* 44 (1993), 63.

13 For an explanation of 'transversal politics', see Nira Yuval-Davis, *Gender & Nation* (London, 1997), pp. 125–32.

14 George L. Mosse, *Nationalism and Sexuality: Middle-Class Morality and Sexual Norms in Modern Europe* (Madison, 1985).

15 George L. Mosse, *The Image of Man: The Creation of Modern Masculinity* (New York and Oxford, 1996), p. 6.

16 Robert A. Nye, *Masculinity and Male Codes of Honor in Modern France* (New York, 1993); Madeleine Hurd, 'Class, Masculinity, Manners and Mores: Public Space and Public Sphere in Nineteenth-Century Europe', *Social Science History* 24:1 (2000), 76–110.

17 Jean Bethke Elshtain, *Public Man, Private Woman: Women in Social and Political Thought* (Princeton, 1981).

18 Nira Yuval-Davis and Floya Anthias (eds), *Woman-Nation-State* (London, 1989), p. 7.

19 Sylvia Walby, 'Woman and Nation', in Anthony D. Smith (ed.), *Ethnicity and Nationalism* (Leiden, 1992), p. 83.

20 Anne Clark, *The Rhetoric of Masculine Citizenship: Concepts and Representations in Modern Western Political Culture* (New York, 2007), p. 4.

21 Catherine Hall, 'Gender, Nations and Nationalisms', in Edward Mortimer (ed.), *People, Nation and State: The Meaning of Ethnicity* (London and New York, 1999), p. 51. See also Georgina Waylen, 'Gender, Feminism and the State', in Vicky Randall and Georgina Waylen (eds), *Gender, Politics and the State* (London and New York, 1998), pp. 12–13; Yuval-Davis, *Gender and Nation*, pp. 68–92; Jean Bethke Elshtain, 'Sovereignty, Identity, Sacrifice',

in Marjorie Ringrose and Adam Lerner (eds), *Reimagining the Nation* (Buckingham, 1993), pp. 159–75.

22 Linda Colley, *Britons: Forging the Nation 1707–1837* (New Haven: Yale University Press, 1992), p. 281.

23 Karen Hagemann, 'Female Patriots: Women, War and the Nation in the Period of the Prussian-German Anti-Napoleonic Wars', *Gender & History* 2 (2004), 397–424.

24 Brigitte Studer, 'Citizenship as Contingent National Belonging: Married Women and Foreigners in Twentieth-Century Switzerland', in Kathleen Canning and Sonya O. Rose (eds), *Gender, Citizenships and Subjectivities* (London, 2002), pp. 196–228; Nancy F. Cott, 'Marriage and Women's Citizenship in the United States, 1830–1934', *American Historical Review* 103:5 (1998), 1440–74.

25 Walby, 'Women and Nation', p. 90.

26 Robert M. Ponichtera, 'Feminists, Nationalists, and Soldiers: Women and the Fight for Polish Independence', *International History Review* 19:1 (1997), 24.

27 Gisela Kaplan, 'Feminism and Nationalism: The European Case', in Lois A. West (ed.), *Feminist Nationalism* (New York and London, 1997), p. 8.

28 Karen Offen, 'The Theory and Practice of Feminism in Nineteenth-Century Europe', in Renate Bridenthal and Claudia Koonz (eds), *Becoming Visible: Women in European History* (Boston, 1977), p. 350; Nicoletta F. Gullace, *The Blood of Our Sons: Men, Women and the Renegotiation of British Citizenship During the Great War* (London, 2002).

29 Kumari Jayawardena, *Feminism and Nationalism in the Third World* (London, 1986); Lois A. West, 'Feminist Nationalist Social Movements: Beyond Universalism and towards a Gendered Cultural Relativism', *Women's Studies International Forum* 15:5–6 (1992), 563–79.

30 Geraldine Forbes, *Women in Modern India* (Cambridge, 1996); Gail Minault, *Secluded Scholars: Women's Education and Muslim Social Reform in Colonial India* (Oxford, 1998).

31 Julia Clancy-Smith and Frances Gouda (eds), *Domesticating the Empire: Race, Gender, and Family Life in French and Dutch Colonialism* (Charlottesville, 1998); Philippa Levine (ed.), *Gender and Empire* (Oxford, 2004).

32 Catherine Hall, 'British Cultural Identities and the Legacy of the Empire', in David Moorley and Kevin Robins (eds), *British Cultural Studies* (New York and Oxford, 2001). pp. 27–40.

33 Roger Chickering, '"Casting Their Gaze More Broadly": Women's Patriotic Activism in Imperial Germany', *Past & Present* 118 (1988), 156–185; Lora Wildenthal, *German Women for Empire, 1884–1945* (Durham, NC, 2001); Nancy Reagin, 'The Imagined *Hausfrau*: National Identity, Domesticity, and Colonialism in Imperial Germany', *Journal of Modern History* 73 (2001), 54–86.

34 Antoinette Burton, *Burdens of History: British Feminists, Indian Women, and Imperial Culture, 1865–1915* (Chapel Hill, 1994).

35 Indira Chowdhury, *The Frail Hero and Virile History: Gender and the Politics of Culture in Colonial Bengal* (Oxford, 1998).

36 Mrinali Sinha, *Colonial Masculinity: The 'Manly Englishman' and the 'Effeminate Bengali' in the Late Nineteenth Century* (Manchester, 1995), p. 1.

37 Anne McClintock, *Imperial Leather: Race, Gender and Sexuality in the Colonial Contest* (New York, 1995).

38 Partha Chatterjee, *The Nation and Its Fragments: Colonial and Postcolonial Histories* (Princeton, 1993).

39 Colley, *Britons*, p. 252.

40 Clark, *The Rhetoric of Masculine Citizenship*, pp. 4–5.

41 Ibid., p. 5.

42 George L. Mosse, *The Nationalization of the Masses: Political Symbolism and Mass Movements in Germany from the Napoleonic Wars Through the Third Reich* (New York, 1975), p. 20.

43 Marina Warner, *Monuments and Maidens: The Allegory of the Female Form* (London, 1985).

44 Eleanor E. Zeff, 'Old Traditions Die Hard: The Influence of Nationalism and European Community on Women's Rights in France, the United Kingdom and Germany', *History of European Ideas* 15:1–3 (1992), 257.

45 Rudy Koshar, *From Monuments to Traces: Artifacts of German Memory, 1870–1990* (Berkeley, Los Angeles and London, 2000), p. 70; Billie Melman, 'Gender, History and Memory: The Invention of Women's Past in the Nineteenth and Early Twentieth Centuries', *History and Memory* 5:1 (1993), 10.

46 Patricia Herminghouse and Magda Mueller, 'Looking for Germania', in Patricia Herminghouse (ed.), *Gender and Germanness: Cultural Productions of Nation* (Providence and Oxford, 1997), pp. 1–8.

47 Joan B. Landes, *Visualizing the Nation: Gender, Representation, and Revolution in Eighteenth-Century France* (Ithaca and London, 2001).

48 Johanna Valenius, *Undressing the Maid: Gender, Sexuality and the Body in the Construction of the Finnish Nation* (Helsinki, 2004), p. 207.

49 Maurice Agulhon, *Marianne au pouvoir: L'imagerie et la symbolique républicaine de 1880 à 1914* (Paris, 1989), p. 345.

50 Eric Jennings, '"Reinventing Jeanne": The Iconology of Joan of Arc in Vichy Schoolbooks, 1940–44', *Journal of Contemporary History* 29:4 (1994), 711–34.

51 Anne Helmreich, 'Domesticating Britannia: Representations of the Nation in Punch: 1870–1880', in Tricia Cusack and Sighle Bhreathnach-Lynch (eds), *Art, Nation and Gender: Ethnic Landscapes, Myths and Mother-Figures* (Aldershot, 2003), p. 15.

52 Koshar, *From Monuments to Traces*, p. 72.

53 Linda Edmondson, 'Putting Mother Russia in a European Context', in Tricia Cusack and Sighle Bhreathnach-Lynch (eds), *Art, Nation and Gender*, pp. 53–64.

54 Suruchi Thapar, 'Women as Activists; Women as Symbols: A Study of the Indian Nationalist Movement', *Feminist Review* 44 (1993), 81–96.

55 Beth Baron, 'The Construction of National Honour in Egypt', *Gender & History* 5:2 (1993), 245.

56 Ida Blom, 'Gender and Nation in International Comparison', in Ida Blom, Karen Hagemann and Catherine Hall (eds), *Gendered Nations*, p. 13.

57 Henrietta Harrison, *The Making of the Republican Citizen: Political Ceremonies and Symbols in China, 1911–1929* (Oxford, 2000), pp. 79–83.

58 S. A. Smith, *Revolution and the People in Russia and China: A Comparative History* (Cambridge, 2008), p. 113.

59 Kathryn Robinson, 'Women: Difference Versus Diversity', in Donald K. Emmerson (ed.), *Indonesia beyond Suharto: Polity, Economy, Society, Transition* (London and New York, 1999), pp. 237–61.

60 Mina Roces, 'Gender, Nation and the Politics of Dress in Twentieth-Century Philippines', *Gender & History* 17:2 (2005), 374.

61 Fatima Mernissi, *Beyond the Veil: Male-Female Dynamics in Modern Muslim Society*. Revised edition (Bloomington, 1987); Leila Ahmed, *Women and Gender in Islam: Historical Roots of a Modern Debate* (New Haven, 1992); Daphne Grace, *The Woman in the Muslin Mask: Veiling and Identity in Postcolonial Literature* (London, 2004).

62 Joane Nagel, 'Masculinity and Nationalism: Gender and Sexuality in the Making of Nations', *Ethnic and Racial Studies* 21:2 (1998), 242–67.

63 Steven Jackson, 'Globalization, Corporate Nationalism and Masculinity in Canada: Sport, Molson Beer Advertising and Consumer Citizenship', *Sport in Society* 17:7 (2014), 901–17.

64 Nancy R. Reagin, *Sweeping the German Nation: Domesticity and National Identity in Germany, 1870–1945* (New York, 2006).

65 Eric Storm, 'The Nationalisation of the Domestic Sphere', *Nations and Nationalism* 23:1 (2017), 173–93.

66 George L. Mosse, 'Nationalism and Respectability: Normal and Abnormal Sexuality in the 19th Century', *Journal of Contemporary History* 17:2 (1982), 222.

67 Keely Stauter-Halsted, 'Moral Panic and the Prostitute in Partitioned Poland: Middle Class Respectability in Defense of the Modern Nation', *Slavic Review* 68:3 (2009), 558.

68 Hans- George Stumke, 'From the "People's Consciousness of Right and Wrong" to "the Healthy Instincts of the Nation:" The Persecution of Homosexuals in Nazi Germany', in Michael Burleigh (ed.), *Confronting the Nazi Past: New Debates on Modern German History* (New York, 1996), p. 155.

69 Nira Yuval-Davis, 'Women and the Biological Reproduction of the Nation', *Women's Studies International Forum* 19: 1–2 (1996), 23.

70 Ruth Harris, 'The "Child of the Barbarian": Rape, Race and Nationalism in France during the First World War', *Past and Present* 141 (1993), 170–206.

71 Alexander Maxwell, 'National Endogamy and Double Standards: Sexuality and Nationalism in East-Central Europe during the 19th Century', *Journal of Social History* 41:2 (2007) p. 417.

72 Gisela Bock, 'Racism and Sexism in Nazi Germany: Motherhood, Compulsory Sterilization, and the State', *Signs* 8:3 (1983), p. 403.

73 Claudia Koonz, *Mothers in the Fatherland* (New York, 1987).

74 George Hawley, *Making Sense of the Alt-Right* (New York, 2017).

75 Kathleen M. Blee, *Women of the Klan: Racism and Gender in the 1920s* (Berkeley, 1992), p. 3.

76 Kathleen M. Blee, 'Becoming a Racist: Women in contemporary Ku Klux Klan and Neo-Nazi Groups', *Gender & Society* 10:6 (1996), 680–702.

77 Michael Kimmel, *Angry White Men: American Masculinity at the End of an Era* (New York, 2015); Diana C. Mutz, 'Status Threat, Not Economic Hardship, Explains the 2016 Presidential Vote', *Proceedings of the National*

   Academy of Sciences, April 2018. Accessed online http://www.pnas.org/
   content/early/2018/04/18/1718155115.
78 Seyward Darby, 'The Rise of the Valkyries', *Harper's Magazine*,
   September 2017. Accessed online https://harpers.org/archive/2017/09/
   the-rise-of-the-valkyries/.
79 Hall, 'Gender, Nations and Nationalisms', p. 51.
80 Walby, 'Woman and Nation', pp. 93–4.
81 See, e.g., Cynthia Cockburn, *The Space between Us: Negotiating Gender and
   National Identities in Conflict* (London and New York, 1998).
82 Melissa Feinberg, 'Dumplings and Domesticity: Women, Collaboration,
   and Resistance in the Protectorate of Bohemia and Moravia', in Nancy M.
   Wingfield and Maria Bucur (eds), *Gender and War in Twentieth-Century
   Eastern Europe* (Bloomington, 2006), pp. 95–110.
83 Margaret R. Higonnet and Patrice Higonnet, 'The Double Helix', in Margaret
   R. Higonnet, Jane Jenson, Sonya Michel, and Margaret Collins Weitz (eds),
   Behind the Lines: Gender and the Two World Wars (New Haven, 1987),
   pp. 31–47.
84 Lucy Noakes, *War and the British: Gender and National Identity 1939–91*
   (New York and London, 1998), p. 50.
85 Matthew Evangelista, *Gender, Nationalism, and War: Conflict on the Movie
   Screen* (Cambridge, 2011), pp. 25–79.
86 Wambui Waiyaki Otieno, *Mau Mau's Daughter: A Life History* (Boulder,
   1998), p. 39.
87 Dagmar Herzog (ed.), *Brutality and Desire: War and Sexuality in Europe's
   Twentieth Century* (Basingstoke and New York, 2009).
88 Jan Jindy Pettman, 'Boundary Politics: Women, Nationalism and Danger',
   in Mary Maynard and June Purvis (eds), *New Frontiers in Women's
   Studies: Knowledge, Identity and Nationalism* (London, 1996), pp. 187–202.
89 Cynthia Enloe, '"All the Men are in the Militias, All the Women Are
   Victims": The Politics of Masculinity and Femininity in Nationalist Wars', in
   Lois Ann Lorentzen and Jennifer Turpin (eds), *The Women and War Reader*
   (New York, 1998), pp. 50–62.
90 Nicoletta F. Gullace, 'White Feathers and Wounded Men: Female Patriotism
   and the Memory of the Great War', *Journal of British Studies* 36:2 (1997),
   178–206.
91 Joanna Bourke, *Dismembering the Male: Men's Bodies, Britain, and the Great
   War* (Chicago, 1996).
92 Timothy Stewart-Winter, 'Not a Soldier, Not a Slacker: Conscientious
   Objectors and Male Citizenship in the United States during the Second World
   War', *Gender & History* 19:3 (2007), 519–42.
93 Teresa Iacobelli, *Death or Deliverance: Canadian Courts Martial in the Great
   War* (Vancouver, 2013).
94 Cynthia Enloe, *Bananas, Beaches, Bases: Making Feminist Sense of
   International Politics* (London, 1989), p. 44.
95 Jane de Hart, 'Containment at Home: Gender, Sexuality, and National Identity
   in Cold War America', in Peter Kuznick and James Gilbert (eds), *Rethinking
   Cold War Culture* (Washington, DC, 2001).
96 Gretchen Ritter, 'Domestic Containment or Equal Standing? Gender, Nationalism,
   and the War on Terror', *Journal of Policy History* 21:4 (2009), 439–47.

97 Allan Bérubé, *Coming Out Under Fire: The History of Gay Men and Women in World War II* (New York, 1990).

98 John D'Emilio, 'The Homosexual Menace: The Politics of Sexuality in Cold War America', in Kathy Peiss and Christina Simmons (eds), *Passion and Power: Sexuality in History* (Philadelphia, 1989), pp. 226–40; Eithne Luibhéid, *Entry Denied: Controlling Sexuality at the Border* (Minneapolis, 2002); Gary Kinsman and Patrizia Gentile, *The Canadian War on Queers: National Security as Sexual Regulation* (Vancouver, 2010).

99 Joan Wallach Scott, 'Gender: Still a Useful Category of Analysis?', *Diogenes* 57:1 (2010), 7–14.

100 Sylvia Paletschek and Sylvia Schraut (eds), *The Gender of Memory. Cultures of Remembrance in Nineteenth and Twentieth Century Europe* (Frankfurt/Main, 2008).

101 Karen Hagemann and Jean H. Quataert (eds), *Gendering Modern German History: Rewriting Historiography* (Oxford, 2007), p. 20.

102 Anthony D. Smith, 'Beyond Modernism', in Anthony D. Smith, *Nationalism and Modernism: A Critical Survey of Recent Theories of Nations and Nationalism* (London and New York, 1998), pp. 199–220; Stefan Berger and Bill Niven, 'Writing the History of National Memory', in Stefan Berger and Bill Niven (eds), *Writing the History of Memory* (London, 2014), pp. 141–42.

103 Joy Damousi, 'Writing Gender into History and History in Gender: Creating a Nation and Australian Historiography', *Gender & History* 11:3 (1999), 612–24. One of the most complex and controversial examples of this is in Japan with regard to military 'comfort women'. Yoshiko Nozaki, 'Feminism, Nationalism, and the Japanese Textbook Controversy over "Comfort Women"', in France Twine and Kathleen M. Blee (eds), *Feminism and Antiracism: International Struggles for Justice* (New York, 2001), pp. 170–92.

104 Christopher Clark, for example, introduces gender to great effect in *The Sleepwalkers: How Europe Went to War in 1914* (London, 2013).

105 Stefan Berger and Chris Lorenz (eds), *The Contested Nation: Ethnicity, Class, Religion and Gender in National Histories* (Basingstoke and New York, 2008).

Further reading

Anthias, Floya and Nira Yuval-Davis (eds), *Woman-Nation-State*. Basingstoke: Palgrave Macmillan, 1989.

Blom, Ida, Karen Hagemann and Catherine Hall (eds), *Gendered Nations: Nationalisms and Gender Order in the Long Nineteenth Century*. Oxford and New York: Routledge, 2000.

Dudink, Stefan, Karen Hagemann and Josh Tosh (eds), *Masculinities in Politics and War: Gendering Modern History*. Manchester: Manchester University Press, 2004.

Levine, Philippa (ed.), *Gender and Empire*. Oxford and New York: Oxford University Press, 2004.

Mosse, George L. *Nationalism and Sexuality: Middle-Class Morality and Sexual Norms in Modern Europe*. Madison: University of Wisconsin Press, 1985.

Ranchod-Nilsson, Sita and Mary Ann Tétrault (eds), *Women, States and Nationalism: At Home in the Nation?* London and New York: Routledge, 2000.

Scott, Joan Wallach. *Gender and the Politics of History*. New York: Columbia University Press, 1988; rev. edn, 1999.

West, Lois A. (ed.), *Feminist Nationalism*. New York and London: Routledge, 1997.

Yuval-Davis, Nira. *Gender & Nation*. London: Sage, 1997.

11

The spatial turn and the history of nationalism: Nationalism between regionalism and transnational approaches

Eric Storm

Introduction

Most historians today agree that nations are constructed and their borders largely arbitrary. So, why should we study nationalism by limiting ourselves to the boundaries of existing nation states or nationalist movements? In fact, since the 1990s historians have been analysing the interaction between local, regional and national identities, mostly by concentrating on the territorial identification processes in a specific city or region. Other scholars examined transborder influences on the nation-building process by focusing on the role of emigrants, borders, transfers or the impact of foreign scholars and tourists. As a consequence, nationalism is now being studied at various geographical levels besides the traditional emphasis on the nation itself: the local, the regional, the transnational and the global (which will be the topic of Chapter 12). This chapter aims to provide an overview of the impact of the 'spatial turn' on the history of nationalism.

Globalization and the spatial turn

The spatial turn in the humanities and social sciences can be understood as a reaction to the globalization that rapidly gained momentum after 1989.

During the Cold War, the division of the world in the capitalist West, the communist Eastern Bloc and the Third World was taken for granted and there seemed to be no signs of imminent change. The basic units of the three blocks were independent nation states. Ethnic strife and secessionist movements still existed, but apart from a few unsatisfied regions in the West – such as Quebec or the Basque Country – this was largely limited to the new nation states in Africa and Asia.

This stable worldview was shattered by the fall of the Berlin Wall in 1989. It seemed as if the lid of the pressure cooker had been removed as ethnic rivalries boiled over in various parts of the world. In the Eastern Bloc, the Soviet Union, Yugoslavia and Czechoslovakia, which for decades had given the impression of being successful nation states, fell apart within a few years. At the same time, regionalist and separatist movements became more active within the West. Existing regionalist (or nationalist) parties scored electoral victories and were joined by new ones, such as the Lega Nord in Italy. In the Third World, separatist movements saw new opportunities and Eritrea, East Timor and South Sudan gained independence. The borders of existing nation states were no longer inviolable.

The nation state was also undermined by the increasing globalization of the economy. Neo-liberal reforms, which from the late 1980s were adopted by most democracies, opened up protected markets and led to growing international competition, large-scale privatizations, the curtailing of the welfare state, the liberalization of financial markets and massive relocations of industries. Moreover, international corporations and banks seemed to have more power than many nation states, particularly the smaller ones. Other factors that undermined the central role of nation states were the rapid increase of travel and migration, the invention of the internet and the growing importance of international organizations such as the European Union. At the same time, global shifts of (economic) power became obvious. In the 1990s, the Soviet Union disappeared as a superpower, while the spectacular economic growth of China began to undermine the dominance of the West.

Many people, at least initially, viewed the growing interconnectedness of the world and the end of the strict divide between East and West with optimism, and this was reflected in the popularity of ideas about the 'global village' (McLuhan), the 'death of distance' (Cairncross) or even the 'end of history' (Fukuyama). Others however doubted whether globalization and the communications revolution would result in a more homogenous and uniform world. In any case, these developments subverted the self-evident nature of nation states as the primary independent actors on the global stage.

A growing number of scholars now became aware that in a world in flux it is not logical anymore to use the nation state as an abstract and fixed geographical container and continue to use it unreflexively as the main unit of analysis in the humanities and social sciences. As a consequence, in the 1990s a reaction began to develop, which is part of a broader 'spatial turn'. The roots for this new critical understanding of space can be found in France, where in the 1970s the Marxist philosopher Henri Lefebvre and the Jesuit Michel de Certeau began to oppose the strong focus on language and discourse by post-structuralists, such as Michel Foucault.

Lefebvre was an unorthodox Marxist, with a strong interest in the impact of capitalism on everyday life, who as a professor of sociology at the University of Nanterre would be a direct source of inspiration for the May 1968 student revolt. In 1974, Lefebvre published *The Production of Space*, in which he criticized post-structuralism for only exploring abstract mental spaces, while ignoring the social spaces where language and discourse had practical effects. He also deplored the disciplinary division between architects, urbanists and regional planners, which each study and act upon a specific spatial domain. Moreover by working within the constraints of capitalist society, they serve the interests of the dominant classes. Lefebvre argued that the interaction between physical, mental and social spaces should be studied together by examining the production of space. Scholars should not focus on the location of things in space and try to come to a rational use of space devising models and typologies, but study the genesis of actual spaces, thus historicizing space. By uncovering the homogenizing forces of capitalism, Lefebvre hoped to stimulate acts of social resistance in which inhabitants, users and artists would struggle to re-appropriate and diversify spaces in everyday life.[1]

Michel de Certeau came from a very different tradition. He was a sociologist from a Catholic background, but was also fascinated by the psychoanalysis of Freud and Lacan. Like Lefebvre, he criticized post-structuralism for favouring discourse over daily life and social practices. Whereas Michel Foucault had focused on the mechanisms of power and discipline,[2] Certeau turned his attention to the way individuals respond to them. Thus, in *The Practice of Everyday Life*, which was first published in 1980, he argued that people are not spineless victims of oppression or passive consumers, but can in their daily activities subvert, manipulate or evade the mechanisms of discipline, as does anyone who makes a ramble in a city. Walkers accept the layout and concrete forms of the city, but take their own route, while making detours and finding shortcuts that were not foreseen by the planners. Thus, every inhabitant or visitor experiences the space of the city in his or her own way. Certeau distinguished between the long-term 'strategies' of institutions, governments, enterprises and other powerful bodies to influence the behaviour of the population and the 'tactics' used by individuals in all kinds of everyday practices, such as dwelling, shopping, walking and talking, to manipulate events and seize the opportunities thus created.[3] In his analysis of society Certeau accordingly prioritized individual agency and concrete places over long-term developments and the structural limitations of discourse, which had been the focus of Foucault. In the 1990s these ideas of both Lefebvre and Certeau were taken over and adapted by geographers like Edward Soja – who introduced the term 'spatial turn' – David Harvey and Doreen Massey, while scholars from other disciplines did the same.[4]

In fact, the spatial turn entails four related ideas which are relevant for historians. The first is that space is not an empty, abstract entity, but that it is understood and used differently in different periods and by different people. Thus, place is not a neutral, empty space, but socially constructed, or produced over time as Lefebvre would argue. A second, related idea is that space is made, reproduced and transformed in daily life. What is of interest in both cases is not geometrical space, like the coordinates of a specific location on the globe, but the way spaces are perceived and lived. A third idea, which is somewhat more controversial, is that spaces also have their own materiality that can enable or delimit certain uses. Rohkrämer and Schulz argue that it matters if someone lives in or experiences an Alpine landscape, an open plain or a forest. Others even plead for a 'moderate geographical materialism'.[5] In line with Massey, I would add a fourth idea that place should not be seen as something static and closed in itself but as a meeting place of movements, communications and networks of social relations.[6]

The first idea of space as a social construct is already part of mainstream nationalism studies since the breakthrough of the modernist and constructivist approaches,[7] although this is now also applied to other territorial units, while the second idea that space is transformed in daily life permeates almost all contributions discussed in this chapter. Most authors conduct a detailed case study in which they implicitly agree with Certeau by not presenting their objects of analysis as passive victims of a nation-building process that was imposed on them from above, but by focusing on the agency they had and on the 'tactics' people used to adapt the national policies and projects to their own needs. The third idea of a geographical materialism is not very popular among historians dealing with territorial identity construction, although recently Andreas Wimmer has argued that geographical conditions influence state-building processes that in the long term had an impact on the feasibility of well-functioning nation states. Thus, the presence of high mountains or inhospitable deserts makes it more difficult for peasants to avoid taxation and thus favours the construction of centralized states, while rugged terrain can be an obstacle for efficient communications needed for state-building.[8] The fourth idea, however, that nation states (or regions) should not be studied as self-contained entities seems to have been widely accepted by almost all authors analysed here.

The spatial turn has been a source of inspiration for many different disciplines and the study of a broad range of topics, but it also had a direct impact on the study of nationalism and national identity construction by a number of social scientists. Highly innovative in this sense is the geographer Anssi Paasi, who in his *Territories, Boundaries and Consciousness* (1996) combined a long-term analysis of the production of the space of the Finnish nation state with a more concrete focus on current-day social practices and individual 'life-histories'.

According to him it is crucial to distinguish between the historical construction of a nation or a region – by drawing boundaries and providing it with symbols and institutions – and the way the inhabitants identify with it through their concrete experiences. In order to study this territorialization of space he focuses on the Finnish perceptions of and experiences with the Russian border and first examines the institutionalization of Finnish territory and its boundaries in official discourse, but also in such heterogeneous sources as periodicals, textbooks, religious hymns and photographs. In addition, he explores how the boundaries were reproduced and transformed in people's everyday life in the border community of Värtsilä. This industrial town was divided between the Soviet Union and Finland after the latter's defeat in 1944 and Finland subsequently had to resettle about 420,000 citizens who left the territories that were ceded to the victor. Through several field trips and dozens of interviews he found that the younger generations, who had no personal memories of the lost homelands, quickly adapted to the new situation and as a consequence developed different 'territorial identities' than the older inhabitants.[9]

In his *National Identity, Popular Culture and Everyday Life* (2002), the sociologist Tim Edensor focuses on the reproduction of national identities in current-day social spaces. In this stimulating book, he argues that national identity is not something fixed; it is represented and performed in all kinds of practices, which are all related to each other. Thus national identity can be reproduced at iconic sites such as the Taj Mahal or the Sydney Opera House, but also at home and in quotidian spaces such as a prairie farm or a red telephone box. The same way, the nation can be performed at several levels; by participating in national holidays, by cheering the national team at the Olympic Games, but also by Turkish wrestling, having a Guinness beer at an Irish pub or enjoying a Finnish sauna. The nation is also represented in film, on websites and in other media. Objects are also frequently associated with nations, from masterpieces of art to cars and sausages. Thus, if we want to know how national identities are constructed and reconstructed on a daily basis we also have to pay attention to popular culture, mundane spaces and all kinds of banal practices.[10]

Social scientists usually focus on recent periods and can conduct surveys and interviews to examine actual life-histories, which is much more difficult for the distant past. As a result, when studying the way people (re)construct their sense of the nation most historians concentrate on small communities and the role of all kinds of associations – which have produced enough primary source material – rather than on the quotidian experiences of individuals. Strikingly, until very recently they did not include direct references to the spatial turn. Most scholars asserted that they merely applied Anderson's concept of 'imagined community' or Hobsbawm's 'invention of tradition' to a case study in order to empirically assess how the nation-building process functioned in a specific region or border community. Thus, their approach can be defined as constructivist and they generally also accepted the view that nationalism was essentially a modern phenomenon. Nonetheless, most of them did not see modernization as an automatic or teleological process. They also moved away from the post-structuralist emphasis on discourse and narrative and preferred to examine the role of agency, social practices and everyday life. The influence of the spatial turn, however, is most obvious in their unease about nationalism and nation-building as being processes that operated in the supposedly uniform and homogenous space of the nation state.

Unlike most of the other chapters in this volume, which focus on a relatively limited number of path-breaking studies, in my field there are almost no classic interpretations with a global impact. Particularly in the studies that explore the interaction between local, regional and national identities there are even various disconnected historiographical traditions. As a result, I will discuss a relatively large number of case studies, beginning with those that focus on the countryside, then regional and local case studies, and finally those that deal with transnational influences.

Agency in the countryside

Inspired by modernization theories, an older generation of scholars, such as Eugen Weber, had presented nation-building as a process of assimilation imposed from above.[11] However, from the late 1980s this view has been criticized in a growing number of regional case studies that showed that the inhabitants of rural areas did not undergo this process passively and, as a consequence, that national integration and homogenization were not an almost automatic process. By awarding agency to the rural population, scholars in fact argued that the nation-building process did not operate in the homogenous space of the existing nation state, but that the nation was made, reproduced and transformed at a local level as well. Thus, in 1993, Caroline Ford examined how Brittany became more integrated into France during the period 1890–1926. In her *Creating the Nation in Provincial France* she made clear that this happened largely as a local response to some of the more controversial policies of the left-wing governments of the Third Republic. New social-catholic parties and associations mobilized broad layers of the population in opposition to the anticlerical measures from Paris and by doing so integrated the region more thoroughly within the national political domain.[12] In a case study on the department of the Loire that appeared two years later, James Lehning equally asserted that peasants actively interacted with the state in matters concerning education, religion and politics. Inspired by anthropological approaches, he argued that during the nineteenth century the inhabitants of the countryside slowly became members of the French nation through a process of negotiation and adaptation.[13] By focusing on the response of local actors, both authors argued that the nation-building process did not have the same outcome everywhere.

Elsewhere, authors also began to pay attention to the agency of the rural population, some of whom even anticipated the studies by Ford and Lehning on France. Thus, Prasenjit Duara argued that the difficult transition to a modern nation state in China could best be explained by zooming in on the local level. He does so by a detailed examination of the nation- and state-building process in six villages in Northern China between 1900 and 1942. Pressured both by nationalists at home and by imperialist encroachment from abroad, the national authorities attempted to strengthen their grip on the countryside. The taxes that had to fund the new agencies of the modernizing state, such as Western-style education, a modern bureaucracy and up-to-date armed forces, had to be collected by the traditional local elites. Through their networks, informal relations and shared norms and beliefs they continued to control village life. However, this 'cultural nexus of power' broke down because the high demands that were placed on local society were not compensated by new, well-functioning state services.[14]

Florencia Mallon was clearly influenced by postcolonial studies and instead of looking at the role of local elites she focused on the agency of the rural 'subaltern classes'.[15] In her *Peasant and Nation* she ambitiously compared the nation-building process in two Mexican with two Peruvian rural areas. In the exceptional circumstances of national crisis and foreign invasion – the French intervention in Mexico in 1861 and the Chilean occupation of Peru between 1881 and 1884 – the rural population actively participated in the national struggle and in three of the regions under scrutiny they even developed their own form of peasant nationalism by embracing the idea of citizenship and legal equality. However, the effects of this rural activism were quite different in the two countries. In Mexico, the memories of this 'alternative national-democratic' project were revived under Porfirio Díaz and during the Mexican Revolution, while in Peru the irregular peasant forces were repressed by the national authorities and in the 1890s the suffrage was restricted, converting the indigenous population of the countryside effectively into second-rate citizens.[16]

Although Keely Stauter-Halsted also focused on the role of peasants in *The Nation in the Village*, like most other scholars writing on the rise of nationalism in East-Central Europe, she did not concentrate much on modern citizenship, but on interethnic rivalry. The emancipation of the serfs in 1848 profoundly transformed social relations in the Galician countryside. The dependency of the peasants on their former lords diminished substantially and they now had to deal directly with Austrian officials. Nonetheless, changes did not happen overnight and it took decades before a modern, rural public sphere was in place. Education, military service, emigration, electoral campaigns, new associations and the rural press all played a role in bringing the peasants into contact with a wider world. However, this modernization process also meant that peasants were mobilized along national lines, while relations between the Poles, Jews, Germans and Ruthenians became tenser. However, as the author argues, the 'discovery' of the Polish nation by the peasants also implied the adaptation of the national idea to a broader public. Thus more attention was given to the needs of the poorer members of the national community living outside of the major cities, while including rural folk culture into a new and broader conception of the Polish nation.[17]

Regional and local identities

While these authors uncovered the role of peasants in the nation-building process, others focused on the interaction between local, regional and national identity formation. Scholars applying modernist or constructivist approaches had until the 1980s been concerned exclusively with nations, while implicitly assuming that separate regional economies, politics and cultures would slowly be absorbed by more encompassing nation states. However, authors who applied a constructivist approach to smaller territorial entities found that regional identities did not disappear but were in fact strengthened by the rise of nationalism.

Surprisingly, several different historiographical traditions can be discerned. Authors dealing with the rather stable Western European nation states concentrated primarily on the role of regional identities in the nation-building process. In areas where state borders had been more fluid, such as Eastern Europe and large parts of Asia and Africa, scholars generally concentrated on the interaction and conflicts between different ethnic groups. In the Americas, where the nation state generally was not contested, most attention was paid to racial discrimination and the formal or informal exclusion from citizenship of large parts of the population. Most of these studies deal with the period between 1870 and 1945 when nationalism became a mass movement, although there are also scholars who concentrate on earlier periods[18] or on the more recent decades.[19]

Groundbreaking for Western Europe was Celia Applegate's *A Nation of Provincials: The German Idea of Heimat* (1990). Instead of choosing one of the 'unhappy regions' or 'stateless nations', which in the neo-Marxist centre-periphery theory were interpreted as being subordinate to the centre, she examined the construction of regional identity in the Palatinate, a rather nondescript region which in 1815 was added to the Kingdom of Bavaria and which, like the rest of Bavaria, became part of the new German Empire in 1871. In her monograph Applegate showed how regionalist sentiment did not disappear with German unification; on the contrary the identity of the region was more closely defined in the subsequent decades. Regionalist associations rapidly grew in number and membership. They were not part of a backward-looking movement, but constituted a modern and largely urban phenomenon. By encouraging the participation of wide strata of the population in collecting and preserving the regional heritage, they had clear egalitarian and democratic implications. They often even embraced the heritage of local minorities, such as the Jews. Love of the local *Heimat* was closely intertwined with loyalty to the German fatherland. What is more, the connection to the large and rather abstract nation was stimulated by strengthening the attachment to the more concrete heritage of regional folk custom, song, dance, dress and nature.[20]

Anne-Marie Thiesse, who a year later published her study on French regionalist literature, had a very different starting point, but her conclusions were similar to those of Applegate. Thiesse applied Bourdieu's theories about the literary field to regionalist literature by not focusing primarily on the aesthetic or ideological motives of the authors, but on their competition for scarce resources. She thus asserted that towards the end of the nineteenth century there was a broad 'réveil des provinces' that was caused by the broadening and democratization of the public sphere. Profiling oneself as a regional author came to be seen as a profitable strategy. However, she not only analysed the structural causes behind the rise of a new literary genre but also discussed how the lost war against Prussia in 1870 and the concerns about the levelling effects of modernization led to growing calls for political decentralization and a new interest in regional folklore, local history and vernacular traditions. Like in Germany, the new and rather diverse regionalist associations were instrumental in constructing new regional identities in all parts of France, thus not only in the unhappy or underprivileged regions.[21]

Both books provided the inspiration for a wave of case studies which focused on the regionalist movements and associations that were instrumental in constructing and disseminating a new awareness of the various regional identities. But even within Western Europe there were two largely separate historiographical traditions. Although in her first book on regionalism, Thiesse still very much underlined its cultural aspects, in *Ils apprenaient la France* (1997), she showed how, in reaction to the defeat of 1870, the Third Republic began to actively promote the exaltation of the regions in French primary education. In history and geography lessons France was explicitly presented as a union of diverse regions which all contributed in their own way to the greatness of the nation. The pupils studied their 'petit patrie' in order to better understand and love the 'grande Patrie'.[22] Likewise, most studies on French regionalism concentrate on the political integration of the regions in the nation and this also happened in neighbouring countries like Spain, Italy and Belgium.[23] Studies on Germany in turn focused on all kinds of associations and had a strong cultural focus. A cultural interpretation of regionalism also seems to prevail in England, the Scandinavian countries and the Netherlands.[24]

Local and regional studies dealing with nation formation in East-Central Europe have made clear that the break-up of the so-called 'multi-ethnic' empires was not an automatic consequence of the modernization process. Interestingly, in a local case study of the impact of nationalism on the Bohemian city of Budweis/Budějovice between 1848 and 1948, Jeremy King also had a keen eye for those who were 'nationally uncommitted' and those who felt loyal to the Habsburg state. He argues against taking pre-existing ethnic identities for granted, as most scholars did, even if they embraced the constructivist view on national identity formation. Thus, in the early nineteenth century it was extremely difficult to distinguish between German and Czech Bohemians, since in both languages there was only one term to refer to them: *Böhme* and *Čech*. Many inhabitants of the town and the surrounding countryside were bilingual and many others were able to make themselves understood. Nonetheless, towards the end of the nineteenth century, inhabitants were increasingly forced to identify with one nationality, as associations, political parties and schools were organized along national lines. Geopolitical shifts, however, determined the fate of the town's inhabitants, as in 1918 they became citizens of a new, independent Czechoslovak Republic. Twenty years later Nazi Germany took over and the implementation of its racial policies indirectly resulted in the expulsion of all ethnic Germans after the end of the Second World War. However, part of the bilingual population switched sides and nationality, sometimes more than once, according to what was opportune.[25]

Other historians, such as Pieter Judson, James Bjork and Tara Zahra, also paid attention to those who – particularly in those parts of East-Central Europe where ethnic and religious cleavages did not overlap – had difficulties in defining themselves in ethnic terms or who were not enthusiastic nationalists, while coining the concept of 'national indifference' to cover this phenomenon. The emphasis of scholars on nationalist discourse, while ignoring myriad indifferent practices, has led to an overvaluation of the strength of nationalism, at least until the First World War. Zahra even argues that the radicalization of the various nationalist movements in Austria-Hungary was largely caused by their relative failure in mobilizing the population.[26]

Most regional case studies on Asia and Africa, like their counterparts in East-Central Europe, also focus on interethnic strife. This can be illustrated with the case of India. In a monograph on the politics of nationality in Assam, which appeared in 1999, Sanjib Baruah argues that the rise of both the anti-colonial nationalism of the Indian National Congress and an Assamese 'imagined community' was the result of the modernization process during the colonial era. The expansion of the tea plantations caused the integration of the region within the capitalist market economy, while profoundly affecting the social structure of the population. Both an Assamese 'subnationalism' and a pan-Indian nationalism coexisted peacefully side by side until in the 1980s the United Liberation Front of Assam tried to 'restore' the region's 'lost independence'. This in turn triggered a reaction by some of the region's ethnic minorities, who now also demanded a separate state. In general, however, most inhabitants cherished their regional or ethnic 'subnationalism' while recognizing the existing framework of the Indian nation state.[27] Other scholars have studied the construction of other regional or subnational identities within India with a more cultural approach, focusing for instance on language, historical memory or religion, while largely confirming Baruah's view that these territorial identities were the product of modernization and developed alongside Indian nationalism.[28]

In the United States, the South is generally seen as a region with an outspoken identity, which was cultivated particularly after its failed attempt to secede from the Union during the American Civil War. As a result the field of Southern Studies is flourishing. The main topic here is the region's traditionalism (or economic backwardness) and the continuing presence of all forms of racial discrimination. Recently, more cultural approaches have also been applied, but apart from the issue of citizenship, the link with nationalism or nation-building is not explicitly made.[29]

Since in the rest of the Americas the nation or nation state is generally not contested, while discrimination of indigenous groups, descendants of African slaves and other people of colour is still very much an issue, regional case studies mainly focus on the relations between the different ethnic communities. Nancy Appelbaum's *Muddied Waters*, for instance, examines the construction of local and regional identities in Riosucio, a town in Colombia's western Coffee Region. The town was founded in 1819 by a 'black' and 'Indian' community, but during the nineteenth century 'white' migrants from the neighbouring department of Antioquia arrived in the region to domesticate an 'empty' wilderness in order to cultivate coffee. They quickly took over power at the municipal and provincial level and they generally presented the region's identity as modern and 'white'. The author, however, makes clear that this was neither a peaceful colonization of virgin lands by hard-working migrants, nor an 'invasion' of outsiders, since the already existing indigenous and black communities actively participated in the process of regional identity formation.[30]

However, there were also other ways of studying the construction of territorial identities in the Americas. In 1993, Robert Dorman published his *Revolt of the Provinces*. Similar to Thiesse, he analyses the rise of regionalist literature in the United States within a broad cultural context. He clearly shows that regionalism was not something that was confined to the South but that intellectuals, writers, folklorists, sociologists and architects all over the country were interested in rural traditions, the tribal cultures of Native Americans and the folklore of new immigrants. Dorman presents regionalism primarily as a reaction against the levelling impact of modernization and the destructive force of unbridled capitalism. Nevertheless, he also underlines that not all activists were nostalgic traditionalists; many of them collaborated actively in Roosevelt's New Deal and attempted to reform capitalism while taking into account regional differences.[31]

Scholars have also paid much attention to the construction of spatial identities of smaller regions and cities within the United States. Again the link with the nation-building process, which is so prominent in European case studies, is not explicitly addressed. In her *Inventing New England*, published in 1995, Dana Brown privileged economic actors and commercial motives over the initiatives and ideas of politicians and intellectuals, thus dealing with themes that would be highlighted by Edensor as well. She clearly showed how the growth of the tourism business during the nineteenth century transformed the image of New England as a highly industrialized region ridden with class conflict into a charming tourist destination, with beautiful fishing villages, rustic cottages and a peaceful countryside, thus profoundly affecting the region's identity.[32] In a similar way, Chris Magoc makes clear how Yellowstone, the world's first national park, became an iconic landscape through the efforts of railway companies, businessmen and local authorities. As a kind of illustration of the frontier myth, and against the backdrop of rather exceptional scenery, wild bison and Native Americans were converted into picturesque tourist objects.[33]

Also dealing with economic motives is Kolleen Guy's monograph *When Champagne became French*. In it she tells the sparkling story of the international success of champagne and its association with both the region and the nation. Around 1900 various groups of wine growers and the large trading houses violently clashed, particularly over the use of grapes and wine from outside the Champagne region. This was opposed by the farmers with the argument that true champagne could only be made with locally grown grapes. As a consequence, they obtained protective measures which after the First World War were extended as the *appelation d'origine contrôlée* to other regional agricultural specialties as well (primarily cheese and wine). This way champagne became closely connected to both the soil and identity of the region, while at the same time it was marketed as a quintessential French beverage.[34]

In the end, we can conclude that there are many similarities between the construction of regional or subnational identities and their relationship with the larger nation-building process in the various parts of the Americas, Europe and Asia. First of all, the rise of nationalism did not weaken existing regional identities; on the contrary, these were strengthened and more closely defined towards the end of the nineteenth century. Everywhere the interest in local history, vernacular traditions, folklore and the cultural and natural heritage of the region grew rapidly. It seemed that in most cases local and regional elites tried to advance the nation-building process by broadening and democratizing the national identity that had to be adopted by including the vernacular culture of the rural population within the national patrimony. Sometimes political considerations had the upper hand; in other cases cultural or even commercial motives seemed to have been more relevant. Nevertheless, almost all existing studies are still firmly embedded within a specific national context and historiographic tradition.

Unfortunately, apart from Mallon's book on Mexican and Peruvian peasant nationalism and a few edited volumes on regionalism in Europe, there are almost no comparative studies.[35] One of the few exceptions is *The Culture of Regionalism* in which Eric Storm compares regionalist painting, neo-vernacular architecture and regionalist exhibits in France, Germany and Spain. In his monograph, he contradicts some of the findings of most existing case studies by arguing that the new interest in regional identities was not so much a 'revolt' or 'awakening' of the provinces, which can be explained from the particular national context, but an innovative cultural trend that arose almost simultaneously in different parts of Europe towards the end of the nineteenth century. Regionalist activists decisively broke with the conventional historicist and academic culture of the nineteenth century – which took the nation as its main frame of reference. As a result, the 'culture of regionalism' became its most important alternative during the first decades of the twentieth century. Moreover, he claims that the construction of regional identities and the integration of the regional cultural heritage within the patrimony of the nation were not primarily the work of local and regional elites, on the contrary many of its early promoters belonged to the highly cosmopolitan national artistic and intellectual elites. This novel interest in the 'authentic' vernacular culture of the countryside could therefore be interpreted as a new transnational phase in the nation-building process.[36]

Next to this comparative interpretation of regionalism as a cultural trend, there is another highly comparative research tradition that focuses more on institutional factors and that is largely dominated by social scientists. Their investigations deal with the 'Europe of the regions', that is to say, the effects of the regional policies that were introduced by the European Economic Community in 1973 with the establishment of the European Regional Development Fund in order to reduce regional disparities in income and wealth. As a consequence, this approach privileges governance and economics over culture, while institutions receive more attention than actors from civil society. Michael Keating is probably the most important expert on this topic and in *The New Regionalism in Western Europe* he shows how from the 1970s onwards the need to attract investors and markets caused increased inter-regional competition, which led to active policies of 'region branding'. At the same time, the growing role of the European Union restructured the relations between the European Commission, the member states and the various substate regions. Regional councils administered the subsidies that were obtained from Brussels. This 'rescaling' implied that nation states ceded power in some fields to the European Union, while devolving other responsibilities to regional or municipal bodies. Nevertheless, this was not a one-way process and in many instances national governments reasserted their position. Region branding, the empowerment of the region by the European Union and the growing assertiveness of some regions on the international stage can strengthen regional identities or reinforce a process of 'region building', and in some cases even have a debilitating effect on existing nation states.[37] Other authors have also stressed the role of globalization in stimulating a somewhat defensive and more cultural-laden 'new regionalism', both in Europe as elsewhere.[38]

Transnational approaches

Possibly even more directly related to the new phase of globalization since 1989 is the rapidly growing interest in global flows and movements of goods, ideas and persons in earlier periods of time, which is now generally known as transnational history.[39] Many scholars are starting to realize that transborder movements had an impact on the rise and development of nationalism, the nation-building process and the construction of national identities around the globe. In fact, the new emphasis on transnational flows even entails a fundamental critique of the older, almost exclusive focus on the nation state. Thus, in 2002 Andreas Wimmer and Nina Glick Schiller launched an attack on what they labelled 'methodological nationalism'. Although they principally dissected the role of methodological nationalism in the social sciences and its impact on migration studies, their critique also applies to the discipline of history and the field of nationalism studies. They distinguish three forms of methodological nationalism. First of all classical social theory downplays the role of nationalism while considering it to be backward, but at the same time accepts a world divided into nation states as a given. Second, sociologists equate society with national society and thus take nation states as the 'naturally given entities of study'. Third, in the social sciences the analytical focus is reduced to the boundaries of the nation state and everything that extends 'over its borders was cut off analytically'. The consequence of this use of the nation state as a container in which developments should be analysed was that transborder migration was seen as an anomaly that – contrary to migration flows within the nation state – should be controlled and monitored. Moreover, foreign migrants were presented as problematic. They either were 'uprooted' and implicitly supposed to return home, or should be naturalized and assimilate into the homogenous national culture that presumably already existed within the host country.[40]

The awareness that transnational influences had been ignored has led scholars dealing with nationalism to direct their attention beyond the existing borders. This can be done by concentrating on the role of migrants, but has expressed itself in other ways as well. Some historians focus on the role of borderlands, others look at transfers and transnational networks, while another group deals with foreign influences on the nation-building process. In all cases, scholars examine how local, regional and transnational actors actively construct and reconstruct territorial identities in everyday life. It is noteworthy that within these four transnational approaches the differences between the various geographical historiographical traditions are much less prominent.

In a lecture in 1992 Benedict Anderson already paid attention to the impact of nationalism on migrants. He argued that because the nation state model became the norm during the twentieth century the identity of immigrants had the tendency to become 'ethnicized'. Anderson also coined the term 'long-distance nationalism' to describe the strong attachment emigrants and many of their descendants feel towards their home country. This has become easier thanks to modern communication technology. Sometimes this led to active political involvement and even support for violent nationalist movements, such as the Tamil Tigers and the Irish Revolutionary Army. In this way citizenship and national feelings became disconnected and some migrants participated in the politics of a country in which they did not live, pay taxes or vote.[41] In 2001, in a more extensive case study Nina Glick Schiller and Georges Fouron demonstrated how Haitian migrants in the United States created 'transnational social fields'. Instead of being uprooted or assimilating in the host country, they remained in contact with those who stayed behind to improve the situation of their 'fatherland'.[42]

While most studies on long-distance nationalism discuss very recent developments, Sebastian Conrad focuses on the decades around 1900. Moreover, in his book he primarily examines the impact of transnational migration flows on the development of nationalism within the motherland itself, in this case the German Empire. With the growing number of German emigrants, especially to the United States, people began to worry about the diminishing strength of the German nation. Emigrants were renamed 'diaspora Germans' and attempts were made to redirect migration flows towards the German colonies. Relations with emigrant groups were intensified and German settlers abroad were even presented as a 'rejuvenation' of the 'race'. Preoccupations, on the other hand, with growing numbers of Polish and Jewish newcomers, together with anxieties over miscegenation in the German colonies, led to a gradual 'racialization' of foreign immigrants. These transnational influences and worries had practical consequences, such as stricter border controls, and in 1913, a new citizenship law stipulated that Germans would not lose their citizenship after leaving the country and could even transfer it to their descendants.[43]

Borders also received more scholarly attention and a very early example is Peter Sahlins's *Boundaries*, a compelling examination of the social construction of a national border in the Pyrenees after half of the Spanish county of Cerdanya was annexed by France in 1659. He analysed how the identity of the rural communities developed over the following centuries, while showing that even before the boundaries became more territorialized and rigid during the French Revolution, the inhabitants of the county already used 'the language and rhetoric of nationality' to protect their interests. They requested specific benefits and privileges that were due to them as Frenchmen or Spaniards, while continuing to use the local Catalan dialect in daily life. Local identities therefore continued to exist alongside a more modern national identity. Only during the late nineteenth and twentieth centuries did differences between the two parts of the valley become more prominent as the modernizing French state offered its citizens more advantages, opportunities and material rewards than its Spanish counterpart. This could possibly explain why all things Catalan merely have a folkloric status on the French side of the border, whereas on the Spanish side Catalan nationalism made significant inroads.[44]

A similar study is Paul Nugent's analysis of the construction of the border between Ghana and Togo during the twentieth century. Although the border was imposed from above, the colonial authorities did take existing realities in this part of West Africa into account. Moreover, the local population not only took the border as a 'theatre of opportunities' for smuggling and cross-border trade but also used it as a protection against persecution by fleeing to the other side. Western-educated elites among the Ewe – the most important ethnic group on both sides of the border – began to advocate the creation of their own nation state. However, the large majority of the population was not interested in this theoretical construct; most local inhabitants preferred the concrete benefits that could be gained from the existing borders, while directing their demands increasingly to the central governments of the new nation states of Ghana and Togo. Here, like in the Cerdenya valley, the local population actively contributed to the strengthening of the new nation states.[45]

Some recent studies pay more attention to cross-border flows. In her monograph on northern Bohemia (Sudetenland) and southern Saxony, Caitlin Murdock begins in 1871, when the border between these two regions became the separation line between two large Central European Empires. For the moment, the dividing effect of the state-building processes was offset by improved communications. Different price levels provided strong incentives to cross the border for work or shopping, while mutual relations were also stimulated by tourism, entertainment – beer was cheaper in Bohemia – and marriages. Until 1914, nation-building on both sides of the border was not so much stimulated by the state as by nationalist organizations and movements. German-speaking workers from Bohemia were not considered foreigners in Saxony's civil society. However, Czech and German nationalist groups in Bohemia began to resent migration to Saxony since it weakened their cause within Austria. The First World War, the intensification of state- and nation-building and the economic upheavals during the interwar period drove Saxony and Bohemia apart. The border was better guarded; those without citizenship were now considered foreigners and economic relations were disrupted.[46] Thus, not only were borders imposed from above, but they also took shape on a daily basis by the actions, ideas and imaginations of thousands of ordinary people.

Another transnational approach is developed by historians who recognize that nationalist movements were influenced by foreign ideas, that many nationalist intellectuals conducted their activities in exile and that many nationalist pamphlets and magazines were published abroad. The most ambitious attempt to literally map the intellectual networks of nationalist activists, their international contacts and the transfer of ideas from one movement to another is undertaken by Joep Leerssen, who advocates a comparative approach to nineteenth-century cultural nationalism in Europe. During the Romantic era, intellectuals began to canonize vernacular cultures by salvaging, producing and propagating all kinds of 'national' cultural manifestations. In 2015, he launched a digital database with over 1200 articles – written by hundreds of scholars – about themes and persons, while showing the links between them on a map of Europe. It also provides access to visual, textual and audio documentation. This *Encyclopedia of Romantic Nationalism* demonstrates the large number of transnational connections between different cultural fields, genres and media.[47]

Somewhat similar is Prasenjit Duara's attempt to study the nation formation in China from the 'outside-in', which means that he puts much emphasis on entangled histories, international transfers, comparisons and transnational influences in order to understand the Chinese case as part of broader global and East-Asian developments. He particularly emphasizes the rise of nationalism in Japan, China, Korea, Manchukuo and Taiwan as an entangled history. This obviously had to do with the Japanese occupation of the other areas, but intellectual trends such as the production of national histories or the adoption of racialist conceptions also developed along common lines. In his book, he also explores the role of the Chinese diaspora and its connections with the 'homeland'.[48]

Surprisingly, all studies discussed until now, whether they focus on peasants, regional activists, migrants or transfer, only award agency to members of the proper nation. This is quite obvious in the case of nationalist movements. However, it is much less logical when analysing the construction of national identities and this brings us to the fourth transnational approach. Influenced by Edward Said's *Orientalism*, many scholars have analysed how collective identities in the non-Western world were imposed or largely shaped from outside. A highly nuanced application of Said's views on a national case is given by Donald Reid in his book on the role of Egypt's rich ancient past in the construction of the country's national identity during the long nineteenth century. Egyptian archaeology was dominated by Western scholars and they also largely determined the way that Egypt's pharaonic, Greco-Roman, Islamic and Coptic heritage was represented in scientific texts and popular guidebooks, at sites, in museums and at world fairs. Nonetheless, Reid also shows how Egyptian scholars, politicians and intellectuals became involved in this process, producing their own histories of ancient Egypt in Arabic, founding a national school of Egyptology and embracing the pharaonic past as part of their national heritage. They were not the passive victims of Western science and imperialist powers, but had an active role in the construction of an Egyptian national identity.[49]

The impact of foreign tourism has also been a topic of research. Anthropologists in particular have examined how local communities interacted with outsiders to reshape their own collective self-image. A fascinating example is provided by Michel Picard's exploration of how the people of Bali became 'Balinized' through the interaction with colonial authorities, Western travellers, the Indonesian state and foreign tourism. First of all, colonial officials considered Bali a 'living museum' of the original Hindu-Javanese civilization of the Dutch East Indies. Foreign visitors created the image of a peaceful paradise and more or less invented Balinese arts and crafts by separating diverse traditions from their original ritual and religious context and packaging them for Western consumption. In the 1960s the independent Indonesian state began to present Bali as one of the highlights of the country's rich cultural and natural treasures in order to attract foreign tourists. In this way, the Balinese were required to be worthy representatives of their supposedly 'authentic' culture. The island's collective identity was thus shaped by the interaction of the local population with the processes of colonization, nation-building and 'touristification'.[50]

Largely ignored, however, is the notion that foreigners also had a substantial impact on the construction of national identities within the Western world. Some recent studies have made this clear for the case of Spain. Foreign scholars, for instance, were the first to historicize the story of Spanish art, thereby contributing in a decisive way to the definition of the country's artistic canon. And during the nineteenth and twentieth centuries, foreign travellers and tourists also played a crucial role in integrating the monuments of Al-Andalus, flamenco music and the figure of Don Juan – each of which initially was seen with suspicion by most domestic elites – into the Spanish national imagination.[51]

Conclusion

The disintegration of the nation as the self-evident unit of analysis in the study of nationalism has had important consequences. First of all, the modernist view of nation-building as a process that was imposed from above has been undermined by a large number of local and regional case studies that show that regional authorities, local elites and even peasants had an active role and could in many instances bend it to their needs. Moreover, existing collective and territorial identities were not absorbed by the more modern identification with the nation, but were transformed and in many cases even strengthened in the process. From the late nineteenth century the vernacular heritage of the countryside became an integral part of both better defined regional identities and of the more encompassing patrimony of the nation. Globalization, tourism and devolution ensured that regions and their territorial identities continue to be a factor at the (inter)national stage.

The growing attention for transnational flows and movements in turn have made clear that the rise of national movements, the nation-building process and the construction of national identities should not be studied in isolation. Borders were not just fixed demarcation lines between two nation states, but were reproduced and transformed by geopolitical developments, governmental decisions, but also on a daily basis by the ideas, practices and transborder movements of the people on the ground. On top of that, it has become evident that migrants and exiles transferred ideas and even foreign scholars and tourists had an impact on nation formation and nation-building processes.

Although many of the main concepts of the spatial turn, such as the idea that spaces are social constructs, the focus on agency, tactics and everyday life and the questioning of the nation state as a neutral, inert box in which developments can objectively be analysed, have become mainstream among historians and social scientists, the nation state remains the main unit of analysis in the humanities and social sciences. Statistical data, archival material and surveys are still collected and classified per country, which as a consequence also functions as the basic unit for comparisons. In public opinion the world is still divided into discrete and bounded nation states, which each have their own identity and are supposed to command their own destiny. Even recent historical overviews that are used for our undergraduate courses continue to focus on the individual trajectories of the various nation states and routinely speak of nations when modern nation states did not yet exist. So a lot of work still needs to be done.

At the same time, the focus on the production of spaces by different social groups and communities over time seems to have its limitations as well. It has resulted in a fast-growing number of historical studies that tend to emphasize the specific circumstances and unique outcomes of each case, thus resulting in a very fragmented overall picture. Moreover, many scholars still do not escape the trap of 'methodological nationalism'; most studies discussed in the first half of this chapter, for instance, were firmly embedded in national historiographical debates and focused almost exclusively on national actors and national turning points, while using national concepts and national primary sources. This makes it even more difficult to arrive at a global overview. Comparative studies could probably make clear that there are many similarities as well in the way nations were constructed, in the way local and regional identities interacted with the nation-building process and in the impact of transnational actors.

Notes

1   Henri Lefebvre, *The Production of Space* (Oxford, 1991).
2   See chapter by Elgenius.
3   Michel de Certeau, *The Practice of Everyday Life* (Berkeley, 1984), pp. xi–xxiv.
4   Barney Warf and Santa Arias (eds), *The Spatial Turn: Interdisciplinary Perspectives* (London and New York, 2009); Jörg Döring and Tristan Thielmann (eds), *Spatial Turn. Das Raumparadigma in den Kultur- und Sozialwissenschaften* (Bielefeld, 2008).
5   See Thomas Rohkrämer and Felix Robin Schulz, 'Space, Place and Identities', *History Compass* 7 (2009), 1338–49; Matthias Middell and Katja Naumann,

'Global History and the Spatial Turn: From the Impact of Area Studies to the Study of Critical Junctures of Globalization', *Journal of Global History* 5 (2010), 149–70. Leif Jerram, 'Space: A Useless Category for Historical Analysis?' *History and Theory* 52 (2013), 400–19.

6   Doreen Massey, *Space, Place and Gender* (Minneapolis 1994), pp. 146–57.

7   See chapters by Breuilly and Wicke.

8   Andreas Wimmer, *Nation Building: Why Some Countries Come Together While Others Fall Apart* (Princeton, 2018), pp. 171–208.

9   Anssi Paasi, *Territories, Boundaries and Consciousness: The Changing Geographies of the Finnish-Russian Border* (Chichester, 1996).

10 Tim Edensor, *National Identity, Popular Culture and Everyday Life* (Oxford, 2002).

11 Eugen Weber, *Peasants into Frenchmen: The Modernization of Rural France, 1870–1914* (Stanford, 1976); see also the chapter by Breuilly.

12 Caroline Ford, *Creating the Nation in Provincial France: Religion and Political Identity in Brittany* (New Haven, 1993).

13 James R. Lehning, *Peasant and French: Cultural Contact in Rural France during the Nineteenth Century* (Cambridge, 1995).

14 Prasenjit Duara, *Culture, Power, and the State: Rural North China, 1900–1942* (Stanford, 1988).

15 See chapter by Seth.

16 Florencia E. Mallon, *Peasant and Nation: The Making of Postcolonial Mexico and Peru* (Berkeley, 1995).

17 Keely Stauter-Halsted, *The Nation in the Village: The Genesis of Peasant National Identity in Austrian Poland 1848–1918* (Ithaca, 2001).

18 For instance: Katherine B. Aaslestad, *Place and Politics: Local Identity, Civic Culture and German Nationalism in North Germany during the Revolutionary Era* (Leiden, 2005).

19 Rogers Brubaker, Margit Feinschmidt, Jon Fox and Liana Grancea, *Nationalist Politics and Everyday Ethnicity in a Transylvanian Town* (Princeton, 2006).

20 Celia Applegate, *A Nation of Provincials: The German Idea of Heimat* (Berkeley, 1990). See also: Alon Confino, *The Nation as a Local Metaphor: Württemberg, Imperial Germany, and National Memory, 1871–1918* (Chapel Hill, 1997).

21 Anne-Marie Thiesse, *Écrire la France. Le Mouvement littéraire régionaliste de la langue française entre la Belle Époque et la Libération* (Paris, 1991).

22 Anne-Marie Thiesse, *Ils apprenaient la France. L'exaltation des régions dans le discours patriotique* (Paris, 1997).

23 Xosé-Manoel Núñez, 'The Region as Essence of the Fatherland: Regionalist Variants of Spanish Nationalism (1840–1936)', *European History Quarterly* (2001), 483–518; Stefano Cavazza, *Piccole Patrie. Feste popolari tra regione e nazione durante il fascismo* (Bologna, 1997); Maarten Van Ginderachter, *Le chant du coq. Nation et nationalisme en Wallonie depuis 1880* (Ghent, 2005).

24 Robert Colls and Bill Lancaster (eds), *Geordies: Roots of Regionalism* (Newcastle, 1992); Goffe Jensma, *Het rode tasje van Salverda. Burgerlijk bewustzijn en Friese identiteit in de negentiende eeuw* (Leeuwarden, 1998). F. Persson, *Skåne, den farliga halvön. Historia, identitet och ideologi, 1865–2000* (Lund, 2008).

25 Jeremy King, *Budweisers into Czechs and Germans: A Local History of Bohemian Politics, 1848–1948* (Princeton, 2002).

26 Pieter Judson, *Guardians of the Nation: Activists on the Language Frontier of Imperial Austria* (Cambridge, MA, 2006); James E. Bjork, *Neither German nor Pole: Catholicism and National Indifference in a Central European Borderland* (Ann Arbor, 2008); Tara Zahra, *Kidnapped Souls: National Indifference and the Battle for Children in the Bohemian Lands 1900–1948* (Ithaca, 2008); Tara Zahra, 'Imagined Non-Communities: National Indifference as a Category of Analysis', *Slavic Review* (2010), 93–119.

27 Sanjib Baruah, *India against Itself: Assam and the Politics of Nationality* (Philadelphia, 1999).

28 Sumathi Ramaswamy, *Passions of the Tongue: Language Devotion in Tamil India, 1891–1970* (Berkeley, 1997); Yasmin Saikia, *Fragmented Memories: Struggling to Be Tai-Ahom in India* (Durham, 2004); Prachi Deshpande, *Creative Pasts: Historical Memory and Identity in Western India, 1700–1960* (New York, 2007); Chitralekha Zutshi, *Languages of Belonging: Islam, Regional Identity, and the Making of Kashmir* (London, 2004).

29 See for instance Martyn Bone, Brian Ward and William A. Link (eds), *Creating and Consuming the American South* (Gainesville, 2015). For the West, see: David M. Wrobel, *Promised Lands: Promotion, Memory, and the Creation of the American West* (Lawrence, 2002). See for a similar study on the Brazilian South: Ruben Oliven, *Tradition Matters: Modern Gaucho Identity in Brazil* (translated from Portuguese; New York, 1996).

30 Nancy P. Appelbaum, *Muddied Waters: Race, Region, and Local History in Colombia, 1846–1948* (Durham, 2003).

31 Robert L. Dorman, *Revolt of the Provinces: The Regionalist Movement in America, 1920–1945* (Chapel Hill, 1993).

32 Dona Brown, *Inventing New England: Regional Tourism in the Nineteenth Century* (Washington, 1995).

33 Chris J. Magoc, *Yellowstone: The Creation and Selling of an American Landscape, 1870–1903* (Albuquerque, 1999). See also Chris Wilson, *The Myth of Santa Fe: Creating a Modern Regional Tradition* (Albuquerque, 1997); Angela M. Blake, *How New York Became American: 1890–1924* (Baltimore, 2006).

34 Kolleen M. Guy, *When Champagne Became French: Wine and the Making of a National Identity* (Baltimore, 2003).

35 Almost all chapters still deal with one national or regional case: Laurence Cole (ed.), *Different Paths to the Nation: Regional and National Identities in Central Europe and Italy, 1830–70* (Basingstoke, 2007); Joost Augusteijn and Eric Storm (eds), *Region and State in Nineteenth-Century Europe: Nation-Building, Regional Identities and Separatism* (Basingstoke, 2012).

36 Eric Storm, *The Culture of Regionalism: Art, Architecture and International Exhibitions in France, Germany and Spain, 1890–1930* (Manchester, 2010); Xosé M. Núñez Seixas and Eric Storm (eds), *Regionalism and Modern Europe: Identity Construction and Movements from 1890 to the Present Day* (London, 2019).

37 Michael Keating, *The New Regionalism in Western Europe: Territorial Restructuring and Political Change* (Cheltenham, 1998); Michael Keating,

Rescaling the European State: The Making of Territory and the Rise of the Meso (Oxford, 2013).

38 Anssi Paasi, 'The Resurgence of the "Region" and "Regional Identity": Theoretical Perspectives and Empirical Observations on Regional Dynamics in Europe', *Review of International Studies* (2009), 121–46; Tim Oakes, 'China's Provincial Identities: Reviving Regionalism and Reinventing "Chineseness"', *Journal of Asian Studies* (2000), 667–92.

39 See Pierre-Yves Saunier, *Transnational History* (Basingstoke, 2013).

40 Andreas Wimmer and Nina Glick Schiller, 'Methodological Nationalism and Beyond: Nation-State Building, Migration and the Social Sciences', *Global Networks* (2002), 301–34; Daniel Chernillo, 'The Critique of Methodological Nationalism: Theory and History' *Thesis Eleven* 106:1 (2011), 98–117.

41 Benedict Anderson, *Long-Distance Nationalism: World Capitalism and the Rise of Identity Politics* (Wertheim Lecture; Amsterdam, 1992), p. 11.

42 Nina Glick Schiller and Georges Eugene Fouron, *Georges Woke Up Laughing: Long-Distance Nationalism and the Search for Home* (Durham, 2001). See for a similar in-depth study of Slovene and Croat migrant communities in Australia Zlatko Skrbis, *Long-Distance Nationalism: Diasporas, Homelands and Identities* (Aldershot, 1999).

43 Sebastian Conrad, *Globalisation and the Nation in Imperial Germany* (translated from German; Cambridge, 2010).

44 Peter Sahlins, *Boundaries: The Making of France and Spain in the Pyrenees* (Berkeley, 1989).

45 Paul Nugent, *Smugglers, Secessionists, and Loyal Citizens on the Ghana-Togo Frontier* (Oxford, 2002).

46 Caitlin E. Murdock, *Changing Places: Society, Culture and Territory in the Saxon-Bohemian Borderlands, 1870–1946* (Ann Arbor, 2010). See also Omar Bartov and Eric D. Weitz (eds), *Shatterzone of Empires: Coexistence and Violence in the German, Habsburg, Russian and Ottoman Borderlands* (Bloomington, 2013).

47 Joep Leerssen, 'Nationalism and the Cultivation of Culture', *Nations and Nationalism* 12:4 (2006), 559–78; Joep Leerssen (ed.), *Encyclopedia of Romantic Nationalism* (Amsterdam, 2018); http://romanticnationalism.net.

48 Prasenjit Duara, *The Global and Regional in China's Nation-Formation* (London, 2008). See also Mark Frost, '"Wider Opportunities": Religious Revival, Nationalist Awakening and the Global Dimensions in Colombo, 1870–1920' *Modern Asian Studies* 36:4 (2002), 937–67.

49 Donald Malcolm Reid, *Whose Pharaohs? Archaeology, Museums, and Egyptian National Identity from Napoleon to World War I* (Berkeley, 2002).

50 Michel Picard, *Bali: Cultural Tourism and Touristic Culture* (translated from French; Singapore, 1996).

51 Eric Storm, 'Nationalism Studies between Methodological Nationalism and Orientalism: An Alternative Approach Illustrated with the Case of El Greco, Toledo, Spain', *Nations and Nationalism* 21:4 (2015), 786–804; Xavier Andreu, *El descubrimiento de España. Mito romántico e identidad nacional* (Barcelona, 2016); Eric Storm, 'Making Spain more Spanish: The Impact of Tourism on Spanish National Identity', in Javier Moreno Luzón and Xosé M. Núñez (eds), *Metaphors of Spain: Representations of Spanish National Identity in the Twentieth Century* (New York, 2017), pp. 239–60.

Further reading

Applegate, Celia, *A Nation of Provincials: The German Idea of Heimat.*
    Berkeley: University of California Press, 1990.
Duara, Prasenjit, *Culture, Power, and the State: Rural North China, 1900–1942.*
    Stanford: Stanford University Press, 1988.
Glick Schiller, Nina and G. E. Fouron, *Georges Woke up Laughing: Long-Distance*
    Nationalism and the Search for Home. Durham: Duke University Press, 2001.
Keating, Michael, *The New Regionalism in Western Europe: Territorial*
    Restructuring and Political Change. Cheltenham: Edward Elgar, 1998.
Leerssen, Joep (ed.), *Encyclopedia of Romantic Nationalism.* Amsterdam:
    Amsterdam University Press, 2018.
Mallon, Florencia E., *Peasant and Nation: The Making of Postcolonial Mexico and*
    Peru. Berkeley: University of California Press, 1995.
Nugent, Paul, *Smugglers, Secessionists, and Loyal Citizens on the Ghana-Togo*
    Frontier. Oxford: Ohio University Press, 2002.
Núñez Seixas, Xosé M. and E. Storm (eds), *Regionalism and Modern Europe:*
    Identity Construction and Movements from 1890 to the Present Day.
    London: Bloomsbury, 2019.

12

The global turn in historical writing and the history of nationalism

Matthias Middell

Over the past three decades, global history has again gained popularity among both professional historians and a wider audience expecting long-term explanations for global processes. In the beginning, the new interest in world history writing as well as in the history of faraway world regions seemed to be on its way to replace an ever more outdated national history writing. However, a closer look at the practice of global history writing demonstrates that states and societies – which were imagined as national even long before the nineteenth century when nation state building came to the fore – remain an important subject in historical investigation. This can take the form of a unit of analysis in comparative studies, especially when state-based statistics and the political archives of such states are used; a collective actor behind arrangements in international organizations as well as international relations; and finally as a necessary point of departure for the study of all flows of goods, capital, people and ideas, transcending national borders that for many scholars make up the core of the new global history. More recently, the once-so-loud prophesiers of the end of the nation state have reversed their prognosis and have insisted on the possibility of a U-turn from globalization to deglobalization, inviting historians to share their historical reference to the crisis of 1929. In this perspective then, a protectionist national policy becomes the goal of a next round in the permanent ups and downs of opening and closure which in this interpretation characterizes world history.

After a long period of enthusiasm for globalization – which was presented as not having any alternative – some commentators on current affairs hasten now, after the British referendum to leave the European Union and the election of a rather protectionist Donald Trump to the White House, to declare the era of growing economic interdependency over, or at least stalled for the time being. In their binary opposition of globalization and (lost) national sovereignty, this moment of 'deglobalization' raises the question if it will be possible to regain control over the many flows that make our borders so porous that they are invisible to some. The term 'deglobalization', however, is ambiguous in many respects. Some applaud it as counter-hegemonic and dream of a democratization of the international system, while others hope for political support for their xenophobic and racist agendas under the label of national sovereignty. Defending the profits from the inclusive patterns of (national) welfare states at times of growing migration flows demonstrates not only a legitimate struggle for well-being among the ordinary people working hard to earn their living, but it also indicates how far behind labour movements are in adjusting to the global character of capitalism that has been advanced by the managerial elites over the past decades. This chapter is about the more nuanced interpretations of processes of de- and reterritorialization provided by the current generation of global historians confronting fantasies of a borderless world based upon global governance without any intermediate instances.

Shifts towards world history writing

The last 25 years of historical scholarship have been characterized by increasing popularity of world and global history approaches. Especially in the 1990s, this went hand in hand with a strong critique towards a tradition of national history writing that was described as outdated at 'times of globalization' and even as a hindrance to a necessary emerging cosmopolitan attitude based upon global historical consciousness. Some social scientists and economists saw the nation state in definite decline and disappearing to the benefit of so-called global governance or a world society. Answers differ when it comes to what may replace the nation state, either regional trading blocs or a world polity that makes the individual state its subunit.[1] Historians, being more familiar with the many facets of state- and nation-building, have taken over the centuries, were a little bit more reluctant to declaring the death of nationalism and in turn became more and more critical towards their own discipline's involvement in nationalist agendas.

Jerry Bentley – for many years the editor of one of the leading academic journals in the field, the *Journal of World History*, and among the most successful authors in the new genre of world history textbooks for American undergraduate programmes[2] – explained the main shift from national to global history through a changing environment. Since historians are no longer needed as heralds of the upcoming nation state – which provided them with the necessary tools for further professionalization, such as access to archives, libraries, museums and collections, as well as influence over policies regarding monuments and collective memory – they now have become partisans of a globalizing academic community promoting the postnational configuration of the world order. As a consequence, parts of historiography have become anachronistic when not following the path from national to world history: 'In many ways, professional historical scholarship is an artefact of what you might call national-state era of world history.'[3]

The polemical undertone of this statement has to be understood within the context of the early years of the new world history movement in the United States of America – the renewal of the 'manifest destiny' topos, which has dominated North American self-perception for a very long time, raised critical concern again during times of unilateralism after the end of the Cold War and the collapse of the Soviet Union.[4] This new constellation provoked sharp conflicts (some even speak of history wars) about the future content of introductory courses at North American colleges. While some insisted on a continuation of the old 'Rise of the West' narrative[5] (often ironically summarized as running 'from Plato to NATO') because it would have been confirmed by America's new leadership role, others heavily criticized the lack of students' intellectual preparation for living a more and more connected world and fought for a renewal of courses with world historical encounters between different civilizations as the basis.[6] As a result, today more than 50 per cent of American colleges have introduced some sort of world history curriculum, which gives more emphasis than the former ones to regions outside the Atlantic world and help to integrate area studies into teaching at history departments. The cosmopolitan intention of such courses is beyond any doubt, but we should not forget that it occurred in the context of a redefinition of the global role to be played by a single nation (as multicultural as it is).

Starting as early as in the late 1980s, the new world history movement emerged in order to influence curricula at universities and high schools. The pioneers of this movement remember a series of forerunners among their own academic teachers.[7] This, however, has connected the new initiative to a particular national tradition in academia. It is not limited to this academic system but it is heavily influenced by its specific features. Patrick Manning, an Africanist by training, summarized this narrative in his book *Navigating World History* (2003) where he recognized a longer tradition of universal and world history writing, but came to the conclusion that the now emerging global (or world) history is something radically new – postcolonial, multicentric and free from teleological Hegelianism. These new characteristics were mainly due to the influence of area studies, which were on the one hand in an institutional crisis after 1989 and 9/11 (criticized for not having foreseen the breakdown of the Soviet Union and the terrorist attacks by radical Islamists) and were on the other hand gaining a stronger institutional position by joining history departments that were increasingly adopting global history approaches. This change allowed for better responses to the demand by immigrant students for representation of 'their' (or their parents) national or continental histories in introductory courses,[8] and helped world history as a new subdiscipline to overcome its often amateurish knowledge basis regarding the non-Western world.

What was presented as new was, however, not completely new, excluding the political success the interest in world or global history won in the 1990s. World history has a long tradition and the remarkable growth rates of international trade and migration, or the circulation of knowledge across the boundaries of 'civilizations' have not only attracted the interest of contemporary commentators but also aroused historical interest in the preconditions and emergence of such waves of 'globalization'. What is often perceived as the zenith of patriotic or national history writing in the nineteenth century was at the same time a period within which a globally oriented anthropology (late eighteenth century),[9] political economy with a similarly global scope (with Marx and others in the mid-nineteenth century) and the academic institutionalization and first professionalization of world history (turn from the nineteenth to the twentieth century) occurred.[10] The dominance of national history writing was in fact never complete, but was disputed and framed at the same time by approaches that have put the one nation or the nation state as a general structure into a global perspective. This global perspective itself has developed in remarkable was – including an ongoing decolonization of our understanding of history and an expansion into social dimensions that are less national and perhaps more regional or transnational than the politics organized by a nation state, think alone of gender relations or cultural patterns and fashions.

The emphasis on border-crossing phenomena was indeed not new. A narrative that claims global history as the quasi-natural product of post-national times only is destined for failure when we look back at the long tradition of world history writing. However, globally oriented historiography had a hard fight to win against the dominant view, which was primarily inward looking and confining history to the limits of national (or better, state) containers. Late-eighteenth-century social theory, very much under the influence of the revolutionary experience stretching at least both sides of the Atlantic, has emphasized the role of domestic structures in explaining historical change. The emergence of a middle class asking for total political participation inspired constitutionalism and thoughts about the best way to organize democracy instead of absolute monarchical power, while continuing social inequality raised concerns about the incongruence of political and social democracy. The great debate between liberal Girondins and the more radically leftist Montagnards, caused by warfare in 1792 over the possibility of exporting revolutionary principles to other territories, ended with Jacobin scepticism and a little bit more than two decades later

Napoleon's grand design of a renewed Europe had failed. The Congress of Vienna finally codified the compromise – containment of a status where in one part of Europe the Bourbons had to accept that there was no way back to a full Restoration, while in other parts all kinds of half-hearted reforms were either confirmed or even reversed.

What is indispensable here for historiography – in contrast to the universal ambitions of enlightened history writing that addressed mankind and its past – is the idea that territorial containers (some of them national, others imperial) are the widely accepted frame for the understanding of history, world history included. It is therefore no wonder that the growing interest in the new features of capitalism that inspired Marx and others in the mid of the nineteenth century to write world history from the angle of economic and social history have done so by starting from the assumption that there is an English, a French, a Prussian, as well as an American path to modern capitalism, all of them distinct from each other due to different domestic constellations between the social and political forces. In the 1850s, Marx widened the perspective to include the colonial world by discussing India and the European periphery by looking at the Spanish case, and 20 years later, in the famous letters to Vera Sasulic, he widened the perspective to include Russia and Eastern Europe in general as well. But in all these cases, he – and with him the emerging sociology, with its mutual inspiration for social history – remained loyal to the point of origin, that is to say, entities characterized by a long history of statehood are the units of analysis for comparison even when it comes to socio-economic questions. This was a decisive precondition for methodological nationalism, which was only fully elaborated upon when these states became instrumental for the fulfilling of nation-building processes (as in the German case where Prussia played such a role). More conservative authors, among them Leopold von Ranke, who became the leading authority for the professional writing of both national and universal history, followed by celebrating the power of the state as the essential element in historical orders.

It was in the 1870s and 1880s that the intellectual programme of anthropogeography gained influence among historians. Friedrich Ratzel, a German professor and one of the founders of human geography and very much interested in questions of geopolitics, already in the second half of the nineteenth century provided an analysis of several continents which inspired scholars to start thinking of the 'world' again as a possible entity. World economy and world politics became terms used to describe a more interconnected world than ever before, based upon the role of international markets and transcontinental competition.[11] This did not abolish national units as the basic unit of the narrative but it brought area studies, having become more institutionalized, into the game and with them the category of civilization – both old and new – became prevalent in world history writing. The case of Karl Lamprecht is telling here in many respects: The Leipzig-based historian started in the 1890s a highly ambitious multivolume book on German history, opening up towards the new trends of social, economic as well as cultural history, which laid the groundwork for a destructive controversy with his colleagues. But after the turn of the century, he became much more interested in questions of how to conceptualize a world history both in writing and teaching. The influence of his colleague Ratzel played out as well as his visit to the United States.[12] Among the intellectual contacts that were crucial for his view on world history were Sinologists, ethnographers, religious studies scholars and early sociologists, which helped him to overcome the classical Eurocentric approach. What made him famous among his contemporaries was his ability to translate the research agenda into an academic institution for world history research that lasted longer than a couple of years only and became the home for more than four generations of world historians at Leipzig University.

But he was by far not the only one among his colleagues all over Europe, as one can see when comparing Lamprecht with Henri Berr's school of historical synthesis in France or Lord Acton's *Cambridge Modern History* around the same time. The concepts, however, remained rather vaguely elaborated upon and the empirical basis was not yet sufficient to consequently replace the leading categories of national history writing. Under permanent attacks by their opponents, who held the central positions in the discipline, world historians of the time produced a series of very popular narratives aiming at satisfying the appetite of the greater audience for such historical foundations of a world this public experienced as further globalizing. What was achieved around the turn of the century was an increasing awareness that the centrality of national entities may be substantially challenged by global economic forces, by newcomers in the field of global politics, as well as by the dynamics of border-crossing learning and appropriation.

The 1920s and 1930s were characterized by a return of ethnonational centrism in world history writing while more liberal versions (like the *Propyläen World History* edited by Walter Goetz) used civilizations as basic units of analysis for the times before the sixteenth century and seemingly national units for the periods after the Renaissance. It was only after the Second World War (and Mahatma Gandhi's glimpses of world history) that Lucien Febvre (on behalf of the United Nations Educational, Scientific and Cultural Organization) took the initiative to liberate modern world history writing from exclusive European authorship and mobilized the oecumene of historians for a new project. Notwithstanding, it turned out to be extremely difficult to satisfy all respective colleagues' insistence on the particular place of their nation, macro-region or continent within the larger narrative. National history worked here as a corrective – or even veto – power to the world historical narrative. At the same time, new categories like the West (in the already mentioned world history by William McNeill) as well as socio-economic formations and the world proletariat (in the Soviet ten volume series on world history edited by Zhukov) were introduced to allow for older categories of civilization and nation state to be transcended; that being said, a look at chapters dealing with times since the late nineteenth century rather provides the impression that the nation state remains an undisputed frame for the explanation of modern history.

It was only since the 1960s that a new wave of world history writing considerably challenged the combination of national and world history that was dominating since the 1920s at least, and can be traced back to the mid-nineteenth century. Fernand Braudel, well known for his interest in *geo-histoire* since the publication of his *Mediterranean World*, wrote world history from a completely different perspective and criticized the emphasis given so far to politics and structures established by politics. He searched for new frames following the logics of regional markets and transregional trade. But he worked mainly on the periods before 1800 and insisted (rightly, as many economic historians nowadays would argue) on the regional and predominantly isolated character of economies that had not yet converged into one global market. Immanuel Wallerstein, in contrast, as well began his narrative around 1450, but went further into the present times. He combined Braudel's rather intuitive description of 'économies-mondes' with the idea of one world system that integrates step by step all these regional economies into core or periphery. National entities remain visible in his narrative but they are no longer the explanatory factor. It is now their position in the world that shall be explained – quite the opposite to what national history most often is interested in.

Methodological nationalism became the object of an eloquent and well-grounded criticism.[13] The nation state, declared definitively dead by parts of the social science-based research on globalization, was no longer self-evident to historians either. This had additional fundamental implications for the ways in which historical theory-building was approached. Comparison, for a long time perceived as the road to success in the social sciences (which have no ability to validate their results with experiments as the natural sciences have), came under critique for inventing the units of analysis it assumed to investigate objectively.[14] Instead, the study of cultural transfers and other kinds of interactions gained prominence and concepts of entangled and connected histories became more and more popular.[15]

This rather sketchy overview on two centuries of world history writing confirms, on the one hand, a long dominance of a methodological nationalism that became disturbed briefly around 1900 and more substantially after the 1960s. It is no coincidence that these two periods have very much been influenced by a growing awareness of the importance of global processes and a growing influence of transnational structures on many dimensions of society. On the other hand, we observe a continuous effort to overcome the limitations of national history writing through renewed attempts to formulate categories for an alternative way of understanding history. But interpretations that took internal processes as the major factor in explaining societal development instead of intersocietal – transnational as well as transregional – interaction as an important cause for historical change persisted for very long.

In brief, we see global history has neither been in the past nor is it in the present completely free from methodological nationalism. Many world historians continue to take the nation state as the basic unit of analysis and rather confirm what they intend to overcome. Rankings that display the assumed performance in global connectedness present (nation) states as the items to be compared. This is, naturally, different from the invention of nations in the nineteenth century, which became a sharp weapon in the hands of nationalists; however, it is much less of an alternative to this tradition than some global historians believe. But, of course, global history is by far not limited to the comparative study of states and macro-regions positioning themselves towards and within global processes. It has more recently complemented such approaches through the study of border-crossing networks and flows.[16] This works subversively against the basic assumptions of nationalisms, where the nation and its state are seen as a unit that is almost completely separated from other such units. The investigation of entanglements between and mutual constituency of societies is an approach that leads to conclusions that are no longer compatible with traditional national history and its relationship with a nationalist agenda.

A re-evaluation of nationalism as reaction to the global condition

There is a second dimension to the relationship between world history and nationalism beyond the rupture with a tradition of national history writing. This is as well the study of nationalism as a phenomenon that can be observed globally and as one of the global ideologies.[17] Michael Geyer and Charles Bright, who both insist on the new character of world history writing after universalism, divide world history between the before and since the emergence of what they call the 'global condition'. In their opinion, it is now no longer the philosopher (and philosophically minded historian, one has to add) who alone creates the unity of the world through theoretical effort; this unity is the very practical results of activities exercised by many, including elites in governments, industries, the banking sector, the cultural sphere, as well as the marginalized migrant, the anonymous spectator of Hollywood as well as Bollywood films, the consumer of goods imported from another continent and so on.[18] Global history, in this sense, is not merely a history of the powerful but is also a post-structuralist history of a multitude that connects all social dimensions across borders of states and continents.

The attempt to put as much distance between old-fashioned universal history, being bound to national history writing and related to a sort of Rankean 'pantheistic state-worship',[19] and the new world and global history has led to an impressive list of innovations with regard to topics, methods and theories in historiography over the past two decades. It has inspired the analysis of border-crossing phenomena of all kinds – migrating people, traded commodities, transferred capital and circulating ideas, as well as viruses bringing about epidemics across continents. Inequalities and injustices are studied transregionally, and international organizations have received much more emphasis than they did before the 1990s. Climate change, demographic patterns and the position in global value chains became explanations for developments that concern more than one society. There was a substantial shift from theory-building that took internal processes as the essential point of departure to an understanding of historical change that may be caused by interaction and interference between many societies – some of them located in neighbourhoods, others at more than an arm's-length distance. The achievements of this new boom in empirical studies as well as in conceptual debates are fascinating and they are so numerous that it is difficult to even keep track of them.[20] Every month there is a new monograph or a collective volume of highest academic quality that helps in discovering the global or transnational dimensions of a phenomenon so far underestimated in its position towards global history.[21]

Of course, national history writing has not disappeared in the meantime. Quite on the contrary, inspired by continuous demand, histories framed nationally have remained popular. In many countries they remain at the centre of school curricula and therefore central to the training of future school instructors. Nowadays, as in former times, history politics – depending heavily on decisions by parliaments and governments about the funding of museums, monuments and other places and media of commemoration – are bound to nationally acting parties, civil society organizations and companies. Political discourses in many countries contain historical references to national historical events and traumas that invite scholars to respond positively or negatively to the use of history for political purposes.

There is ample evidence that national history has even seen a revival, particularly in African universities after the major crisis of academia in the 1990s that was due to the massive reduction of public spending in the educational sector and in the humanities, especially as a consequence of the so-called structural adjustment policies.[22] A similar boost can be observed in Asian and Latin American countries, either connected to nationalism inspired by pride in economic success and growing international recognition or quickened by postcolonial views along the ongoing asymmetries in the relationship with the former imperial metropolis. Such nationalism may sometimes find forms of expression, and therefore looks, similar to nineteenth-century nationalism in Western and Central Europe; however, it has been rightly argued that emancipation from colonialism adds a specific feature to nationalist arguments and makes it attractive to other audiences (and for other reasons) than nationalism a century ago. Charles Mayer has convincingly pointed out that the historical culture of the twenty-first century will be impacted much more by the remembrance of colonialism and postcolonial arguments than it was during the second half of the twentieth century, when the Holocaust was at the centre of attention in all remembrance activities either as a subject or as a standard for comparison, or as an essential doubt in global civility.[23]

National history as a field has therefore undergone important changes too and has largely disengaged itself from the strong connection to nationalist agendas. This has led, for example, to the more intense debate of differences between nation states and other forms of statehood, for example, empires. In the beginning of the post-Cold War era, a European framing[24] of narratives seemed to be the most obvious way to overcome evident limitations of the national container within which history was considered for a long time.

The imperial turn and the interest in spatial formats

But around the year 2000, imperial histories gained more prominence as a tool connecting the former practice of national history writing with the new standards of border-transcending explanations.[25] Interestingly, this was not only limited to those empires that had lost their colonial extensions in the 1960s,[26] but was also echoed by transnational views on the German Empire before the First World War,[27] the discovery of possible postcolonial perspectives on the Habsburg Empire[28] and a debate on a possible impact of imperial pasts having ended more than four centuries ago, for example, the Polish–Lithuanian Union.[29] 'Empire' also became a metaphor for worldwide capitalism[30] as well as for unilateralism and global hegemony,[31] and thus partly identified with the analysis of powerful nation states. In these perspectives, nationalism and imperialism are to a certain extent identified with each other.

The re-emerging interest in imperial history and its relationship with the nation state, which seems to be much more complicated than the traditional expression 'from empire to nation' suggests,[32] in fact encourages, a re-evaluation of the status of nation states and nations in a longer historical perspective instead of taking it for granted as the quasi-natural framework of historical action. This re-evaluation has several aspects. One of these is a critical reassessment of the status of the national within world histories in the past. What were the entities with which world historians since the late eighteenth century tried to manage the chaotic mass of material in order to provide reasonably accessible narratives and explanations? It is not only national historians that fall into the trap where states of the past were presented as if they are fully integrated national states, economies and societies of the twentieth century. This anachronistic backward reading of the state is most prevalent in the famous series on gross domestic product estimated and published by Angus Maddison and the successors in his project.[33] Here, a category that was only introduced at the beginning of the twentieth century (gross domestic product) on the basis of state formation processes and these states' policies towards social integration and economic performance is presented as existing forever, or at least since the year 0. Some of the confusion that comes with the otherwise very important debate about the preconditions for the so-called Great Divergence[34] – in the economic performance between East Asia and parts of Western Europe after 1800 – is due to the anachronistic comparison of different kinds of states and economies across historical periods. The debate about empire has various effects on the discussion about nations and nation states: it makes us understand that nation states are of a different quality with respect to the management of territory, border and people than empires are. This new quality became effective rather late even in Europe. Empires have not simply dissolved and were replaced by nation states. On the contrary, leading powers of the later eighteenth century have transformed into (different kinds of) nation states at home while establishing new imperial features. Nationalization and empire-building went hand in hand, and it is therefore not surprising that both forms of statehood coexisted not only into the nineteenth century but for most parts of the twentieth as well. Nationalism as one of the widespread global ideologies is not simply a reflection of the emergence of nation states but has developed its many different features in reaction to the complex intertwinement of national and imperial tendencies in modern organization of political and social spaces.

Statehood has for sure a much longer history than the nation state. At the same time, the history of the same nation state does not end with the emergence of transnational ties between economies and societies. On the contrary, recent transnational history has been able to demonstrate that nation states and transnationality went hand in hand since the late eighteenth century.[35] And they continue to do so, even after the prematurely declared death of the nation state, as the experience of the recent financial crisis has shown, when states saved, on the one hand, banks and coordinated, on the other, with global financial agencies on transnational strategies.

The history of spatial frameworks is obviously more complex than previously thought. While traditional historiography followed the idea of an extraordinary centrality of the national among the many scales at which territoriality is at work, scholars investigating global processes often underestimated the reputation of the national by assuming that one scale is simply replaced by another – the national disappears and the global comes to the fore. But it turned out that there is always more than one spatial pattern at work. To complicate the story further, the focus on global or at least border-crossing processes invites for a reassessment of the role of networks and chains compared to the often overemphasized territory.

Territory, as all historical phenomena, is not simply a given but rather the product of a lengthy and contradictory process.[36] It entails the construction of borders as well as the homogenization of space and of the people living there through the help of bureaucracies, law, violence, cultural hegemony and exclusionist practices. Territorialization does not just start with the emergence of the nation state; conversely, it often begins under the quite different circumstances of empire, where neither clear-cut border nor equal access to power and resources for all inhabitants belong to the general principles. What is even more important, territorialization does not occur in isolation. It is historically accompanied and complemented by processes of exchange, encounter, conflict, war and other forms of interaction with neighbouring and even faraway societies. Defining borders takes place synchronously by making them porous again for the purpose of trade and migration.

It was the specific crisis at the end of the eighteenth century that somehow radicalized the already ongoing process of territorialization – through anti-colonial emancipation and in reaction to the global race of empires that had started in the Seven Years' War and continued from 1792 onwards for another 25 years of belligerency. The outbreak of the French Revolution, as it has been argued, was due to the lack of resources for the next round in this worldwide competition.[37] Territory now became fully defined and constitutions promised all people living on the territory the same rights and access to power; although in reality the inclusive promise was realized step by step and not without severe setbacks.[38] The invention of the nation – transnational right from its beginning – turned out to be an extremely powerful tool in the inter-imperial competition for global influence, profit and hegemony.[39] It legitimized the appropriation of resources from the formerly privileged, who lost their exemption from taxation, and consequently the distribution of higher rates of state income (for the navy, army and national guards). It facilitated both in the United States and in France land reform – by opening the frontier land in the American West or by redistributing church and emigrant possessions – to gain farmers' support for the project. And it offered an extensive toolkit for cultural policies that have strengthened the sense of belonging among the inhabitants of the territory and mobilized sacrifices for the 'nation'. The mythical invention of common cultural resources (ranging from a common past to a shared language as well as to a rich reservoir of symbols) played less of a role during the Atlantic revolutions than it did in the fight against Napoleonic expansionism.[40]

Strikingly, the imperial context of the nation-building has not disappeared. Far beyond Napoleon's masquerade as the almighty emperor who crowned himself in the presence of a pope condemned to inactivity, empire remained the dominant spatial framework of the exercise of power during the nineteenth century and even for larger parts of the world in the twentieth.[41] The spread of nationalism was not at the expense of imperialism; just the opposite, both were closely associated, especially during the second wave of colonialism at the end of the nineteenth and the beginning of the twentieth century, just before American president Wilson (and the Russian revolutionary leader Lenin) heralded a world of self-determination of the people. But even this claim has only slowly opened the doors of decolonization that materialized primarily after the Second World War and gave rise to a new wave of emancipatory nationalisms full of hope for independent development. However, it took the ongoing dependencies not very much time to become painfully visible to the new elites in the former colonies.

National territorialization has never been a stand-alone process but was complemented by imperial contexts; by processes of (sub- and supra-state) regionalization; by direct contacts between cities; by border-crossing networks of experts, artists and all kinds of transnational family ties established across the global migratory systems that came into existence. And not to forget, the transnational value chains of capitalist production and consumption of more and more sophisticated goods as well as their coordination in international organizations of standardization and at stock exchanges, which have provided the production sites with capital. None of these spatial formats have existed completely independent from the other (sometimes analytically separated for the purpose of historiographical description) nor have they continuously existed unchanged. On the contrary, the various spatial formats relate to each other over time in many different ways – continually forming spatial orders.

The somewhat abstract language of the considerations above helps us to empirically investigate concrete configurations of various spatial formats and their interaction as historically changing spatial orders. The breakthrough of a terminology concerning the 'national' in the first months of the French Revolution (with the Estates-General calling themselves a national assembly) indicated that something fundamental had changed. This does not mean that there were nations everywhere. But a new standard was emerging. John Breuilly insists on the paradox that nationalist ideology combines the claim to the uniqueness of an individual nation with the claim to the universal applicability of nationhood everywhere.[42] But it took a while until nationalism became a global ideology and we should not fall into the trap of confusing a possible origin with the full story afterwards. It is true that the declaration of North American independence became a sort of blueprint for future documents with the same intention,[43] but this does not mean necessarily that the idea of independence was already universally accepted in the late eighteenth century. The new arrangement between the national (at home, with constitutional rights for all citizens) and the imperial (for abroad, where the old differentiated access to rights was continued as colonial rule) became attractive for many but by far not for all: Russian rulers and feudal authorities in Central and Southeast Europe were none too happy with the revolutionary principles, and slave holders from Chili to Virginia were by a large majority not willing to give up their privileged position in the plantation economy.

A second such critical juncture around 1800 was needed to push national territorialization to the forefront again. The global chain of revolutions, (civil) wars and social upheavals between the 1840s and the 1870s shattered the spatial order on the world scale again.[44] In contrast to the period half a century before, the means of communication and transportation now had connected the world in a more compressed and faster manner[45] so that the exchange of information across oceans took minutes instead of months. This brought continents and cultures, and people and their productive capacities closer together so that one can speak, according to Geyer and Bright, of a global condition that was insofar a new quality that from then on societies across the globe were unable to escape from, including interaction with others unless they were ready to risk decline and marginalization. The period in the midst of the nineteenth century was a fundamental transformation towards this global condition. But against what one might expect, this has not led to absolute deterritorialization. On the contrary, the more the flows of goods, people, capital and ideas were not simply silently at work but became visible to everyone, the more sovereignty became an issue. Or in other words: it was not about stopping the flows from which one was to expect material profit and intellectual inspiration but it was about gaining control over such flows, either in traditional or innovative forms. Such control had to respect the demand for an increasing proportion of – increasingly educated and at least partly urbanized – people becoming politically active. The result was a rearrangement of spatial formats with a further strengthening of the national level by elements of welfare states. The social question that had been put forward by the labour movement thus became spatialized – workers of the Western world got a share via state redistribution and increasing payment for their (skilled) work from profits taken from the colonies, from the differential in wages and from an advantageous legal position for truly free workers in contrast to the many forms of indentured labour.[46]

Nationalism as a global phenomenon

The history of the first half of the twentieth century has added further chapters concerning the enormous power of nationalisms to mobilize masses – two world wars later, nationalism was interpreted in a much more sceptical manner, at least in Europe. However, historians did not, and have not, stopped framing history nationally and liberation movements in former colonies insisted on the productive force of the idea of a nation to be independent. It is perhaps not by accident that one of the most stimulating interpretations of nationalism, Benedict Anderson's book about 'imagined communities', was inspired by the analysis of not only European but also of Southeast Asian cases.[47] Nationalist movements did not emerge in complete isolation. They reacted to the same wake-up call for decolonizing efforts described by Erez Manela as the 'Wilsonian moment' and read in newspapers and pamphlets about parallel attempts to get their respective cases approved by the dominant powers after 1918.[48] Activists of anti-colonial nationalism met at places like London or Paris in the interwar period to formulate their agendas and to create their networks.[49] But other places like Berlin or Hamburg, Vienna and Moscow as well became such hotspots of transnational nationalism.[50]

What the global history of spatial formats and spatial orders has already brought to the fore is the relative importance of nationalism as a tool to mobilize for (in fact, imperial) competition as well as for internal integration. There is obviously an interplay between the national, as the result of a process of territorialization that arrives at a substantially new quality, and nationalism, which proves to be helpful in managing the crisis emerging with that process as a global one. Only when taking a global perspective – instead of looking from within the society how it reformats its relevant spatial framings (from imperial to national territory) and how it reformulates its self-description (as nation) – can we understand why and under which circumstances such transformation occurred.[51]

Global history, as practiced nowadays, has overcome a simple denial of the national and instead advocates taking it seriously as a spatial format that was able historically (that means within a certain time span and a certain geographical framework) to gain a sort of definitive dominance over the other formats – the border-crossing activities become the international[52] or the transnational, and the sub-state region appears, at best, as a smaller version of the nation.[53] But this is a historically contingent valorization of spatial formats against each other. The period of the 1970s – with its still rather critical emphasis on transnational companies and the most recent enthusiasm about a world that becomes flat (Friedman), networked (Castells) and all the time further shrinking into a sort of global village (McLuhan) – has seen a devalorization of the spatial format of the national but never its disappearance. This went side by side with the negative connotation of nationalism as a major source of self-destructive conflict.

But the national was not just a spatial format among others; the nation state has been interpreted also as a portal of globalization.[54] With this category, recent global history writing approaches consider the fact that global flows are not simply everywhere. They arrive at certain points – at harbours for a long time already, and at train stations and airports more recently. These points of entrance play an important role in the process of globalization, not only because they are places where there is a high density of commodities and people arriving from (are leaving for) faraway places but also because a specific culture emerges at those places where people are in a particular way familiar with the 'global' (whatever the term may represent at a given historical moment). Here, the global flow is recognized as such, it is managed in a certain way and it is channelled further to other destinations. This goes hand in hand with the development of new cultural techniques from naming to ordering things. The emergence of modern ways of economic calculation is a case in point. They have been the product of early modern ports where merchants adapted traditional ways of calculation to the needs of far-distant (and therefore long-term) trade.

Under the global condition, these portals changed their character. With border guards and huge administrations for the handling of migration, trade and later on also capital flows, the nation state intervenes. From the single place that can be called a portal of globalization, states now develop a much larger and more sophisticated set of institutions managing the incoming and outgoing flows. Passports, statistics and maps become instruments for the management of belonging – and simultaneously exclusion. Nationalism – as a phenomenon that can be found all over the world[55] and that has become focused into a global ideology – is an obvious product of the many attempts to secure a position within a globalizing world and to run flows in a controlled manner. Insofar nationalism is not in opposition to global processes but it is an inherent element of certain political or societal projects to manage global flows.

Understood as an inherent reaction to projects of globalization, nationalism is researched nowadays at various angles. One is of course the long history of protectionist policies intended to help not yet competitive industries to gain a position suitable for international markets. Napoleon's blockade declared in 1806 against British commodities and spanning large parts of Europe is a well-known example.[56] Recent research on British behaviour towards Indian textile industries in the late eighteenth and early nineteenth centuries demonstrates a similar protectionist intervention by the state against the competitor.[57] Economists like the German Friedrich List formulated some decades later a doctrine of national economies as a space securing development under the supremacy of the British free trade empire, ironically long before the respective infrastructures allowed for the effective integration of such economies at the scale of nation states (and replacing the early modern trade networks that were largely independent from territorialization).[58] The debate has not stopped in the nineteenth century but continues until today, with controversies over the capacities of the developmental state in Asia, Latin America and Africa.

A second stream of nationalism emerged out of the restructuration of social welfare, being transferred to the national level and replacing at least in parts welfare organized at the level of family obligations and village communities. This implied a stricter distinction between those belonging to the nation and others. Administrations were built to secure this more and more sophisticated differentiation. However, this process happened only in parts of the world. Both the colonial state and societies depending on (settler-)immigration were much less inclined to follow the European model of welfare statehood.

Immigration formed nevertheless a permanent challenge to nationalist agendas so that a set of tools had to be developed that brought the two into a manageable relationship. Assimilation and inclusionist strategies can be found on the one side, exclusion with arguments of xenophobia and racism on the other. Interestingly, while each society searched for its own mix in the application of these tools, the ideological elements circulated easily across borders with the help of academic internationalism and transnational organizations. The discrimination against people of non-white descent at the same time spurred nationalism in their countries of origin, as the example of Chinese nationalism proves among many others. Both anti-imperial revolutions and warfare as part of the global competition for a better position in the international system inspired nationalism in its recourse to violence and protection against the effects of violence. Nationalism is based upon a sharp demarcation between the 'us' and the 'them', which is not always in line with the confusing alliances that had to be built for successful revolution or warfare but influencing the imaginaries. While this experience of the violent 'origins' of one's own nation had effects on a rather 'heroic' discourse, the second half of the twentieth century has seen a competition for greater 'victimhood' that has characterized nationalist discourses. 'Victimhood' has addressed various dimensions of the struggle for global hegemony, represented not only by colonialism, genocidal warfare and criminal extermination of people but also the inclusion into the bloc system of the Cold War and cultural marginalization by different kinds of (often Western) universalisms.

It becomes evident that nationalism is an important aspect of global history.[59] It can be seen from different angles, a reaction to the global condition emerging during the nineteenth century as well as a product of the global condition, which enabled the flourishing of border-crossing entanglements and mutual inspirations.

The more recent development in global history writing has ended a less and less fruitful opposition of nation and mankind, of nation state and world. It has become clear that nationalization of state and society in parts of the world has been a successful strategy to cope with the global condition of increasing interdependencies. Such nationalization has, however, not entirely replaced imperial strategies but big powers of the nineteenth and twentieth centuries have combined nation-building at home (where elites had to accept equal rights to all people belonging to the nation and thus making them citizens) with imperialism abroad. The consequence was not a world of nicely separated nation states where everyone knows his home, but violence and war.[60] Not simply a series of local conflicts, but a broad international crisis across various continents produced dynamics against which the spatial order defined at the Vienna Congress in 1815 with its mix of empires, nation states and zones of imperial influence was no longer defendable.[61]

Anti-colonial nationalism seems to have similarities with Western European nationalism of the late nineteenth and twentieth centuries but its international context is quite different and the socio-structural conditions for nation-building are different as well. Examples from Latin America after Independencía to Africa after the liberation from colonialism in the beginning of the 1960s demonstrate these differences and raise a fundamental question of comparative history. Is it appropriate to measure against with the yardstick of 'successful' nationalism in Western Europe or the United States or is it more enlightening to put the conditions under which such nationalism has been developed for the purpose of internal integration, resistance to ongoing economic and political dependency or defence of a never fully achieved sovereignty again endangered by the intervention of transnational companies, foreign powers or international organizations?

Another dimension of comparison, which brings the concepts of the imagined and invented community back into discussion but in rather new ways, concerns the question of resources that are at disposal to elites to make such an invention work. While Anderson, Hobsbawm or Gellner had argued that the nation was nothing that existed already since mythical and obscure origins but that was made (rather late) by purposeful action to the profit of certain groups in society,[62] studies following this innovative approach published since the early 1980s have demonstrated how sophisticated this process was and what an understanding of modern culture, media, technology, arts and sciences, mobilization and self-organization of civil society as well as organization of the political sphere from above it presupposes. Examples were most often taken from countries where such efforts were successful in the sense that an often aggressively self-confident nation emerged.[63] This supported both the impression that the nation state is the only remaining spatial format and nationalism a global ideology that can be found everywhere. But the new perspectives established by global historians that insist on the complexity of spatial formats and spatial orders with the nation state being only one among many established and combined with each other in order to find an appropriate answer to the global condition invite for a more nuanced interpretation. The toolkit of nationalist symbols and rhetoric is at the disposal of many actors but not all of them have the means or even the will to use it effectively for the purpose of nation-building.

Some concluding remarks

Nationalism as a distinct orientation in the world[64] has emerged at the same time as the global condition, when processes of globalization came to a point where no society in the world was any longer able to develop economically and politically without going more and more connected to other parts of the world. The conclusion which has been drawn by global history so far is that nationalism is neither independent from global connectedness nor a simple reaction to globalization in general (which began long before the modern times).[65] Its massive emergence in the last third of the nineteenth century was a reaction to a substantial turn in the development of globalization. At this particular moment, which of course has its roots in a longer history as well, the formation of nation states cum imperial annexes seemed to be the logical consequence of growing proximity between societies and growing mobility as a result of technological innovation in communication and transportation, of increasing competition across the globe and along trans-regional commodity chains. There was a need for a world order that organized both a stronger identification of people with territories on the one hand and allowed for further expansion of capitalist economic activities. When defining nationalism as the ideology that accompanied and legitimated this attempt to organize a certain world order, we are able to understand its historicity. This nationalism of the leading powers in the international system of the late nineteenth century was followed and answered by the claim for sovereignty of an increasing number of former colonies. But instead of a linear development towards a world of independent and self-determining nations (as American president Woodrow Wilson was willingly misinterpreted by anti-colonialists and other representatives of not yet free nations), we see new imperial ambitions emerging as well as the problem of multi-ethnic states and the phenomenon of transnational nations (a term that characterizes the dilemma of Jewish people). The denial of independence as well as the refusal of equal rights within the existing states inspired new waves of resistance against the existing power relations and searched for legitimation in anti-Western nationalism. Protectionism and the closing of borders, as for the United States in the 1920s, remained in the repertoire as well. To strengthen the power of nationalist arguments the ideology took inspiration from an ever-growing set of historical references but merged also with as many other ideologies as possible, ranging from racism and social Darwinism to (Ordo-)liberalism and socialism, not to speak of the liaison with all kinds of religions.

Any handbook of the history of nationalism gets thicker and more complex with each of its editions. This indicates that the story is not over and new chapters are just written by new actors. Global history has refreshed the field by putting nation-building and nationalism into a new, global perspective. But it has also gained a lot by no longer simply opposing the global and the national but rather investigating the complexities of the spatial order which reflects the changing features of a global condition under which we live already for a while.

Notes

1 Kenichi Ohmae, *The End of the Nation State. The Rise of Regional Economies* (New York, 1996); Connie L. McNeely, 'World Polity Theory', in George Ritzer (ed.), *The Wiley-Blackwell Encyclopedia of Globalization* (Hoboken,

2012). See also: John W. Meyer, John Boli, George M. Thomas and Francisco O. Ramirez, 'World Society and the Nation-State,' *American Journal of Sociology* 103 (1997), 144–81.

2 Jerry H. Bentley and Herbert F. Ziegler, *Traditions & Encounters: A Global Perspective on the Past* (Boston, 2000).

3 Jerry H. Bentley, 'From National History toward Word History', in Matthias Middell (ed.), *Vom Brasilienvertrag zur Globalgeschichte. Zum 70. Geburtstag von Manfred Kossok* (Leipzig, 2002), pp. 169–82, here p. 169.

4 Jerry H. Bentley, 'Myths, Wagers, and Some Moral Implications of World History', *Journal of World History* 16:1 (2006), 51–82.

5 William McNeill, *The Rise of the West: A History of Human Community* (Chicago, 1963).

6 William Hardy McNeill, 'The Rise of the West after Twenty-Five Years', *Journal of World History* 1:1 (1990), 1–21.

7 Kenneth R. Curtis and Jerry H. Bentley (eds), *Architects of World History. Researching the Global Past* (Chichester 2014).

8 Hanna Schissler and Yasemin Nuhoğlu Soysal (eds), *The Nation, Europe, and the World. Textbooks and Curricula in Transition* (New York, 2005).

9 Hans Erich Bödeker, Philippe Büttgen and Michel Espagne (eds), *Die Wissenschaft vom Menschen in Göttingen um 1800. Wissenschaftliche Praktiken, institutionelle Geographie, europäische Netzwerke* (Göttingen, 2008); Hans Erich Bödeker, 'The Debates about Universal History and National History around 1800: A Problem-Orientated Historical Attempt' *Proceedings of the British Academy* 134 (2006), 135–70.

10 Matthias Middell and Lluis Roura (eds), *Transnational Challenges to National History Writing* (New York, 2013).

11 Jürgen Osterhammel, 'Raumbeziehungen. Internationale Geschichte, Geopolitik und historische Geographie', in Wilfried Loth and Jürgen Osterhammel (eds), *Internationale Geschichte. Themen-Ergebnisse-Aussichten* (München, 2000), pp. 287–308.

12 Karl Lamprecht, *Americana* (Freiburg, 1905).

13 Andreas Wimmer and Nina Glick-Schiller, 'Methodological Nationalism and Beyond: Nation-State Building, Migration and the Social Sciences', *Global Networks* 2:4 (2002), 301–34.

14 Michel Espagne, 'Sur les limites du comparatisme en histoire culturelle', *Genèses* 17 (1994), 112–21.

15 Sanjay Subrahmanyam, 'Connected Histories: Notes toward a Reconfiguration of Early Modern Eurasia', *Modern Asia Studies* 31 (1997), 735–62.

16 Pierre Yves Saunier, *Transnational History* (London, 2013).

17 John Breuilly (ed.), *The Oxford Handbook of the History of Nationalism* (Oxford, 2013).

18 Michael Geyer and Charles Bright, 'For a Unified History of the World in the Twentieth Century', *Radical History Review* 39 (1987), 69–91; Michael Geyer and Charles Bright, 'World History in a Global Age', *The American Historical Review* 100:4 (1995), 1034–60.

19 Peter Novick, *That Noble Dream: The 'Objectivity Question' and the American Historical Profession* (Cambridge, New York, Melbourne, 1988), p. 27.

20 See Merry E. Wiesner-Hanks (ed.) *The Cambridge World History*, 9 vols (Cambridge, 2015).

21 See the e-journal *Connections: A Journal for Historians and Area Specialists* at http://www.connections.clio-online.net/.

22 Damtew Teferra and Heinz Greijn (eds), *Higher Education and Globalization: Challenges, Threats, and Opportunities for Africa* (Maastricht, 2010).

23 Charles S. Maier, 'Consigning the 20th Century to History: Alternative Narratives for the Modern Era', *The American Historical Review* 105 (2000), 807–31.

24 Rolf Petri and Hannes Siegrist (eds), *Probleme und Perspektiven der Europa-Historiographie* (Leipzig, 2004).

25 Dane Kennedy, 'The Imperial History Wars', *Journal of British Studies* 54:1 (2015), 5–22; Durba Gosh, 'Another Set of Imperial Turns?' *American Historical Review* 117:3 (2012), 772–93.

26 Martin Thomas, *Fight or Flight. Britain, France, and Their Roads from Empire* (Oxford, 2014).

27 Sebastian Conrad and Jürgen Osterhammel (eds), *Das Kaiserreich transnational. Deutschland in der Welt 1871–1914* (Göttingen, 2004); Sebastian Conrad, *Globalisierung und Nation im Deutschen Kaiserreich* (München, 2006).

28 Moritz Czaky and Johannes Fiechtinger/Ursula Prutsch (eds), *Habsburg postcolonial. Machtstrukturen und kollektives Gedächtnis* (Innsbruck, Wien, München, Bozen, 2003); Clemens Kaps and Jan Surman (eds), *Post-Colonial Perspectives on Habsburg Galicia* (Krakow, 2012).

29 Frank Hadler and Mathias Mesenhöller (eds), *Lost Greatness and Past Oppression in East Central Europe: Representations of the Imperial Experience in Historiography since 1918* (Leipzig, 2007); for the 'long history' of empire see Peter F. Bang and C. A. Bayly (eds), *Tributary empires in global history* (New York, 2011) and Peter Fibiger Bang and Dariusz Kołodziejczyk (eds), *Universal Empire. A Comparative Approach to Imperial Culture and Representation in Eurasian History* (Cambridge, 2012).

30 Michael Hardt and Antonio Negri, *Empire. Die neue Weltordnung* (Frankfurt/Main, 2002).

31 Niall Ferguson, *Empire. The Rise and Demise of the British World Order and the Lessons for Global Power* (New York, 2002); Niall Ferguson, *Colossus. The Rise and Fall of the American Empire* (London, 2005); Charles S. Maier, *Among Empires. American Ascendancy and Its Predecessors* (Cambridge, 2006).

32 Joseph Esherick, Hasan Kayalı and Eric van Young (eds), *Empire to Nation: Historical Perspectives on the Making of the Modern World* (Lanham, 2006).

33 Angus Maddison, *Monitoring the World Economy* (Paris: OECD, 2003). The 'Maddison Project' database is constantly being updated and revised. See http://www.ggdc.net/maddison/maddison-project/home.htm. See also Francesco Boldizzoni, *The Poverty of Clio. Resurrecting Economic History* (Princeton, 2011).

34 Kenneth Pomeranz, *The Great Divergence: China, Europe, and the Making of the Modern World Economy* (Princeton, 2001).

35 Jürgen Osterhammel, *Geschichtswissenschaft jenseits des Nationalstaats. Studien zu Beziehungsgeschichte und Zivilisationsvergleich* (Göttingen, 2001); Kiran Klaus Patel, *Nach der Nationalfixiertheit. Perspektiven einer transnationalen Geschichte* (Berlin, 2004); Ian R. Tyrrell, *Transnational nation. United States history in global perspective since 1789* (Basingstoke, 2007); Akira Iriye and Pierre-Yves Saunier (eds), *The Palgrave dictionary of transnational history* (New York, 2009). Frank Hadler and Matthias Middell (eds), *Handbuch einer transnationalen Geschichte Ostmitteleuropas: Von der Mitte des 19. Jahrhunderts bis zum Ersten Weltkrieg*, vol. 1 (Göttingen, 2017).
36 Stuart Elden, *The Birth of Territory* (Chicago, 2013).
37 Suzanne Desan, Lynn Hunt and William Max Nelson (eds), *The French Revolution in Global Perspective* (Ithaca, 2013).
38 Charles S. Maier, *Once within Borders: Territories of Power, Wealth, and Belonging since 1500* (Cambridge, 2016).
39 Bailey Stone, *Reinterpreting the French Revolution: A Global-Historical Perspective* (Cambridge, New York, 2002); Alan Forrest and Matthias Middell (eds), *The Routledge Companion to the French Revolution in World History* (London, 2015).
40 Alan Forrest, Karen Hagemann and Janet Rendall (eds), *Soldiers, Citizens and Civilians: Experiences and Perceptions of the Revolutionary and Napoleonic Wars, 1790–1820* (Basingstoke, 2009).
41 Jane Burbank and Frederick Cooper, *Empires in World History: Power and the Politics of Difference* (Princeton, 2010).
42 John Breuilly, 'Introduction: Concepts, Approaches, Theories', in John Breuilly (ed.), *The Oxford Handbook of the History of Nationalism* (Oxford, 2013), p. 2.
43 David Armitage, *The Declaration of Independence. A Global History* (Cambridge, 2007).
44 Michael Geyer and Charles Bright, 'World History in a Global Age', *The American Historical Review* 100:4 (1995), 1034–60.
45 Roland Wenzlhuemer, *Connecting the Nineteenth-Century World: The Telegraph and Globalization* (Cambridge, 2013); Simone M. Müller, *Wiring the World: The Social and Cultural Creation of Global Telegraph Networks* (New York, 2016).
46 Marcel van der Linden, *Workers of the World: Essays Toward a Global Labor History* (Leiden, 2008).
47 Benedict Anderson, *Imagined Communities: Reflections on the Origin and Spread of Nationalism* (London, 1983); Benedict Anderson, *The Spectre of Comparison. Nationalism, Southeast Asia, and the World* (London, 1998).
48 Erez Manela, *The Wilsonian Moment: Self-Determination and the International Origins of Anticolonial Nationalism* (New York, 2007).
49 Michael Goebel, *Anti-Imperial Metropolis: Interwar Paris and the Seeds of Third World Nationalism* (New York, 2015); Marc Matera, *Black London: The Imperial Metropolis and Decolonization in the Twentieth Century* (Berkeley, 2015) as well as a related AHR Roundtable in *American Historical Review* 121:5 (2016), 1435–519.
50 Holger Weiss, *Framing a Radical African Atlantic: African American Agency, West African Intellectuals and the International Trade Union Committee of Negro Workers* (Leiden, 2014); Holger Weiss, 'The Road to Moscow: On

Archival Sources Concerning the International Trade Union Committee of Negro Workers in the Comintern Archive' *History in Africa – A Journal of Method* 39 (2012), 361–93.

51 Jürgen Osterhammel, 'Nationalism and Globalization', in John Breuilly, *Handbook*, pp. 694–709, here p. 694.

52 Jost Dülffer and Wilfried Loth (eds), *Dimensionen internationaler Geschichte* (München, 2012).

53 Anne-Marie Thiesse, *Ils apprenaient la France. L'exaltation des régions dans le discours patriotique* (Paris, 1997); Anne-Marie Thiesse, *La création des identités nationales. Europe XVIIIe-XXe siècle* (Paris, 1999).

54 Michael Geyer, 'Portals of Globalization', in Winfried Eberhard/Christian Lübke (eds), *The Plurality of Europe. Identities and Spaces* (Leipzig, 2010), pp. 509–20.

55 See the many examples in John Breuilly, *Handbook*, who distinguishes between nationalisms in empires and nationalisms in a world of nation states, and ends with the blending of nationalisms with internationalist and pan-movements.

56 François Crouzet, *L'économie britannique et le blocus continental, 1806–1813* (Paris, 1987); Katherine B. Aaslestad and Johann Joor (eds), *Revisiting Napoleon's Continental System. Local, Regional and European Experiences* (Basingstoke, 2015); discussing the effects on British industries: Patrick K. O'Brien, *The Contributions of Warfare with Revolutionary and Napoleonic France to the Consolidation and Progress of the British Industrial Revolution* (London, 2011).

57 Prasannan Parthasarathi, *Why Europe Grew Rich and Asia Did Not. Global Economic Divergence, 1600–1850* (Cambridge, 2011).

58 On German debates about the role of the state when dealing with the challenges of global processes see Sebastian Conrad and Jürgen Osterhammel (eds), *Das Kaiserreich transnational. Deutschland in der Welt 1871–1914* (Göttingen, 2004); Cornelius Torp (ed.), *Die Herausforderung der Globalisierung. Wirtschaft und Politik in Deutschland 1860–1914* (Göttingen, 2005); Sebastian Conrad, *Globalisierung und Nation im Deutschen Kaiserreich* (München, 2006).

59 Additionally to Jürgen Osterhammel, 'Nationalism and Globalization', in John Breuilly, *Handbook*, pp. 694–712, see also Mike Featherstone (ed.), *Global Culture, Nationalism, Globalization and Modernity* (London and New Delhi, 1990); Anthony D. Smith, *Nations and Nationalism in a Global Era* (Cambridge, 2000).

60 Andreas Wimmer, *Waves of War: Nationalism, State Formation, and Ethnic Exclusion in the Modern World* (Cambridge, 2013).

61 Charles Bright and Michael Geyer, 'Globalgeschichte und die Einheit der Welt. Weltgeschichte als Globalgeschichte – Überlegungen zur einer Geschichte des 20. Jahrhundert' *Comparativ. Leipziger Beiträge zur Universalgeschichte und vergleichenden Gesellschaftsforschung* 4:5 (1994), 13–46.

62 Anderson, *Imagined Community*; Eric John Hobsbawm and Terence Ranger (eds), *The invention of tradition* (Cambridge, 1983); Ernest Gellner, *Nations and Nationalism* (Ithaca, 1983).

63 Gerard Delanty and Krishan Kumar (eds), *The SAGE Handbook of Nations and Nationalism* (London, 2006).

64 Jürgen Osterhammel, 'Nationalism and Globalization', in John Breuilly, *Handbook*, pp. 694–712.
65 Christopher A. Bayly, '"Archaic" and "Modern" Globalization in the Eurasian and African Arena, c. 1750–1850', in Anthony G. Hopkins (ed.), *Globalization in World History* (London, 2002), pp. 47–73; Charles Bright and Michael Geyer, 'The Global Condition 1850–2010', in Douglas Northrop (ed.), *A Companion to World History* (Oxford, 2012), pp. 285–302.

Further reading

Anderson, Benedict, *Imagined Communities: Reflections on the Origins and Spread of Nationalism*. London: Verso, 1991.

Armitage, David, *The Declaration of Independence: A Global History*. Cambridge, MA: Harvard University Press, 2007.

Bentley, Jerry H. (ed.), *The Oxford Handbook of World History*. Oxford, New York: Oxford University Press, 2011.

Breuilly, John (ed.), *The Oxford Handbook of the History of Nationalism*. Oxford: Oxford University Press, 2013.

Burbank, Jane and F. Cooper, *Empires in World History: Power and the Politics of Difference*. Princeton, NJ: Princeton University Press, 2010.

Geyer, Michael, 'Spatial Regimes', in Akira Iriye/Pierre-Yves Saunier (eds), *The Palgrave Dictionary of Transnational History*. New York: Macmillan, 2009, pp. 962–6.

Middell, Matthias and L. Roura (eds), *Transnational Challenges to National History Writing*. New York: Palgrave Macmillan, 2013.

INDEX

This Index was compiled by Sebastian Braun, Alessandra Exter, Jannik Keindorf, Riccarda Schirmers and Fabian Wallaschkowski.

Abdul Hamid II 141
absolutism 84
Abulof, Uriel 99, 115
Abu-Lughod, Lila 183
Adorno, Theodor W. 9, 110–12, 132
Africa 7, 9, 76, 138, 162, 182, 184–5, 198, 216, 222, 224–5, 247, 254, 256
  East-Central Africa 77
  West Africa 230
Al Qaeda 122
Algerian War 133
American Civil War 225
American Revolution 161
ancestry 86, 89
Anderson, Benedict 3, 5, 7–8, 12, 53–4, 64, 66–8, 70, 75–6, 87, 93, 114, 138–41, 144, 181–2, 219, 228–9, 252, 256
Annus mirabilis 64, 136
Anthias, Floya 195–6
anthropogeography 243
anti-Semitism 27, 113, 122
anti-Tsarism 45
Appelbaum, Nancy 225
Applegate, Celia 222–3
area studies 241, 243
Argentina 3, 201
  Falklands war 3
Arminius 85, 200
Arnold, Edward 76
Asia 8–9, 46, 95, 172, 182, 184, 216, 222, 224, 226, 247
  East Asia 231, 249
  South Asia 76
  South-East Asia 76, 96, 139, 145, 253–4

Soviet Central Asia 77
Atatürk, Mustafa Kemal 141
Athena 199
Augustus 21
Australia 7, 32, 161
  aboriginals 150
  Sydney 219
Austria 45–7, 71, 221, 230
  Austria-Hungary 48, 224
  Habsburg Empire 49, 66, 84, 86, 98, 146, 224, 248
  Vienna 48, 133, 136, 243, 253
authoritarianism 9, 27, 31, 73–4, 86, 110–11, 120
Authoritarian Personality thesis 110, 120
autonomy 7, 13, 46, 49, 65, 74, 116, 176, 178, 203

Badran, Margot 183
Balibar, Etienne 140–2
Balkans 74
Baltic States 27
Baron, Beth 183
Barthes, Roland 133, 157
Baruah, Sanjib 224–5
The Battle of Algiers (1966) 205
Bauer, Otto 7, 46–8, 51–2, 64
Baycroft, Timothy 4
Bayly, Christopher A. 4, 96
Beaune, Colette 94
Beauvoir, Simone de 10, 193
Becker, Ernest 9, 113–14
Beethoven, Ludwig van 67
Belgium 26–7, 31, 223
  Flanders 2
Bentley, Jerry 240

Berger, Peter L. 133–4
Berger, Stefan 6, 14, 76, 147
Berr, Henri 244
Beyen, Marnix 149
Bhabha, Homi 9, 160
Bible, the 22, 91
Billig, Michael 9, 112, 120, 148, 159
Bismarck, Otto von 138, 191, 200
Bjork, James 224
Blair, Tony 77
Blee, Kathleen 203
Bock, Gisela 203
Bolshevism 74
border 10–11, 14, 27, 143, 205,
        215–16, 219, 222, 228–30,
        239, 240, 242, 244, 246–51,
        253–5, 257
    borderland 22, 228
    borderless world 240
    control 229
Bourbons 243
Bourgeoisie 7, 23, 41, 43–52, 54–5, 65,
        141, 173–7, 180, 183, 195, 199
Bourke, Joanna 205
Braudel, Fernand 245
Braun, Rudolf 137
Brazil 24
Breuilly, John 3–4, 7, 251
Brexit 164, 240
Bright, Charles 246, 252
Britain 64, 71, 73, 91, 118, 135, 138,
        141, 162, 164, 173, 175–6,
        193, 196–8, 201, 205, 240, 254,
        52–53. See also England
Britannia 199
Brown, Dana 225
Brubaker, Rogers 142–3, 148
Bull Sr, Edvard 29
Burma 96, 145
Burton, Antoinette 197
Butler, Judith 193
Butterfield, Herbert 29

Calhoun, Craig 9, 163
Canada 31, 201
    Quebec 216
capitalism 6–7, 42, 44–6, 51, 64, 65,
        77, 110, 171, 176, 179, 185–6,
        217, 225, 240, 243, 248

market economy 224
pre-capitalist 48
print capitalism 53, 66, 68, 93,
        139–40
Castro-Klaren, Sara 184
Catholicism 21, 24, 71, 73, 84, 86, 91,
        94, 132, 146, 199, 217
Celtic fringe 53
Certeau, Michel de 11, 217–18
Chakrabarty, Dipesh 176, 186
Chatterjee, Bankimchandra 181
Chatterjee, Partha 9, 95, 158, 178–9,
        198
China 7–8, 13, 64, 76–7, 96–7,
        145–6, 182–3, 185, 202, 216,
        221, 231
    Han Empire 77
    Northern China 221
    Qing dynasty 77, 96, 145–6, 200
    Republican China 200
Christianity 91, 94, 118, 142
citizenship, citizen 10, 12, 49, 55,
        68–9, 94, 99, 114, 120, 125,
        149, 160, 163–4, 181, 194–200,
        203–4, 206, 219, 221–2, 224–5,
        229–30, 251, 255
    and equality 120, 163, 221
    exclusion from 222, 230
    and gender 10, 149, 194, 196–8, 200,
        204, 206
Code Civil 196
Cohen, Edward 92, 144–5
Cold War 1, 3–3, 30, 63, 69, 74, 86, 90,
        97–8, 122, 131, 142, 206, 216,
        241, 248, 255
Colley, Linda 196, 207
Colombia 225
    Riosucio 225
colonial authorities 174, 230–1
colonialism 34, 53, 162, 171–5, 181,
        186, 248, 251, 255, 256
    anti-colonialism 50, 171, 173, 178,
        180–6, 224, 250, 255, 257
    colonization 225, 232
    decolonization 19, 31–2, 52, 74, 97,
        131, 140, 185, 242, 251
    and emancipation 34, 53–4
Comaroff, Jean 185
Comaroff, John 185

communication
  modernization of 63, 216, 229–30,
    252, 257
  and national identity 134–5
  social 10, 53, 55, 70, 118, 124, 133
  theory of 52
communism 1, 3–4, 30–1, 33, 49, 63,
    123, 142, 174–5, 183, 216
  anti-communism 30
  fall of 31, 123, 142
  post-communism 1, 90
Confucius 32
Congress of Vienna (1815) 243, 255
Conrad, Sebastian 229
constitutionalism 29, 48, 84, 88, 95,
    117, 119, 134, 156–8, 161–2,
    164, 173, 174, 176, 179, 193–4,
    222, 242, 246, 251
constructivism 3–6, 8, 12, 49, 53–4, 86,
    110, 115, 118, 131–40, 144, 147,
    148–50, 155, 218–19, 222, 224
  social constructivism 86–7, 118, 131,
    133, 135, 144–5, 193, 218, 229
Continental blockade 254
Cosmopolitanism 49, 111, 136, 139,
    227, 240, 241
Counter-Reformation 86, 91
counter-revolution 44
Croce, Benedetto 28
culture
  cultural transfer 11, 144, 245
  cultural turn 3, 8, 93, 155–7, 165
  microcultures 201
  national, see national, culture
  political 131, 184
  public 89, 93
  shared 48, 88, 106, 160, 163
  vernacular 66, 75, 223, 226–7,
    231–2
Cyprus 162
Czechoslovakia 27, 44–5, 52, 66, 74–5,
    86, 98–9, 143, 204, 216, 230
  Bohemia 99, 224, 230
  Budweis 223
  Czech Republic 1
  Prague 133, 136

Darwin, Charles 108
Deleuze, Gilles 157

democracy 2, 3, 15, 28–30, 32, 34–7, 51,
    54, 73–4, 93, 119–20, 123, 135,
    142, 150, 157–8, 162, 176, 178,
    181, 216, 221–3, 226, 240, 242
  liberal 29–30, 73–4, 142
  parliamentary 74
  social 29, 51, 242
democratization 29, 54–5, 158, 162,
    223, 240
Denmark 162
Deringil, Selim 141
Derrida, Jaques 8, 133, 157–8
Deutsch, Karl 7, 52, 64, 70, 72, 133
developing world 31
diaspora 229, 231
Diaz, Porfirio 221
Dickens, Charles 67
discrimination 158, 160, 222, 225, 255
Don Juan 232
Dorman, Robert 225
Duara, Prasenjit 96, 150, 185, 221, 231
Durkheim, Emile 63, 108
Dutch Revolt 146

Eastern Bloc 216
East Timor 216
Edensor, Tim 219, 226
Egypt 33, 146, 200, 231
  ancient 90
Elgenius, Gabriella 162
Elias, Norbert 124
Elliott, Mark 96, 145
Engels, Friedrich 7, 43–4, 46
England 8, 49, 52, 64, 67, 91, 93–5,
    118–19, 135, 144, 161–2, 164,
    183, 199, 223, 243. See also
    Britain
  London 77, 136, 253
enlightenment 6, 9, 21, 25, 63, 91, 114,
    132, 139, 158, 171–2, 184–5
empire 8, 11, 13–15, 25–6, 28–9, 45,
    54, 63, 65–6, 70–1, 74, 77, 97,
    136, 140, 146, 197, 207, 223,
    248–50, 254–5
equality 15, 24, 53, 158, 162–3, 176–7,
    193, 221
  inequality 100, 139, 161, 164, 172,
    176, 242
Erdogan, Recep Tayyip 77

Eriksen, Thomas Hylland 148
Erikson, Erik 109
Eritrea 216
essentialism 8, 35, 48, 84, 87, 98, 119,
	178, 185, 192
Estonia 52
Ethiopia 96
Eurasia 142
eurocentrism 31, 97, 158, 184, 244
Europe
	Central Europe 44, 49, 75, 95, 136,
		139, 230, 247, 251
	East-Central Europe 49, 221, 223–4
	Eastern Europe 49, 69, 90, 222, 243
	history, see history
	interwar 143
	medieval 93–4, 147
	Nazi-occupied 204
	nineteenth-century 138, 144, 149,
		227, 231
	post-war Europe 74
	Western Europe 49, 69, 94–5, 222,
		247, 249, 255–6
European Commission 227
European Economic Community 227
European Regional Development Fund
	227
European Union 1, 13, 98, 118, 164,
	216, 227, 240

fascism 5–6, 27–33, 63, 72, 110–11, 204
	anti-fascism 30
Febvre, Lucien 244
Feischmidt, Margit 148
femininity 193, 195
	and nationalism 10, 198, 200
Ferguson, Adam 63
feudalism 7, 44, 46–7, 93–4
	semi-feudal 175–6
Fichte, Johann Gottfried 2, 5
Financial crisis (2008) 249
Finland 162, 218–19
Five Factor Model 111
Ford, Caroline 220–1
Foucault, Michel 8, 133, 156–7, 172,
	180, 217
Fouron, Georges 229
France 2, 8, 10, 11, 15, 20–1, 25–7,
	30–1, 49, 64, 70–3, 94, 135,

	141, 145, 196–6, 199, 202, 217,
		220–1, 223, 227, 229, 244, 250
	Alsace 86, 132
	Bretons 44
	Champagne region 226
	French Revolution 11, 86, 135, 229,
		249–51
	Hundred Years' War 94
	July Monarchy 71
	late-medieval 8, 94
	Napoleonic Wars 135, 196, 198, 250
	Paris 71, 135, 220, 253
	Paris Peace Conference (1919)/
		Versailles Peace Treaty 13, 74, 27
	Provencal 44
	rural 70, 135, 220
	Third Republic 72, 199, 220, 223
	Vichy France 30, 199
Franco, Francisco 28
Franco-Prussian War 26
Frankfurt School 110–11, 132
Freikorps 113
Freud, Sigmund 9, 107–13, 116, 122–3,
	217
Frevert, Ute 124
frontier myth 226
Fukuyama, Francis 216

Gandhi, Mahatma 181, 244
Gat, Azar 88
Gaullist resistance 30
Gellner, Ernest 3, 5, 7–8, 12, 51, 62,
	64–9, 72, 76, 87, 89, 93, 96,
	107, 115, 136, 138–9, 140, 144,
	256
gender roles 10, 149, 195, 197,
	199–201, 206
	transgression of 204
gender stereotype 199, 205
genocide 19, 34, 69, 87, 203
geopolitics 142–3, 150, 232, 243
	geopolitical shift 224
George V 29
Germania 62, 191, 199
German Michel 201
Germany 2–3, 5–7, 9, 13, 26–30, 35,
	64, 71, 73–4, 76, 86, 113, 133,
	135, 138, 147, 191, 194–5, 203,
	223–4, 227

Bavaria 222
Berlin 27, 135–6, 253
Fall of the Berlin Wall 216
Federal Republic of Germany 30
First World War 1, 2, 4–5, 13, 72, 88,
    113, 135, 140, 147, 197, 202,
    205, 224, 226, 230, 248
German Empire 29, 74, 132, 138,
    202, 222, 229, 248
German Unification 222
Holy Roman Empire 95
Nazi Germany 5, 7, 13, 28–30, 135,
    203, 224
Prussia 194, 196, 223, 243
Southern Saxony 230
Weimar Germany 113, 194
Geyer, Michael 246, 252
Ghana 74, 230
Girard, Rene 116, 122
Glick Schiller, Nina 228–9
globalization 4, 10, 11–13, 42, 46, 50,
    87, 90, 147, 158, 164, 173, 186,
    215–16, 227–8, 232, 239–42,
    245, 253–4, 256–7
of concepts 42, 147
cultural 90
deglobalization 239–40
economic 13, 90, 216, 256
    and nationalism 11–13, 158, 216,
    227, 256
and nation-state 10, 40, 253–4
Goetz, Walter 244
Gorski, Philip 146–7
Gramsci, Antonio 49, 175
Grancea, Liana 148
Great Britain. See Britain
Great Divergence 249
Greece 8, 162
Athens 20, 92–3, 144–5
Grosby, Steven 92
Grotius, Hugo 147
Guha, Ranajit 173–6
Gurminder, Bhambra 164
Guy, Kolleen 226

Habermas, Jürgen 142
Hagemann, Karen 194, 196
Haidt, Jonathan 111
Hall, Catherine 204

Harvey, David 218
Hastings, Adrian 90–1, 93–5, 144
Haussmann, Georges-Eugène 135
Hayes, Carlton 5, 51, 74, 132
Hearn, Jonathan 149
Hebraic Political Studies 91
Hebraism 91–2, 94, 146–7
Hechter, Michael 53, 165
Heeren, August Ludwig von 25
Hegel, Georg Wilhelm Friedrich 43, 241
Heimat 15, 222
Herder, Johann Gottfried 2, 5, 21–2
heritage 24, 86, 88
    of minorities 222
    national 231
    precolonial 77
    regional 222–3, 226–7
    vernacular 232
Hewitson, Mark 4
Higonett, Patrice 204
Higonnet, Margaret 204
Hill, Christopher 175
Hindenburg, Paul von 201
hinduism 33, 197, 232
Hirschi, Caspar 93
historian
    economic 245
    feminist 195, 207
    gender 23, 193–4, 196, 198–9, 204,
        207
    global 240, 246, 256
    Historikerinnenstreit 203
    Marxist 65, 175
    national 6, 22–4, 26–7, 241, 249
    professional 15, 25–6, 31, 77, 147,
        239
    world 244, 246, 248
historical
    consciousness 26, 28, 240
    culture 138, 248
historiography
    colonialist 173, 175
    Enlightenment 19–20
    Marxist 175
    national 20, 25–6, 31–3, 64, 233
    nationalist 19, 28, 32, 34, 77, 137,
        147, 175, 178
history
    cultural 31, 67, 244

economic 28, 243–4
of emotions 5
European 55, 62, 158, 186
gender 193–4, 207
global 4, 11, 25, 30–1, 176, 229–42,
    246–7, 253, 255–7
imperial 25–6, 31, 248
labour 30
memory 31
national 14–15, 20–2, 25–6, 28, 30,
    32–3, 35, 50, 74, 76–7, 149,
    156, 159–60, 163, 195, 207,
    228, 239–40, 242–8
non-European 76
people's 23, 28
regional 22, 25
social 30, 32, 193, 243–4
transnational 25, 30, 228, 249
universal 20, 185, 243, 247
Whig history 29
women's 10, 30, 193, 207
world 11, 15, 20–1, 25–6, 28,
    239–46
history of nationalism 3–4, 7, 77
    constructivist approach, see
        constructivism
    cultural turn 8, 93, 155–7, 165
    gender approach 10, 197, 206
    global turn 5, 11
    modernist approach, see modernism
    neo-imperial turn 97
    psychoanalytic approach 6, 9, 114,
        124
    spatial turn 6, 10–12, 207, 215,
        218–20, 233
    transnational approach 11, 143, 228,
        230–1
History Wars 22, 150
history writing
    bourgeois 175
    enlightened 20–1, 243
    global 4, 6, 239, 253, 255
    national 4, 6–7, 11, 13–16, 19–23,
        25–7, 31–4, 75, 239–40, 242,
        244–8
    and nationalism 6, 19, 24, 29, 31–4,
        70, 73
    professional 6–7, 25, 32
    Romantic 19, 21, 23

socialist 23, 29
world 239, 241–6
Hitler, Adolf 113, 136, 203
Hobsbawm, Eric 3–5, 7, 12, 50–4, 64,
    76, 86, 106, 136–41, 175, 219,
    256
Holocaust 110, 133, 248
homeland 89, 139, 143, 219, 231
Hope, Anthony 136
Horkheimer, Max 132
Hroch, Miroslav 7, 52, 75
humanism 93, 177
Hume, David 63
Hungary 44, 143, 148
Hussite 86, 98–9
Hutchinson, John 123

Iceland 162
identity
    collective 99, 106, 134, 231–2
    construction of 3, 8, 14, 109, 133,
        142–3, 147, 150, 159, 197, 199,
        218, 222, 224–8, 231–2
    ethnic 8, 11, 89, 96, 141, 145–6, 224
    gender 194
    imperial 197
    local 11, 145, 215, 220, 222, 225,
        229
    national, see national, identity
    politics 78
    regional 11, 215, 220, 222–3, 225–7,
        232–3
    subnational 224, 226
    territorial 218–19, 225, 228, 232
immigration 12, 15, 70, 225, 228–9, 254
imperialism 27, 32, 77, 96–7, 141, 174,
    194, 197–8, 221, 231, 248, 251,
    255
    anti-imperialism 50, 255
India 2, 77, 97, 171, 173–4, 176, 182,
    187, 197–8, 225, 243
    Assam 224
    Bengali 198
    colonial 175, 183, 224
    Independence Day 162
    Indian National Congress 176, 178,
        224
Indonesia 74, 232
    Bali 231–2

Industrial Revolution 86, 171
industrialization 6, 52, 55, 66, 99, 133,
    136, 148, 226
Ingle, David 118
international
    First 45
    Second 45
    Third 49
Iorga, Nicolae 26
Iranian revolution 68
Iraq 33
    Iraq War 123
Ireland 53
    Irish Free State 27
Irish Revolutionary Army 229
Iron Curtain 2
Islam 33–4, 86, 141–2, 197, 200, 231,
    242
Islamism 33, 242
Israel 91–2, 146
    First Temple era 92
    Jerusalem 147
Israelites 91
Italy 3, 6, 15, 27–8, 30–1, 64, 70, 223
    Florence 21
    Lega Nord 216
    Risorgimento 15, 30
    Rome 21, 147

Japan 2, 7, 32, 63–4, 74, 76, 86, 96,
    145, 182–3, 185, 231
    Manchukuo 231
    Meiji Restoration 15, 32, 182
    Revolution of the 1860s 86
Jaures, Jean 73
Jews 92, 113, 122, 133, 135–6, 139,
    148, 221–2, 229, 257
    ancient Jews 90
Jie, Huang 33
Jiegang, Gu 33
Joan of Arc 94, 199–200
John Bull 201
Jouissance 116–23
Judson, Pieter 149, 224
Jusdanis, Gregory 106

Kandiyoti, Deniz 183
Kant, Immanuel 5, 21
Karamchand, Mohandas 181

Kautsky, Karl 45–6
Keating, Michael 227
Kedourie, Elie 5, 62–4, 180
Kenya 77
King, Jeremy 149, 223
Koenigsberg, Richard 113
Kohl, Helmut 3
Kohn, Hans 5, 52, 74, 133, 139
Koht, Halvdan 29
Koonz, Claudia 203
Korea 96, 231
Kristeva, Julia 10, 115, 157
Kuhn, Thomas 179
Ku Klux Klan (KKK) 203

Lacan, Jaques 10, 116, 118, 120, 123,
    157, 217
Lambros, Spyridon 26
Lamprecht, Karl 243–4
Latin America 9, 67–8, 184, 247, 254,
    256
Lavisse, Ernest 25
Lawrence, Paul 4
Leerssen, Joep 3, 12, 143, 230
Lefebvre, Henri 10, 217–18
Lehning, James 220–1
Leipzig University 244
Lelewel, Joachim 24
Lenin, Wladimir Illjitsch 7, 45–6, 48,
    65, 251
Leonard, Philip 158
liberalism 15, 28, 65, 70, 257
    illiberalism 29, 73
    neo-liberalism 3, 69
    ordo-Liberalism 257
Lieberman, Victor 8, 96, 145
List, Friedrich 254
Lithuania 44, 248
Longue duree 23, 88
Lord Acton 83–4, 86, 99–100, 244
Louis XIV 20
Luckmann, Thomas 133–4
Luxemburg, Rosa 45–6

Maddison, Angus 249
Magoc, Chris 226
Maier, Charles 11
Major, John 118–19
Mallon, Florencia 184, 221, 226

Malthusian discourse 202
Manela, Erez 12–13, 253
Mann, Michael 54, 68
Manning, Patrick 241
Maoism 175, 178
Marvin, Carolyn 118
Marx, Karl 1, 3, 5–9, 41, 43–4, 46, 52,
    63, 65, 242–3
Marxism 3, 5–9, 32, 41–56, 65, 74–5,
    86–7, 93, 173, 175, 177–8, 217,
    222
  Austro Marxists 7, 42, 46, 48–9
  neo Marxists 42, 49, 222
  orthodox Marxists 41–2, 45–6, 50,
    54, 74, 217
Marxism-Leninism 28, 30, 33, 42, 48
masculinity 193–5, 198, 207
  colonial 198
  hegemonic 194, 198
  and nationalism 32, 201, 205–6
Massey, Doreen 218
master narrative 24–5, 28–30, 32–5,
    91, 160
Mau Mau Uprising 205
Maxwell, Alexander 143
Mayer, Charles 248
Mbembe, Achille 186
McClintock, Anne 194, 198
McNeill, William 244
memory 9, 31, 96, 106, 139, 195,
    206–7, 225, 241
Mexico 184, 201, 221
  French Intervention (1861) 221
  Mexican Revolution 221
Middle East 76, 78, 183
migration 13, 161, 216, 228, 230–2,
    242, 250, 254
  flow 229, 240
  studies 228
militarism 10, 63, 86, 204
Mill, John Stuart 99–100
Miller, David 142
Minogue, Kenneth 50
modernism 3–8, 12–13, 61–5, 67–71,
    73, 76–8, 83, 86–90, 92–3, 95–9,
    107, 132, 134, 136, 140, 143–4,
    147, 185, 218, 222, 232
monarchy 22, 94, 138–40, 199
Mongols 28

Monumenta Germaniae Historica 25
Mosse, George 135, 195–6, 207
Motherland 28, 145, 229
movement
  Arab Renaissance Movement 33
  "alt-right" movement 203–4
  Communist movement 49, 183
  democratic movement 73
  fascist movement 204
  feminist movement 193
  Islamic movements 33–4
  labour movement 74, 240, 252
  liberal movement 73
  liberation movement 9, 50, 174, 252
  nationalist movement 1, 3–4, 31, 67,
    74, 78, 96, 110, 141, 195, 197,
    200–1, 203, 215, 224, 229–31,
    253
  national movement 7, 12, 44–6,
    52, 54, 75, 99, 138, 146, 194,
    232
  Negritude movement 34
  new world history movement 241
  Pan-African movement 34
  pan-nationalist movement 77
  secessionist movement 216
  socialist movement 45
  Solidarity movement (Poland/
    Solidarnosc) 91
Murdock, Caitlin 230
Mussolini, Benito 30

Nagel, Joane 201
Nairn, Tom 7, 50–2, 180
Namier, Lewis 29
Napoleon Bonaparte 22, 72, 196, 243,
    250, 254
Napoleon, Louis 71
Nasser, Jamal Abdul 33
nation
  building 6–7, 8, 11–12, 15, 26, 50,
    64–5, 201, 206, 215, 218–20,
    222, 225–6, 228, 232–3,
    239–40, 243, 250, 256
  construction of 137, 139, 144–5
  disintegration of 47–8, 52, 232
  as imagined community 67, 93, 139,
    198, 222, 252–3
  reproduction of 159, 196

state 3, 4, 8, 13–15, 22–3, 25, 27–9,
    34–5, 195, 201–2, 216, 218, 224–
    5, 228, 233, 241, 245, 248–50
national
    character 20–3, 27, 47, 86, 105, 110
    community 55, 106, 114, 120–2,
        194–5, 201, 206, 222
    consciousness 6, 48, 75, 97–8
    culture 14, 33, 54, 134–5, 139, 144,
        180, 183, 196, 228
    identity 3, 5–6, 8, 11–12, 14, 35, 52,
        55, 62–5, 69–70, 73, 75–6, 86–7,
        90–9, 109, 111, 118–20, 122,
        132–6, 142–3, 145, 147–50,
        158, 161–2, 183, 194, 196–7,
        199, 204, 206, 216, 218–32
    question 7, 42, 46, 48–9, 56, 181
    Socialism 28–30, 63, 110–11, 131–3,
        203–4
    symbol 115, 135, 141, 148, 159, 162,
        194, 198–9, 201
nationalism
    anti-colonial 171, 173, 178, 180–6,
        224, 250, 255
    banal 4, 9, 12, 78, 112, 159, 201
    emergence of 19, 62, 78
    ethnic 4, 74, 90, 131, 145
    European 4, 92, 255
    and gender 5, 10, 195–8
    as (global) ideology 1, 5, 249, 251,
        256–7
    in a global context 253–4
    methodological 14–15, 19, 30–1, 35,
        72, 147, 163, 228, 233, 243,
        245–6
    peasant 221, 226
    racial 6, 194
    romantic 12, 21, 31, 99, 231
    studies 2–6, 194, 207, 218
    transnational 144, 253
nationalist discourse 9, 25, 86, 106,
    141, 155–65, 178–80, 185, 195,
    197, 202, 206, 224, 255
nationality 14, 43, 46, 49, 62, 69, 74,
    83–4, 103, 136, 143, 1612, 196,
    203, 224, 229
nationalization 8, 14, 23, 26, 30, 135–8,
    141, 143–4, 147–9, 161, 197–8,
    201, 203, 249, 255

denationalization 12, 16, 20, 30
renationalization 20, 30–1, 142
nationhood 33, 84, 89–90, 92, 94–5,
    98–9, 137, 140–1, 144–5, 147–9,
    162, 165, 197, 199, 251
    construction of 140, 148
Nazism. See national, socialism
Nehru, Jawaharlal 181
Netherlands 146, 223
    Dutch Republic 91, 146–7
    Leiden 147
    States of Holland 147
networks 10–12, 124, 135, 143, 161,
    218, 221, 228, 230, 246, 250–1,
    253–4
New Zealand 32
Niethammer, Lutz 106
Northern Ireland 86, 162
Norway 29, 162
Nugent, Paul 230

Occident 32, 172
O'Hanlon, Rosalind 177
Orient 32, 172
Orientalism 141, 172, 179, 198, 231
Orwell, George 118–19
Osterhammel, Jürgen 4
'othering' 15, 142
Ottoman Empire 28, 45, 71, 86, 141–2
    Tanzimat Reforms 15, 142
Özkirimli, Umut 4

Paasi, Anssi 218
Pakistan 33, 137
Palestine 133
parliament 22, 29, 68, 74, 247
participation 119, 142, 163, 196, 222,
    242
patriotism 2–3, 28, 49, 96, 135, 149,
    160
perennialism 4, 6, 8, 47, 54, 61, 77, 84,
    86, 89, 90, 98–9, 114
Persia 20
Peru 184, 226
    Chilean occupation (1881–4) 221
Philip II, King of Spain 146
Philippines 200
Picard, Michael 231
Pirenne, Henri 27

Plamenatz, John 180
Pokrovski, Mikhail 28
Poland 24, 52, 91, 197, 221–2, 229,
     248
Polish-Lithuanian Union 248
Political Parties 61, 68, 86, 179–80,
     224, 247
  communist parties 49
  nationalist parties 148, 216
  social-catholic parties 220
Portugal 24, 28
  Estado Novo 28
postcolonialism 6, 9, 12, 155, 158,
     171–3, 175, 179, 181, 183–5,
     207
postmodernism 6, 12, 42, 64
post(-)structuralism 8, 10, 93, 120, 155,
     157–8, 165, 172, 178–9, 194,
     217, 220, 246
primordialism 4, 8, 78, 87–8, 98, 119,
     125, 139, 141
privatization 13, 216
proletarians 43–4, 46, 48–50, 244
protectionism 239–40, 254, 257
protestantism 91, 94, 133, 146
Puritans 91

Queen's University Belfast 90

racism 87–8, 120, 185–6, 203, 240,
     255, 257
  apartheid 69, 134
  sexist racism 203
Ranger, Terence 3, 64, 76–7, 136
Rank, Otto 113
Ranke, Leopold von 22, 243, 247
Ratzel, Friedrich 243–4
Reagan, Ronald 68
Reagin, Nancy 201
reformation 23, 53, 86, 91, 93–4, 140
regionalism 2, 71–2, 95, 215–16,
     222–3, 225–7
regionalization 11, 251
Reid, Donald 231
religion 21–3, 54, 73, 84, 86, 88, 90–6,
     98–9, 106–8, 110, 114, 221,
     132–3, 135, 139–41, 149, 162,
     175, 194, 196, 204, 219–20,
     224–5, 232, 244, 257

renaissance 2, 3, 33, 93, 244
Renan, Ernest 51, 83, 86, 93,
     106, 132
Renner, Karl 64
republicanism 28, 30–1, 68, 71, 73, 94,
     146, 183, 199–200
resistance 30, 71–2, 86, 158, 176, 204,
     217, 256–7
Revue Historique 26
Reynolds, Susan 94
right-wing movements 2, 27–9, 31,
     72–3, 113, 159
  Alternative für Deutschland 2
  Front National 2
  Lega Nord 3, 216
  Swedish Democrats 2
  True Finns 2
  UK Independence Party 2
"Rise of the West" 98, 241
Robertson, William 21
Rokkan, Stein 54
Romania 26–7, 72, 135, 148
  Cluj-Napoca 148
romanticism 5–6, 12, 19, 21–4, 31, 99,
     132–3, 138, 231
Roper, Michael 193
Rude, George 175
Ruritania 66, 136
Russia 26, 28, 45–6, 71, 145, 219, 243,
     251
  Moscow 253
  October Revolution 48
Rwanda 194

Sahlin, Peter 229
Said, Edward 9, 133, 172, 178–80, 231
Samuel, Raphael 3
Sarkar, Sumit 178
Sasulic, Vera 243
Sayer, Derek 98–9
Scales, Len 95
Scandinavia 29, 162, 223
Schmitt, Guido 191–2
Schniedewind, William 92
Scotland 44, 52–3, 138, 149, 162
  Nairn 180
Scott, Joan 193, 206–7
secularization, secularism 7, 73, 91, 98,
     132, 142

self-determination 13, 15, 46, 49, 63, 65, 74, 84, 87, 91, 99, 145, 163, 197, 251
Senegal 34
separatism 49, 69, 159, 216
Serbia 64, 75
Sestakov, Andrej Vasilevic 28
Seven Years' War 250
sexuality
  discourse of 10, 113, 156, 177, 203
  endogamy 203
  exogamy 203
  homosexuality 202–3
  as reproduction of the national body 112, 195, 198, 201, 206
  women's sexuality 201–3, 205–6
Shi, Hu 33
Significant Other 122
Sinha, Mrinali 198
Slovakia 1
Slovenia 44
Smith, Adam 63
Smith, Anthony D. 4, 8, 53, 69, 84, 87–90, 92, 94, 98–9, 106, 114, 144–5, 164
social
  class/group 23, 42, 51, 55, 149, 177, 233
  Darwinism 257
  democracy 29, 46, 47, 51, 242
  Identity Theory 121
  justice 73
  mobility 52, 54, 66, 74, 133
  question 252
  Revolution 7, 28, 42
socialism 7, 23, 28, 33, 42–51, 65, 73, 199, 203, 257
  class struggle 43, 47–8, 50, 52
sociological theory 179
Socrates 145
Soja, Edward 217
South Africa 69
South Sudan 77, 216
sovereignty
  national 83, 89, 93, 142–3, 180–2, 240, 252, 256–7
  popular 84, 87, 91, 99, 135, 163
Soviet Union 28, 48–9, 63, 78, 122, 194, 216, 219

Brezhnev Years 69
  collapse of 67, 69, 194, 241
Spain 15, 21, 26, 28, 31, 64, 146, 162, 223, 227, 232, 243
  Basque Country 162, 216
  Catalonia 53, 230
  Cerdanya 229
  Falange 28
  Opus Dei 28
space
  homogenization of 11, 140, 220, 250
  as social construct 12, 218, 234
  territorialization of 11, 219, 240, 250–4
special path (Sonderweg) 30, 62, 73, 133
Spillman, Lyn 161
Spivak, Gayatri 177–8
Sri Lanka 92
Stalin, Josef 28, 48–50
state formation 23, 64–5, 194, 249
statehood 23, 43–4, 54, 74–5, 142, 173, 243, 248–9
Stauter-Halsted, Keely 221
stereotype 50, 121, 123, 141, 195, 199, 205
Stewart-Winter, Timothy 205
Storm, Eric 226
Subaltern Studies 9, 95, 171, 173, 175–8, 184–6
Subaltern classes 9, 174, 176, 178, 221
Suharto, Haji Mohamed 200
swadeshi 15
Sweden 28, 162
Switzerland 137
Syria 33
  Damascus 33
Systems Justification Theory 115

Taiwan 231
Tajfel, Henri 121
Tamil Tigers 229
Tatars 28
territorialization 11, 219, 240, 250–4
  deterritorialization 252
territory 22–3, 46, 250, 253, 257
Terror Management Theory 114, 125

Thailand
  Siam 145
Thatcher, Margaret 2, 68
Ther, Philipp 97
Theweleit, Klaus 113
Thiesse, Anne-Marie 143–4, 223, 225
Third World 7, 216
Thompson, E. P. 175
Tilly, Charles 54
Togo 230
Tosh, John 193
totalitarianism 28
tourism 13, 215, 226, 230–3
  Invented tradition 50, 54, 67, 136–7,
    139, 141
transnationalism 26, 31
Treitschke, Heinrich von 27
Trevelyan, George 29
Trump, Donald 2, 240
Turkey 77, 141, 162
  Turkish Republic 141

Ukraine 52
Uncle Sam 201
United Liberation Front of Assam 224
United Nations 1, 65
United Nations Educational, Scientific
    and Cultural Organization 244
United States of America (USA) 2, 6–7,
    15, 31–2, 63, 68, 91, 122, 133,
    135, 176, 184, 200–1, 205, 225,
    241, 244, 250–1, 256–7
  New England 91
  Yellowstone 226
unity 9, 14, 27, 46, 49, 118, 146, 155,
    160–2, 165, 192, 246
Universal History 20, 185, 243, 247
universalism 21–2, 94, 246, 255
University of Cambridge 161

van den Berghe, Pierre 87–8
van Ginderachter, Maarten 149
Varnhagen, Francisco Adolfo de 24
Vietnam 96, 145
  Dai Viet 96
Voltaire 20–1

Walby, Sylvia 196
Wales 53, 162
Wallerstein, Immanuel 7, 54, 140, 142,
    245
World War
  First World War 1, 2, 4–5, 13, 72, 88,
    113, 135, 140, 147, 197, 202,
    205, 224, 226, 230, 248
  Second World War 1–2, 4, 41, 49, 88,
    105, 110, 131, 133, 150, 199,
    204, 224, 244, 251
Warner, Marina 199
Warwick University 89
Weber, Eugen 8, 65, 70–3, 135, 220
Weber, Max 63, 106
Westernization 33, 95, 182
Wehler, Hans-Ulrich 73
welfare state 11, 13, 68, 197, 216, 240,
    252, 254
White House 240
Wimmer, Andreas 13, 218, 228
Wilson, Woodrow 13, 15, 65, 74, 251,
    253, 257
  Fourteen Points 13
Woolf, Virginia 204
working class 7, 23, 49, 65, 67, 119,
    162, 164, 194, 205
world economy 243
Wormald, Patrick 95

xenophobia 255

Yalom, Irvin 113
Yongzheng (Chinese emperor) 146
Yugoslav War 1
Yugoslavia 69, 74, 77, 86, 133, 194,
    216
Yukichi, Fukuzawa 32
Yuval-Davis, Nira 195–6, 202

Zaghloul, Safiya 200
Zahra, Tara 149, 224
Zimmer, Oliver 4, 95
Zionism 91
Zizek, Slavoj 10, 115, 118, 123
Zurayq, Constantine 33

www.ingramcontent.com/pod-product-compliance
Lightning Source LLC
Chambersburg PA
CBHW070240290326
41929CB00046B/2119